THE LAW AND REGULATION OF FRANCHISING IN THE EU

ELGAR INTELLECTUAL PROPERTY LAW AND PRACTICE

Series Editors: Trevor Cook, *Partner, Bird & Bird* and Johanna Gibson, *Herchel Smith Professor of Intellectual Property Law, Queen Mary University of London*

The *Elgar Intellectual Property Law and Practice* series is a library of works by leading practitioners and scholars covering discrete areas of law in the field of intellectual property. Each title will describe the law in detail, but will also be deeply analytical, highlighting and unpicking the legal issues that are most critical and relevant to practice. Designed to be detailed, focused reference works, the books in the series aim to offer an authoritative statement on the law and practice in key topics within the field, from *Trade Marks* to *Pharmaceuticals*, from *Patent Standards* to *Trade Secrecy* and from *IP Licensing* to *IP Valuation*.

THE LAW AND REGULATION OF FRANCHISING IN THE EU

MARK ABELL
PhD, Partner in a law firm in the city of London, UK

ELGAR INTELLECTUAL PROPERTY LAW AND PRACTICE

Edward Elgar
Cheltenham, UK • Northampton, MA, USA

Published by
Edward Elgar Publishing Limited
The Lypiatts
15 Lansdown Road
Cheltenham
Glos GL50 2JA
UK

Edward Elgar Publishing, Inc.
William Pratt House
9 Dewey Court
Northampton
Massachusetts 01060
USA

A catalogue record for this book
is available from the British Library

Library of Congress Control Number: 2012944475

This book is available electronically in the ElgarOnline.com Law Subject Collection,
E-ISBN 978 1 78195 235 1

FSC
www.fsc.org
MIX
Paper from
responsible sources
FSC® C018575

ISBN 978 1 78195 220 7

Typeset by Columns Design XML Ltd, Reading
Printed by MPG PRINTGROUP, UK

CONTENTS

EXTENDED TABLE OF CONTENTS

ABBREVIATIONS

ANCC	Australian Competition and Consumer Commission
BAG	Bundesarbeitsgericht (Federal Supreme Court for Labour Law)
BB	Betriebsberater (Business Advisor)
BFA	British Franchise Association
BGB	Bürgerliches Gesetzbuch (Civil Code)
BGH	Bundesgerichtshof (Federal Supreme Court for Civil Law)
CA	Court of Appeal
CFR	The Common Frame of Reference recommended by the Study Group on a European Civil Code under the EU Commission's Action Plan. Resolution of 1989, OJC 158/400
DStR	Deutsches Steuerrecht (German Tax Law)
EFF	European Franchise Federation
FCA	Franchise Council of Australia
FFF	French Franchise Federation
FSA	Financial Services Authority (UK)
FSMA	Financial Services and Marketing Act 2000 (UK)
FTC	Fair Trade Commission (USA)
GWB	Gesetz gegen den unlauteren Wettbewerb (Anti-trust law)
HGB	Handelsgesetzbuch (German Commerical Code)
HL	House of Lords
IFA	International Franchise Association (USA)
KG	Kammergericht (Court of Appeal in Berlin)
KSchG	Kündigungschutzgesetz (Termination Protection Act)
LG	Landesgericht (Lower Court)
NGO	Non-governmental Organization
NJW	*Neue Juristische Wochenzeitschrift* (New Judicial Weekly Journal)
NJW-RR	*Neue Juristische Wochenzeitschrift* Rechtsprechungsreport (New Judicial Weekly Journal Case Reports)
OECD	The Organisation for Economic Cooperation and Development
OJ	Official Journal of the European Community
OLG	Oberlandesgericht (Court of Appeal)
SME	Small and Medium-Sized Enterprise
TFEU	Treaty on the Functioning of the European Union
TPA	Trading Practices Act (Australia)
UNIDROIT	The International Institute for the Unification of Private Law
VerbrKrG	Verbraucherkreditgesetz (Consumer Protection Act)
WFC	World Franchise Council

‘The strictest law often causes the most wrong’

Marcus Tullius Cicero – 106–43 BC

Dedication

For Jane.

Much loved, much missed, never forgotten.

'From light to light, through a brief darkness'

Henry Wordsworth Longfellow, The Golden Legend

FOREWORD

This book focuses upon the law and regulation of franchising in the European Union, but its conclusions are equally applicable to other jurisdictions if their legislatures and judiciaries are to help enable franchising to fulfil its full potential in their economies. It is my hope that my research, analysis and conclusions will inspire other enquiring minds to also question the orthodoxy of franchise regulation and so lead to a more homogeneous, enlightened and commercially appropriate approach to the way that franchising is regulated around the world.

This book is the result of five years of hard work. It has been a long personal journey that has seen me pass through an unusual number of travails: an unscheduled and enforced extended stay in a Mumbai hotel room, the tragic and untimely loss of a much loved sister and the premature and unexpected death of a close friend and colleague. Through all of that, this work has been not only a burden but also a form of intellectual support.

The researching and writing of this book has also been a rich and meaningful professional experience. I found myself ending it with a far broader, more sophisticated and commercially relevant understanding of franchising and its regulation in the EU than I had expected. Indeed, on some issues, such as unconscionability, my views have fundamentally changed as a result. Consequentially, I find myself significantly better educated, even if some may think me no wiser.

The journey has been literal as well as metaphorical with parts of the book having been researched and written by me not only in the UK, but also in the USA, Germany, France, Japan and China. That has also enriched the experience for me.

Like all long journeys, this one would not have been possible without the active and much appreciated support of a host of generous people and it is my pleasure to be able to thank them for their support in this foreword.

The list of those who have in some way helped me is endless and space does not permit me to name them all, but particular thanks are due to the following people:

My dear wife Shizuka, who has always encouraged and supported me in my labours and cheerfully put up with endless weekends and holidays during which I was locked in my study with piles of paper.

Our wonderful children, Emma and Benjamin, who uncomplainingly accepted my attention being shared between them and my research over weekends and holidays and who have served as a constant reminder to me that one's real priorities are to be found in neither one's profession nor academia.

My loving parents, Philip and Bea, who have always encouraged me to follow my dreams and go wherever my passion takes me.

My dear departed friend and colleague, Moira Gilmour, for her encouragement and support during the more challenging moments.

My long suffering, hard working and ever cheerful secretary, Caroline Flambard, without whose typing skills and ability to deliver against even the most demanding of deadlines this book would have never seen the light of day.

My colleagues Babette Marzheuser-Wood and Vicky Reinhardt, whose advice, guidance and linguistic skills helped me come to grips with the intricacies of how the German legal system deals with franchising.

Professor Uma Suthersanen, who took me on as an 'orphaned' academic and helped me shape a mountain of raw data and strong opinions into a scholarly book.

Professor Alison Firth, for her helpful suggestions, particularly on the more challenging aspects of the uneasy relationship between intellectual property rights and EU competition law.

Professor Guido Westkampff, for his suggestions on the more arcane aspects of the German Civil Code.

And finally, many professional friends from around the world who have kindly answered my occasional questions about the more technical aspects of franchise regulation in their jurisdictions, including Stephen Giles, John Sier, John Baer, Franck Veiss, Yu Yan and Ran Yanling.

All opinions and any errors and omissions are, of course, entirely down to me.

Mark Abell

TABLE OF CASES

Australia

Austria

Belgium

Finland

France

Germany

United Kingdom

United States of America

European Union

TABLE OF STATUTES

Germany

Greece

Hungary

Indonesia

Italy

Japan

Kazakhstan

United States of America

Venezuela

Vietnam

European Union

1

INTRODUCTION

Franchising is a commercial mechanism for re-engineering businesses by enabling them to unlock the commercial value and potential of their intellectual property rights in domestic and international markets. 1.1

Franchising substantially contributes to the GDP of a number of EU member states. In the UK in 2009 it contributed £11.8 billion,[1] in Germany €48 billion[2] and France €47.6 billion.[3] The estimated turnover of franchising in the EU is over €215 billion (US$300 billion) generated by over 9971 franchises.[4] 1.2

> Franchising normally stimulates economic activity by improving the distribution of goods and/or the provision of services as it gives franchisors the possibility of establishing a uniform network with limited investment, which may assist the entry of new competitors in the markets particularly in the case of small and medium sized enterprises. It allows independent traders to set up outlets more rapidly and with a higher chance of success than if they were to set up without the franchisor's experience and assistance. Franchisors therefore have a better opportunity to compete with larger distribution undertakings.[5]
>
> Franchising also generally allows consumers and other end users a fair share of the resulting benefits, as they combine the advantage of a uniform network with the existence of traders personally interested in the efficient operation of their business. The homogeneity of the network and the constant co-operation between the franchisor and the franchisees ensures the constant quality of the products and services. The favourable effect of franchising on inter brand competition and the fact that consumers are free to deal with any franchisee in the network guarantees that a reasonable part of the resulting benefits will be passed on to consumers.[6]

---

1 The NatWest/BFA 2010 Franchise Survey – The British Franchise Association.

2 Deutsche Bank. Report on Franchising, January 2008.

3 French Franchise Federation Report, 2010.

4 European Franchise Federation Statistics – www.eff.franchise.com (viewed 23/12/2010). See 2.9 below.

5 Commission Regulation (EEC) No. 4887/88 (OJ 1988 L 359/52).

6 Ibid.

It is therefore a significant economic activity in the EU. However, a comparison with the level of franchising activity in the US[7] and Australia[8] suggests that it is markedly underdeveloped in the EU. This in turn suggests that franchising has potential for substantial further growth in the EU.

1.3 A mixture of economic, cultural and historical factors account for much of this comparative underdevelopment of franchising in the EU. The lack of a supportive, pan-EU, homogeneous regulatory environment is also a contributory factor. It is suggested that a uniform and supportive regulatory environment would help to facilitate and encourage the further growth of franchising in the EU, particularly between member states and so support the single market in a significant manner. As stated in existing EU legislation,[9] the differing approaches to regulating commerce found in EU member state laws are detrimental to the functioning of the single market and substantially reduce its ability to stimulate trade between member states by improving the distribution of goods and provision of services within the EU. This heterogeneous regulatory environment is detrimental to both the protection available to franchisors and franchisees vis-à-vis each other and to the security of commercial transactions. These differences substantially inhibit the conclusion and operation of franchise agreements where franchisor and franchisee are established in different member states.

1.4 The trade in goods and services between member states should be carried on under conditions which are similar to those of a single market. There is therefore a need to approximate the legal systems of the member states to the extent required for the proper functioning of franchising in the common market.

In pursuing the goals of economic growth, job creation, consumer satisfaction and commercial innovation franchising needs to be encouraged. Franchising contributes to the establishment of a single European Market. It facilitates cross-frontier development as it is based on the leverage which an established name or idea can give a relatively small investment to enable the product or

---

7 600 000 franchised businesses generating an estimated total turnover of US$12 trillion in 2005 according to Iuliana, S. and M. Mihaela, 2009, 'The High Impact of Franchising on Economic Affairs in Some of the EU Members', *Annals of Faculty of Economics*, volume 1, issue 1, pages 251–6 (Published by the University of Oradea, Faculty of Economics). The turnover of franchised businesses in the USA is estimated at US$868.3 billion, in Australia US$130 million and the EU$300 billion; see 2.9 below for fuller analysis. http://steconomice.uoradea.ro/anale/volume/2009/v1-international-relations-and-european-integration/39.pdf

8 An estimated turnover of US$130 billion in a country with a GDP that is less than 10% of that of the EU (Franchise Council of Australia – www.franchise.org.au).

9 Council Directive (EC) 861 653 on the co-ordination of the laws of the member states relating to Self Employed Commercial Agents [2004] OJ L 382.

service involved to spread quickly, far and wide.[10] Franchising is a commercial phenomenon particularly well suited to the challenges of the single market. The combination of a franchisor's know-how and a franchisee's enterprise can boost economic activity and employment, while enlarging the range of goods and services on offer to the public. Franchising makes products and services available to a wide public and does not have to stop at national frontiers. The regulatory environment should therefore be re-engineered to enable franchising to fulfil this potential. Given the heterogeneous policy legacies in the EU member states as well as the diverse preferences of national governments and other domestic actors, a one-size-fits-all approach is neither politically feasible nor normatively desirable. A certain amount of flexibility and variation will therefore be needed to successfully re-engineer the regulatory environment. It is therefore suggested that a directive would be the appropriate catalyst for the required re-engineering.

There is a rich seam of commentary on the regulation of franchising but there is **1.5** little work which considers franchising's under-contribution to the EU's economy or the extent to which the EU regulatory environment contributes to this and could be re-engineered to increase cross border business by promoting the use of franchising in the EU. In 'Franchise Sector Regulation: The Australian Experience'[11] Terry concludes that 'a healthy franchising sector requires adequate and appropriate infrastructure to which the legal environment is central'. Unfortunately there is little research into the legal environment in the EU.

Much academic research into the role of franchising in inter state trade within the EU has focused upon its vertically integrated nature and potential to prevent, restrict and distort competition between member states. This line of analysis focuses upon the *Pronuptia* decision of the European Court of Justice,[12] the various decisions of the Commission on the impact of what was then Article 85 of the Treaty of Rome,[13] the Franchise Block Exemption,[14] the two Vertical

---

10 The Rt Hon Sir Leon Brittan, QC, Vice President of the European Commission in Abell, M., 1991, *European Franchising: Law and Practice in the European Community*, pp. xi.

11 Terry, A., 'Franchise Sector Regulation: The Australian Experience', EMNet-Conference on 'Economics and Management of Franchisors Networks', Vienna, Austria, 26–28 June 2005, http://emnet.univie.ac.at/fileadmin/user_upload/conf_EMNet/2003/papers/Terrypaper.doc, accessed 19 August 2009.

12 *Pronuptia de Paris GmbH* v. *Pronuptia de Paris Irmgard Schullgallis* (Case 161/84) [1986] 1CMLR 414.

13 *Computerland Europe SA* (Case IV/32–34) (87/407/EEC) [1989] 4CMLR 259; *Sociéte Anonyme des Chausseures Seducta Charles Jourdan et fils, Charles Jourdan Holdings AG and Xavier Danaud SA* (Case IV/31.697) [89/94/EEC] [1989] 4 CMLR 591; *Service Master Limited* (Case IV/32.358) (88/604/EEC) [1989] 4 CMLR 581; *Yves Rocher* (Case IV/31.428–31.432) [1988] 4 CMLR 592; *Pronuptia de Paris SA* (Case IV/30.937) (97/17/EEC) [1989] 4 CMLR 355.

14 Regulation (EEC) 4087/88.

Restraint Block Exemptions that superseded it[15] and relevant member state decisions such as *Crehan*.[16]

1.6 Crossick and Mendelsohn,[17] Schmitz and Hamme,[18] Ritter, Rawlinson and Braun[19] and a long catalogue of other commentators have gone into great detail about the need for franchisors to be able to impose certain restrictions on their franchisees to protect their image and reputation, grant exclusive territories, tie in goods and services and so on. Korah[20] and Mendelsohn and Rose[21] in particular have produced long, valuable and detailed texts. However, all of these commentaries are concerned solely with the Vertical Restraints that exist in a franchise relationship and how and in what circumstances they can, or should be seen as, being pro-competitive. They do not consider how the differing legal provisions of EU member state law or typical provisions found in franchise agreements support or undermine the economic drivers of franchising or reduce the consequential risks.

1.7 This book analyses the way in which competition law protects the public interest in franchising by preventing distortion of the market but in contrast to existing works, looks beyond the technical way in which anti-trust laws are applied to franchising. It places the regulation of vertical restraints in franchising into the bigger picture of how franchising can be best regulated. It concludes that the 'per se' approach adopted by the European Commission is inappropriate. Instead it recommends one more in line with the Chicago School's 'rule of reason' approach – as recommended by the Organisation for Economic Cooperation and Development (OECD) and evidenced in the *Leegin* decision of the US Supreme Court. This would mean focusing less on intra brand competition and allowing franchise chains to compete on a level playing field with corporate chains in terms of retail price maintenance, and harmonised multi-channel strategies, including use of the internet. This 'Exchange of Benefits' approach will help promote and encourage the use of franchising and be pro-competitive.

---

15 Regulation (EC) No. 2790/1999.

16 Case C-453/99 *Courage Ltd* v. *Bernard Crehan* [2002] QB 507, [2001] All ER CEC 886.

17 Mendelsohn, M. and S. Crossick, 1986, 'Franchising in Europe: Consequences of Pronuptia', 14 *Int'l Bus. Law* 220.

18 Schmitz, D.A. and A.V. Hamme, 1988, 'Franchising in Europe: The First Practical EEC Guidelines', 22 *Int'l Bus. Law* 717.

19 Ritter, L., F. Rawlinson and D. Braun, 2000, *European Competition Law: a Practitioners Guide*, 2nd edition, Kluwer Law International, pp. 263–78.

20 Korah, V., 1990, *An Introductory Guide to EEC Competition Law and Practice*, Oxford: ESC Publishing (4th edn) and Korah, V., 2002, 'The New Vertical Restraints Block Exemption', *Intereconomics*, Vol. 37, Number 1, 4–11, DOI: 101007/BF02927395.

21 Mendelsohn, M. and S. Rose, 2002, *Guide to the EC Block Exemption for Vertical Agreements*, Kluwer Law International.

The UNIDROIT Study of Franchise Regulations[22] is not restricted to the EU but is applicable to it. Unlike this book it is limited to pre-contractual disclosure and does not analyse the contents of franchise agreements and how they might be regulated. Its consideration of the issues involved in disclosure is somewhat shallow and its conclusions are little more than a patchwork based upon the preferences of the individual practitioners involved in the study. This study is not restricted to consideration of pre-contractual disclosure. Its consideration of disclosure is based upon how it can be formulated to best protect the interests of both franchisor and franchisee. Its conclusions on disclosure are far more radical than those of UNIDROIT, recommending for example franchisee disclosure at the request of the franchisor and considering whether liability for non-disclosure should be strict or dependent upon 'defective consent'. **1.8**

The Report of the Study Group on a European Civil Code ('the Study Group') seeks to identify how to overcome obstacles to the functioning of the internal market. It, inter alia, proposes a way in which to harmonise the regulation of franchising in the EU. It does so based upon its stated objective to produce 'a set of codified principles which constitute the most suitable private law rules for Europe wide application'.[23] **1.9**

Since the Commission on European Contract law (led by Professor Ole Lando) in 1982, the European Parliament's first resolution on private law in 1989 and the Commission's subsequent communication on European contract law in 2001 there has been a good deal of academic debate about the development of private law. This led to the establishment of various research projects[24] and the European Commission's Action Plan for a more coherent European Contract law.[25] Reactions to the Action Plan were summarised in 'European Contract Law and the revision of the acquis: the way forward'[26] ('The Way Forward'). The second part of The Way Forward dealt with the preparation of a common frame of reference (CFR) to 'improve the quality and consistency of the acquis in the area of contract law'.[27] Academics have played a central role in elaborating the CFR:[28] the so-called 'Network of Excellence'.[29] **1.10**

---

22 UNIDROIT Model Franchise Disclosure Law – September 2002.

23 http://www.sgecc.net accessed 14 August 2009.

24 Such as the Trento Common Core Project of European Private Law and the Research Group on the Existing European Community Private law (Acquis Group).

25 Communication from the Commission to the European Parliament and the Council, A More Coherent European Contract Law, An Action Plan, COM (2003) 68 final.

26 Communication from the Commission to the European Parliament and the Council, European Contract Law and the revision of the acquis: the way forward, COM (2004) 651 final.

27 The Way Forward, pp. 9–13.

28 The Acquis Group and the Insurance Group.

29 See www.copecl.org. The Network of Excellence was funded by the Commission in May 2005 under the Sixth Framework Programme for Research.

1.11 This produced specific recommendations for the regulation of franchising in the EU. This study group ('the Study Group') has stated that the principles impacting upon franchising have not been drafted with a specific protection aim, but to save transaction costs for the parties by providing for 'possible problems, solutions which parties would presumably agree to'.[30] Nevertheless the Study Group aimed to achieve a balance between the competing interests of the parties and so did not only seek to reflect the common core of solutions in the EU member states as regards franchising but other sources such as the UNIDROIT model disclosure law[31] and the International Chamber of Commerce's model for International Franchising Contract.[32]

1.12 The 'Amsterdam Group' was established to work with national reporters who were asked to answer several questionnaires concerning the main legal issues as regards commercial agency, franchising and distribution.[33] After formulating its proposals the Amsterdam Group discussed them with an Advisory Council consisting of various academics.[34] The Working Party's recommendations were then reviewed by the Co-ordinating Committee which comprises some 50 professors from around the EU.

1.13 The recommendations can therefore be seen as an authoritative academic work on the regulation of franchising in the EU. However, it is not free of political influence and some commentators feel that its exclusion of other stakeholders coupled with the Commission's clear political agenda of 'Europeanisation' undermines its objectivity and value.[35] The Amsterdam Group's proposal can be seen as little more than a distillation of existing jurisprudence in EU civil law jurisdictions. It fails to consider the valuable insights offered by non legal academic analysis of the nature of franchising. This results in an extremely narrow understanding of how legal regulation can support and encourage the

---

30 Introduction to Study Group on a European Civil Code. Proposal for a European law on Commercial Agency, Franchising and Distribution Contracts, pp. 93.

31 See the Report on the Fourth Meeting of the Study Group on Franchising held on 9–10 December 1999, Study LXVIII – Doc 20, p. 2.

32 See ICC Model International Franchising Contract, 2000. ICC International Contract Series, ICC Publishing, Paris, 2000.

33 The Dutch group of reporters consisted of researchers of different European jurisdictions who provided information on their own legal systems: Georgios Arnokourous (Greek Law), Odavia Bueno Diaz (Spanish Law), Rui Miguel Patricio Cascao (Portuguese Law), John Dickie (Common Law), Christoph Jeloschek (Austrian Law), Roland Lohnert (German Law), Andrea Pinna (French Law), Manola Scotton (Italian Law), Hanna Sivesand (Swedish Law), Muriel Veldman (Dutch Law), Aneta Wiewiorowska (Polish Law).

34 The members of the Advisory Council on Commercial Agency, Franchise and Distribution Contracts are Professor Johny Herre (Stockholm), Professor Jérôme Huet (Paris), Professor Ewan McKendrick (Oxford), Professor Peter Schlechtriem (Freiburg i.Br.), Professor Hugh Beale (London/Warwick) and Professor Christina Ramberg (Stockholm).

35 Hesselink, M.W., 2004, 'The Politics of a European Civil Code', *European Law Journal*, Vol. 10, No. 6, 675–97.

efficient exploitation of the single market by companies through the medium of franchising.

However, some commentators believe that applying the recommendations of the Amsterdam Group will 'most probably lead to a win-win situation for the parties on franchising ...'[36] Bueno Diaz's consideration of *Franchising in European Contract Law*[37] is a prime example. It is focused on the Study Group's proposals for commercial agency, franchising and distribution contracts. It restricts itself to comparing it with the provisions of the French Loi Doubin (Article 330 of the Civil Code) and the Spanish Retail Law (Article 62 of Law No. 7/1996). It compares the policies that underpin the respective laws in franchising in France and Spain and identifies the Study Group's proposals as the rational choice for parties involved in franchising in the EU. This study takes a much broader focus. It identifies the reasons for franchising's popularity, analyses the way it is currently regulated in the EU, recommends the re-engineering of the regulatory environment so that the legal eco-systems more closely reflect the impact of three commercial imperatives – market confidence, pre-contractual hygiene and protecting the interests of franchisors and franchisees through a mandatory taxonomy for franchise agreements. **1.14**

The most fundamental difference is that, whereas the Study Group does not meaningfully distinguish franchising from commercial agency and distribution, this book argues that franchising is markedly different to them and should be recognised as a 'type-agreement' in its own right. This study also identifies good faith as an important 'doctrinal tool' in dealing with the franchise relationship and disputes that arise out of it. After considering the influential German approach to good faith based on BGB 242, the French concept of *Bonne Fois* and England's ad hoc approach, it recommends a more refined approach based upon prohibiting unconscionable conduct and misleading and deceptive behaviour. **1.15**

In contrast to the Study Group's proposal for a European Commercial Code, this book proposes the enactment of a Directive that will harmonise EU member state law by making franchising a recognised 'type-contract' with mandatory, non-mandatory and essential rules. By dealing with detailed obligations and rights of the parties this approach will allow a level of flexibility that is likely to promote the use and sustain the success of franchising within the **1.16**

36 Diaz, O.B., 2007, *Franchising in European Contract Law. A comparison between the main obligations of the contracting parties in the Principles of European Law on Commercial Agency, Franchise and Distribution Contracts*, Sellier European Law Publishers, p. 51.

37 Ibid.

context of each member state's legal tradition. This contrasts with the techno-cratic and politically driven agenda of the Study Group.

A. THE SCOPE OF THIS BOOK

1.17 This book studies the regulation of Business Format Franchising in the European Union. It analyses the way in which it is currently regulated by both franchise specific and general commercial law. It also considers how the current regulatory environment might be improved. As the UK, Germany and France together accounted for 50% of the €215 billion (US$300 billion) franchising turnover in the EU in 2009, it focuses on these three member states. It contextualises this focus by a comparative reference to the US and Australia (both of which are Federal States with highly developed regulatory regimes).[38] It also tests its conclusions against empirical research amongst the relevant stakeholders, including franchisors, franchisees, potential franchisees and professionals engaged in franchising. The desirability of protecting the rights of franchisees is not disputed within this book. However, it will be underlined how this should not be the only purpose of regulation and that a balance must be struck between the protection of the rights of franchisees and the need to re-enforce the economic drivers that encourage both franchisors and franchisees to become involved in franchising in the first place. It is suggested that excessive protection of franchisees can have detrimental effects on both franchising and on the Single Market. This book suggests that such a critical balance can be achieved through a directive which re-engineers the regulatory environment in the EU by accentuating the impact of three commercial imperatives (market confidence, pre-contractual hygiene and a mandatory taxonomy of rights and obligations) upon the various legal eco-systems. These commercial imperatives re-enforce the economic drivers that attract franchisors and franchisees to franchising and reduce the inherent consequential risk to an appropriate level.

This book suggests that franchising has failed to fulfil its potential in the EU, that this is in part due to the regulatory environment and that this failure can be remedied by re-engineering the legal eco-systems that comprise the regulatory environment in the EU. It draws three basic conclusions.

38 And (mostly in footnotes) to the other 24 EU jurisdictions and the 21 jurisdictions outside of the EU that have franchise specific laws.

The first conclusion is that franchising is a specific, distinct and uniform type of commercial activity with positive influence in the EU, which stimulates economic activity by offering economic advantages to all those involved and improving distribution and giving businesses increased access to other member state markets. However, it is not fulfilling its full potential to contribute to the realisation of the single market. This book reaches this conclusion after considering franchising's basic architecture, its historical development, its rationale and its contextualisation, differentiating it from other business models and identifying why franchisors and franchisees are attracted to franchising and are prepared to accept the inherent consequential risks. It then benchmarks the contribution of franchising in the EU against its contribution in the USA and Australia and concludes that it is not fulfilling its potential in the EU. **1.18**

The second conclusion is that the regulatory environment in the EU is responsible for this underachievement of franchising in the single market. This book concludes that regulation of franchising in some form is required and considers the difficulties encountered by member states in seeking to regulate it. It considers the differing approaches of EU member states to constructing franchising's contractual environment, its impact on the risks to which franchisors and franchisees are exposed and the commercial drivers that attract them to franchising. It considers the impact of the self-regulatory system in the EU and then considers both the lack of homogeneity between the legal eco-systems that comprise the regulatory environment within the EU and the failure of those legal eco-systems to re-enforce the economic drivers that attract franchisors and franchisees to franchising or to reduce the inherent consequential risk. It analyses the nature of these shortcomings and the difficulties they impose upon franchising. **1.19**

The third conclusion is that the regulatory environment in the EU can be re-engineered to enable franchising to better fulfil its potential in the EU. This book proposes that this should be done by re-engineering the regulatory environment so that it imposes a harmonised approach across the EU which aims to accentuate the impact of three commercial imperatives; promoting market confidence, pre-contractual hygiene and imposing a mandatory taxonomy of rights and obligations on to the franchise relationship. The harmonisation of laws within the EU has always been difficult. This book also considers whether the trend amongst some academics and the EU 'technocracy' to advocate the abandonment of the traditional methods of achieving this (Directives and Regulations) in favour of a European Civil Code is an appropriate way in which to re-engineer the regulatory environment for franchising. **1.20**

1.21 The heterogeneous approach of EU member states to protecting franchisees is at odds with the political and economic desirability of encouraging the use of franchising in the single market. It is suggested that the solution should be based upon accentuating the impact of three commercial imperatives upon the legal eco-systems in the EU. These are the need to re-enforce market confidence, the need to ensure an appropriate level of pre-contractual hygiene and the need to impose a mandatory taxonomy of rights and obligations upon the franchise relationship. A draft EU Franchise Directive is proposed in Appendix 1. This work then explores whether and how such a new regulatory environment could solve the problems under consideration, and how it could be implemented on an EU-wide basis. This involves analysis of the contractual architecture, economic drivers, commercial interests and, most importantly, the EU member state and other legal eco-systems.

1.22 The subject matter at hand has been approached from the perspective of (1) the law impacting upon the use of franchising as a way of doing business across European Union member state borders and so promoting the single market, and (2) the business efficacy of the regulatory environment of the EU as it relates to franchising. The issues relating to intellectual property and the constitutional law of the European Union reach beyond the scope of this book, and are therefore mentioned throughout the work, but are not deeply analysed. Where deemed necessary, various references have been made to contract law, the duty of good faith, anti-trust law, commercial agency law, distribution law, unfair competition law, consumer protection law, employment law, private international law, and other member state law. Nevertheless this book does not purport to deliver a broad in-depth or authoritative analysis of any of these. This book does not purport to provide a full and in-depth analysis of German or French law.

2

DECONSTRUCTING THE CONTEXTUALISATION, ARCHITECTURE, RATIONALE AND RISKS OF FRANCHISING

A. INTRODUCTION

This chapter seeks to show that although franchising is a specific, distinct and uniform type of commercial activity with a positive influence in the EU which stimulates economic activity by offering economic advantages to all those involved, improves distribution and gives business increased access to other member states, it is not fulfilling its full potential to contribute to the realisation of the single market. In order to understand the reasons for this underperformance in the EU and the way in which the regulatory environment might be re-engineered to improve franchising's contribution to the single market, this book endeavours to better understand what franchising is. It does this by analysing both the economic and legal features of the architecture of franchising, **2.1** distinguishing it from agency and distribution, identifying the tensile stresses that arise within franchising and deconstructing the economic and sectoral contextualisation of franchising and its economic rationale and risks. It concludes that, despite the impact of variable determinants such as the value of the investment required from franchisees and the commercial sectors in which the business operates, the architecture of franchising comprises six fundamental features that are always present. These are independence of the parties, economic interest, use of a brand, use of a business format, control of the franchisee by the franchisor and assistance provided to the franchisee by the franchisor. This architecture withstands the tensile stresses placed upon franchising by its long term and dynamic nature. It also suggests that those economic drivers that constitute the commercial rationale for franchisors using franchising as part of their business strategy are distinct from those which attract franchisees to buy a franchise and that the risks inherent in franchising also differ between the parties.

1. The historical contextualisation of franchising in the EU

2.2 Business format franchising has evolved over many centuries to what is now a distinct and commercially impactful way of doing business.

Table 2.1 Chronology of the historical development of franchising

Date	Milestones
The Middle Ages[1]	**Source of Franchising's Historical DNA** 1215 Magna Carta 'enfranchises' Barons to collect taxes until ended by Council of Trent in 1562 1600 onwards 'Norenkai' system of restaurant chains developed in Japan during the Tokugawa Shogunate[2]
1700s	**Need for Distribution Channels Promotes early form of Franchising** 'Tied House' system develops to secure the distribution of beer by brewers in the UK
1800s[3]	**Technical Demands Promote use of Primitive Forms of Franchising** US Manufacturers such as Singer, Coca-Cola and McCormick adapt franchising as method of distribution
	Franchising Develops as a distinct Retail Channel • Harper Beauty Shops (US) (1920) • US automobile manufacturers adopt franchise model
1900–1950[4,5]	• Rexall Pharmacy (US) (1902) • Howard Johnson Ice Cream Parlours (US) (1925) • Pingouin Stores (France) (1930)

Date	Milestones
1950s	**Classic Franchise Structures Developed in the US and a few expand into Europe** • McDonalds (USA) (1955)[6] • KFC (USA) (1955)[7] • Service Master (USA) (1958) • IHOP (USA) (1959)[8] • Wimpy master franchisee opens in UK (1955)[9] • Service Master master franchisee opens in UK (1958)[10]
1960s	**First Wave of Business Format Franchising Growth** • Franchising flourishes in the USA • In the UK – Golden Egg Restaurants (1965); Dyno Rod (1966) open • In Germany[11] – Ihr Platz (drugstore), Nordsee (fish restaurant) and OBI (D-I-Y Store) open • More US concepts begin to enter Europe (e.g. Ziebart) • Regulatory problems arise in the UK[12]
1970s	**Second Wave of Business Format Franchising Growth** • First Franchise Regulation adopted – California (1971)[13] • 14 US States adopted franchise relationship laws • FTC Disclosure Rules implemented • European Franchise Federation founded (1972)[14] • French and German Franchise Associations founded (1973) • British Franchise Association founded (1978)[15]
1980s	**First Wave of Franchise Legislation Outside of USA** • EU Franchise Block Exemption adopted (1988) • French 'Loi Doubin' adopted (1989)
1990s	**Second Wave of Franchise Legislation Outside of USA** • Romania (1992) • Mexico (1998) • Brazil (1993) • Spain (1998) • Russia (1997) • Australia (1998)
2000s	**Third Wave of Franchise Legislation Outside of the USA** • Kazakhstan (2002) • Sweden (2006) • Estonia (2002) • China (2006) • Italy (2004) • Vietnam (2007) • Indonesia (2007) • Belgium (2006)

Notes:

1 Early references to franchising include 'All franchises and liberties of the bisshopericks... deryvid from the crowne 1559. and Fairs, Markets and other franchises c.1630' (Oxford English Dictionary, 1933). The origins of franchising lie in the mercantile codes and common law of the Middle Ages when the crown offered feudal lords the right to maintain civil order, determine and collect tax revenues, and make other special tax assessments. The barons paid the crown a specified sum from the tax revenues collected. In 1562 the Council of Trent ended this system of patronage.

2 The 'Norenkai' system in Japan has existed for several hundred years. It involves a long-term employee of a restaurant being allowed by the employer to set up a restaurant in a different location under the same name and using the same menu. 'Noren' is the Japanese word for the small curtain that lies across the entry of traditional Japanese restaurants and houses. 'Kai' is the Japanese word for club or association. 'Mai Toi' or table rent agreements have long existed in Chinese communities around the world. These enable individuals to run a small number of tables in a restaurant owned by another party.

3 One of the earliest examples of franchising in the United States was the McCormick Harvesting Machine Company. This manufacturer commissioned local agents to sell and service its machinery around 1850 (Mendelsohn, M., 1999, *The Guide to Franchising*, 6th Edition, Cassell). This gave birth to what the US Department of Commerce calls 'traditional franchising'. The Singer Sewing Machine Company (Ibid. Mendelsohn and Stanworth, J. and B. Smith, 1991, *Barclays Guide to Franchising for Small Businesses*, Blackwell) was another early franchise business that sprung up in the US during the 1850's. Agents working on commission demonstrated, sold, and repaired the Singer sewing machines. Both the McCormick and Singer franchises were after some years replaced by a company-owned network. Coca-Cola was conceived in 1886 as a non-alcoholic alternative to 'hard' drink such as beers and spirits. It was dispensed from a soda fountain by mixing syrup with carbonated water. It was not portable and so this severely limited the size of its market and growth (Felstead, A., 1993, *The Corporate Paradox: Power and Control in Business Franchise*, Routledge, p. 41). The advent of bottling technology changed all that and the rights to bottle and sell Coca-Cola everywhere in the US (other than New England, Mississippi and Texas, where prior arrangements were in place) were granted to two traditional franchisees – Messrs Thomas and Whitehead in 1899. The franchisees were granted the rights to make up and bottle Coca-Cola from syrup provided by the franchisor which also provided them with bottles, labels and advertising matter. Whitehead soon after sold out to John Thomas Lupton, after realising that he did not have sufficient capital to set up the bottling plants. In due course the franchisees were granting sub franchises across the US (Ibid. Felstead). Pepsi-Cola followed suit and by 1910 had 280 bottlers across the USA (Ibid. Felstead). US Department of Commerce (USDOC), various years, 'Franchising in the Economy', ed, Kostecka.

4 At the turn of the century, William E. Metzger of Detroit became the first franchisee of the General Motors Corporation. Ford, and then other manufacturers, followed suit. Similar trends developed in the petroleum industry (Felstead, 1993, p. 42).

5 The first true business format franchise was created by Martha Matilda Harper, who developed her network of Harper Beauty Shops at the turn of the century into over 500 shops in the USA, Canada and Europe by the mid-1920s. Plitt, J.R., 2000, *Martha Matilda Harper and the American Dream: How One Woman Changed the Face of Modern Business*, New York: Syracuse University Press. Other businesses followed suit. Rexall drugstores began in 1902 as a co-operative of some 40 druggists organised by Louis Ligget who set up a company to manufacture private-label drugs which would be distributed and sold exclusively by these druggists under a franchise (Felstead, 1993, p. 42). In 1925, Howard Johnson established an ice cream business in Massachusetts and expanded it by franchising it to a group of restaurants on the East Coast. By 1940 the first Howard Johnson Restaurant appeared, and in 1954 the first motor lodge opened. The Howard Johnson franchise system has since grown internationally to over 200 restaurants and about 500 motor lodges (Felstead, A. – Ibid. p. 42). Hertz Car Rental and A&W Restaurants are just two of the businesses that began franchising in the 1920s and are still doing so (Blair, R. and F. Lafontaine, 2005, *The Economics of Franchising*, Cambridge University Press, p. 7).

6 Love, J.F., 2008, *McDonalds: Behind the Arches*, p. 45.

7 Felstead, 1993, p. 42.

8 Ibid., p. 42.

9 Stanworth, J. and B. Smith, 1991, *Barclays Guide to Franchising for Small Businesses*, Blackwell.

10 ServiceMaster, the carpet and upholstery cleaning franchise, was another American import which came to the UK in 1958 when Raymond Crouch bought the master licence for Europe from ServiceMaster Industries Inc, a Chicago based company (ibid.). Mr Softee and Lyons Maid are also credited with offering franchises during the 1950s (ibid.).

11 Between 1970 and 1985, franchising grew steadily and the number of franchise systems increased from a mere 40 to 200. Over the last 25 years the rate of growth has accelerated, reaching a number of some 980 franchisees in 2009. This growth can be attributed in part to German Reunification, even though many in the East suffered from a lack of capital with which to invest in franchise systems (*Giesler, Nauschütt, Franchiserecht*, 2.ed. 2007, pp. 10–11. According to Köhler, NJW 1990, p. 1689, there were 140 franchising systems with 7750 franchisees in 1986).

12 Events in the UK slowed the growth of franchising in the 1960s. The public linked franchising with pyramid selling, a fraudulent marketing scheme (Adams and Prichard Jones (1997), *Franchising: Practice and Precedents* business format franchising). Pyramid selling involves the sale of distributorships to purchasers, who are encouraged with financial incentives to subdivide their distributorship to 'sub-distributors' and so on. The system can be likened to the chain letter principle. At one end of the chain, a door-to-door sales force found the unknown product very difficult to sell, while at the top of the pyramid a fortune had been amassed from the effective sale of multi-level distributorships rather than products.

13 The California Franchise Investment Law (California Corporations Code, Division 5, Parts 1 through 6, Sections 31000 through 31516) was adopted in 1970 to be effective January 1 1971. Code of Federal Regulations, Title 16, Chapter 1, Subchapter D, Part 436 (16 CFR 436), promulgated December 21 1978, effective October 21 1979 (effective date extended from July 21 1979, 44 Federal Register 31170, May 31 1979). Cited as 'FTC Rule'.

14 www.eff-franchising.com. Its purpose has been to uphold a self-regulatory approach to good and fair business practice in franchising in Europe and promote franchising in Europe by protecting the Franchise Industry by promoting the European Code of Ethics, influencing and encouraging the development of Franchising in Europe, representing the interests of the Franchise industry to international organisations such as the European Commission, the European Parliament etc., promoting and representing the European Franchise industry and its members world-wide; the exchange of information and documentation between national Associations or Federations in Europe and in the world and serving its member Associations (the EFF currently represents 16 national Franchise Associations; Belgium, France, the Netherlands, Italy, the United Kingdom, Austria, Finland, Portugal, Sweden, Denmark, Finland, Hungary, Germany, Slovenia, Greece and the Czech Republic).

15 The following organisations are founder members: Budget Rent-a-Car Limited, Dyno-Rod plc, Holiday Inns Inc, Kentucky Fried Chicken Ltd, Prontaprint Limited, ServiceMaster Limited, Wimpy International Limited and Zeibart Mobile Transport Service Limited (*Barclays Guide to Franchising for Small Businesses*).

Although franchising is mentioned in historical texts dating back to the Middle Ages and the 'tied house system'[1] was widely used by brewers in the UK from the mid-18th century until the mid-1980s,[2] it only really came 'of age' and became a popular form of doing business in the EU in the early 1970s.[3] Despite its rapid growth, for a long time there remained much suspicion of franchising in the European establishment. For example, in the Fraud Trials Committee 1986 Report,[4] Lord Roskill, the Chairman, described franchising as an enterprise in which 'fraudsters induce investors to buy franchises, holding out the prospect of large returns on investment. But once the payment has been made the franchise proves worthless'. Nevertheless, franchising has continued to **2.3**

1 The widespread availability of alcohol was causing social concern. Legislation was introduced to restrict the sale of alcohol to those with licences and also to require innkeepers to improve the drinking environment. As a result the value of those inns with licences greatly increased. However, those with licences often had insufficient funds to improve their properties and were therefore likely to go out of business. It was out of this economic difficulty that the tied house system developed. By granting a landlord a loan or leasing its own property out to prospective landlords brewers, such as Whitbread, were able to retain and expand the number of outlets for their beer (Ritchie, B., 1992, *An Uncommon Brewer: The Story of Whitbread 1742–1992*, James and James). This 'tied house' system proved itself as an efficient business mechanism until the competition authorities undermined it in the 1980's ('The Supply of Beer – A Report on the Supply of Beer for Retail Sale in the United Kingdom' – Mergers and Monopolies Commission).

2 Ibid. Ritchie, B., 1992, p. 17.

3 When the British Franchise Association was established, followed by the French Franchise Federation and the European Franchise Federation.

4 Fraud Trials (Roskill Report) HMSO, 1986.

grow. In 2010 the estimated turnover of franchised businesses in the USA was US$868.3 billion[5] and an estimated US$300 billion in the EU.[6] Its presence around the globe is evidenced by the waves of franchise-specific legislation that occurred in the 1990s and the new millennium. Business format franchising encompasses a wide range of goods and services across many sectors whilst traditional franchising is evident in automobile and petroleum distribution, US sports franchises such as the NFL, NHL and NBA and national infrastructure with rail and TV franchises being granted to operators.[7] The difference between traditional and business format franchising endures today.[8] This book focuses upon business format franchising.

2. The institutional contextualisation of franchising in the EU

2.4 The potential for franchising to help make the EU's single market dream a reality for small and medium sized enterprises (SMEs) that might otherwise find entering other member states too daunting a prospect, has clearly been identified by the movers and shakers in the EU Commission.[9] The International Chamber of Commerce considers that 'franchising has proved over many years to be an extremely successful commercial vehicle for the distribution of products and services, making a considerable contribution to growth in business sectors that use this type of distribution channel'.[10] Prominent member state politicians have hailed franchising as being 'an important incentive for the recovery of the economy'.[11] Indeed, in Italy the government has invested over €350 million in franchising by sponsoring franchisees with investment

5 Price Waterhouse Coopers 2010 Franchise Business Economic Outlook. The International Franchise Association's Educational Foundation www.franchise.org (viewed 29/12/2010) (142) European Franchise Federation Statistics 2010 – www.eff-franchise.com (viewed 23/12/2010).

6 See 2.18 below.

7 However, whereas both forms of franchise are often considered together in the US (so greatly inflating the figures for franchising, e.g. US Department of Commerce. Various Years. *Franchising in the Economy*, Kostecka, A.), in the EU the two forms are kept separate when considering the economic importance of franchising (e.g. The BFA/National Westminster Bank Survey of Franchising in the UK. Various Years. BFA). In the EU automobile distribution is dealt with separately from business format franchising from the legal perspective.

8 Although some believe that the difference between traditional and business format franchising is more a matter of degree and that although traditional franchising tends to be a simpler financial arrangement there is little real difference between the two in terms of the basic legal relationship. Dnes, A., 1992, *Franchising: A case study approach*, Aldershot, Ashgate Publishing Ltd, and Klein, B., 1995, 'The Economics of Franchise Contract', *Journal of Corporate Finance*, Volume 2:9–37.

9 Rt Hon Sir Leon Brittan, Q.C. – President of the European Commission, Abell, *European Franchising* (Vol. 1).

10 Maria Livanos Cattaui, Secretary General of ICC on the ICC Model International Franchising Contract.

11 Senator Asciutti commenting upon bill no. 2093 of 6 March 1997 in the Italian senate stated that 'franchising has the potential to be an important element in the recovery of the economy'. He also observed that 'particularly during a period of sluggish economic performance, the regulation of franchising can play a noteworthy role in the creation of new enterprises, especially in the central and southern regions of the country'.

grants and soft loans.[12] The World Intellectual Property Organization recognises franchising's 'rapid growth and success' and comments upon its ability to ensure that 'a large and stable organisation is able to grow and develop, motivated by or indeed driven by the spirit of small business'.[13] Yet at the same time reports of the legislature and political debate in member states in which franchising is well developed condemn it as an enterprise in which 'fraudsters induce investors to buy franchises, holding out the prospect of large returns on investment. But once the payment has been made the franchise proves worthless'.[14] Others seek to 'explode the myth that the franchise industry is a relatively safe industry in comparison with other fully fledged business'.[15] Despite this difference of opinion however, franchising continues to grow and the International Institute for the Unification of Private Law (UNIDROIT) has identified franchising as 'playing an ever greater role in a wide range of national economies'.[16]

B. THE ECONOMIC CONTEXTUALISATION OF FRANCHISING IN THE EU

> Franchising normally stimulates economic activity by improving the distribution of goods and/or the provision of services as they give franchisors the possibility of establishing a uniform network with limited investments, which may assist the entry of new competitors in the markets particularly in the case of SMEs. It allows independent traders to set up outlets more rapidly and with a higher chain of success than if they were to set up without the franchisor's experience and assistance. Franchisors therefore have a better opportunity to compete with larger distribution undertakings[17] ... It also generally allows consumers and other end users a fair share of the resulting benefits as they combine the advantage of a uniform network with the existence of traders personally interested in the efficient operation of their business. The homogeneity of the network and the constant co-operation between the franchisor and the franchisees ensures the constant quality of the products and services. The favourable effect of franchising on inter brand competition and the fact that consumers are free to deal with any franchisee in the network guarantees that a reasonable part of the resulting benefits will be passed on to consumers.[18] **2.5**

12 Legislative Decree No. 185 of 21 April 2000 and Decree No. 295 of 28 May 2001 (Italy).
13 WIPO, *Franchising Guide.*
14 Lord Roskill, Chairman of the Fraud Trials Committee 1986, *Roskill Report.*
15 Brian H. Donohoe (Central Ayrshire), Hansard HC vol 450 col 1493 (24 October 2006).
16 UNIDROIT, *Model Franchise Disclosure Law*, Preamble.
17 Commission Regulation (EEC) No. 4887/88 p. 12.
18 Ibid.

In pursuing the goals of economic growth, job creation and consumer satisfaction, commercial innovation such as franchising needs to be encouraged. Franchising can contribute to the establishment of a unified European Market. It facilitates cross-frontier development as it is based on the leverage which an established name or idea can give a relatively small investment to enable the product or service involved to spread quickly, far and wide.

2.6 Franchising is a commercial phenomenon particularly well suited to the challenges of the single market. The combination of a franchisor's know-how and a franchisee's enterprise can boost economic activity and employment, while enlarging the range of goods and services on offer to the public. Franchising makes products and services available to a wide public and does not stop policy making at national frontiers within the EU.

It is suggested that the regulatory environment in the EU should therefore support and re-enforce the economic drivers that attract franchisors and franchisees to franchising and reduce the inherent consequential risks they expose themselves to.

However, given the heterogeneous policy legacies in the EU member states as well as the diverse preferences of national governments and other domestic actors, a one-size-fits-all solution is neither politically feasible nor normatively desirable.

2.7 Although franchising is a positive influence in the EU and stimulates economic activity by improving distribution and giving business increased access to other member state markets, it is not fulfilling its full potential to contribute to the realisation of the single market. The following is critical analysis towards proving this objective. Business format franchising is 'a distinct and remarkably effective method of conducting business activities that is particularly appropriate in current economic conditions, due mainly to the advantages to both parties in the contract'.[19] It is a significant part of the economy of a number of EU member states. However, the economic data available is poor and incomplete. There is no up-to-date, uniform and complete set of economic data for franchising in all or even the majority of EU member states. This in itself suggests that franchising is not achieving its full potential in the EU. According to the 2010 NatWest/BFA Franchise Survey, franchising contributed £11.8 billion to the UK's GDP in 2009, an increase of £400 million from 2008.[20] The same publication indicates that despite the economic climate, nine out of ten

---

19 The Belgian House of Representatives, 17 March 2004 Doc 51 0924/001.

20 UK: Natwest/BFA Survey 2010: http://www.thebfa.org/fpnews/natwestbfasurvey10.asp.

franchise businesses are profitable. The survey also states that the number of individuals employed in franchising in the previous twelve months stands at 465 000 across a total of 34 800 franchised units in the UK. This means that on average each unit employs 13 people.

The European Franchise Federation (EFF) indicates that the total 2009 turnover of franchising in Germany was €48 billion.[21] A report in January 2008 by Deutsche Bank stated that the sector has tripled its nominal turnover in the ten preceding years.[22] By comparison, Germany's nominal GDP has only grown by 25% over the same period. As a result, the franchising share of GDP increased by nearly 1% to 1.6% between 1996 and 2006. This figure is likely to be higher now as the industry's turnover has continued to rise. Indeed, Deutsche Bank expects the sector to grow until 2015 at a rate of 7% per annum to around €70 billion. Deutsche Bank also reported that between 1996 and 2006 the number of people working in the sector nearly doubled. By comparison the total workforce only increased by 4%. In its 2010 report, the EFF estimates that 452 000 people are employed in 58 000 units. On average this means that each unit employs 7.8 people.[23] According to Guy Gras, Chairman of the French Franchise Federation, the 2008 total turnover of franchising in France was €47.6 billion.[24] The number of franchise networks in France has doubled over the past ten years, with steady growth of 8–10% over the last four years. In 2009 693 194 people were employed by 51 600 units[25] in France. This equates to 8.25 people being employed per franchise unit. 2.8

1. Estimating the size of franchising in the EU

Although franchising makes a substantial contribution to the economy of the European Union, in order to measure whether it is as well established as it could be and is making its full potential contribution to the single market, it is necessary to first of all examine how well developed it is in the EU member states and then to benchmark this against its development in the USA and Australia. There is a lack of full and accurate information about the scale of 2.9

21 European Franchise Federation – www.eff-franchise.com (viewed 23/12/2010).

22 Deutsche Bank Research: 'Franchising Coming of Age in Germany' (January 2008) http://www.franchiseverband.com/fileadmin/user_upload/MAIN-dateien/Studien/Franchising_in_Germany_coming_of_age.pdf.

23 Ibid.

24 FFF Press Pack for the 2009 Franchise Expo in Paris. http://lb7.reedexpo.fr/Data/kmreed_franchise/block/F_23316ac8f1472bf8d16e0ce274b508624c124d19ed45d.pdf. The Franch Franchising Association excludes company-owned outlets from this figure and therefore concluded there were only 53 002 franchised outlets in 2009.

25 Ibid. The French Franchising Association excludes company-owned outlets from this figure and therefore concluded there were only 53 002 franchised outlets in 2009.

franchising in the whole of the EU. The most recent figures published by the EFF are in respect of 2009, but they only deal with 18 member states[26] and the information given for them is incomplete[27] and in places incorrect.[28] There are no other recent figures for franchising in the EU. The most recent figures for franchising in the whole of the EU are from 2005. 'Franchising Europe' estimated that there were 5000 franchises operating in Europe, that supported 300 000 outlets with an estimated total turnover of US$200 billion.[29] Unfortunately this figure is not broken down into figures for individual member states, save for the turnover figure for France, which is given at US$51.6 billion (€38.6 billion). The premises made and data used in arriving at the estimated figure are not given. It is therefore not particularly reliable, but it is the only figure available.

2.10 In order to establish the turnover of franchising in the EU it is therefore necessary to extrapolate a figure based upon the EFF's 2009 statistics and the Franchising Europe 2005 statistics. This paucity of current statistics about franchising in the EU of itself suggests that franchising may not be as well established in the single market as a whole, as it is in the larger member states. In 2009 the EFF estimates that there were 9971 franchises accounting for 405 000 outlets. The EFF estimates the turnover of franchising in 2009 in Germany, Italy, Spain, Portugal, the Netherlands and the UK[30] at US$188.1 billion. Add to that the French Franchise Federation's figure for France (US$62.3 billion) and it totals US$250.4 billion. The figures below clearly suggest that franchising in the EU is underperforming when compared to those for the USA and Australia.[31]

---

26 Austria, Belgium, Croatia, Czech Republic, Denmark, Finland, France, Germany, Greece, Hungary, Italy, Netherlands, Portugal, Poland, Slovenia, Spain, Sweden, Turkey and the UK. Turkey is not a member of the EU. However, four of these (Belgium, Denmark, Finland and Germany) are estimates and the gross total of 11 731 is arbitrarily discounted by 15% to take into account the fact that brands that exist in several countries may be costed more than once in these statistics. The figure for Turkey is given at 1640 and so that must be removed. Consequently the estimated figure of 8330 is deemed to be unreliable. The statistics do not give details of even estimated turnover for franchising. The estimated number of franchised outlets in the EU is around 405 000 but again this is unreliable as figures for Austria, Belgium, Czech Republic and Portugal are missing.

27 For example, no turnover figures are given for 12 member states.

28 The turnover figure for the UK in 2009 is given as €9.42 billion rather than the €11.8 billion given by the BFA.

29 Iuliana, S. and M. Mihaela, 2009, 'The High Impact of Franchising on Economic Affairs in Some of the EU Members' *Annals of Faculty of Economics*, 2009, Vol. 1, Issue 1, 251–6 (Published by the University of Oradea, Faculty of Economics) http://steconomice.uoradea.ro/anale/volume/2009/v1-international-relations-and-european-integration/39.pdf.

30 The EFF figure wrongly put the UK's 2009 turnover at €9.4 billion rather than £11.8 billion (€14 billion or US$18.7 billion) reported by the BFA.

31 See 'Price Waterhouse Coopers 2010 Franchise Business Economic Outlook' – The International Franchise Association's Educational Foundation www.franchise.org (viewed 29/12/2010) and Franchise Council of Australia www.franchise.org (viewed 29/12/2010).

Table 2.2 Key statistics about franchising those member states referred to in the EEF's 2009 Survey

	Population	GDP[1] (US$)	Estimated 2009 turnover of franchising in local currency	Estimated 2009 turnover of franchising in US dollars (exchange rate as at 23/12/10)
The UK	62 million	2.2 trillion	£11.8 billion[2]	US$18.7 billion
Germany	81.7 million	3.3 trillion	€48 billion[3]	US$62.9 billion
France	64.7 million	2.5 trillion	€47.6 billion[4]	US$62.3 billion
Italy	60.4 million	2.1 trillion	€21.77 billion	US$28.5 billion
Spain	45.9 million	1.46 trillion	€24.7 billion	US$32.4 billion
The Netherlands	16.5 million	0.77 trillion	€29.2 billion	US$29 billion
Portugal	10.6 million	0.2 trillion	€5 billion	US$6.6 billion
Total	341.8 million	12.54 trillion	–	US$250.4 billion

Notes:
1 International Monetary Fund.
2 BFA/NatWest Survey 2010.
3 European Franchise Federation – www.eff-franchise.com (viewed 23/12/10).
4 FFF Press Pack.

The paucity of current, complete and consistent data for all 27 EU member states means that it is impossible to definitely state the turnover of franchising in the EU. Nevertheless, it can be estimated in three ways. All three ways lead to estimates that suggest that franchising in the EU is underperforming compared to the USA and Australia. **2.11**

Firstly, Franchise Europe's 2005 figure US$200 billion can be increased by the same percentage as the number of outlets are reported to have increased by the 2009 EFF Survey. Assuming that each new outlet on average has the same turnover as the average outlet in 2005, it is logically justifiable.[32] Applying this methodology the increase of outlets from 3000 in 2005 to 4000 in 2009 represents a 33.3% increase. If the same percentage increase is applied to the turnover of franchising the US$200 billion figure for 2005 would become US$266 billion in 2009.[33] This methodology produces a figure which wrongly assumes that retail prices are the same in all EU member states and ignores the number of outlets in a number of smaller member states in 2009 but it does produce a working figure. **2.12**

32 However, as explained below this assumption is incorrect due to the differing resale prices in member states.

33 This methodology underestimates the increase in the number of outlets in the EU in 2009, as the EFF figures do not include all EU member states – although it does include all those in which franchising is well established.

Table 2.3 Increase in franchising in the EU between 2005 and 2009

	2005	2009	Percentage increase
Number of outlets	3000	4000	33.3
Turnover	US$200 billion	US$266 billion	33.3

2.13 The second way of estimating the turnover of franchising in 2009 using 2005 figures involves increasing the total 2005 turnover figures by the same percentage as the turnover for France has increased in the same period. This assumes a uniform level of growth in all EU member states which is logically defensible. The French Franchise Federation's 2009 turnover figure of €47.6 billion represents an increase of €9 billion on the Franchise Europe 2005 figure of €38.6 billion, which is approximately a 25% increase. If that percentage increase is applied to the US$200 billion figure it suggests that the turnover of franchising in the EU in 2009 should be approximately US$250 billion. That is more or less the same as the figure that EFF's 2009 survey produces for the UK, Germany, France, Italy, Spain, the Netherlands and Portugal. It can therefore be concluded that it is an underestimate.

Table 2.4 Increase in the turnover in franchising in France and the EU between 2005 and 2009

	2005	2009	Percentage increase
Turnover in France	€38.6 billion	€47.6 billion	c25%
Turnover in EU	US$200 billion	US$250 billion	25%

2.14 The third way of estimating the turnover of franchising in 2009 is to compare the number of outlets in the seven EU member states that have a turnover of US$250.4 billion according to the EFF figures with those in the other 11 member states referred to in the EFF's 2009 figures. (For some reason no turnover figures are given for these 11 member states.)

2.15 Six of the member states that account for a turnover of US$250.4 billion account for 283 115 outlets. There are no outlet figures given for Portugal. However, as Portugal's turnover is approximately 25% of Italy's, it is reasonable to assume that it may have around 25% of the outlets Italy has. That would mean that the seven EU member states account for approximately 300 000 outlets of the 405 000 – around about 75%. As the remaining eleven member states have approximately one third of the outlets of the seven EU member states which have a turnover of US$250.4 billion, it is reasonable to suggest that they also have a turnover which is roughly equivalent to one third of that figure, that is US$83.2 billion. That would mean that the turnover of the 18 EU member states listed by the EFF is estimated at approximately US$333.6 billion.

Table 2.5 Breakdown of number of Outlets in 18 member states in 2009

		Percentage of Outlets in the 11 member states
Number of Outlets in 18 EU member states in 2009 according to the EFF	405 000	100%
Less		
Estimated number of Outlets in the 7 EU member states that had a turnover of US$250.4 billion in 2009*	Approx 300 000	c66.6%
Number of Outlets in other 11 EU member states	105,000	c33.3%

Notes:
* The EFF gives no number of outlets for Portugal. This is calculated by reference to Italy. Italy's turnover is €21.77 billion. Portugal's turnover is €5.05 billion, i.e. approximately 25% of Italy's. Italy has 53 300 outlets. If Portugal has 25% of that number, this would be 13 325.

Assuming that on average outlets turnover an equal amount, approximating the number of outlets in the 11 EU member states as being 33.3% of those in the 7 member states accounting for turnover of US$250.4 billion and applying that same percentage to turnover suggests a turnover figure for franchising in 2009 of US$333.6 billion. **2.16**

33.3% × US$250.4 billion = US$83.2 billion

US$250.4 billion + US$83.2 billion = US$333.6 billion

There is no evidence to suggest that there is any substantial franchising in the remaining nine member states[34] and so for the purpose of this calculation it will be assumed that they account for no significant franchising turnover. However, the problem with this calculation is that it is unlikely that outlets in the 11 member states for which estimates are being made will be turning over the same amount as those in Germany, the UK and France which have a much higher cost of living.[35] The most relevant way of testing this is to consider the relative cost of a particular product sold by a franchise network in the EU.

34 Malta, Cyprus, Finland, Norway, Slovakia, Ireland, Lithuania, Latvia and Estonia.

35 The EU Statistics on Income and Living Conditions (EU-SILC) (see http://epp.eurostat.ec.europa.eu) suggest that there is a wide range in the cost of living in the EU member states. (Framework Regulation 1177/2003 of the European Parliament and of the Council of 16 June 2003 concerning community statistics on income and living conditions.)

2.17 The Big Mac Index[36] gives the cost of a Big Mac in a number of different EU member states. In the UK it costs US$3.65, in France US$3.20 and in Germany US$3.96. The cost in the eight other EU member states that are not included in the seven that had a turnover of US$250.4 billion are considerably lower.

An analysis of the cost of a Big Mac in these 11 EU member states yields the following data set out in Tables 2.6, 2.7 and 2.8.

Table 2.6 Selection of member states included in those which had a turnover of US$250.4 billion in 2009

EU Member State	Cost of Big Mac as at 2006 in US$
The UK	3.65
Germany	3.96
France	3.20

Table 2.7 Selection of member states included in EFF outlets statistics for which no turnover figure is available

EU Member State	Cost of Big Mac as at 2006 in US$
Hungary	2.71
Poland	2.10
Czech Republic	2.67
Slovenia	2.76
Greece	2.40

Table 2.8 Selection of member states for which the EFF has no statistics

Latvia	2.47
Lithuania	2.41
Slovakia	2.76

These figures suggest that it is unlikely that the outlets in the 11 EU member states included in the 2009 EFF Statistics (but not included in the seven member states that account for the US$250.4 billion turnover) have a turnover of US$83.2 billion.

36 The Big Mac index was introduced in *The Economist* in September 1986 and gave rise to 'Burgernomics' (Daley, J. (6/9/2008), 'Burgernomics: Why the price of a Big Mac may hold the key to better investment returns', *The Independent*) www.investment.com (viewed 16/1/2011).

The above three methodologies produce a range of the estimated turnover of franchising in the EU in 2009 from US$250 billion to US$333.6 billion. None of the figures can be considered to be totally accurate, but they are all the result of a logical use of the data available. It is therefore suggested that a figure somewhere in the middle of the range between US$333.6 billion and US$250 billion is a fair and reasonable estimate of the likely turnover of franchising in the EU during 2009. Thus, these methodologies suggest that the turnover of franchising in the EU in 2009 can reasonably be estimated at around US$300 billion or €215 billion.[37] Further critical analysis of the figures also suggests that franchising in the EU is heavily concentrated in a minority of member states. Those EU member states other than the UK, Germany, France, Italy, Spain, the Netherlands and Portugal probably account for a turnover of around US$50 billion (€35 billion) at most. **2.18**

Estimated 2009 turnover of franchising in the EU	cUS$300 billion
Less	
2009 turnover of seven EU member states identified	US$250.4 billion
Estimated 2009 turnover of other 20 EU member states	US$49.6 billion

This suggests that franchising is heavily focused in around a quarter of the EU member states which account for US$250.4 billion (€180 billion) out of a total estimated turnover of US$300 billion. In other words 25% of the EU member states account for an estimated 83.5% of franchising's turnover in the EU.

Having established the scale of franchising in the EU and that franchising is not well developed in the majority of EU member states, it is appropriate to benchmark its turnover in the EU against that in the USA and Australia. This is critical analysis towards establishing the first objective of the book. The EU has a population of around 500 million[38] compared to the USA's 310.9 million.[39] The EU's Gross Domestic Product[40] in 2010 was US$16 106 896 000 000 (16.1 trillion) compared to the USA's GDP of US$14 624 184 000 000 (14.6 trillion), according to the International Monetary Fund.[41] One might therefore expect the estimated turnover of franchising in the EU and the USA to be similar. However, this is not the case. The estimated 405 000 franchised outlets in the EU and the generous estimated turnover of US$300 billion are dwarfed by the equivalent figures in the United States, where in 2010 there were an **2.19**

37 Exchange rate as at 12 March 2011.

38 International Monetary Fund. World Economic Database, October 2010.

39 Ibid.

40 The market value of all final goods and services from a nation in a given year.

41 International Monetary Fund, 2010.

estimated 901 093 business format franchise outlets employing 9 558 000 and accounting for an output of US$868.3 billion.[42] Even Australia, with a population of only 22.5 million and a GDP of US$1.2 trillion, has an estimated franchise turnover of US$130 billion.[43]

Table 2.9 Key statistics about franchising in the EU, the USA and Australia

	Population	GDP 2010	Estimated turnover of franchising	Franchising as a percentage of GDP	Turnover of franchising per head of population
EU	500 million	US$16.1 trillion	US$300 billion	1.86%	US$600
USA	310.9 million	US$14.6 trillion	US$868.3 billion	5.95%	US$2792
Australia	22.5 million	US$1.2 trillion	US$130 billion	10.83%	US$5777

There are no up-to-date figures for the number of franchisors in the USA. None are published by the International Franchise Association (IFA), which focuses instead upon the number of franchised outlets.

2.20 The figures are very stark. Although the USA has only 60% of the population of the EU and a lower GDP, franchising's estimated turnover in the USA is considerably more than double that in the EU. Compared to both the USA and Australia (both of which have sophisticated and well developed franchise laws), franchising in the EU is markedly underdeveloped. Despite a broad range of differing attitudes to business format franchising, it has developed into a channel to market that makes a significant contribution to the economy of the European Union. However, it is underperforming in the single market relative to its contribution to other markets, namely the USA and Australia. Also, with some 83.5% of franchising being concentrated in just 25% of the 27 member states, franchising is clearly not promoting trade between member states as much as it could.

42 'Price Waterhouse Coopers 2010 Franchise Business Economic Outlook' – The International Franchise Association's Educational Foundation www.franchise.org (viewed 29/12/2010).

43 Franchise Council of Australia www.franchise.org (viewed 29/12/2010).

C. DECONSTRUCTING THE ECONOMIC RATIONALE OF FRANCHISING – WHY DO PEOPLE GET INVOLVED IN FRANCHISING?

Franchising stimulates economic activity by offering advantages to those involved in it. There are inherent economic advantages of franchising which attract franchisors and franchisees to become involved in it. **2.21**

1. The economic drivers of franchising for franchisors

Businesses, other than sole traders, involve a relationship between a principal and the individuals he hires to provide a service or manufacture/distribute goods – his 'agents'. The principal delegates decision-making authority to those agents.[44] The interests of the principal and its agents do not always coincide, so there is potential for conflict. The agent may not always act in the principal's best interests[45] and underperforming agents are not uncommon.[46] In order to reduce the risk of a poor employee, a non-franchised business will need to institute a costly management system. Franchising, on the other hand, replaces much of the need for such a management system with powerful financial incentives, namely the benefit of the profits created by his/her endeavours and the risk of losing the capital that they have invested in the business.[47] Because franchising creates a better financial synergy between the two parties, there is less need for monitoring and a greater probability for maximum performance by the franchisee.[48] There is evidence that increased managerial ownership improves performance.[49] The corollary of the franchisee's better performance is improved performance by the franchisor, as the franchisor's performance depends to a large extent on its franchisees' performance. **2.22**

The relationship between principal and agent can be described or explained in mathematical models.[50] Agents are generally assumed to be risk averse i.e. **2.23**

---

44 Klock, C., 2004, *Franchising a Good Strategy for a company operating throughout Europe – Case Study Benetton*, University of Abertay Dundee.

45 Jensen, M.C. and W.H. Meckling, 1976, 'Theory of the Firm, Managerial Behavior, Agency Costs, and Ownership Structure', *Journal of Financial Economics*, October, 305–60. Eisenhardt, K., 1989, 'Agency Theory: An Assessment and Review', *Academy of Management Review*, Volume 14, Issue 1, 57–74.

46 Rubin, P., 1978, 'The Theory of the Firm and the Structure of the Franchise Contract', *Journal of Law and Economics* 21, 223–33. Brickley, J. and F. Dark, 1987, 'The Choice of Organizational Form: The Case of Franchising', *Journal of Financial Economics*, Volume 18, 401–20.

47 Ibid. Brickley and Dark.

48 Bradash, J.L., 1997, 'Using the Plural Form in the Management of Restaurant Chains', *Administrative Science Quarterly*, Vol. 42, No. 2, 276–303.

49 Bruton, G.D., J.K. Keels and E.L. Scifres, 2002, 'Corporate Restructuring and Performance: An Agency Theory Perspective on the Complete Buyout Cycle', *Journal of Business Research*, Vol. 55, Issue 9, September, 709–24.

50 Op cit, Jensen and Meckling, 1976, 305–360.

they prefer a low but secure income whilst principals are risk neutral.[51] Many commentators have highlighted the advantages of franchising a business using this 'Agency Theory'.[52] Another analysis proposed is that franchising is a solution to the capital, managerial and information constraints faced by expanding businesses:[53] the so-called 'Resource Scarcity Theory'. It is suggested that growing businesses use franchising as a way of accessing capital that would otherwise be unavailable to them in a cost-effective way that offers fair reward to the financier (the franchisee). Support for this analysis is provided by the former president of Kentucky Fried Chicken, John Y. Brown, who estimated that it would have cost KFC $450 million to establish its first 2700 stores, an amount of capital that was not available to KFC in the early stages of its expansion.[54] The traditional ways for new businesses to access capital are to either sell equity or raise a loan, although raising a loan may not be possible in the early stages of a business's development due to lack of collateral and a proven track record. Therefore, franchising is often a more cost effective and realistic option.[55] Indeed, franchisees may be able to provide capital to the franchisor at a lower cost than passive investors can.[56] In addition to capital, franchising also provides an efficient way to obtain the managerial expertise needed to grow the business. Because a franchisee puts a significant amount of her/his assets and time into her/his unit, she/he is likely to purchase a franchise only if she/he is confident in her/his managerial abilities.[57] Several commentators stress the fact that franchising facilitates much more rapid growth for companies,[58] suggesting that franchisors have used franchising to secure a large

---

51 Williamson, O. and S.E. Masten, 1999, *The Economics of Transaction Costs*, Cheltenham, Edward Elgar Publishing Ltd.

52 E.g. Dourma, S. and H. Schreuder, 2002, *Economic Approach to Organisation*, 3rd edn. Edinburgh, Pearson Education; Brousseau, E. and J.-M. Glachant, 2002, *The Economics of Contracts: Theory and Application* 1st edn. Cambridge, Cambridge University Press; Brickley, A., F. Dark and M. Weisbach, 1991, 'An Agency Perspective on Franchising', *Financial Management*, Volume 20, Issue 1.

53 Oxenfeldt, A.R. and A.O. Kelly, 1968, 'Will Successful Systems Ultimately Become Wholly-Owned Chains?', *Journal of Retailing*, Volume 44, Issue 49, 69–83; Norton, S., 1988, 'An Empirical Look at Franchising as an Organizational Form', *Journal of Business*, Volume 61, Issue 2, 197–218; Carney, M. and E. Gedajlovic, 1991, 'Vertical Integration in Franchise Systems: Agency Theory and Resources Explanations', *Strategic Management Journal*, Volume 12, 607–29; Shane, S.A., 1996, 'Hybrid Organizational Arrangements and Their Implications for Firm Growth and Survival: A Study of New Franchisors', *Academy of Management Journal*, Volume 39, No. 1, pp. 216–34.

54 Tikoo, S., 1996, 'Assessing the Franchise Option', *Business Horizons*, May–June, 78–82.

55 Dant, R.P. and P.J. Kaufmann, 2003, 'Structural and Strategic Dynamics in Franchising', *Journal of Retailing*, Volume 79, Issue 2, 63–75.

56 Combs, J.G. and D.J. Kitchen, 1999, 'Explaining Interfirm Cooperation and Performance: Toward a Reconciliation of Predictions from the Resource-Based View and Organizational Economics', *Strategic Management Journal*, 20, 867–88.

57 Op cit, Shane, 1996, 216–34.

58 Barrow, C., 1989, 'Franchising', in: P. Burns and J. Dewhurst, eds, *Small Business and Entrepreneurship* (London, Macmillan) and Thompson, R.S., 1994, 'The Franchise Life Cycle and the Penrose Effect', *Journal of Economic Behaviour and Organisation*, 24, 207–18, North Holland.

market share much more rapidly than they otherwise could achieve.[59] The reason for this is largely the so-called 'Penrose Effect', that is managerial capacities pose a static limit to a firm's expansion and rapid recruitment of staff raises operating costs. Franchising is a device that circumvents this constraint by externalising the management functions to the franchisee.[60] Thus franchising addresses the adverse selection problem of firms hiring managers who may overstate their qualifications to secure employment. On the international front franchising also allows a firm to leverage the local market knowledge of its franchisees as it expands into new geographic areas.[61] Thus the 'Resource Scarcity' school of thought suggests that low cost capital, motivated managerial expertise and better local market knowledge are three key resources that should reduce a franchisor's overall risk and have a significant positive impact on a franchisor's financial performance.

A third hypothesis is 'Value Creation' or 'Transaction Cost'. Aliouche and Schlentrich suggest the real value of franchising to a business is the improvement in business performance due to its choice of growing through franchising instead of growing through its own means.[62] Their study of the US restaurant sector over the ten-year period 1993–2002 suggests that US public restaurant franchisors have created more value than their non-franchising competitors in that they have a higher propensity to create market value and economic value than non-franchisors and generate on average higher added value than non-franchisors.[63] Commentators also suggest that other economic factors that cause businesses to franchise their business model are based upon its ability to give smaller, less well capitalised businesses access to some of the commercial advantages enjoyed by their larger, better capitalised competitors. These include lower costs through bulk purchasing, economies of scale, new product development and advertising campaigns.[64] Its ability to combine the chains' comparative advantages in creating brand recognition and capturing economies of scale with the local entrepreneur's local knowledge and commercial drive is seen as a key element in franchising's success and attractiveness to growing business.[65] This leads to a conclusion that the capacity of franchising to harness the effort 2.24

59 Hall, P. and R. Dixon, 1988, *Franchising*, London, Pitman.

60 Thompson, 1994.

61 Minkler, L.P., 1990, 'An Empirical Analysis of a Firm's Decision to Franchise', *Economic Letters*, 34, 77–82.

62 'Does franchising create value? An analysis of the financial performance of US public restaurant firms', Aliouche, and Schlentrich, Working Paper No. 2005–02 presented at the 19th Annual Conference of the International Society of Franchising, London, England, May 20–22, 2005.

63 Also see Pilat, D., 1997, 'Regulation and Performance in the Distribution Sector': OECD Economics Department Working Papers No 180.

64 Blair and Lafontaine, 2005, p. 1.

65 Caves, R.E. and W.F. Murphy, 1976, 'Franchising: Firms, Markets and Intangible Assets', *Southern Economic Journal*, Volume 42, 572–86.

of a central entity, the franchisor, and a number of local entrepreneurs, the franchisees, explains much of franchising's prevalence and popularity as a way of organising certain economic activities.[66]

2.25 All three of these analyses are cogent and in practice combine to produce a powerful reason for businesses choosing franchising. A survey of 25 franchisors in the UK, Germany, France and Spain[67] supported the theories with the majority of the sample surveyed identifying elements of the Agency theory, Resource Scarcity theory and the Transaction Cost theory together with other economic drivers as the reasons that they franchised their businesses.

2. The economic drivers of franchising for franchisees

2.26 Whilst some franchisees become substantial multi-unit operators or operate high investment businesses such as hotels, most franchisees are small, family owned and family run businesses.[68] All franchisees, regardless of their size, are attracted to franchising by certain common factors. Regardless of the scale and type of the franchisee, research suggests that the economic reasons for a franchisee buying a franchise include access to a national brand,[69] franchisor support[70] such as ongoing operational assistance, marketing/advertising and bulk purchasing, use of a proven business format[71] (that is continually developed) and independence.[72] All of which, regardless of the franchisee's size, increase its chances of success compared to those of an independent start-up business. The BFA states that one reason that franchisees buy a franchise is that 95% of franchises are in profit after 5 years compared to only 45% of other independent small firms. The other reason given is that franchisors are benevolent business partners with 86% of franchisees satisfied with their franchisor relationship.[73] The EFF[74] agrees with this analysis. Mendelsohn also agrees and

---

66 Blair and Lafontaine, 2005, p. 2.

67 See Appendix at end of Chapter 3.

68 Kaufmann, P. and J. Stanworth, 1995, 'The Decision to Purchase a Franchise: A Study of Prospective Franchisees', *Journal of Small Business Management*, 22033.

69 Stanworth, J., 1977, *A study of Franchising in Britain*, London, England, University of Westminster.

70 Hough, J., 1986, 'Power and Authority and their Consequences in Franchise Organisations – A Study of the Relationship between Franchisor and Franchisees', unpublished PhD book. London, England: University of Westminster.

71 Withane, S., 1991, 'Franchising and Franchise Behaviour: An Examination of Opinions, Personal Characteristics and Motives of Canadian Franchisee Entrepreneurs', *Journal of Small Business Management*, Volume 29, Issue 1, 22–29.

72 Knight, R., 1986, 'Franchising From the Franchisor and Franchisee Points of View', *Journal of Small Business Management*, July 8–15.

73 www.british-franchise.org/casestudies.asp.

74 www.eff-franchise.com accessed 3 February 2009. A franchisee's principal motive in joining a franchise network is 'to improve his chances of success during the initial start-up period, and to ensure his business's rapid expansion by virtue of the fact that he: buys into a brand-name, has immediate access to a market via the right to

adds improved product sourcing, advertising and marketing and increased access to funding as the banks tend to regard franchisees as lower risk than independent operators.[75] There are clear economic reasons for franchisees investing in a franchise, but it must be borne in mind that 'non-institutional' franchisees (i.e. individuals rather than corporations) are also subject to a 'large number of situational, personality and economic correlates ... likely to influence their perceptions'.[76] The situational, personality and economic correlatives referred to by researchers include a desire to own and operate one's own business and lack of other attractive options (for example redundancy).[77]

There is much support for the belief that the franchisee has the incentive of owning his own business with the additional benefit of continuing assistance from the franchisor.[78] The franchisee is an independent businessman operating within the framework and structure of the franchise system. This provides the opportunity to the franchisee through hard work and effort to maximize the return from his business and the value of his investment.[79] 2.27

D. DECONSTRUCTING THE RISKS INHERENT IN FRANCHISING

1. Inherent risks in franchising to which the franchisor is exposed

Both parties to a franchise agreement expose themselves to certain risks that are inherent in franchising. The risks to which the franchisor is exposed are different to those to which the franchisee is exposed. The agency theory identifies the risks of franchising as including 'information asymmetry' and 'moral hazard'. Information asymmetry means that it is impossible for both parties to observe all of the relevant information they need for the decision making process and so the franchisee is able to behave opportunistically in a manner that the franchisor would deem inappropriate.[80] Moral hazard is the 2.28

---

utilise the parent company's trademark or brand name, and benefits from both the transfer of know-how (professional, management and marketing skills) and on-going assistance. In return for which the franchisee pays the franchisor a fee or royalty, or a combination of fees, which often includes an entrance fee and/or a fixed percentage of annual turnover for the period of the contract.'

75 Mendelsohn, 1999.

76 Peterson, A. and R. Dant, 1990, 'Perceived Advantages of the Franchise Option From the Franchise Perspective: Empirical Insights from a Service Franchise', *Journal of Small Business Management*, Volume 28, Issue 3, 46–61.

77 Kaufmann and Stanworth, 1995.

78 Mendelsohn, 1999.

79 Ibid.

80 Lafontaine, F., 1992, 'Agency Theory and Franchising: Some Empirical Results', *Rand Journal of Economics*, Volume 23, Issue 2, 263–83.

influence of the environment on the franchisee's willingness to work effectively.[81] 'Free riding', where the franchisee does not behave in accordance with the rules of the franchise, is therefore a risk.[82] Certainly the degree of risk involved for the franchisor can be substantial. It is disclosing all of its business know-how to an independent party that is also permitted to use the franchisor's brand. In doing so it is opening the brand to potential abuse by another and creating an extremely effective future competitor which after the expiry of the franchise agreement and any post-termination restrictive covenants will be able to freely compete with the franchisor and its other franchisees in a manner that no other competitor can.

2.29 Recent research in the US[83] suggests that 'due to the public good nature of the franchise trademark, franchisees have an incentive to shirk by providing a sub-optimal level service since they do not bear the full cost of any resulting deterioration of the trademark's value'.[84] There is a risk of free riding. These failings risk damaging the franchisor's brand. UK, German, French and Spanish franchisors[85] were asked how significant various risks resulting from their entering into the franchise relationship were to them. Their responses seem to add further support to the belief that information asymmetry and moral hazard are the main risks to franchisors. These areas of very significant risk were identified as competition from franchisees during the term of the franchise agreement,[86] competition from franchisees after the term of the franchise agreement,[87] underpayment of monies due from franchisees,[88] franchisees not complying with the system[89] and damage to the franchisor's intellectual property.[90] Areas of less significant risk were identified as protection of know-how from unauthorised use by franchisees or their agents outside of the franchise system in France and Spain[91] and in the UK underperformance by franchisees during the term of the franchise agreement which has a significant impact on the brand.[92]

---

81 Besanko, D., D. Dranove and M. Sharley, 1996, *Economics of Strategy*, 1st edn, New York, John Wiley & Sons.
82 Lafontaine 'Agency Theory'.
83 Klick, Kobayashi and Ribstein, George Mason Law & Economics Research Paper No. 07–03.
84 Ibid, pp. 31–2.
85 See Appendix at end of Chapter 3.
86 Ibid – 80% of UK Franchisors, 72% of German Franchisors, 80% of French Franchisors, 4% of Spanish franchisors (72% thought that it was 'insignificant').
87 96% UK, 56% German, 88% French, 40% Spanish (56% thought it was a 'significant risk').
88 36% UK (60% thought that it was a 'significant risk'), 88% German, 96% French, 100% Spanish.
89 12% UK (80% thought that it was a 'significant risk'), 84% German, 48% French, 72% Spanish.
90 92% UK, 92% German, 88% French, 64% Spanish.
91 80% French, 68% Spanish.
92 72% UK.

It is important to bear in mind that the franchise relationship is not merely a bilateral one. It is a multilateral relationship. This potentially changes the dynamics of the relationship and creates a new and substantial risk for franchisors. As the franchise network increases, so the balance of power in the franchisor/franchisee relationship can start to tip away from the franchisor. The changes are subtle and at first not always easy to identify, but the fact that the franchisees can come to account for the majority if not all of the franchisor's income inevitably means that the franchisees have the potential to influence the actions of the franchisor. 2.30

This leads to a fundamentally complex relationship and can mean that the franchisor comes to rely on the good working relationship it establishes with the majority of its more successful franchisees. A case in point was Domino's Pizza UK. In 1995 it had in the order of 35 franchised outlets in the UK of which approximately 30% were owned by one franchisee. When the franchisee was thwarted in its bid to purchase the failed UK master franchise, it took a belligerent stance against the new master franchisee making the running of the master franchise far more difficult than it should have been until its eventual exit in 2000. Franchisors are exposed to a number of risks that are inherent in franchising. 2.31

2. Inherent risks in franchising to which the franchisee is exposed

Some of the risks to which franchisees are exposed tend to vary depending upon their size and sophistication. Less sophisticated and experienced franchisees, particularly small and mid-sized unit franchisees, can sometimes invest substantial amounts of money into a new business based almost entirely upon the representations made to it by the franchisor. Not all such potential franchisees are experienced enough to carry out appropriate levels of pre-contractual due diligence on their own initiative, and there is no doubt that unscrupulous individuals sometimes seek to use franchising as a way of taking unfair advantage of inexperienced potential franchisees, so depriving them of the basic benefits that they were hoping to enjoy from becoming a franchisee. The most important of these benefits include an established brand name, access to a business format that will increase their chances of success, and ongoing assistance and support including effective marketing/advertising, ongoing development of the business format and the benefits of bulk purchasing discounts. Other areas of risk impact on all franchisees regardless of their size and sophistication. The failure of the franchisor to deliver the promised level of support, know-how or brand recognition can lead to system-wide failure of franchisees. The case of 24 Self Video is a case in point. The franchisor made 2.32

some £4 million profit whilst 15 of its 30 franchisees went out of business[93] due to a lack of real business format and support from the franchisor and the tying in of overpriced, poorly selected products. The case of *MGB Printing & Design Ltd* v. *KallKwik UK Ltd*[94] details another such failure by a franchisor to deliver the promised level of support and advice. The collapse of the Pierre Victoire Franchise[95] and the Rymans and Athena franchises,[96] which all left orphaned franchisees with no franchisor to maintain the brand or develop the know-how, shows the vulnerability of the franchisees to the franchisor's commercial failure, so underlining the need for franchisees to conduct full pre-contractual due diligence.

2.33 Franchisees are also susceptible to what the Klick, Kobayashi and Ribstein research[97] identifies as a tendency for franchisors to 'seek to expropriate the franchisee's investments in market discovery and development in markets that turn out to be particularly profitable'. That is territorial encroachment. The contractual asymmetry inherent in the franchise relationship also adds to the risks. The nature and frequency of franchise disputes underlines the need for pre-contractual due diligence and suggests that there is a high level of mismatch between what some franchisees feel they bought into as a franchisee and what they are delivered. The delivery of inadequate support and territorial encroachment by the franchisor also seem to be common causes of dispute between franchisees and their franchisor, so exposing franchisees to a high level of risk and supporting Klick, Kobayashi and Ribstein's findings. As Emerson comments:[98] 'The focus for many disputes is the aggrieved franchisee's expectations, whether those expectations are based in contract terms or more general concepts of fairness. At its core, the merits of a franchisee's argument may rest on the legitimacy – the reasonableness – of its expectations.'[99] Franchisees are exposed to a number of risks that are inherent in franchising.

E. DECONSTRUCTING THE ARCHITECTURE OF FRANCHISING

2.34 Franchising is a specific, distinct and uniform commercial activity within the EU. The architecture of franchising comprises several distinct features (economic interest, independence, the business format, the brand, control by the

93 Hansard HC Vol 450 Col 1493 (24 October 2006).
94 QBD – 31 March 2010 – [2010] EWHC 624 (QB).
95 Scotland on Sunday 23 May 2010.
96 Franchise World Feb/March 1994.
97 Klick, Kobayashi and Ribstein, George Mason Paper 07–03.
98 Emerson, R., 2010, 'Franchise Territories – A Community Standard', *Wake Forest Law Review*, Vol. 45, No. 3, 1.
99 Ibid.

franchisor and ongoing support of the franchisee by the franchisor) and can therefore be differentiated from both commercial agency and distribution. The architecture needs to withstand a number of tensile stresses that result from the long-term nature of the franchise relationship. Although franchising is used in a wide variety of commercial sectors and although the balance of economic power between franchisor and franchisee can vary substantially from franchise to franchise, it does not materially impact upon the fundamental features of the architecture of the franchise relationship.

1. An economic perspective of the architecture of franchising

Franchising is a long-established commercial strategy that has evolved over the years and is represented by some 9971 different systems in the EU.[100] Some economic-based explanations of franchising, such as that offered by Housden,[101] add little to our understanding of it as they are so general that they include other third party contractual relationships, such as commercial agency and distributorship. Rather than define franchising they identify the basic characteristics of a third party commercial arrangement. Franchising can be seen as 'a contractual bond of interest in which an organisation, the franchisor, which has developed a pattern or formula for the manufacture and/or sale of a product or service, extends to other firms, the franchisees, the right to carry on the business, subject to a number of restrictions and controls. In almost all cases of significance, the franchisee operates using the franchisor's name as a trade name.'[102] This suggests that the elemental parts of franchising are a format, a brand, restrictions and control. **2.35**

R.S. Thompson takes a different approach and focuses primarily upon the independence of the parties and their respective assets, suggesting that franchising is 'an organisational form which combines the decentralised ownership of physical assets with centralised brand name ownership and provision of operational know-how'.[103] Rubin also focuses on decentralisation, describing franchising as a system that 'partitions decisions between two legally independent but economically linked entities ... and allocates to each the appropriate level of residual claims. The franchisee alone makes decisions regarding local operating policies such as location, pricing, hours of service and hiring. And the **2.36**

100 See Section 2.10 above.

101 'A right to do or use something which is granted by one party (the franchisor) to another party (the franchisee) for a consideration.' Housden, 1986, *Franchising and Other Business Relationships in Hotel and Catering Services*, Heinemann.

102 Thompson, D.N., 1971, *Contractual Marketing Systems*, Heath Lexington Books.

103 Thompson, R.S., 1994, 'The Franchise Life Cycle and the Penrose Effect', *Journal of Economic Behaviour and Organisation*, 207–18, North Holland.

franchisee bears the residual claims from these decisions – the net profit of the unit after expenses.'[104] This decentralisation point is well made and is consistently present in all franchising relationships but Rubin's failure to consider other elements is disappointing. Gerstenhaber's view of franchising echoes part of Thompson's analysis and focuses instead upon the key role of the business format as 'a system leasing arrangement under which the franchisee acquires from the franchisor the licence to duplicate the franchisor's existing and successful system of providing a product/service to the end user'.[105] However, it does not refer to the use of a brand or autonomy of the parties. Nevertheless, it captures much of the commercial essence of the franchising relationship – the replication of the franchisor's business 'blueprint' by the franchisee – and reflects those elements that are important to those in business who utilise the franchise model. In doing so it identifies another fundamental element of the franchise relationship.

2.37 The Franchising Council of Australia (FCA) definition of franchising[106] fails to identify the business format as a fundamental element and focuses instead on the use of the brand and the independence of the parties. The importance of the brand is echoed in many other analyses including that of both the IFA[107] and the EFF. Like Rubin, the IFA focuses upon the independence of the parties, but also identifies the brand and the format as being of elemental importance. However, it also suggests a further element – the ongoing support of the franchisor.[108] The EFF also focuses on the brand, the business format, the independence of the parties and ongoing support by the franchisor, but also adds control by the franchisor.[109]

---

104 Rubin, P., 1978, 'The Theory of the Firm and the Structure of the Franchise Contract', *Journal of Law and Economics*, 21, 223–33.

105 Moshe Gerstenhaber, the Managing Director of the KallKwik printing chain in the UK between the years 1975 and 1998, *Directory of Franchising 1989* (Franchise World).

106 'A business relationship in which the franchisor (the owner of the business providing the product or service) assigns to independent people (the franchisees) the right to market and distribute the franchisor's goods or service, and to use the business name for a fixed period of time', http://www.franchise.org.au/lib/pdf/aboutfranchising/WhatIsFranchisingBrochure.pdf accessed 21 August 2009.

107 Which is in fact the franchise association of the USA (the 'IFA').

108 'A contractual relationship between the franchisor and franchisee in which the franchisor offers or is obliged to maintain a continuing interest in the business of the franchisee in such areas as know-how and training; wherein the franchise operates under a common trade name, format and/or procedure owned or controlled by the franchisor and in which the franchisee has or will make a substantial capital investment in his business from his own resources.'

109 'A system of marketing goods and/or services and/or technology, which is based upon a close and ongoing collaboration between legally and financially separate and independent undertakings, the Franchisor and its individual Franchisees, whereby the Franchisor grants its individual Franchisee the right, and imposes the obligation, to conduct a business in accordance with the Franchisor's concept. The right entitles and compels the individual Franchisee, in exchange for a direct or indirect financial consideration, to use the Franchisor's trade name, and/or trademark and/or service mark, know-how, business and technical methods, procedural system, and other industrial and/or intellectual property rights, supported by continuing provision of

Blair and Lafontaine bring all of those elements together in their explanation of franchising but also expressly state an element which is implied in all of the other definitions – economic interest. They suggest that: 2.38

> the franchisor maintains ownership over the trade name and marks and ... develops a complete 'recipe' to run each outlet. It then licences the right to operate under the central trade name and business format in a given market for a certain period of time to individuals or small firms in exchange for various fees. The ownership stake of the franchisee in current and future profit leads him to put significant effort into the outlet. At the same time, the ongoing fees he pays to the franchisor ensure that the latter has incentives to maintain the value of the brand by, amongst other things, screening and monitoring the franchisees and keep abreast of market trends.[110]

It amounts to a synthesis of the various elements identified by other sources into a balanced compound that identifies the brand, the business format, independence, ongoing support to the franchisee by the franchisor, the economic interests of both parties and the control and enforcement of the brand standards by the franchisor.

2. A legal perspective of the architecture of franchising

Whereas an economic analysis of franchising focuses upon how the parties organise their economic interests, a legal analysis is more concerned with the rights and obligations they allocate to each other in the relationship. There is a continuum of control and independence which is interpreted in different ways in different jurisdictions to define what amounts to franchising. However, this different approach to analysing franchising ultimately leads to the identification of the same key elements. Some legal definitions are extremely wide and barely distinguish franchising from other third party relationships such as distributorship and commercial agency. For example, the UK's Financial 2.39

---

commercial and technical assistance, within the framework and for the term of a written franchise agreement, concluded between parties for this purpose.' 'A particular form of associated commerce, in other words a business partnership, between a franchisor and his independent partners – the franchisees. Together they form the franchise network. Of the many forms of business partnerships, franchising is the most sophisticated both in the business concept construct as in the scope of the franchisor–franchisee relation. A franchisor seeks to duplicate, as many times as possible, a tested and successful business or system with a network of independent partners, the franchisees. A franchisee is legally and financially separate and independent of the franchisor and of the other franchisees in the network.' 'The franchise business is generally built around a brand name which may be a trademark, a service mark and/or trade name. During the term of a franchise contract, the franchisor gradually transfers to his franchisee all the know-how and assistance necessary to efficiently and profitably run the franchisee's independent outlet. The packaging of these elements – the brand name, the transfer of know-how and constant assistance and support – summarises the distinctive elements of franchising with regard to other forms of associated businesses.' http://www.eff-franchise.com/spip.php?rubrique6, accessed 27 October 2009. http://www.eff-franchise.com/spip.php?rubrique6, accessed 27 October 2009. http://www.eff-franchise.com/IMG/article_PDF/article_13.pdf accessed 7 September 2009.

110 Blair, R. and F. Lafontaine, 2005, *The Economics of Franchising*, Cambridge University Press, p. 294.

Services Act[111] describes franchising as 'arrangements under which a person earns profits or income by exploiting a right conferred by the arrangements to use a trade name or design or other intellectual property or the goodwill attached to it…'. It identifies only the independence, brand and economic interest as elemental parts of franchising. The 'Community of Interest' approach used in the US in states such as Wisconsin[112] and New Jersey[113] identifies the same three elements. It defines a 'franchise' as an agreement between two or more persons in which (1) the franchisee is granted the right to engage in the business of offering or distributing goods or services using the franchisor's trade name or marks, (2) the franchisor and franchisee share a community of interest in the marketing of the goods or services, and (3) the franchisee pays a franchise fee. 'Community of interest' generally means a continuing financial interest between the parties in the operation of the franchisee's business or the resale of the franchisor's products. The Wisconsin statute explicitly defines a community of interest as a 'continuing financial interest between the grantor and the grantee in either the operation of the dealership business or the marketing of such goods or services'.[114] However, the 1987 *Ziegler* decision by the Wisconsin Supreme Court[115] lists ten factors that should be considered in determining whether a community of interest exists.[116] Although the primary factor in this equation is interdependence (which generally arises when the franchisee invests heavily in the franchise business so that its economic health hinges on the continuation of that business), other elements include the franchisor's control of the franchisee. The now defunct Block Exemption Regulation for Franchise Agreements (which was adopted by the European Commission on 30 November 1988[117] and exempted franchise agreements which came within its bounds from Article 81 of the Treaty of Rome) focused only on the vertical restraints in the franchise agreements. It therefore identified know-how (the format) and the brand as the key elements defining a franchise as 'a package of industrial or intellectual property rights

111 Financial Services Act 1986 Section 75; the Act was repealed by the Financial Services and Markets Act 2000 (Consequential Amendments and Repeals) Order 2001.

112 Wisconsin Fair Dealership Law.

113 New Jersey Franchise Practices Act.

114 Fair Dealership Law, Chapter 135.02(1).

115 *Ziegler Co.* v. *Rexnord Inc.* [1987] 139 Wis.2d 593 N.W.2d 873.

116 These factors include: (1) the duration of the parties' relationship; (2) the extent and nature of the parties' obligations; (3) the percentage of time or revenue devoted to the grantor's products or services; (4) the percentage of the grantee's gross proceeds or profits derived from the grantor's products or services; (5) the extent and nature of the grantee's territory; (6) the use of the grantor's trademarks or logos; (7) the grantee's financial investment in the inventory, facilities, and goodwill of the alleged dealership; (8) the personnel devoted to the alleged dealership; (9) the amount of money and time spent on advertising and promotions for the supplier's products and services; and (10) the extent of supplemental services provided by the grantee to purchasers of the grantor's products or services.

117 Commission Regulation (EEC) 4087/88 on the application of article 85(3) of the Treaty to categories of franchise agreements.

relating to trademarks, tradenames, shop signs, utility models, designs, copyrights, know-how or patents, to be exploited for the resale of goods or provision of services to end users'.

a) *Business format, control and assistance*

The importance of the brand, the business format and economic independence are also identified in the other approach to defining franchising commonly found in the US, the so-called 'Marketing Plan' or 'Prescribed System' approach. This is more successful than the Community of Interest approach in distinguishing franchising from other third party relationships. Its influence is evident in all of the other 26 countries[118] that have a franchise law which defines franchising and the work of numerous legal commentators.[119] The Marketing Plan Approach deals with not only the business format, the brand and economic interest but also the issues of 'control and assistance'. It therefore distinguishes franchising from other third party relationships. The State of California's franchise legislation was the USA's first franchise law when it was introduced in 1970.[120] It adopts the Marketing Plan Approach, defining a franchise as a contract or agreement, either express or implied, whether oral or written, between two or more persons by which: **2.40**

1. a franchisee is granted the right to engage in the business of offering, selling or distributing goods or services under a marketing plan or system prescribed in substantial part by a franchisor;
2. the operation of the franchisee's business pursuant to such plan or system is substantially associated with the franchisor's trademark, service mark, trade name, logo type, advertising or other commercial symbol designating the franchisor or its affiliate; and
3. the franchisee is required to pay, directly or indirectly, a franchisee fee.

It involves a symbiotic relationship between two legally independently owned businesses based upon the use of a brand and a business format with which it is closely associated. Each has its own differing rights and obligations. Franchisees can only succeed when the system as a whole succeeds. Franchisors

118 There are 28 other countries with franchise laws but two of them – France and Belgium – do not seek to define franchising.

119 Mendelsohn 1999, adopts a marketing plan approach and suggests that franchising consists of four elements and must exhibit eight different features. The four basic elements are the ownership by the franchisor of a trademark, an idea, a secret process, a patent or a specialised piece of equipment and the goodwill and know-how associated with it; the grant of a licence by the franchisor to the franchisee permitting it to exploit these elements; the imposition of controls relating to the operation of the franchisees and the payment of a fee to the franchisor by the franchisee. The basic features Mendelsohn believes must be present are a written contract; a successful business format which is identified with a brand name which may be a trademark, service mark and/or trade name; training; on-going support; use of the franchisor's brand by the Franchisee; a substantial capital investment by the franchisee into its own independent business.

120 Cal. Corp. Code Section 31005(a)(1).

therefore have to provide a system, a brand and support. The franchisor's success depends upon operating a successful network of franchisees. Franchisees must therefore diligently follow the franchise system. However, what is implicit in this is that whilst franchisor and franchisee have a common interest in the brand being successful what they own and therefore care about is different. The franchisee is focused on maximising the profits of its outlets. The franchisor is focused on the profits of the overall chain. Those two objectives, whilst broadly similar are not the same, and they do not always imply the same desired behaviour. Control by the franchisor is a key element in the relationship. This dichotomy is at the heart of franchising. It is what the franchise agreement attempts to reconcile in a mutually satisfactory manner. It is what a regulatory regime must seek to deal with.

2.41 The Federal Trade Commission Franchise Rule's definition takes a similar approach as do[121] other US states. Section 4(1) of the Australian Franchise Code[122] also focuses upon the brand, the business format, control, assistance and the economic interests of the parties.

---

121 FTC Rule Section 436.1(h).

122 The Trade Practices (Industry Codes-Franchising) Regulations (1998). It defines a franchise agreement as an agreement:

'(b) in which a person (the franchisor) grants to another person (the franchisee) the right to carry on the business of offering, supplying or distributing goods or services in Australia under a system or marketing plan substantially determined, controlled or suggested by the franchisor or an associate of the franchisor; and

(c) under which the operation of the business will be substantially or materially associated with a trade mark, advertising or a commercial symbol:

(i) owned, used or licensed by the franchisor or an associate of the franchisor; or

(ii) specified by the franchisor or an associate of the franchisor; and

(d) under which, before starting any business or continuing the business, the franchisee must pay or agree to pay to the franchisor or an associate of the franchisor an amount including, for example:

(i) an initial capital investment fee; or

(ii) a payment for goods or services; or

(iii) a fee based on a percentage of gross or net income whether or not called a royalty or franchise service fee; or

(iv) a training fee or training school fee; but excluding

(v) payments for goods or services at or below their wholesale price; or

(vi) repayment by the franchisee of a loan from the franchisor; or

(vii) payment for the wholesale price of goods taken on consignment; or

(viii) payment of market value for purchase or lease of real property, fixtures, equipment or supplies needed to start business or to continue business under the franchise agreement.'

The definition then goes on to state that a transfer, renewal or extension of a franchise agreement and motor vehicle dealerships (The Trade Practices (Industry Codes-Franchising) Regulations (1998)) are included within the definition. A list of other relationships, such as employer/employee, landlord and tenant and co-operatives are excluded from the definition (Trade Practices (Industry Codes-Franchising) Regulations Section 4(3)). Certain limited types of franchise agreements are also exempted from the Code (Trade Practices (Industry Codes-Franchising) Regulations Section 5). The two main types of exempted franchise agreement are where the franchisor is resident outside Australia and only grants one franchise or master franchise to be operated in Australia. The other main exemption is 'fractional franchises' where the franchise agreement is for

In the EU Member States' franchise laws there is a marked lack of homogeneity in the definition of franchising. Although France[123] and Belgium[124] have franchise laws, both have declined to define franchising.

Italy's definition of franchising focuses on the brand and other intellectual property rights, commercial assistance and the economic interests of the parties. Although it does not expressly deal with a business format or with control,[125] these are implied by the reference to intellectual property rights, which includes know-how. Spanish law[126] focuses only upon the business format and fails to identify the brand, control/support or the economic interest of the parties. The International Institute for the Unification of Private Law[127] has drafted a definition which follows the Marketing Plan approach referring to a business format (prescribed system), the brand, assistance and control, independence and the economic interests of the parties. Interestingly, despite providing a fairly well-rounded definition of franchising it has not been adopted by any of the legislators which have sought to define franchising. **2.42**

b) Other perspectives

In Germany, some legal commentators take a somewhat different approach to examining the architecture of franchising. They focus upon how the different elements of the franchise agreement might determine how they should be dealt with by German law. Instead of identifying independence, the brand, economic interest, the business format, control and assistance as key elements in the legal architecture of franchising, they suggest that it can be viewed in a number of different ways. It can be seen as a licence of intellectual property to the franchisee, the provision of business services by the franchisee to the franchisor, the provision of support by the franchisor to the franchisee, the sale of goods to the franchisee or even the leasing of real estate to the franchisee by the franchisor in some cases. Franchise agreements are therefore compared to these other agreement types, namely service agreements, licences, stakeholder agreements and 'mixed' agreements. Some consider that the franchisee's duty to promote the franchisor's goods and services are the predominant elements of **2.43**

---

goods or services substantially the same as those previously supplied by the franchisee and the sales under the franchise are likely to provide no more than 20% of the franchisee's gross turnover.)

123 Law No. 89–1008 31 December 1989, French Commercial Code Article L.300–3.

124 'Law relative to pre-contractual information in the framework of agreements of commercial partnership' adopted on 19 December 2005, modified on 27 December 2005.

125 Law of 6 May 2004, No. 129 Article 1.1.

126 Article 62 of Act 7/1996. An activity which 'is carried out by virtue of an agreement or contract by which a company, known as the franchisor, grants to another, known as a franchisee, the rights to exploit its own system of commercialisation of products or services'.

127 UNIDROIT, *Model Franchise Disclosure Law*, Article 2.

franchise agreements. They therefore classify them strictly as business management contracts similar to agency agreements.[128] Although it is true that, in most franchises, the franchisee's duty to promote the goods and/or services of the franchisor will be one of the main obligations under the franchise agreement the simple classification as a business management contract underestimates the importance of the other obligations which are central to the franchise agreement such as the licence of the intellectual property rights. Others see franchise agreements as simple licence agreements[129] (*Rechtspacht*), as the transfer of know-how and licensing of the trade mark and business format are key elements of the franchise relationship. However, this view fails to take into account the other key elements of franchising – particularly the support provided by the franchisor and the franchisee's obligation to perform under the brand.[130] Franchisees, as opposed to licensees, are not mere beneficiaries,[131] but have extensive duties under the franchise agreements in particular regarding promoting the goods and/or services of the franchisor under the trade name and the trade marks of the franchisor. Other commentators compare franchise agreements with shareholders' agreements.[132] There are two main flaws with this classification. Firstly, most franchise systems are characterised by a strict hierarchy and control by the franchisor. The franchisor directs, through guidelines, the operations manual and so on how the franchise business should be operated. Shareholders on the other hand, even if they have different rights under the shareholders' agreement, tend to (co-)operate on the same level. It is also questionable if the intention to make a profit is sufficient to conclude that a franchisor and a franchisee share a common purpose, as both parties try to achieve this by very different means and have conflicting interests.[133] The simple aim to make a profit is a common feature in all commercial contracts.

2.44 The preferred view[134] is that franchise agreements are mixed contracts[135] that contain a mixture of elements found in other forms of agreements[136] (*Mischvertrag* or *Typenkombinationsvertrag*). There are five basic different types of agreement felt to be relevant:

---

128 Emmerich, JuS 95, 761, 763.

129 Skaupy, NJW 1992, 1785, 1789.

130 Vergl. etwa Flohr, Franchisevertrag, 3. Auflage 2006, S. 73 Nr. 5; S. 118 Nr. 1.

131 Martinek in Martinek/Semler, 2010, *Handbuch des Vertriebsrecht*, §4 Rn. 44.

132 Giesler, in Giesler/Nachschütt, Franchiserecht, 2. Auflage 2007, Chapter 5, Rn. 82.

133 Ibid, Rn. 84.

134 BGH, Judgment dated 03.10.1984 – VIII ZR 118/83, NJW 1985, 1894, 1895.

135 BGH NJW 1985, 1894, 1895; OLG Hamm, Urteil vom 13.03.2000 = NZG 2000 1169.

136 OLG München, Urteil v. 26.06.2002 = BB 2002, 2521; OLG Frankfurt a.M., Urteil vom 27.09. 1994 – 11 U (Kart.) 30/94 = NJWE-WettbR 1996, 142, Stadler in Jauernig, *Bürgerliches Gesetzbuch*, 13. Auflage 2009, § 311, Rn 30.

(i) business management contracts (*Geschäftsbesorgungsvertrag*), the main feature of which is the obligation of the agent or manager to pursue a commercial activity for the financial benefit and in the financial interest of the principal.[137] The franchisee's duty to promote the franchisor's goods and services under the franchisor's trade name and trademark, and the franchisor's obligations to support and assist the franchisee in the operation of its business, are seen as obligations which are characteristic of business management contracts;

(ii) service agreements: services as are provided under the franchise agreement without them being directly for the financial benefit or the financial interest of the other party, such as conducting training sessions for the franchisees, or to develop new goods and/or services or to continue to further develop the franchise concept;

(iii) lease agreements: when the franchisor also acts as landlord of the franchisee and makes the premises available to the franchisee by way of lease or sub-lease or leases equipment to the franchisee;

(iv) licence agreements: in respect of the use of the trademark, the know-how and the franchise concept; and

(v) depending on the nature of the franchise in question also contracts for the sale of goods if the franchise agreement contains an obligation on the franchisee to purchase goods and/or equipment from the franchisor.

How many and to what extent these different agreement types are reflected in the franchise agreement will depend on the underlying franchise concept and the requirements of the parties. Although the German approach has some similarities with the other approaches discussed in that it identifies the brand and assistance by the franchisor as key elements, it suggests an implied reluctance to recognise franchising as a specific, distinct and uniform business model and fails to identify the importance of the business format, independence, economic interest or control of the franchisee by the franchisor. It is suggested that such an approach is incomplete. It fails to identify key elements of the franchise relationship and is perhaps too constrained by its desire to place franchising into the German legal system's existing taxonomy of third party relationships. 2.45

137 This is also the reason why the agency compensation upon termination is applied by analogy to franchise agreements.

3. Architectural features that distinguish franchising from distribution and commercial agency

2.46 Some academics seem oblivious to the fundamental difference between franchising on the one hand and commercial agency and distributorship on the other.[138] They certainly have a number of characteristics in common. They are third party relationships that involve a 'principal' and an 'agent'. They all come within Housden's[139] ill-informed definition of franchising as 'a right to do or use something which is granted by one party to another for a consideration', but from there onwards fundamental differences between these three channels to market emerge. Franchising consists of a brand, control and assistance by the franchisor, a business format, independence and economic interest. The use of a brand, independence, some level of control and possibly even assistance and economic interest can sometimes be found in both commercial agency and distribution. A business format cannot. Commercial agency and franchising both 'generally bring together a strong party (the principal) and a weaker party (the agent/franchisee). Both parties are consistently, before, during and after the collaboration, in this unequal position with each other.'[140] This perception of an imbalance of economic bargaining strength between the parties is what seems to persuade academics[141] and some Courts[142] that franchising and commercial agency are the same thing. However, although there can be some overlap in certain circumstances, the two are quite distinct. A commercial agency is defined as 'a self employed intermediary who has continuing authority to negotiate the sale or purchase of goods on behalf of another person ("the Principal") or to negotiate and conclude the sale or purchase of goods on behalf of and in the name of the Principal'.[143] The key elements are independence and the power to negotiate sale and purchases for, on behalf of or in the name of the Principal. Franchisees are independent and certainly have the right to negotiate sales and purchases under the brand. However, that is fundamentally different from negotiating for or on behalf of the Principal. Franchisees are inevitably obliged under the terms of a franchise agreement to give notice to the public that it is an independently owned and operated business operating under licence from the franchisor.[144] Further, franchisees generally sell goods or services on their own behalf under the brand, not on behalf of the franchisor. Franchisees generally own the goods they sell. It is of course possible for

138 *Commercial Agency, Franchise and Distribution*, Amsterdam Team Draft (21 May 2003)..

139 Housden, J., 1986, *Franchising and other Business Relationships in Hotel and Catering Services*, Heinemann.

140 The Belgian House of Representatives, 28 Jan 2004 – draft parliamentary bill relating to Franchise Agreements (lodged by Mme t. Pieters – Doc 510747/0001).

141 E.g. the Amsterdam Team.

142 BGH Judgment of 12 Nov. 1986 I ZR 209/84 ('Aquella').

143 Commercial Agents (Current Directive) Regulations 1993.

144 This is certainly the case in the sample franchise agreements.

franchisees to sell goods or services to be provided by the franchisor (e.g. a travel agency franchise, such as TUI or Thomas Cook). However, there are some other fundamental differences between a franchise and a commercial agency. The franchise is run in accordance with a business format. A commercial agency is not. Further, although a Principal will give some low-level assistance and assert a low level of control over the agent, a franchisor will deliver a higher level of assistance and assert a substantially greater level of control over the use of the brand and the business format. Commercial agency is concerned with the legal process by which the title of goods or services is passed to purchasers by the agent. Franchising is more concerned with the manner in which they are sold – that is the business format. It is theoretically possible that a franchise involves a commercial agreement by which the way in which the title to goods is passed from one party to the other and then to the consumer amounts to commercial agency. But despite this theoretical co-existence, the two are fundamentally different.

Distribution is also different to franchising. It is where 'one party agrees with the other to supply certain goods for resale within the whole or a defined area of the common market'.[145] It covers a broad spectrum of commercial practices. They range from 'straight distribution' to 'selective distribution'. Straight distribution involves nothing more than the wholesale of goods by the manufacturer to an independent party which sells those goods in such manner at its sole discretion as it deems appropriate. Selective distribution arrangements impose qualitative requirements upon the environment in which the goods are sold. The differences between straight distribution arrangements and franchising are stark. Straight distribution involves no use of the brand, no control or assistance and no business format. 2.47

Selective distribution is far more like franchising. It involves the use of the brand, and a certain level of control. However, it rarely involves assistance from the principal and, most fundamentally, there is no business format. Business format is the franchisor's know-how of how to run the business, its 'blueprint' for success. The perception that the principal and the franchisor both have a much stronger bargaining position than the distributor and franchisee again persuades some commentators and courts that distribution and franchising are the same thing. Again this perception does not accord with reality. For example, the toy shop Hamleys' franchisee in India, 'Reliance', is many times larger than Hamleys; likewise Fortnum & Mason and its distributor in Japan, Mitsukoshi. Selective distribution can at times look like franchising at a superficial level, but 2.48

145 Reg 1983/83.26 O.J. Eur Com. (No L173).

the assistance provided by the franchisor and its provision of a business format are the key difference.

2.49 Franchising is a flexible commercial tool used by a wide variety of companies in a large range of sectors. Although some academics, legislators and courts struggle to differentiate it from distribution and commercial agency, franchising is a fundamentally different species of third party commercial relationship. Franchising is a specific, distinct and uniform type of commercial activity which is fundamentally different to commercial agency and distribution because only franchising comprises the fundamental elements of independence, economic interest, a business format, a brand, control and assistance.

4. The tensile stresses that the architecture of franchise agreements needs to withstand

2.50 The specific, distinct and uniform nature of franchising is, in part, due to the fact that the relationship between a franchisor and its franchisees is of a fluid and dynamic nature and changes with the passage of time, thereby challenging the franchise agreement.[146] The architecture of the franchise agreement has to withstand the tensile stresses that result from these on-going changes. The franchise relationship changes firstly as the foundations of the franchisor/franchisee dynamics harden through commercial interaction between the two and secondly as the structural elements of the relationship expand and contract in response to environmental changes. Some compare the relationship to that between a parent and child.[147] During the initial period the franchisee is relatively 'helpless'; as the young infant is heavily reliant on the parent, so is the franchisee reliant upon the franchisor. As the franchisee gains more experience and confidence it adopts an attitude similar to that of the adolescent child. It rebels, it no longer feels that the franchisor gets everything right. It pushes the boundaries of the relationship to test it to the full. Disputes and arguments are common, often forcing both parties to re-evaluate the relationship in a forthright and sometimes final manner. However, as the franchisee further matures into adulthood it begins to see the value of the relationship with the franchisor and establishes a mature and mutually beneficial rapport with it – one that is substantially different from that it enjoyed in its 'infancy' and 'adolescence'.

---

146 Gudel, P., 1998, 'Relational Contract Theory and the Concept of Exchange', *Buffalo Law Review*, Vol. 46, 763 and Leichtling, A., 1994, 'Why Burger King Cannot Have Its Own Way with Its Franchisees', *University of Miami Law Review*, Vol. 48, 671.

147 Seid, M. and D. Thomas, 2006, *Franchising for Dummies*, 2nd edn, Wiley Publishing, p. 22.

The only way that the franchise agreement can accommodate these changes and at the same time seek to balance the interests of itself and all the franchisees is to allow the franchisor to unilaterally make changes. However, that leaves the relationship open to potential abuse. **2.51**

The franchise relationship's ongoing nature differentiates it from 'one-off' transactions such as the sale of goods, which are 'discrete transactions ... of short duration, involving limited personal interactions and with precise party measurements of easily measured objects of exchange'.[148] Franchise relationships are fundamentally different. They are relational and are characterised by 'long duration, personal involvement by the parties and the exchange, at least in party, of things difficult to monetize or otherwise measure'.[149] As a result 'obligations are not frozen in an initial bargain. They evolve over time and circumstances change. The object of contracting is to establish and define a co-operative relationship, not merely to allocate risk.'[150] This means that 'parties are obliged to behave in a way that promotes the relationship, and ... is consistent with the needs and expectations of both parties'.[151] This change introduces tensile stresses into the franchisor/franchisee relationship. However, franchise agreements do not evolve or change over the years as the franchise system develops. They are static documents fixed for a term of years. They require mutual performance over a number of years and therefore do not always define the parties' full obligations. They need a degree of flexibility to accommodate these tensile stresses. Because of their longevity and the multilateral nature of franchising they inevitably vest the franchisor with an amount of discretion as to how the rights and obligations of both parties will be performed. How the franchisor exercises its discretion will inevitably impact upon the franchisee's operation of its business. 'In making discretionary decisions, franchisors can extract value from the franchisees in many ways, such as granting additional franchises in close proximity, raising the price of goods sold to franchisees, increasing rent on the franchisee's locations, increasing inventory and growth requirements, as well as increasing advertising funds. Conflicts invariably arise when the franchisee perceives the franchisor's exercise of discretion to be unfair.'[152] **2.52**

148 Op cit Gudel, 763.
149 Ibid.
150 Op cit Leichtling, 671.
151 Leichtling quoting Parritt at 717.
152 Whitner, Brito, Spandorf, paper at ABA Franchising Forum Oct. 2007.

5. The impact of sectoral contextualisation upon the architecture of franchising

2.53 Despite the differing nature of the sectors in which franchising is used, it is a specific, distinct and uniform type of commercial activity and as a result sectoral differences do not impact upon its architecture. Regardless of the tendency of trade associations and commentators to speak of the 'Franchise Industry' and the 'Franchise Sector', it is not a business sector in its own right. Rather, it is a strategic tool that is adopted by businesses in a large variety of different business sectors as part of their market channel strategies. The 2010 edition of the *Franchise Directory*,[153] the leading directory of the UK franchise sector, provides a panorama of the types of businesses that have franchised themselves in the UK. It lists 12 different categories of franchises in the United Kingdom.[154] Ten of the categories cover services, two cover goods and one covers food. The reason that this totals 13 rather than 12 is that one category (Catering and Hotels) covers both service and food. The IFA's PWC 2010 Franchise Economic Outlook Report[155] suggests a similar spread of franchising in the USA. There is a wide range of commentary on the use of franchising in various sectors. It is 'very successful in the food distribution market and the manufacturing and DIY and also the car maintenance, travel agency, hotels and hair dressing business sectors' according to one bill placed before the Belgian Parliament,[156] whilst Blair and Lafontaine[157] observe that franchising 'dominates retailing' in the US and has a strong representation in a broad range of sectors, particularly the restaurant sector. Adams and Prichard Jones[158] suggest that it is important to consider the different types of franchising that exist and identify the basic elements of each type. They believe that there are essentially two basic types of business format franchising,[159] namely goods and service franchises. They suggest that, from an economic point of view, goods franchises can be divided into three subcategories and that all service franchises have one thing in common with each other – there is only one market level. This analysis seems to omit one common form of franchising: the type of franchise which

153 *British Franchise Directory and Guide 2010*, 26th edition.

154 Ibid p. 68: 1. Property and maintenance services, home improvements; 2. Catering, Hotels; 3. Cleaning and renovation services; 4. Commercial services; 5. Direct selling, distribution etc.; 6. Domestic, personal, health and fitness, caring and pet services; 7. Employment agencies, executive search, management consultancy, training and teaching; 8. Estate agents, mortgage brokers etc.; 9. Parcel and courier services; 10. Printing, copying, graphic design; 11. Retailing; 12. Vehicle services.

155 Op cit PWC. It lists the Automotive, Commercial and Residential Services, Quick Service Restaurants, Table/Full Service Restaurants, Retail Food, Lodging, Real Estate, Retail Products and Services and Personal Services.

156 The Belgian House of Representatives, 28 Jan 2004 – Development [Doc 510747/001].

157 Op cit Blair and Lafontaine, p. 8.

158 Op cit Adams and Prichard Jones, p. 23.

159 Ibid.

consumers in the EU are probably most familiar with – food franchises. Whether they are family restaurants, takeaways or home delivery businesses, all food franchises are a hybrid between goods franchises and service franchises and cannot properly be classified as either. However, regardless of the omission of the restaurant sector in their analysis, the main issue is that Adams and Prichard Jones do not conclude that the architecture of franchises in each of these sectors varies from one to another in any fundamental manner and their subsequent analysis of the franchise agreement makes no suggestion that this is the case. Analysis of a sample of 25 franchise agreements from the UK, Germany, France, the USA and Australia was undertaken to examine whether or not sectoral contextualisation of franchising does have any impact upon its fundamental elements.[160] The sample comprises franchises in five sectors. The food/restaurant sector, the retail sector, the hotel/leisure sector, the services sector and car rental sector as detailed in the following table:

Table 2.10 Categorisation of sample by sectors

	Australia	UK	Germany	France	USA
Hotel	1	1	1	1	1
Car Rental	0	1	1	0	1
Retail	1	1	2	2	1
Other Services	2	1	0	1	1
Food/Restaurant	1	1	1	1	1
Total	5	5	5	5	5

The sample agreements all identify independence, economic interest, the brand, the business format, control of the franchisee by the franchisor and the provision of assistance by the franchisor to the franchisee, as features of the franchises' architecture regardless of the sector in which they operate. Sectoral contextualisation therefore does not impact the fundamental features of the architecture of franchising. **2.54**

6. The impact of economic contextualisation upon the architecture of franchising

Although value of the investment required from the franchisee inevitably defines the type of franchisee attracted to each franchise system, franchising remains a specific, distinct and uniform type of commercial activity and as a **2.55**

160 Appendix 2.

result the scale of economic investment required does not change the fundamental features of its architecture. The investment required to buy into a franchise immediately disqualifies those franchisees who cannot access sufficient capital. This in turn has a substantial impact upon the nature of the relationship between the franchisor and its franchisees particularly in terms of the ability of the franchisee to negotiate the commercial terms of the franchise.[161] For example, whilst a franchisee of a hotel concept such as Ramada[162] will be investing several millions of pounds in bricks and mortar and fit out costs for each hotel, and may pay the franchisor to operate the hotels through a management agreement, a franchisee for a contract cleaning business such as Jani-King[163] needs to find only a few hundred pounds and is able to pay that by way of instalments over the life of the franchise agreement.

2.56 From a commercial point of view, the difference between such a sophisticated hotel 'investment' franchisee and a contract cleaning 'job' franchisee could not be bigger. One is typically sophisticated, experienced in the ways of business, and wealthy, looking for substantial returns on its capital investment. The other is doing little more than buying himself a job of manual labour that will secure him a modest level of ongoing income for the life of the franchise. Between these two extremes there is a broad spectrum of franchisees varying from the seasoned businessman who is buying a franchise to add to his portfolio, to the former teacher or bank manager who has decided to enter the commercial world in their middle years. These differences inevitably impact upon the franchisor/franchisee relationship – US franchise law exempts large and/or sophisticated franchisees from the requirement for pre-contractual disclosure[164] – but do not impact upon the technical legal components of the contractual relationship.

2.57 Some commentators have focused upon this disparity in the balance of economic power between franchisors and different types of franchisee to categorise franchising. The categorisation of franchise systems according to the balance of power and alignment of interests between the parties was first developed by Martinek in the 1980s and has since been further modified.[165] This approach categorises franchise agreements into two basic types: subordination and partnership franchising. It then suggests a further subdivision in respect of partnership franchising. The analysis suggests that so-called 'Subordination Franchising' exists where there is a hierarchical relationship between franchisor

161 Martinek, 2010.
162 Included in Appendix 2 survey group.
163 Ibid.
164 See Chapters 4 and 5 below.
165 Martinek, 2010, ss 18 Rn 18ff.

and franchisee and the cooperation between the parties is limited to the distribution of the goods and/or services on a vertical level. As such it resembles other distribution arrangements and is 'the further development and refinement of the classic authorised dealer model'.[166] A franchised outlet is distinguished from an authorised dealership due to its look and feel which are identical to those of the corporate outlets of the franchisor. The cooperation between the parties is limited to the franchisor making available to the subordinate franchisee the necessary know-how and providing the services set out in the franchise agreement.[167] The franchisee itself becomes an instrument of the franchisor in its distribution system.[168] The counter-point to Subordination Franchising is so-called 'Partnership Franchising', which according to Martinek can be divided further into three subcategories – 'Co-ordination Franchising', 'Coalition Franchising' and 'Confederation Franchising'. In 'Partnership Franchising' there is more of an economic balance between the franchisor and its franchisees. 'Co-ordination Franchising' is characterised as a uniform exchange agreement between the franchisor and its franchisees who are considered equal partners.[169] The franchisees are not mere instruments of the franchisor who carry out their commercial activity mainly for the benefit and in the interest of the franchisor. They act in their own interests using the franchise model. Opposing interests between the franchisor and franchisees are co-ordinated and a common marketing strategy for the products and/or services is developed.[170] The franchisee uses the franchise concept for its own benefit without being subjected to the directions of the franchisor. Big ticket franchises such as hotel franchise systems are co-ordination franchises, according to Martinek. 'Coalition Franchising', according to Martinek, is characterised by a balance of power and both parties not only sharing a common interest (making a profit by exploiting the franchise concept), but also a common purpose in that both the franchisor and franchisee take on the mutual obligation to optimise the distribution of the goods and/or services of the franchised outlets on the basis of a system-specific marketing concept.[171] As this mutual duty of optimisation is considered as the overarching purpose of the franchise agreement, they are seen as transcending mere obligations of a common purpose and the franchisor and franchisee are deemed to form a very primitive

166 Ibid § 4 Rn. 52.

167 Ibid § 18 Rn. 18ff.

168 For that reason, Martinek considers the business management element in these types of franchise relationships to be predominant with additional service agreement elements and, depending on the type of franchise, sales contract, lease agreement, licence agreement and know-how transfer elements. This means that subordination franchise agreements are mixed contracts with business management agreement features as their core element. (Ibid § 4 Rn. 60).

169 Ibid § 4 Rn. 63.

170 Ibid § 4 Rn. 64.

171 Ibid § 4 Rn. 69.

form of company.[172] 'Confederation Franchising' goes one step further than coalition franchising. The balance of power is marked and the common purpose is extended from a bilateral relationship between franchisor and franchisee to a multilateral relationship between the franchisor and all franchisees in the network. The suggestion is that some sort of unwritten umbrella agreement amongst all participants is concluded.[173] The overarching purpose of this hypothesised umbrella agreement covers everyone in the network and consists in the increase in the goodwill of the products and/or services and competitiveness of the franchise system, the exploitation of group purchasing opportunities and the breakdown of the market into different segments for each participant. This manifests itself in the 'optimisation of the intercompany cooperation in all areas which are relevant for the distribution (of the goods and/or services) for the benefit of all'.[174] The group interests in confederation franchising systems form the core of the franchise that all participants undertake to develop. Whilst it is clearly correct that (largely as a result of the size of the investment the franchisee makes) there are variances in the degree of hierarchy in franchise systems, these do not impact upon the key architectural features of franchising already identified, namely the duty of the franchisor to support the franchisee, its ability/right to control the franchisee, the brand, the business format, independence and economic interest.

2.58 Using Martinek's analysis, the 25 franchises considered in this book[175] based upon the commercial reality of the relationship between franchisor and franchisee could be categorised as follows:

Table 2.11 The categorisation of sample franchises according to Martinek's analysis

	Subordinated Franchises	**Partnership Franchises**
Australia		Choice Hotels
		BB's Coffee & Muffins
		Bartercard
		Cash Converters
		Expense Reduction Analyst
USA	Coverall	Intercontinental Hotels
		National Car Rental
		Dominos Pizza
		Snap on Tools

172 Ibid § 4 Rn. 68.
173 Ibid § 4 Rn. 72.
174 Ibid § 4 Rn. 73.
175 Appendix 2.

	Subordinated Franchises	Partnership Franchises
UK	Jani King	Costa Coffee Hertz Ramada KallKwik
Germany	Eisman	Applebees Starwood Hotels Hertz Polo Ralph Lauren
France	Arteria	Ibis Yves Rocher Pronuptia La Bôte a Pizza

Based upon the commercial reality of the relationship, the distinction between subordinated and partnership franchises reflects the investment required. Low investment franchises are subordinated franchises. All others are partnership franchises.

Table 2.12 The categorisation of Partnership Franchises

	Co-ordination Franchising	Coalition Franchising	Unclear whether co-ordination or confederation franchise	Confederation Franchising
Australia	–	–	Cash Converters Bartercard BB's Coffee and Muffins Expense Reduction Analyst	Choice Hotels
USA	–	–	Dominos Pizza	Intercontinental Hotels National Car Rental
UK	–	–	KallKwik Costa Coffee	Hertz Ramada
Germany	–	–	Applebees Polo Ralph Lauren	Starwood Hotels Hertz
France	–	–	Yves Rocher Pronuptia La Bôte a Pizza	Ibis

2.59 The identification of confederation franchises based upon the commercial reality of the relationship is relatively straightforward and reflects a high investment. Identifying co-ordination and coalition franchises is far more problematic and is impossible to do with the sample agreements considered, or indeed, on the information available, on the commercial reality of the relationship. The conclusion which is drawn from this is that Martinek's categorisation of subordinated and partnership franchises can be justified based upon the commercial reality of the relationship. It reflects low investment franchises on the one hand and medium, substantial and high investment franchises on the other. The categorisation of high investment franchises as confederation franchises is sustainable based upon the commercial reality of the relationship. However, the categorisation of other partnership franchises as co-ordination and coalition franchises is not borne out by the commercial reality of the sample agreements considered. More importantly though, regardless of how the agreements can be categorised using Martinek's approach, such categorisation was not reflected in the actual agreements themselves. The distinction between subordinated and partnership franchises is to some small extent reflected in the agreements considered. The Jani-King and Coverall agreements were distinctly more controlling than the other agreements in the sample. However, the distinction between Co-ordinated, Coalition and Confederation franchises was not reflected in the sample agreements considered at all. All of the agreements considered, regardless how Martinek would categorise them, have the same basic legal architectural features. Martinek's analysis therefore seems somewhat contrived and is certainly not supported by an analysis of the sample franchise agreements. None of the agreements in the sample give any hint of the mutuality that is characteristic of Coalition Franchising let alone the overarching purpose imposed on the franchisor and all of its franchisees which is supposed to be found in Confederation Franchising. The differences suggested between Subordination Franchises and Co-ordination Franchises may in some circumstances be similar to the 'de facto' commercial relationship between economically stronger franchisees and their franchisors on the one hand and economically weaker franchisees and their franchisors on the other but they do not impact upon the basic architectural features of franchising; independence, economic interest, business format, brand, control and assistance.

F. CONCLUSION

2.60 This chapter has established that although franchising is a specific, distinct and uniform type of commercial activity with a positive influence in the EU and which stimulates economic activity by offering economic advantage to all those involved, improving distribution and giving business increased access to other member states, it is not fulfilling its potential to contribute to the realisation of the single market. Business format franchising is the latest incarnation of a long-established business structure. Its importance is acknowledged by a wide range of institutions and it has emerged as an important vehicle for entrepreneurship that appeals to large corporations and small businesses alike. The 9971 or so franchise networks operating in the EU and the 405 000 or so outlets make a substantial contribution to the GDP of a number of member states, with a roughly estimated total turnover of €215 billion (US$300 billion). It has great potential to stimulate economic activity within the EU by improving the distribution of goods and/or services within and between member states. However, it is overconcentrated in a small number of EU member states[176] and a comparison with the size of franchising in the USA and Australia suggests that its potential to contribute to the single market and promote trade between member states is far from being fulfilled at present:[177] an estimated 83.5% of its turnover is concentrated in only 25% of the member states. The economic drivers that lead franchisors and franchisees to become involved in franchising and the consequential inherent risk differ. Improved access to both appropriately qualified managerial resource and capital (the Agency, Resource Scarcity and Transaction Cost theories) and other economic drivers such as bulk purchasing, economies of scale and enhanced product development explain why businesses use franchising as part of their commercial strategy. A number of economic incentives resulting in an increased chance of success (such as access to a proven format, a nationally recognised brand, ongoing support, economies of scale and so on), supported by various situational, personality and economic correlatives, explain the attraction of franchising to franchisees. There are a number of different risks inherent in franchising for franchisors and franchisees. Franchisors are exposed to risks arising from information asymmetry and moral hazard (such as underpayment, in-term competition, abuse of the franchisor's brand and non-compliance with the business format), whilst franchisees are exposed to the risk of misrepresentation, encroachment, poor quality business formats and inadequate support. Franchising is a symbiotic relationship between two legally independent businesses that is used in a wide range of sectors and on a broad spectrum of scale and value which can be differentiated from commercial agency and distribution. The architecture of franchising comprises six basic features: independence of the parties involved, economic interest, a business format, a brand, control of the franchisee by the franchisor and the provision of assistance to the franchisee by the franchisor. It is distinct from agency and distribution, the main difference being the business format and the ongoing support. These features are not impacted by either

176 See 2.18.
177 See 2.19.

economic or sectoral contextualisation. The legal architecture is uniform regardless of the legal system in which the franchise operates. Despite the differing nature of the sectors in which franchising is used these differences do not impact upon the architecture of franchising. Likewise although the value of investment required from franchisees inevitably defines the type of franchisee attracted to each franchise system, the resulting differences in economic bargaining power do not change the fundamental architectural features of franchising.[178] This architecture is subjected to tensile stresses as a result of the long term and ever changing nature of the franchise relationship. In order to withstand these stresses the franchise agreements give the franchisor a degree of flexibility that can result in abuse of the franchisee.

178 See 2.55–59.

3

DOES THE CONTRACTUAL AND REGULATORY ENVIRONMENT SUPPORT AND PROMOTE FRANCHISING?

3.1 This chapter suggests that franchising does need regulating and that the economic determinants and the interparty dynamics of the franchisor/franchisee relationship lead to a contractual environment that transcends sectoral divergence and the differing legal traditions of EU member states. This contractual environment tends to support and re-enforce the economic drivers that encourage franchisors to become involved in franchising and reduces their consequential inherent risk to a reasonable level. However, although it tends to re-enforce some of the economic drivers that encourage franchisees to become involved in franchising it does not re-enforce them all and it fails to reduce all the consequential inherent risks for franchisees to an adequate level. The regulatory environment in the EU within which franchising operates (which comprises a series of legal eco-systems) does not adequately protect and reinforce the economic attractions that drive franchisors and franchisees to become involved in franchising. Nor does it adequately reduce the consequential risks. It is therefore to some extent responsible for the underachievement of franchising in the EU.

A. THE DIFFICULTIES EXPERIENCED IN SEEKING TO REGULATE FRANCHISING IN THE EU

3.2 Those intimately involved in franchising in the EU exhibit differing approaches to the regulation of franchising. Franchise trade associations in some member states[1] have fought long and hard to have franchise-specific laws enacted in their jurisdictions. At the same time, in other member states, such trade associations have expended a great deal of time, energy and money to ensure that franchise laws are not enacted in their jurisdiction.[2] This is despite all such trade associations being members of the European Franchise Federation (EFF) and therefore supposedly sharing a common view of how franchising should be regulated. The regulation of franchising on a purely national level in certain EU member states has created barriers which restrict the ability of

1 E.g. the Italian Franchising Association.
2 E.g. the British Franchise Association.

franchisors to freely expand from one member state to another.[3] There is a wide divergence of opinion and even conflict as to the form and approach that those laws take. A degree of political cynicism towards franchising is noticeable in the EU. It seems that franchising is 'big enough' for its regulation to make an impact on the public consciousness but not important enough to matter to the government concerned if that regulation is not as positive or as appropriate as it might be. It has been treated as a political plaything: a palliative to potentially troublesome politicians who, although outside of the political mainstream, have the potential to create irritating diversions for the main players.[4] It took seven years and eight bills in Italy,[5] 24 years and five bills in Belgium[6] and 19 years

3 Italy, Spain, France, Lithuania, Estonia, Sweden, Belgium and Romania.

4 Belgium, France, and Italy.

5 In Italy, there was a seven-year battle involving eight separate bills proposing a franchise law. The President, a gaggle of the Italian parliament's numerous political parties (particularly the Communist and the Left Democratic parties), the Italian Franchise Association, the FIF Confeserienti (the National Association of Traders), the Commission for Constitutional Affairs and the Italian Justice Commission were all actively involved in the process. (A) Resolution of 24 July 2000: (B) Bill of law no. 19 of 30 May 2001 from Senators Maconi, Grosso, Pasquini and Piatti; (C) Bill of law no. 25 of 30 May 2001 from Senator Asciutti ; (D) Bill of law no. 103 of 6 June 2001 from Senators Marino, Muzio and Pagliarulo; (E) Bill of law no. 842 of 14 November 2001 from Senator Costa; (F) Bill of law no. 95 of 30 May 2001 from Deputy Gambini and others; (G) Bill of law no. 1523 of 24 August 2001 from Deputy Mazzocchi and others; (H) Bill of law no. 4702 of 13 February 2004 from Deputy Perrotta.

6 On 4 February 1982 (Wetsvoorstel tot regeling van de franchise overeenkomst, zitting 1981–1982, 4 February 1982, Parl. Doc. 90, no.1) a proposal was made which focused on regulating the franchise relationship rather than pre-contractual disclosure and was rather cumbersome. It proposed that franchising be regulated by a Public Commission, which would approve franchisor's standard agreements. All modifications agreed with the franchisee had to be approved by the Commission. The Commission would have had the ability to require franchisors to prove to it that they had the necessary financial and technical means to guarantee the normal performance of the agreement. One of the 2003 bills proposed establishment of a Commission of Franchise Arbitrators (the Belgian House Of Representatives, 30 October 2003, Clause 16) to deal with any disputes between franchisors and franchisees. This was perhaps the most unusual and eccentric provision. The Commission would have consisted equally of representatives from organisations protecting the interests of franchisees and of representatives from organisations protecting the interests of the franchisors. On 8 October 2003 Anne Barzin (Reform Movement member of the Belgian House of Representatives), Serge Van Overtveldt and Philippe Collard proposed a draft Parliamentary Bill 'Concerning pre-contract information in relation to contracts by which one person grants to another the right to carry on commercial activities' (the Belgian House of Representatives, Extraordinary Session, 8 October 2003 Doc 51 0265/001 First Sitting of 51st Parliament). The sponsors of the bill decided that the precedent set by the French ('Loi Doubin', Law No. 89–1008 dated 31 December 1989) and Spanish (Article 62 of Act 7/1996) franchise laws should be followed in Belgium and so drafted a bill that imposed a pre-contractual disclosure obligation on the franchisor, failure to comply with which would result in the agreement being void if the franchisee could show that the information which was not properly disclosed induced the franchisee to enter into the agreement (the Belgian House of Representatives, Extraordinary Session, 8 October 2003 Doc 51 0265/001 First Sitting of 51st Parliament). This was followed in rapid succession by three further draft bills. On 30 October 2003 Jan Peeters (International Socialist Party member of the Belgian House of Representatives) and Jean-Marc Delizée (Socialist Party member of the Belgian House of Representatives) proposed (The House of Representatives, 30 October 2003, Draft Parliamentary Bill concerning regulations governing the grant of franchise – Second Sitting of 51st Parliament) a draft Parliamentary Bill 'Concerning Regulations Governing the Grant of Franchise' (The Belgian House Of Representatives, 30 October 2003, Extraordinary Session 2003, Introduction to Draft Parliamentary Bill – Summary). The proponents took the view that franchisors usually offer franchises on a 'take it or leave it basis' and that there is a clear imbalance between the rights and obligations of the franchisor compared with those of

and 12 bills in Sweden[7] to produce a franchise law. Even when governments do become involved in the regulation of franchising a degree of cynicism is evident. For example, when the 'Rainbow coalition'[8] in Belgium introduced a draft bill into Parliament in 2001 it was proposed, at least in part, because the vast majority of franchisors present in Belgium are not Belgian and so any protection afforded to franchisees was seen as having little political risk and being a potentially populist move.[9]

---

the franchisees (The Belgian House Of Representatives, 30 October 2003, Extraordinary Session 2003, Introduction to Draft Parliamentary Bill – Summary). They therefore proposed that franchises need to be specifically regulated, particularly in relation to pre-contractual disclosure, transfer of the agreement, the nullity of certain clauses, the franchisor's right of pre-emption, the duration of the contract and the manner in which the contract is terminated. They also proposed a dispute resolution procedure. On 28 January 2004 Mme Trees Pieters (Christian Democrat Party member of the Belgian House of Representatives) proposed a draft Parliamentary Bill relating to franchise agreements (The Belgian House of Representatives, 28 January 2004 – Summary Doc 51 0747/001 Second sitting of 51st Parliament), which praised franchising as a form of distribution of goods in wide and successful use, but saw it as a relationship between a stronger party, the franchisor and a substantially weaker one, the franchisee. She therefore proposed to bring in 'a number of clear and flexible provisions to correct the imbalance in the contractual relationship, and to introduce minimum trading protection for the franchisee without adversely affecting the development of this system of distribution' which include pre-contractual disclosure and the imposition of mandatory terms in the franchise agreement (The Belgian House of Representatives, 28 January 2004 – Summary Doc 51 0747/001 Second sitting of 51st Parliament). On 17 March 2004 Alain Mathot (Socialist Party member of the Belgian House of Representatives), Jean-Marc Delizée and Sophie Pécriaux (all three Socialist Party Members of the Belgian House of Representatives) proposed a draft Parliamentary Bill 'Regulating Franchise Agreements with a View to Improving Commercial Practices in this Sector' (The Belgian House of Representatives, 17 March 2004 Doc 51 0924/001 Second sitting of 51st Parliament). The sponsors of the bill declared that franchisors offer their franchises on a 'take it or leave it' basis and that there is a clear imbalance between the rights and obligations of the respective parties. They therefore proposed that franchise agreements should be regulated as regards pre-contractual disclosure, the void effect of certain provisions, the franchisor's right of pre-emption, the period of the franchise agreement and the manner in which it can be terminated (The Belgian House of Representatives, 17 March 2004 Doc 51 0924/001 Second sitting of 51st Parliament – Summary).

7 A Swedish franchise law was first mooted in a public report in 1987: Statens offentliga utredningar (SOU) 1987:17 'Franchising'. However it was another 19 years before it was adopted by the Swedish parliament. It was largely the result of the dogged determination of a particular MP who during that period was able to ensure that no less than 12 bills proposing a franchise law were presented to the parliament and several public reports made. The mandate of the 1987 public report was to survey the extent of franchising in Sweden, and describe and analyse the advantages and drawbacks of franchising. Against this background the report considered the need for and possible content of a specific law on franchising. The areas of law focused on in the resulting report were labour law, contract law, competition law, intellectual property and consumer law. The report proposed a definition of franchising and took the view that franchise agreements are often characterised by being one-sided, and consequently include clauses which might be considered to be unfair. However, the overall conclusion of the report was that franchise agreements should be subject to general law of contract rather than franchise-specific regulations. Nevertheless, the report did suggest a mandatory notice period of one year upon termination of the agreement by the franchisor, save in the case where the grounds for termination were misrepresentation by the franchisee. The report suggested that in order to protect consumers franchisees and franchisors should be obliged to notify the public that their business was part of a franchise and that employees of franchisees should have the right to negotiate directly with the employer's organisation to which the franchisor was connected. Following the Government's decision to dismiss the 1987 Report, a series of private member's Bills proposed by Mr Stig Gustafson, which called for a new government study on the need for legislation to protect the weak franchisees, were raised in Parliament between 1992 and 2003 (Lagutskottets (LU): 1992/93: LU2, 1998/99: LU7, 2000/01: LU17, 2001/02: LU12, 2002/03: LU4 and 2003/04: LU7). However, these private member's Bills were all rejected by Parliament.

8 A coalition of the Liberals, Socialists and Greens.

B. THE NEED TO REGULATE FRANCHISING IN THE EU – ABUSE, SHARP PRACTICE AND FAILURE

The growth of franchising seems to have brought with it a degree of sharp practice, abuse and commercial failure that has led the authorities in some member states to conclude that specific regulation was required. There are many examples of abuse, sharp practice and failure in franchising in EU member states. In the UK in 2007 there was an uproar in the press[10] about the Self Video 24 franchise. Fifteen of the 30 franchisees were forced to cease trading due to their poor financial performance caused by lack of any support from the franchisor, whilst the franchisor itself made an alleged £2 million profit.[11] Labour MP Brian Donohoe raised the matter in the House of Commons, stating that it was 'a myth' that investing in a franchise was safe.[12] The collapse of the Pierre Victoire restaurant chain in 1998 was another example of a franchise chain going into receivership, leaving 104 franchisees in dire financial straits.[13] Likewise the collapse of the Pentos Group Plc – franchisor of the Athena and Rymans retail brands.[14] In Germany there have also been a number of franchise failures. For example, Foto Quelle, a mail order business with more than 1000 franchises, failed due to poor management; the master franchisee of Hooters in Berlin, Brandenburg, North Rhine Westfalia and Hesse (Wings of Germany) was declared bankrupt in 2006. In 2007 Kindervilla (children's nurseries) was declared bankrupt, resulting in criminal proceedings in 2009 due to 20 franchisees having lost around €150 000 each; and Zwo24, a dry cleaning business, failed in 2004 due to overambitious expansion. The restaurant Wienerwald failed three different times: in 1982 with 1600 restaurants due to overaggressive expansion; in 2003 due to adverse market conditions and in 2007 due to insufficient capitalisation. It is currently being relaunched for a fourth time.[15] In France, Law n° 89–1008 of 31 December 1989 was adopted due to the proliferation of abuse, sharp practice and commercial failure in franchising. Franchisors such as the Letter Station (which embezzled funds from some 60 franchisees in 1985) took advantage of franchising's growing popularity, whilst several legitimate franchises such as VO 9, Allo-Video, Dermo Vital, Climat de France, Plein Pot, La Taste, Relais Bleus, La Sweaterie and Sporteus[16] failed. These incidents seriously damaged 3.3

9 Pascal Hollander, 'Possible Legislative Developments: Is Belgium Doomed to Become a Hell for Franchisors?', *International Journal of Franchising and Distribution Law*, Vol. 3, Issue 1, pp. 47–51.

10 Penman and Sommerlad, 'Fleeced by 24 Self Video Franchise', *Daily Mirror*, 13 September 2007.

11 Ibid.

12 Hansard HC Vol 450 Col 1493 (24 October 2006).

13 Scotland on Sunday 23 May 2010.

14 Franchise World Feb/March 1994.

15 Marzheuser-Wood, B., 2009 'Franchising in Germany', EfN Conference (London).

16 Celeya, M., 2007, 'Good Faith & Franchising under French Law', EfN Conference (Paris).

the public image of franchising and led the authorities to consider regulating franchise agreements. A similar record of abuse[17] led to the adoption of the Spanish franchise law.[18] It was a record of abuse that also led to the regulation of franchising in Italy, although there was no particular big scandal or case of abuse which made the headlines. Many small players on the market were granting 'franchises' without having any significant formula, brand, trademark, know-how or business format for the franchisee and without providing the potential franchisee with the information necessary to take an informed decision about the advantages of joining the franchisor's network.[19] The much-publicised dispute over the Singer Sewing Machines company's termination of its franchisees led to the suggestion that franchising be specifically regulated being raised in the Swedish Parliament for the first time in its 1982/83 session.[20] Franchising is therefore subject to abuse, sharp practice and failure and so needs to be regulated.

C. ANALYSIS OF THE CONTRACTUAL ENVIRONMENT

1. The differing approaches of EU member states to constructing the contractual environment

3.4 The differing approaches of EU member states have no substantial impact on the basic elements of franchising's contractual environment. The fundamental economic and relational elements of franchising mean that, despite the different approach that civil and common law jurisdictions take to the drafting of commercial contracts, franchise agreements exhibit a common contractual architecture that transcends these differences and creates a uniform contractual environment for franchising in the EU.

(a) An analysis of franchise-specific laws in the EU

3.5 The heterogeneous nature of the regulatory environment is contributed to by the franchise-specific laws of eight EU member states. It is important to consider

---

17 A number of so-called 'empty franchises' (fraudulent schemes to extract money from unsuspecting individuals) SAP Valencia of 21 May 1993 (AC\1993\1024).

18 Act 7/1996, 15 January 1996 regarding Retail Commerce Planning (the 'LRCP'), as later developed by Royal Decree 2485/1998, 13 November 1998, as updated by Royal Decree 419/2006 of 7 April 2006 which came into effect on 17 May 2006.

19 Interview with Prof. Aldo Frignani, Professor, University of Turin (March 2009).

20 An attempt to obtain compensation for them under Sweden's protectionist employment laws failed. However, the lawyer who represented the franchisees, Mr Stig Gustafsson soon after entered the Swedish parliament as an MP, and spurred on by his failure to obtain compensation for the franchisees, dedicated himself to introducing a franchise regulation that would deliver the protection that he had failed to obtain for them under the employment law. After 21 years of campaigning by Mr Gustafsson, the Swedish parliament adopted a franchise-specific law (Statens offentliga utredningar (SOU) 1987:17 'Franchising').

their lack of any common approach. Although France provided initial momentum to the move towards franchise-specific laws in the EU, its approach has not been copied wholesale by any of the other member states. This may well be because, although the French law predates the other EU member state franchise regulations by some years, many of those member states began considering the need for such a law several years before the Loi Doubin was enacted.[21] Each member state has taken a markedly different approach. Six of the member state franchise-focused laws are concerned with pre-contractual disclosure. Two member states require the franchise agreement and the other relevant documents to be registered. One of the member states (Belgium) follows the French example and does not mention the word franchising. The two laws that do not require pre-contractual disclosure are more concerned with trying to define a franchise and the rights and obligations it gives rise to. These eight laws are outlined in Table 3.1. A draft franchise law was also considered in Greece in 2006 and 2007 but was dropped in 2008 because of a lack of governmental interest.

The fundamental economic and relational elements of franchising mean that, despite the different approach of civil and common law jurisdictions to the drafting of commercial contracts, franchise agreements exhibit a common contractual architecture that transcends these differences and creates a uniform contractual environment for franchising. This conclusion is drawn from considering the architecture of a sample of 25 franchise agreements. In order to avoid any jurisdiction-specific issues the sample comprises the agreements of five UK franchisors, five German franchisors, five French franchisors, five US franchisors and five Australian franchisors.[22] These are all agreements of franchisors established in the EU and doing or seeking to do business in more than one EU member state. In order to avoid any distortion due to focusing upon a particular sector, franchises in the retail, commercial and personal services, food/restaurant, contract cleaning, renovation services, printing, car rental and hotel sectors were included. In order to avoid any distortion due to the type of franchisee involved or the level of capital investment required a broad selection was included ranging from low-budget contract cleaning businesses (minimum investment of £500)[23] to large hotel businesses requiring an investment of many millions of pounds.[24] The sample evidences a distinct difference between those franchise agreements drafted for use in civil jurisdictions and those drafted in common law jurisdictions, but that they exhibit a common architecture and address common issues.

21 The first Franchise Law Bill introduced into the Belgian Parliament dates back to 1982 and that in Sweden to 1987.

22 See Appendix 2.

23 Jani-King.

24 Intercontinental.

Table 3.1 Summary of EU member state franchise laws

EU Member State	Title of Law	Pre-contractual Disclosure	Specification of Contractual Terms	Registration of Documentation on a Public Register	Comments
France	Law No 89–1008 dated 31 December 1989 (the Loi Doubin). New Article 330 of Civil Code.	20 days before executing contract	n/a	n/a	It does not refer to franchising but to 'any person who places a commercial name, a trade mark or sign at the disposal of another person in consideration for an undertaking of exclusivity or quasi-exclusivity for the exercise of his business'.
Spain	Article 62 of Act 7/1996 and Royal Decree 2485/1998	20 days before executing contract	n/a	Yes, at regional or central registries	

Italy	Law No 129 – 6 May 2004	30 days before executing contract	Details of the following must be provided; – Fees due – Investment requested – Territory – Details of know-how – Services to be provided by franchisor – Renewal – Termination – Transferability It imposes (1) Mandatory conciliation before legal proceedings (2) The concept must be tested and the results disclosed to the franchisee	n/a	A full copy of the franchise agreement replaces the need for a summary of the agreement's terms.
Sweden	The Disclosure Act 2006 (2006:484)	14 days before executing contract	n/a	n/a	
Belgium	Law Governing Pre-Contractual Information Within the Framework of Commercial Partnership Agreements – 19 December 2005, modified 27 December 2005 (Doc:51 1687/006)	One month before executing contract	n/a	n/a	It does not refer to franchising but to 'commercial partnership'.

EU Member State	Title of Law	Pre-contractual Disclosure	Specification of Contractual Terms	Registration of Documentation on a Public Register	Comments
Romania	Ordinance 52/1997 as modified by Law No. 79/1998	No time specified	Must specify – object of agreement – rights and obligations of parties – term – termination – financial provision	n/a	
Estonia	Law of Obligations Act 2002 Section 375–378	n/a	– duty of good faith – grant of rights to franchisee by franchisor	n/a	
Lithuania	Civil Code Article 6.766–6.779 (200)	n/a	– duty of good faith – automatic transfer of franchise to franchisee's heir in the event of death – franchisor can be held liable for claims against franchisee regarding the quality of goods or services supplied – automatic right of renewal	Yes, but it can be contracted out of (although this results in the agreement being unenforceable against third parties)	

(b) Contrasting the civil and common law approaches

The civil law agreements considered were all shorter than their common law counterparts. The civil law agreements range between 15 and 30 single-spaced A4 pages whereas the common law agreements range between 60 and 90 single-spaced A4 pages. Whilst all of the agreements considered address generally the same commercial issues, the common law agreements go into far more detail on technical legal issues. It has been suggested that common law agreements are generally more verbose than civil law agreements, not because common law agreements address more issues but because in common law countries the drafting style of contracts is heavily influenced by the drafting style of statutes and the tendency of the courts to interpret contracts and statutes in a literal manner.[25] As a consequence, contracts are very detailed because the parties try to take into account all possible events that may occur in the future and lay down an adequate contractual discipline to deal with them. This seems to be borne out by the sample. By contrast, it has been suggested that in civil jurisdictions the codes are usually 'general and abstract' as they state general principles concerning relevant subjects which are designed to prevail over the will of the parties and then add specific rules which are to be applied in those cases where nothing has been stated by the parties. As a result, civil law franchise agreements are brief and concise and the parties rely on relevant statutory provisions.[26] Again, this seems to be borne out by the sample. Other explanations, in addition to the impact of substantive law, include a tradition of succinctness in legal drafting in civil jurisdictions, and the limitations imposed by civil procedure.[27] Article 242 of the German Civil Code, which imposes a general duty of good faith on the parties to a contract, is cited as an example of why civil law agreements do not need to be as detailed as their common law counterparts.[28] The application by analogy of the rules applying to 'type-contracts', such as commercial agency to franchise agreements, is another reason for the brevity of the civil law franchise agreements in the sample. 3.6

(c) Differentiating features of the civil law approach

Unlike common law, civil law distinguishes between those contracts that are of a recognised type of agreement ('type-contracts' or 'nominate' contracts) and those that are not.[29] The reason for this difference is mainly a historical one and 3.7

25 Frignani, A., 1996, 'Some Basic Differences Between the Common Law and Civil Law Approach' – IBA-IFA 13th Annual Seminar on International Franchising.

26 Ibid.

27 Hill, C. and C. King, 2004, 'How Do German Contracts do as much with Fewer Words?', *Chicago-Kent Law Review*, Vol. 79, 889.

28 Whittaker, S. and R. Zimmerman, 2000, *Good Faith in European Contract Law*, Cambridge University Press.

29 For example, the German Civil Code inter alia categorises the following types of agreement: Business Management Agreements, Service Agreements, Lease Agreements and Licence Agreements.

the type-contracts are those which were most common at the time the civil codes were drafted, the belief being that as and when any new types of contracts become more common the rules applying to type-contracts could be applied to them by analogy as and when appropriate. If this proved to be inadequate then specific laws could be adopted for them.[30] The crucial point for this book is that the European civil codes do not usually have franchise-specific laws or type-contracts.[31] Franchise agreements are atypical or innominate agreements (*innommé* in French).[32] General contract law and, where deemed appropriate, by analogy the law applicable to other 'type-contracts' or 'nominate contracts' are applied to them, for example commercial agency and consumer law.[33] Civil law comprises mandatory and non-mandatory rules. The function of the 'non-mandatory rules' is to replace the silence of the parties on specific issues but they can be opted out of by the parties. They are essentially template or precedent terms that are deemed generally appropriate to a specific type of contract. This means that the parties need only deal with the specific issues arising in a particular contract. Mandatory rules cannot be avoided by the parties and include general concepts or principles such as public policy and good faith. The incorporation into a contract of terms that conflict with mandatory rules will be void as may be the entire agreement. Void clauses may be replaced by corresponding mandatory rules. Civil codes usually list terms which are considered to be essential elements of type-contracts, the lack of which invalidates the agreement. They also usually list other terms which are felt to be a natural consequence of a certain type of contract, but which can be opted out of. Civil codes distinguish between contracts for exchange (such as sale of goods) and contracts for co-operation (or adhesion[34]) (such as franchising). Contracts of exchange are usually type-contracts, whereas generally contracts for co-operation are not, as is the case with franchise agreements. As a result contracts for exchange tend to be shorter than contracts for co-operation. Franchise agreements, being contracts for co-operation which are not type-contracts are therefore generally longer than other civil agreements.[35] Civil courts are generally more comfortable interpreting legal rules than the will of

30 Op. cit., Frignani, A., 1996.

31 The exceptions are Lithuania, Estonia and Romania, all of which specifically refer to franchise agreements in their civil code and list mandatory, non-mandatory and essential terms for them.

32 Clément, 1994, p. 13; Michel Jéol, conclusions to the decisions of the Assemblée Plénière de la Cour de Cassation of 1 December 1995, D. jur., 1996, p. 13 ff; Leloup, 2004, p. 11.

33 In Spanish law there are four key decisions of the Supreme Court (Tribunal Supremo) about franchising: STS 27 September 1996, RJ 1996\6646; 4 March 1997, RJ 1997\1642, 30 April 1998, RJ 1998\3456 and 21 October 1005, Id Cendoj 28079110012005100801.
They recognise franchise agreements as an innominate atypical agreement, the norms of which are framed by analogy and characterise franchising in the same manner as to ECJ's judgment in *Pronuptia*.

34 Le Tourneau, 2003, 'Le Contrat de franchisage' Litec, Paris. Bueno Diaz, O., 2007 'Franchising in European Contract Law': Sellier, European Law Publishing, p. 43.

35 Op. cit., Frignani, A., 1996.

the parties and so prefer to apply mandatory and non-mandatory rules by analogy and general concepts such as good faith[36] to franchising agreements.

(d) Common key features

An analysis of the sample agreements leads one to conclude that franchise agreements, be they civil or common law agreements, and regardless of the economic and sectoral contextualisation, exhibit certain common key features. 3.8

Olson, Weinberg and Spencer[37] suggest that

> although there is no 'cookie cutter' approach to drafting a franchise agreement ... there are key provisions commonly found in franchise agreements, regardless of industry or business ... (although) ... every industry, business and relationship has unique considerations and each consideration may affect and alter those provisions.

They identify key terms to include the grant, the financial terms (including targets and product ties), the term and renewal, the franchisor's obligations, the franchisee's obligations, confidentiality, restrictive covenants/non-competition, transfer of the business and termination. The *Encyclopaedia of Forms and Precedents*[38] identifies the same key common terms in franchise agreements. Analysis of the sample agreements suggests that these key terms are indeed found in all franchise agreements as they are in all those comprising the sample. Some agreements in the sample present targets and product ties separately from other financial terms. Others combine confidentiality with restrictive covenants and provisions about the manual. However, these are a matter of form rather than substantive content. One can therefore conclude that regardless of whether agreements are drafted in the civil or common law idiom and despite economic and sectoral contextualisation franchise agreements comprise certain key terms.

2. Analysis of the contractual environment as regards the economic drivers

The contractual environment of franchising has a differing impact on the economic drivers that attract franchisees to franchising and those that attract 3.9

36 Op. cit., Frignani, A., 1996.

37 Olsen, Weinberg and Spencer (2010) 'The Annotated Franchise Agreement'. American Bar Association 33rd Annual Forum on Franchising, p. 1.

38 Abell, M. and D. Bond, *Butterworths Encyclopaedia of Forms and Precedents* (2003) Vol. 16(4). Franchising, Agency and Distribution Fifth Edition. Ed. Millet 96.

franchisors. The contractual environment created by the architecture of franchise agreements generally protects the economic drivers that attract franchisors to franchising. It also protects many (but not all) of the economic drivers that attract franchisees to franchising. Considering each of the key features of the architecture of a franchise agreement in turn within the context of those agreements comprising the sample, one is able to extrapolate upon the adequacy of the contractual environment in supporting and re-enforcing the economic drivers in the franchisor/franchisee relationship.

(a) The grant

3.10 The franchisee is granted the right to use the franchisor's business format (know-how) and trade marks. These are two of the key elements of a franchise. The integrity of this intellectual property is fundamental to the relationship. If the franchisor does not have the right to license the franchisee to use it, if it infringes the rights of others or is insufficient or otherwise unfit for the intended purpose, the franchisee will be deprived of the main benefit of the transaction. However, only two of the agreements in the sample warranted their ownership of the trade mark, and none warranted the mark's validity or their ownership of or the effectiveness of the know-how. The rights granted are often, but not always, restricted to either a specific area or a stated location.[39] They can either be exclusive or non-exclusive.[40] The territory is usually a geographical area that allows a planned approach to exploitation of the franchise. 'Encroachment' on the franchisee's business by franchisors has been identified as a substantial problem.[41] However, it is not always fully prohibited by the agreement. The franchisor's placement of a new company-owned or franchised unit too close to an existing one has emerged

> to be one of the most vexing, emotional and yet least understood franchising problems in mature markets such as the US.[42]

The grant of geographical exclusivity to franchisees is aimed at preventing this. In the sample, just over half of the franchisors grant geographical exclusivity of some kind. The others have no geographical protection at all – probably for good commercial reasons such as the prevalence of national, non-geocentric, accounts in the customer base. Encroachment is usually considered to exist

---

39 18 of the 25 agreements.

40 13 of the 25 agreements were exclusive.

41 Purvin, R., 1994, *The Franchise Fraud*, The American Association of Franchisees and Dealers, 129.

42 Barkoff, R. and W. Garner, 1994, 'Encroachment: The Thorn in Every Successful Franchisor's Side': Annual Forum on Franchising. American Bar Association.

> If a franchisor develops, or grants to a franchisee the right to develop, a new outlet or location which sells essentially the same goods or services under the same trademark, service mark, trade name, logotype or other commercial symbol as an existing franchisee and the new outlet or location is in unreasonable proximity to the existing franchisee's outlet or location and has an adverse effect on the gross sales of the existing franchisee's outlet or location, the existing adversely affected franchisee has a cause of action for monetary damages ... [43]

Deliberate cannibalisation of a franchisee's business by the franchisor is clearly inappropriate. However, encroachment is sometimes the unintended consequence of the franchisor embracing new technologies in an endeavour to maintain and increase the business's competiveness for the ultimate benefit of not only itself but also its franchise network. For example, the advent of the worldwide web has meant that encroachment can be by way of a multi-channel approach to the market. The impact on the franchisee's business of this electronic intra brand competition is regulated by only 60% of the agreements in the sample,[44] so raising a potential concern over the violation of the franchisees' business interests through 'non-traditional' encroachment. Encroachment is an issue which many of the agreements in the sample fail to deal with in an appropriate manner.

(b) Term and renewal

All of the agreements in the sample were granted for a period of between five **3.11**
and ten years. A conditional right of renewal is often included.[45] The franchisee must be confident that it will be able to amortise its investment in the franchise and make a reasonable return within the initial term. It was not possible to judge whether or not the terms granted by the franchise agreements in the sample allowed this. Research in the US suggests that the vast majority of franchisees do seek and are allowed by the franchisor to exercise the right of renewal.[46]

(c) Targets

In order to try and ensure the optimum exploitation of the rights granted to the **3.12**
franchisee, minimum performance levels are sometimes agreed.[47] Others simply place an obligation on the franchisee to use best or reasonable endeavours to grow the business.[48] The consequences of failure to meet the targets vary. Termination of the agreement is the most common option, although there is

43 Iowa Code 2001 Supplement, Section 537A.10.
44 15 of the 25 agreements.
45 21 of the 25 agreements.
46 Op. cit., Blair, R. and F. Lafontaine, 2005, p. 263.
47 9 of the 25 agreements.
48 10 of the 25 agreements.

almost always an opportunity to remedy the breach in some way.[49] This can be 'catching up' and meeting the following year's target and/or paying liquidated damages to compensate the franchisor for its resulting loss of income. It follows from this that the targets should be reasonable, but none of those agreements with targets gave any rationale for them, so it was not possible to judge whether or not they are reasonable.

(d) The franchisor's obligations

3.13 The franchisor is obliged to provide training and ongoing support to the franchisee and to keep it fully appraised of developments in the business format.[50] This training in the business format and the ongoing support are key elements of a franchise. There is sometimes also an obligation to supply goods or services to the franchisee.[51] However, the franchisor's obligations are generally minimal and the agreements usually do not go into detail.[52] Several refer to the manual which is stated to contain details of the franchisor's obligations.[53] Frequency of visits to the franchisee is sometimes stated.[54] None of the agreements impose an obligation for the franchisor to provide a minimal, objective, qualitative level of support to the franchisee. The number of days that training will be given for is often stated.[55] The vague nature of the franchisor's obligations and the lack of any qualitative rather than quantitative metric means that franchisees have no real contractual right to challenge the franchisor if it fails to deliver a reasonable level of support. This lack of any objective measurable standard of performance in any of the agreements means that providing that the franchisor delivers some support the franchisee will not be able to challenge its adequacy or relevance. The ever-changing nature of all businesses, particularly due to the impact of new technologies, means that the franchisor must be able to develop and adapt the business format and, as a consequence, the type of support it provides to the franchisee. That is perhaps why the agreements do not detail the support to be provided. However, the total lack of any qualitative measure in the agreements does expose the franchisee to the risk that the franchisor provides it with inadequate support. An example of the problems that this lack of appropriate support by the franchisor can create is given by the case of *MGB Printing and Design Ltd* v. *KallKwik UK Ltd*.[56] In this case the franchisee was obliged in the franchise agreement to provide the franchisee 'from time to time with advice, know-how and guidance'.

---

49 7 of the 11 sample agreements with targets.
50 All of the agreements in the sample imposed these obligations.
51 12 of the 25 sample agreements.
52 Only 5 of the 25 agreements go into any great level of detail about the franchisor's obligations.
53 8 of the 25 sample agreements.
54 6 of the 25 sample agreements.
55 15 of the 25 sample agreements.
56 QBD – 31 March 2010 – [2010] EWHC 624 (QB).

The court ruled that there was a duty of care which meant that the franchisor was obliged to exercise reasonable skill and care in providing such know-how and advice, which the franchisor had breached. This failure to deliver an appropriate level of skill and care was evident throughout the franchise causing a further 92 franchisees in the franchisor's KallKwik and Prontaprint businesses to threaten proceedings on the same grounds as their fellow franchisee, Mr Bibby.[57] The long-term nature of the franchise agreement and the need to accommodate the resulting tensile stresses within the franchise relationship are discussed in Chapter 2. They result in the franchisor having a good deal of flexibility although this is markedly less so in the German sample. This is due to the impact of the German law of good faith. This flexibility can be misused by franchisors and as a result the contractual environment does not adequately reduce the risks to franchisees or support the economic drivers that attract them to franchising.

(e) The franchisee's obligations

By contrast to those of the franchisor, the obligations of the franchisee are generally voluminous and include use of the know-how and the brand, following the franchisor's system and meeting brand standards. This control is a fundamental element of the franchise. In order to ensure this as far as possible, the franchise agreement goes into detail on issues such as use of the trade marks, staff training and operational procedures. Common law agreements go into more detail than those from civil jurisdictions. The strength of franchise systems typically does not lie in the absolute quality of the products or services offered. Instead it resides largely in the capacity of the franchised chain to offer a uniform product at a reasonably uniform price. Quality and service variation have external effects that damage other franchisees as well as the franchisor and this creates tension between the franchisor and individual franchisees. The individual franchisee's incentives are not aligned with those of the franchisor and other franchisees. **3.14**

> The profit-maximising behaviour of an individual can have adverse external effects on the franchisor and other franchisees.[58]

These provisions of the franchise agreement are designed to remove or at least mitigate the fundamental incentive issue because franchisees care more about the profits of their own outlet while the franchisor cares more about the profits

57 www.printweek.com/news/1040784/kall-kwikfranchisees-continue-legal-against-against-ODC viewed 13/11/2010.

58 Op. cit., Blair, R. and F. Lafontaine, 2005, p. 118. See also op. cit., Caves, R. and W. Murphy, 1976 and Klein, B., 1980, 'Transaction Cost Determinants of Unfair Contractual Arrangements' *American Economic Review*, 356–62.

of the system as a whole. The provisions also provide for the franchisor's right to monitor the performance of the franchise through regular inspections, audits and so on. The manual, which is expressly incorporated in the agreement, also imposes innumerable operational obligations on the franchisee and details the franchisor's know-how. The copyright in both the original and translated manual is stated to vest in the franchisor.[59]

(f) Confidentiality

3.15 A franchisor must disclose a considerable amount of confidential information (the business format) to each of its franchisees. The franchise agreements prevent the franchisee from disclosing the confidential information or using it to compete with the franchisor.[60] These restrictions endure for the duration of the franchise and thereafter. A number of EU member states also impose a duty of confidentiality upon both parties to the franchise agreement,[61] so further re-enforcing this point.

(g) Non-competition

3.16 Franchise agreements forbid franchisees to compete with the franchisor during the term of the agreement[62] and for a limited period with a limited geographical area thereafter.[63] The post-termination restrictions are limited by law in all EU member states. This clause is essential to protect the integrity of the franchisor's business.

(h) Transfer of the franchisee's business

3.17 Franchise agreements usually allow the franchisee to sell its business to a third party that has been previously approved by the franchisor, subject to the franchisor's pre-emptive right to purchase the franchisee's business on the same terms as the bona fide third party offer (provided this right is exercised within a reasonable time).[64] This is necessary to enable franchisees to realise a 'capital profit' on their investment whilst at the same time enabling the franchisor to ensure the quality of its franchisees. The pre-emptive right is necessary to enable the franchisor to retain control (which is an essential element of a franchise).

---

59 19 of the 25 sample agreements.

60 These terms are in all 25 sample agreements.

61 E.g. Article 18 of the German Unfair Competition Act and BGB Sections 675(1), 611 and 241(2).

62 All of the agreements in the sample.

63 22 of the agreements in the sample. The two exceptions in the sample were hotel franchises, where the franchisee still retains the hotel at the end of the franchise and needs to be able to operate it under another brand.

64 23 out of the 25 sample agreements.

(i) Product or service tie

There is often a product or service tie which obliges the franchisee to purchase specific brands and/or purchase goods or products from the franchisor or approved suppliers.[65] The justification for such a tie is that it helps to ensure product consistency across the network. It can relate to goods that are sold on without modification (e.g. ice cream in a Baskins-Robbins franchise) or ingredients that are used to make the final product (e.g. the dough in a Domino's Pizza). Such a provision could, of course, be abused to deliver additional inflated income streams to the franchisor. Likewise the products or services supplied could be of a poor standard and so be problematic. However, not all of the agreements in the sample provided for redress in such circumstances.[66] It is possible that some franchisors supply such goods or services under their standard terms and conditions which do provide for such redress, but the sample did not enable this to be considered. **3.18**

(j) Goodwill

Goodwill survives a defunct business[67] and under the terms of common law franchise agreements it is stated to accrue to the franchisor[68] not the franchisee. However, this is not the case in the civil law agreements, which are silent on the issue. This is presumably because most civil law jurisdictions follow the German lead and take the view that goodwill accrues to the franchisee by analogy to the position as regards commercial agents. **3.19**

(k) Termination

The franchise agreements give the franchisor the express right to terminate the franchise agreement for breach. A distinction is often made between a remediable and irremediable breach, with the right for the franchisee to remedy remediable breaches. The franchisee is not given any express right to terminate the agreement (although this does not impact upon its right to do so under the law of contract). The civil law agreements tend to have less draconian rights of termination. **3.20**

65 12 out of the 25 sample agreements.

66 8 of the 12 sample agreements.

67 In *Ad-Lib Club Ltd* v. *Granville* [1971] 2 All ER 300, [1972] RPC 673 goodwill sufficient to found an action of passing off was held to survive a well-known nightclub by some years.

68 Usually there will be an express term requiring the franchisee to hold the goodwill as bare trustee for the franchisor, but, even in the absence of such a term, it would appear that the goodwill accrues to the franchisor: see *J H Coles Pty Ltd* v. *Need* [1934] AC 82, PC.

3. Analysis of the contractual environment as regards risk

3.21 The contractual environment created by the architecture of franchise agreements generally reduces the inherent risks for franchisors but is less successful in reducing them for franchisees.

(a) Risks to the franchisor

3.22 The franchisor is exposed to information asymmetry and moral hazard potentially resulting in 'free riding'. It is suggested that these are reduced to an appropriate level by the contractual environment. The franchisor is also subjected to abuse of its intellectual property and non-payment of fees. These are generally dealt with in a satisfactory manner by the contractual environment. In order to reduce the impact of 'free riding' and information asymmetry the franchise agreements in the sample impose an obligation on the franchisee to comply with the system and grant the franchisor the right to audit their business for compliance. Non-compliance can lead to termination by the franchisor. This is clearly a strong incentive for franchisees to follow the system. Any fetter on the right to terminate is problematic in that it reduces the effectiveness of the incentive.[69] A prohibition on in-term competition by the franchisee reduces that particular risk for the franchisor. However, although a prohibition on using the franchisor's trade secrets after the term of the agreement helps to prevent competition from former franchisees a permanent prohibition on competing without using the franchisor's trade secrets is restricted to a short period only. This is due to a general prohibition on long-term restrictive covenants in EU member states. Indeed in some member states post-term restrictive covenants are only permissible if the franchisee is paid compensation. The franchise agreement generally gives robust protection to the franchisor's intellectual property. However, the franchisor's ownership of goodwill which is clearly stated in common law franchise agreements is contrary to the law in some member states such as Germany, Austria and Greece and so is not included in the German agreements in the sample. The agreement incentivises the franchisees to pay monies due to the franchisor by way of the imposition of interest on late payments and a right to terminate the agreement in the event of non-payment. When franchisors were asked which obligations were important in protecting their business from franchise abuse there was general agreement that they were non-competition by franchisees

69 Several member states do impose fetters on the franchisor's right to terminate e.g. Germany.

during the agreement;[70] non-competition for a reasonable period after termination;[71] no challenge of the franchisor's intellectual property by franchisees;[72] franchisees being obliged to follow the system;[73] and payment of monies due to the franchisor.[74] The majority of franchise lawyers surveyed[75] felt that following the franchisor's system,[76] not challenging the franchisor's intellectual property rights[77] and not competing with the franchising during the term of the franchise agreement[78] were the most important restrictions that should be placed on the franchisor.[79] This is similar to the results of other research. For example, according to Pratt,[80] of the 129 franchisors that he questioned, the majority felt that being involved in a competing business, passing on confidential information, non-payment of fees, underdeclaration of turnover and encouraging other franchisees to take action against the franchisor, were the issues on which they were willing to litigate. So, the agreements in the sample (unsurprisingly, as they are all drafted by the franchisor) suggest that the contractual environment does reduce the risk of being involved in franchising for the franchisor to an appropriate level, providing member state law does not fetter the contractual rights in any way.

(b) Risks to the franchisees

Franchisees are exposed to inappropriate pre-contractual representations, brand failure, inadequate business formats, encroachment and poor quality support. It is suggested that these are not reduced to an adequate level by the contractual environment. None of the franchise agreements in the sample gave contractually binding effect to pre-contractual representations made to the franchisee. **3.23**

70 UK – 80% of sample; Germany – 72% of sample; France – 80% of sample but only 47% in Spain where 68% thought it to be insignificant.

71 UK – 96%; Germany – 56%; France – 92%; Spain – 40% – in Spain 52% thought that it was 'significant' rather than 'very significant'.

72 UK – 96%; Germany – 84%; France – 80%; Spain – 100%.

73 Germany – 84%; France – 52%; Spain – 76%; only 12% of those in the UK thought it was 'very significant' although 84% thought it was 'significant'.

74 UK – 48%; Germany – 24%; France – 60% and Spain none.

75 Appendix 2.

76 56% of the sample.

77 20% of the sample.

78 16% of the sample.

79 48% of the sample felt that not competing with the franchisor during the term was the second most important obligation, 24% that it was following the franchisor's system and 20% that it was not challenging the franchisor's intellectual property. 56% of the sample felt that not competing with the franchisor for a reasonable period after the end of the agreement was the third most important obligation, 28% felt that it was non competition with the franchisor during the term and 20% that it was not challenging the franchisor's intellectual property. 36% felt that not challenging the franchisor's intellectual property was the fourth most important obligation, 20% that it was following the franchisor's system, 16% that it was not competing after the term and 8% not competing during the term. 12% felt that non competition for a reasonable period after the term was the fifth most important obligation and 4% not challenging the franchisor's intellectual property rights.

80 Pratt, *Franchise World* Dec/Jan 2007, p. 9.

Franchisees are therefore obliged to rely on non-contractual remedies if they have entered into the franchise agreement on the basis of incorrect information. Indeed, many of the agreements in the sample[81] expressly excluded liability for at least some of the pre-contractual representations made by the franchisor to the franchisee. These are mostly common law agreements.[82] This inability to rely on representations made to the franchisee during the sales process does nothing to reduce the risks imposed on them. All of the agreements clearly state the extent of the rights granted to the franchisee as regards duration, and territory. However, only some[83] of them (regardless of whether the grant is exclusive) restrict the franchisor from using multi-channel strategies to exploit the market in competition with the franchisee. Encroachment is not adequately dealt with in many agreements. In the fast-changing era of multi-channel marketing and electronic commerce, it is perhaps reasonable that the franchisor does not restrict its long-term ability to exploit the market in ways that it is not yet familiar with. Indeed, such a restriction could have an extremely damaging impact on its business and that of the franchise network as a whole. However, there is clearly an opportunity here for unethical or opportunistic franchisors to take advantage of the franchisee. This encroachment issue is not dealt with adequately in the franchise agreement. The obligation of the franchisor to provide support to the franchisee during the term of the agreement is stated in all agreements in the sample. However, none of them give any detail about the extent or quality of that support. The support provided to the franchisees by the franchisor is a fundamental part of the communal relationship between the parties. That is why the obligation to support the franchisee is imposed on the franchisor. However, none of the agreements in the sample impose a set standard for the support or go into detail about what the support entails. This is because franchise agreements are long-term agreements and (as detailed in Chapter 2 above) during that term market, economic and technological changes can mean that the franchisor will need to further develop and adapt its concept, making the level and type of support that needs to be delivered to its franchisees change. However, no such obligation was found in any agreement in the sample. This means that franchisees can find it very difficult to hold the franchisor to a set standard of support. If the franchisor fails to provide the franchisee with use of the brand, access to the know-how or any support, all the agreements in the sample permit the franchisee to terminate the agreement. However, none of the agreements give that right to the franchisee if the franchisor greatly reduces the level of support it delivers to the franchisee, even

81 15 of the 25 sample agreements.

82 12 of the 15 agreements are from common law jurisdictions.

83 15 of the 25 sample agreements.

if that reduced level of support is clearly inadequate. Unethical and opportunistic franchisors could take advantage of the lack of any qualitative provision in the agreement and decrease the support given merely to increase its own margins. The franchisor generally has broad discretion to take decisions that have an impact upon the franchise at its sole discretion in the common law agreements and the French agreements. Only the German agreements caveat the franchisor's discretion with an obligation of reasonableness. This exposes franchisees to the risk of exploitation by the franchisor.

The franchisee's ability to sell on its rights, subject to the franchisor's pre-emption rights found in many agreements in the sample, merely balances the rights of both franchisor and franchisee.

The tying of franchisees to purchase certain goods and/or services from the franchisor or approved third parties presents unethical or opportunistic franchisors the opportunity of selling overpriced and substandard products to a captive market.

> Buying into a franchise system with an unproven product, an unknown trademark and/or an untested operating system may constitute the only 'catastrophe' necessary to cause (franchisees) to lose (their) entire life savings ... Investing in a franchise enterprise that provides little support but takes much in the way of royalties, fees and other charges can ensure failure rather than success.[84]

The franchise agreements in the sample suggest that the contractual environment does not adequately reduce the risks of franchising for franchisees, largely due to the long-term nature of the relationship and the dynamic and changing nature of the markets in which the franchised business operates.

D. ANALYSIS OF THE SELF-REGULATORY ENVIRONMENT

The self-regulatory environment in the EU does not adequately support the 3.24 economic drivers or reduce the consequential risks inherent in the franchisor/ franchisee relationship. There can be no doubt that 'a healthy franchising sector requires adequate and appropriate infrastructure'[85] and that

84 Op. cit., Purvin, R., 1994, p. 4.

85 'Franchise Sector Regulation: The Australian Experience', Andrew Terry, The EMNet-Conference on Economics and Management of Franchising Networks, Vienna, Austria, 26–28 June 2003.

> central to this infrastructure is the legal environment in which franchising operates an environment providing for the orderly development of franchising for the benefit of franchisors, franchisees and the wider community.[86,87]

The big question is how such an environment can be best achieved within the EU. Self-regulation as a way of regulating commerce has been subject to severe criticism from lawyers and other social scientists.[88] As Alistair Darling, then the UK government minister with responsibility for the financial services, stated, one of

> the problem(s) with self-regulation is the public's perception that trade interest dominates which is extremely damaging.[89]

Certainly the Australian experiment with the self-regulation of franchising between 1993 and 1996 does not inspire confidence in it and supports the view that

> it can prevent abuses by 'dishonest franchisors' only to a very limited extent and (its main) purpose is to prevent the interference of the regulator in the sector.[90, 91]

However, others argue that when there is market failure, private law remedies are inadequate or too costly and self-regulation is a better/cheaper option: self-regulation can be in the public interest.[92] As a result, in the past, bills

86 Ibid.

87 See Appendix at end of Chapter 3. The vast majority of franchisors surveyed believe that complete transparency in the recruitment process avoids most of the problems that franchisors face with their franchisees.

88 Ogus, A., 1995, 'Rethinking Self Regulation', *Oxford Journal of Legal Studies*.

89 Steward, E., 'The Four Horsemen of the Apocalypse – The Financial Services Authority and its Statutory Objectives', *BLR*, Vol. 22, Number 11, 258–61.

90 The Belgian House of Representatives, 17 March 2004 Doc 51 0924/001 Second sitting of 51st Parliament – Draft Parliamentary Bill regulating franchise agreements with a view to improving commercial practices in this sector (lodged by MM Alain Mathot and Jean-Marc Delizée and Mme Sophie Pécriaux).

91 Despite being declared by the Australian government on its launch as the most progressive industry/government franchising initiative undertaken in the world the Australian self-regulatory code proved to be a failure and 'Within a year of its commencement concerns were being raised about its effectiveness' (Schacht, 'Creating a better business environment: a package for Australian small business', 21 December 1995, p. 3) and after only 14 months the Australian government initiated an independent investigation into it. The Gardini Report was released to the public in March 1995. It estimated that approximately 40% to 50% of franchisors had not registered under the Code and concluded that it was unlikely that more than 70% of franchisors ever would. It also concluded that a significant number of those franchisors that did not register failed to provide adequate pre-contractual disclosure, to offer a cooling-off period or to observe the standards of conduct contained in the Code. The Code was also found to not have been successful at dealing with serious franchise disputes (The Gardini Report to Senator the Hon. Chris Schacht on the effectiveness of the self-regulatory framework, March 1995). The report concluded that 'a system of mandatory self-regulation or co-regulation' was necessary and recommended ' ... specific franchising legislation providing for compulsory registration of franchisors and compliance with codes of practice ... The legislation should provide for adequate disclosure documentation, the establishment of appropriate independent code administration bodies, and dispute resolution procedures ... '

92 Op. cit., Ogus, A., 1995 and Breyer, S., 1982, *Regulation and Its Reform*, Cambridge, MA: Harvard University Press.

designed to regulate franchising in both Belgium and Sweden have been defeated. The abuse, sharp practice and commercial failure in franchising can certainly be ascribed to a degree of failure in the market. Private legal remedies are without doubt beyond the reach of smaller franchisees on the basis of cost. Self-regulation does offer a cheaper and more focused alternative. In addition it can be argued that self-regulation gives access to a greater degree of expertise and technical knowledge[93] and so can provide a more targeted and commercially appropriate result.

1. The determinants of the self-regulatory environment

The self-regulation of franchising in the EU is implemented through the EFF and its 16 member state franchise associations. The EFF's Code of Ethics has been adopted by all of its member associations (with a number of small differences). It provides a useful benchmark for prospective franchisees when seeking to evaluate a particular franchisor's behaviour. It also helps franchisors to understand best practice and so increases the chance that franchisors will conduct themselves in an ethical and fair manner. In that sense the Code is extremely important. The Code of Ethics requires franchisors who are members of the national franchise associations to follow best practice. They must disclose to their potential franchisees information concerning the franchise concept, the people with decision-making power in the system's head office, the franchise offer, outlook on profitability (if available), the franchise contract (including all standardised attachments), information on membership of professional associations and information on other distribution channels of the franchise products or services.[94] **3.25**

2. The self-regulatory environment's relationship with the legal regulatory environment

The British Franchise Association (BFA)[95] claims credit for establishing the current 'favourable regulatory climate for franchising',[96] asserting that the European Commission is satisfied with the EFF and its member association's self-regulatory arrangements based on the EFF's Code of Ethics – although it **3.26**

93 Cane, P., 1987, 'Self Regulation and Judicial Review', 6 *Civil Justice Q.*, 324, 328–33.

94 a) Branches, wholesale trade, specialist trade, mail order, internet sales etc.
b) Sales to corporate clients and large customers through the franchisor.

95 The British Franchise Association ('BFA') asserts that it is 'the largest and most successful franchise association in Europe'. With 350 franchisor members, 115 affiliate (non-franchisor) members and reserves of over £1 million, it is the biggest franchise association in the EU. It is therefore an appropriate and very accessible case study both of the issues facing franchise associations in the EU and the current and potential effectiveness of the self-regulation of franchising by national franchise associations in the EU.

96 *One Vision, 2008 – Strategic Option for the Association's Future*, p. 29.

acknowledges that this needs to be 'actively managed'. It believes that 'Regulation is not just about ivory towers and idiots making up rules',[97] and that over the past 10 years it has

> successfully prevented several misguided attempts to regulate franchising which would have seriously damaged franchising throughout the common market.[98]

That is an exaggerated claim, but there certainly is a substantial body of opinion that firmly believes that

> only the versatility of a self-regulatory regime will enable franchising to grow in a manner that strongly encourages ethical practice. Laws can only seek to offer redress to those wronged. Ethical practice however prevents them being wronged in the first place.[99]

Market forces are deemed to be the best means of ensuring that franchising's needs are met. It is believed that the shackles of legal regulation will inevitably retard the commercial development and success of franchising because of its inevitably cumbersome and commercially divisive nature. An appropriate self-regulatory regime is thought to be able to prevent rather than cure problems by promoting ethical franchising, with caveat emptor still applying throughout. The problem here is that the difference between ethical and non-ethical franchising

> is not always apparent until too late and then often at great expense to the franchisee.[100]

3. The key elements of the self-regulatory environment

3.27 An analysis of the self-regulatory regime of the franchising sector in the EU suggests that it focuses upon pre-contractual disclosure, the resolution of disputes between franchisors and their franchisees, the enforcement of best practice and education. The BFA, as Europe's largest and most influential franchise association, offers a useful case study. It believes that it can 'self-regulate' franchising by promoting best practice and endeavouring to deal with disputes between franchisors and their franchisees.

---

97 *Franchise World*, Feb/Mar 2007, 16–18.

98 Sir Bernard Ingham, BFA Annual Convention, 2005.

99 Brian Smart, Director General of the BFA speaking at the BFA Annual Conference 2005.

100 Broadhurst, N., *Franchise World*, Aug/Sept 2004, 26–30.

(a) Disclosure

Appropriate disclosure requirements could reduce some of the risks of pre-contractual misrepresentation and inadequacy of the business format and support. However, the BFA is against set form regulation disclosure on the grounds of adequacy, cost and complexity. 3.28

It believes that

> a franchisor's obligation to disclose to a potential franchisee should not be limited by a list of items in a statute. It should be determined by the facts of a particular set of circumstances.[101]

The BFA has therefore not followed the lead of the French and Italian associations and recognised that there is a legitimate role for statutory regulation of disclosure. It believes that disclosure laws only limit a franchisor's duty to disclose to what in some circumstances may be an inappropriately low level, claiming that in France the Loi Doubin

> operates to the benefit of franchisors who can 'prove' through the disclosure document that they told an aggrieved franchisee what they were statutorily obliged to tell them.[102]

As a result the BFA has failed to impose even a low level of mandatory, standard form pre-contractual disclosure on its membership. It also comments that franchisors face substantial financial and administrative burdens due to legislation.[103] However, the Director General of the BFA insists that his organisation has never set itself against disclosure, only disclosure that is too complex to be effective.[104] The benefits of pre-contractual disclosure are clear even to the BFA's membership.[105] However, despite these being 'dangerous times for franchising',[106] it is not on the BFA's agenda. As a result many of the risks to which franchisees are exposed are not adequately reduced.

(b) Enforcement of best practice

Best practice could, in theory, create a self-regulatory environment that supports the economic drivers and reduces the consequential risks inherent in franchising. However, without rigorous enforcement of them the credibility of 3.29

101 Brian Smart in interview with the author, 18 September 2008.

102 *One Vision, 2008 – Strategic Option for the Association's Future*, p. 29.

103 Quoting the initial cost to franchisors in the USA of complying with the disclosure law as more than $25 000 with an annual updating cost of $5000.

104 Brian Smart in interview with the author, 18 September 2008.

105 At the 1996 BFA Annual Convention the majority of attendees voted decisively in favour of the BFA adopting a mandatory set form disclosure document for its members.

106 Brian Smart, The British Franchise Association's Director-General – *Franchise World*, Feb/Mar 2007, 16–18.

the BFA as an efficient agent of self-regulation is limited. The BFA's record to date does not inspire confidence.[107]

(c) Dispute resolution

3.30 If it is to be able to support the economic drivers and reduce the consequential inherent risk, an effective and obviously impartial dispute resolution procedure is essential for a self-regulatory regime. The BFA's current 'franchisee-friendly, three-tiered dispute handling procedures, offering a choice of conciliation, mediation and arbitration'[108] are the jewel in its self-regulatory crown. However, their success is somewhat limited.[109] Franchisors that have used the procedures have mixed views and experiences. When interviewed, one stated

> I am always willing to use the conciliation and mediation services offered by the BFA as they are not binding and only increase the chance of avoiding serious conflict with a franchisee.[110]

The BFA's dispute resolution procedure is a mixed success. The conciliation and mediation services are seen as having a role in dispute resolution, although the arbitration has in effect been abandoned and in any event is restricted in the type of dispute it can consider.

(d) Education

3.31 Educating franchisors and potential franchisees should enable the regulatory environment to better support the economic drivers and reduce the consequential inherent risk in franchising. In order to do so, educational programmes must ensure that potential franchisees fully understand what they will be buying into and the need to take and follow appropriate advice. The BFA's educational initiatives include its website,[111] a host of hard copy publications, several series

---

107 In 2007 it expelled three members for breach of its Code of Ethics – more than in the previous ten years put together (Brian Smart, Director-General of the British Franchise Association speaking at the BFA's Annual General Meeting on 6 December 2007 at the Hyatt Regency Hotel, Birmingham). In 2008 it expelled one member (Duckett, *Franchise World*, Feb/Mar 2008, 8). However, these four franchises are apparently still trading and the BFA will not name them or the grounds for their expulsion, presumably for fear of legal action. (It is understood that the grounds for expulsion were complaints by their franchisees and their financial standing.) Whether or not their expulsion will discourage potential franchisees from investing in one of their franchises is doubtful as it is unlikely that they will know about it and if they do, it will depend upon the potential franchisees' due diligence and the value they perceive in BFA membership. Thus self-regulation's focus on best practice does not create an environment which supports the economic drivers and reduces the risks inherent in franchising.

108 *Franchise World*, Dec/Jan 2003, 11.

109 The arbitration system has only been used six times and fell into disuse after one of the arbitrators (Gordon Harris, a partner in the law firm Wragge & Co.) was successfully sued for negligence by a franchisor, Pirtek, in respect of a case that he arbitrated on under the BFA scheme.

110 Steve Mills, CEO of MRI Limited. Interview with author, April 2005.

111 www.bfa.org.

of ongoing seminars and a presence at the franchise exhibitions in London, Birmingham, Manchester and Glasgow. It also co-sponsors with the National Westminster Bank Plc, an annual survey of the franchise industry in the UK. The importance of this role is underlined by 'One Vision 2008' but the limited impact of its 'Proud to Franchise' initiative in the same year underlines the difficulties involved. Educating franchisors to act for the greater good of franchising is always going to be a difficult and never ending task. The BFA is seeking to meet this challenge and broaden its funding base through its 'One Vision' Strategy,[112] but its failure to gather momentum suggests that this will do little to reduce the risks inherent in franchising or support its economic drivers.

4. Failings in the self-regulatory environment

Whatever the self-regulatory environment might aspire to its prospects of success are compromised by a number of fundamental difficulties. The problems that self-regulation encounters are conflict of interest, finance, enforcement of their decisions, competition from other self-regulatory bodies and an inability to have any impact on non-members. The BFA again offers a useful case study. **3.32**

(a) Conflict of interest

Franchise associations primarily exist to protect and promote the interests of their members.[113] Promoting franchising itself is very much a secondary role for them. There is a clear conflict of interest. This is well illustrated by the BFA. For the first 24 years of its existence, there was not even a suggestion that franchisees should be involved in the BFA.[114] It saw itself as a trade body or pressure group, the sole function of which was to further the interests of its members. This has seriously undermined its stance on self-regulation.[115] **3.33**

112 *One Vision, 2008 – Strategic Option for the Association's Future.*

113 E.g. see the German Franchise Association (DFV)'s home page www.dfv-franchise.com which addresses itself entirely to franchisors and their interests rather than franchising as a whole and states that its main duties include supporting franchise systems in establishing themselves in the German market.

114 The BFA members are all franchisors. To become a member, a franchisor has to be accredited. In 2008, 59 new members were admitted (compared to 55 in 2007), ten applications were rejected (compared to 31 in 2007) and one member was 'managed out' or terminated (compared to three in 2007). BFA affiliates comprise professionals involved in franchising such as lawyers and bankers. They also have to be 'accredited'. The inter-relationship of all these parties and franchisees was explained by the current Director General, Brian Smart, at the BFA's 2008 Conference (at the Savill Court Hotel, Ingleton Green, Windsor on 3–4 July 2008) as being 'a matrix of mutual contribution and benefit underpinned by money, standards and business'.

115 It was the experienced eye of Sir Bernard Ingham which, in 2002, saw this lack of franchisee involvement as a serious flaw that undermined the BFA's claim to represent the interests of franchising rather than franchisors. He championed the creation of a Franchisee Forum. This Franchisee Forum has taken two different forms during its short life. In its first form it was based upon individual membership and the second upon delegate members from franchise networks. The Forum was launched in a blaze of publicity in October 2002 when it 'held its first historic solo meeting' (*Franchise World*, Dec/Jan 2003, 11). It is currently made up of 11

The Director-General has expressed his confidence that

> there is a great deal to gain from the combined force of franchisees and franchisors for the protection and promotion of franchising.[116]

However, effective self-regulation of franchising is far from straightforward.

> In order to secure in the UK, Europe and the rest of the world, a legislative and regulatory environment for ethical franchising which encourages its profitable quest,[117]

the BFA must be

> and be recognised as, the authoritative voice of business format franchising in the UK, representing its ethical franchise community, in particular its franchisors, franchisees and professional advisors.[118]

The BFA faces several difficult challenges in achieving this. The first is encouraging a number of franchisees to invest time in the BFA for the greater good of franchising in a truly representative way, rather than merely to promote their own parochial interests. The second is the simple economic fact of life that the BFA relies on funding from franchisors for its survival. If it does anything which a significant number of its franchisor members disagree with, it risks losing their funding and potentially ceasing to exist. The BFA cannot justify a claim that it is the voice of franchising until franchisees are a fully integrated part of it with something approaching the same amount of influence as

---

franchisees from the systems of the franchisors who serve on the BFA policy board (by contrast the French Franchise Federation admitted franchisees to its main board, causing some franchisors to resign from the organisation). Shortly after the Forum's initial meeting, the BFA's Director General stated that 'We will in the future look to franchisees for input and support when it comes to the protection of good franchising in the face of any clumsy attempts at legislation' (*Franchise World*, Dec/Jan 2003, 11). These good intentions suggested a real intent for the BFA to move from being a franchisor pressure group to an association that more genuinely represents the interests of all of those involved in franchising. The Franchise Forum's first task was to assist in considering whether franchise brokers can have a legitimate and ethical role to play in the sale of franchises. The BFA's decision to consult over such an important matter was hailed as 'a significant step in (the BFA's) endeavour to embrace franchisees and thus become truly representative of the franchise sector as a whole, rather than only that of the most powerful partner in the franchise relationship'.

116 However, despite these good intentions, the initial impetus was lost and seven years on there is no evidence to suggest that the Franchisee Forum has had any substantial impact upon the BFA. Indeed, the BFA President has confessed that 'We have still not found the mechanism by which we can tap the energies of franchisees and are thrashing around trying to understand how to involve them' (at the BFA 2008 Conference). The association's initiative did not capture the hearts and minds of its franchisor members. The cynical view of the majority of its members was perhaps well illustrated by one member of the BFA Board, who, speaking on a no-name basis, expressed the view that the Franchisee Forum 'is only a bit of window dressing to give the impression that the BFA represents franchising rather than franchisors' (BFA Annual Conference 2008, interview with the author).

117 *One Vision, 2008 – Strategic Option for the Association's Future*, p. 5.

118 Ibid.

franchisors. This would be a tremendous change, which it is doubtful that many franchisors will have an appetite for. Of all the EU national franchise associations[119] only France actively involves franchisees in any meaningful way.[120] No other national franchise association in the EU purports to involve franchisees.

(b) Enforcement of decisions

The BFA's existence and position of influence over franchisors is fragile and is not in any way guaranteed. As the Director General of the BFA once said, its role is 'rather like treading on egg shells'.[121] **3.34**

As a consequence it rarely exercises its right to expel members due to their failure to comply with its Code of Ethics.

(c) Finance

In order to give self-regulation any chance of success the franchise association must be properly financed. Finance is a big issue for the BFA.[122] Without an appropriate level of funding it is powerless to do anything. Its sole source of income is its membership. Members pay a single fee regardless of their size.[123] Whilst this prevents those with 'deep pockets' from dominating the association it limits the overall income to what the smallest member can afford.[124] Without strong finances the ability of the BFA is limited in what it can do to educate and regulate its members. **3.35**

(d) Impact on non-members

The EFF estimates that there are 9971 franchise brands in Europe.[125] Although the EFF and its 16 member state franchise associations seek to **3.36**

119 The Franchise associations that are members of the EFF are those in Sweden, Finland, Denmark, Bulgaria, Spain, Italy, Slovenia, Romania, Portugal, Poland, The Netherlands, Ireland, Germany, France, The Czech Republic, Belgium, Austria, Hungary and the UK. Many were founded in the 1970s (the BFA, the Spanish Franchise Association, the German Franchise Association, the French Franchise Federation). Others are far more recent (e.g. the Romanian Franchise Association was established in 2006).

120 Since early 2008 it has appointed two franchisees to its Board of Directors. All of its member networks (as it refers to franchise systems) are invited to nominate franchisee candidates and the franchisors then elect two of the shortlist to the board. This initiative was controversial and led to at least one franchisor resigning from the FFF (Brian Smart in interview with author on 18 September 2008).

121 SOAS, London University, IPL Seminar, 1998.

122 In the 2008 Annual Report it showed turnover to be down 5% on 2007 to £1.25 million, with administrative costs of £885 280 (down 8% in 2007) and a profit of £141 344 (up 18.9% on 2007). Reserves were £1.02 million.

123 Unlike the French Franchise Federation which generates far higher membership fees by charging members based upon the size of their networks.

124 In order to facilitate a more representative approach the BFA is considering restructuring itself and has suggested four alternatives to its members, each of which will have an impact on its finances, although two years on, no change has been agreed by its members. *One Vision, 2008.*

125 European Franchise Federation Statistics 2009 – www.eff-franchise.com (viewed 23/12/2010).

self-regulate franchising in the EU, they represent less than 1577 franchised brands,[126] which is less than 16% of the franchises in the EU.[127] The remaining 8300 or so franchised brands[128] have nothing to do with the EFF or its member state national franchise associations. This inability to regulate non-BFA members undermines the credibility of the BFA's Director General, Brian Smart's view that

> we have got a robust *(self)* regulatory framework (*sic*), that can defend your way of doing business in the public domain.[129]

The Australian experience clearly shows that a voluntary regime lacking any means of compelling compliance will always be preaching to the converted. The unarguable paradox is that those franchisors who most need to be regulated are the ones who are least likely to comply with a voluntary code. The BFA believes that by establishing itself as the authority on what is 'good' and what is 'bad' franchising, it can place 'bad' franchisors at a substantial commercial disadvantage by directing potential franchisees only to 'good' franchisors. It may well be that its influence could become such that it does make franchise recruitment more difficult for franchisors that do not meet its standards. However, between there and schemes that are clearly criminal, there remains a grey area in which non-BFA member franchisors, free of the restrictions imposed by the BFA, might take advantage of naïve or inexperienced potential franchisees. The BFA believes that most such abusive schemes are either large but short lived or very small and so have minimal impact,[130] although it lacks any empirical evidence to justify this belief. That may or may not be so, but it is cold comfort to the franchisees who suffer and does little to inspire confidence in self-regulation.

(e) Competition between self-regulatory bodies

3.37 Another problem with self-regulation of franchising in the EU is that there is no limit to the number (or control of the integrity) of associations that purport to regulate the sector. The national franchise associations in the EU vary in size, resource and professionalism. Some, such as the BFA, owe their origins to franchisors coming together to protect and promote their best interests and have become increasingly sophisticated and well-resourced over the years. Others, such as the Bulgarian Franchise Association are still in their very early

---

126 It has a membership of 19 national franchise associations in all. The Spanish Association is not a member as it is not a 'not for profit' organisation. Seven EU member states do not have a franchise association. The Swiss, Croatian and Turkish associations are members of the EFF but are obviously not EU associations. The EFF therefore represents 16 national associations in the EU.

127 The aggregate membership is approximately 1577. See Appendix 13.

128 There is great uncertainty about the number of franchises in the EU.

129 *Franchise World*, Feb/Mar 2007, 16–18.

130 Brian Smart, Director General of the BFA in interview with the author, 18 September 2008.

days. A number, like the Danish and Greek Franchise Associations were started by professional advisers seeking to use the association to promote their services to franchisors. The Spanish Franchise Association, although long established and comparatively well-resourced is actively involved in running exhibitions and trade missions and so is deemed not to be a 'not for profit' organisation and is therefore not allowed to join the EFF. In Germany, the Franchise Association was decimated when many of its members deserted it to join the Co-Operatives Association, which boasts large influential members such as TUI. The Danish Franchise Association is currently teetering on the edge of insolvency. The EFF is a somewhat uneven mix in terms of size, influence, resources and outlook and cannot claim to fully represent either franchising or franchisors even in all those member states in which franchising is most prevalent. This has resulted in occasional anarchy amongst the various franchise associations.[131] This lack of order amongst the organisations that would self-regulate franchising does not stop there. Periodically other, self-appointed, would-be self-regulatory organisations pop up, such as the European Franchise Committee.[132]

E. ANALYSIS OF THE LEGAL REGULATORY ENVIRONMENT

Although individual member state law can create a national regulatory environment that to some degree supports the economic drivers and reduces the consequential risk inherent in the franchisor/franchisee relationship, the heterogeneous nature of the legal regulatory environment in the EU makes it difficult for it to do so adequately on an EU-wide basis. The disparity between franchising in the EU and franchising in both the USA and Australia is marked. A mixture of economic, cultural and historical factors probably account for much of this relative underdevelopment of franchising in the EU and its overconcentration in the five largest economies. However, it is also, in part, due to the failure of the regulatory environment in the EU to support franchising 3.38

131 For example, in 2006 the BFA 'managed to secure the resignation of the full board of the EFF' and appoint a replacement board and Chairman so that it was fit to 'take us forward into the renegotiation of the EC block exemption regulation next year' (*Franchise World*, Feb/Mar 2008, 29). In 2007, the EFF and the World Franchise Council (WFC) had a bitter dispute because the WFC wanted to grant direct membership to franchisors and so compete with national franchise associations in the EU.

132 This UK-based 'Pretender' declares that its primary mission is 'to promote fair franchising, franchise broker and dealer practices, to promote trade and exemplary trade practices and to provide members with programs, training courses, workshops, services and products which enhance their ability to conduct their individual businesses and careers with competence and integrity'. It goes on to state that it advocates 'beneficial legislation and legal doctrines' and promotes ethical franchising. It also boasts a 'franchising Bill of Rights'. It invites membership from other organisations but gives no details of who its members are. www.efcommittee.eu; this site no longer exists, so further suggesting the transient nature of the organisation.

and its expansion across member state boundaries. Most academic commentators agree that franchising has emerged as an important vehicle for entrepreneurship[133] which, whilst endorsed as a way for large firms to become nimble and more responsive to customers,[134] retains its appeal as the preferred method for small businesses to grow.[135] The heterogeneity found in the legal eco-systems constituting the regulatory environment substantially impacts upon franchising within the EU. It is detrimental to both the protection available to franchisors and franchisees vis-à-vis each other and to the security of commercial transactions. This heterogeneity amounts to a technical barrier to trade. It means that the regulatory environment in the EU does not support and re-enforce the economic drivers that attract franchisors and franchisees to franchising. It substantially inhibits the conclusion and operation of franchise agreements where franchisor and franchisee are established in different member states. In order to encourage business to use franchising for interstate trade, the trade in goods and services between member states should be carried on under conditions which are similar to those of a single market and this necessitates the approximation of the legal systems of the member states to the extent required for the proper functioning of franchising in the common market. An analysis of the legal regulatory environment of franchising in all 29 countries that have franchise-specific laws[136] suggests that it comprises four different legal 'eco-systems': anti-trust;[137] foreign trade/investment;[138] the

133 Michael, S., 1996, 'To franchise or not to franchise: An analysis of decision rights and organisational form shares', *Journal of Business Venturing*, Volume 11, 57–71.

134 Matusky, G., 1990, 'The Competitive Edge: How franchisees are teaching corporate elephants to dance', *Success* (September), 58–66.

135 Huber, J., 1992, 'Franchising puts small business in the fast lane', *Entrepreneur* (January), 117–23.

136 Australia, Barbados, Belarus, Belgium, Brazil, Canada, China, Estonia, France, Georgia, Italy, Indonesia, Japan, Kazakhstan, Lithuania, Malaysia, Mexico, Moldova, Romania, Russia, South Korea, South Africa, Spain, Sweden, Taiwan, Ukraine, USA, Venezuela, Vietnam.

137 Anti-trust regulations are aimed at preventing restraint of trade and generally focus upon classical competition law issues such as tying, full-line forcing, retail price maintenance, exclusivity and so on. These are found in Japan (Japan Fair Trade Commission Guidelines, April 2002 – These provide for disclosure and offer guidance on vertical restraints) and Venezuela (The Venezuelan Pro-Competition Agency's Guidelines for the Evaluation of Franchise Agreements, January 7, 2000 – These are based upon the previous EU Franchise Block Exemption from 4087/88). The EU has this type of regulation in the form of Article 101 of the TFEU and the Vertical Restraints Block Exemption.

138 Foreign trade/investment regulations are typical of developing markets with either a protectionist economic policy or distinct political aims, such as the distribution of wealth. These are found in China, Indonesia, Kazakhstan, South Korea, Malaysia, Moldova, Russia, Ukraine, Belarus, Barbados and Vietnam. Typically they seek to regulate the entry into their domestic market of foreign business systems that escape the restraints placed upon direct foreign investment. Clearly the EU would not want to adopt this type of law as it is contrary to its general approach to free trade.

franchisor/franchisee relationship;[139] and hybrids.[140] The EU legal regulatory environment of franchising comprises several legal 'eco-systems': those created by franchise-specific laws[141] which focus on the franchisor/franchisee relationship and those created by eight distinct other types of EU member state law, each of which is interpreted according to the legal traditions of the relevant jurisdiction. These are good faith; misrepresentation; anti-trust; consumer protection; employment; commercial agency; restrictive covenants; and breach of contract. Their impact on franchising is considered below in three parts: first the pre-contractual relationship, then the contractual relationship and finally the termination of the relationship.

1. The pre-contractual relationship – franchise-specific disclosure laws

The franchise-specific pre-contractual regulatory environment in the EU fails both to adequately re-enforce the economic drivers that attract franchisors and franchisees to franchising and to reduce the inherent consequential risk to an appropriate level. **3.39**

(a) The architecture of the franchise-specific laws

The regulatory environment in the EU offers a lack of homogeneous pre-contractual protection for franchisees against inadequate pre-contractual disclosure on an EU-wide basis and so does not adequately support the economic drivers that attract franchisees to franchising or reduce the consequential risks they assume. The drivers that attract franchisors to franchising are supported, although the risks they assume are not reduced. **3.40**

139 Pure franchise regulations focus upon areas of potential abuse in franchising, namely pre-contractual disclosure and the in-term relationship between the franchisor and its franchisees. These are generally symptomatic of more developed markets and are found in the USA, Australia, Canada, Brazil, Taiwan, Georgia and Mexico. They have much in common with the franchise laws of France, Spain, Italy, Belgium and Sweden. The laws of the USA and Australia are of particular relevance. Some of these pure franchise regulations have their roots in consumer protection law (e.g. the California Franchise Investment Law (1970) (Cal. Corp. Code Sections 31000 to 31516).

140 Some countries have adopted laws which are hybrid in form in that they are best placed in one category but also show characteristics of another. Two examples are Malaysia and China: both have foreign trade/investment franchise laws with a strong element of pure franchise regulation in them. Croatia defines franchise agreements but does not regulate them (Croatian Regulation on block exemption granted to certain categories of vertical agreements, Article 3(6)). The South African Consumer Protection Act 2009, which will come into force in 2010, is a hybrid between anti-trust regulations (it prevents or limits full-line forcing) and pure franchise regulations (focusing on pre-contractual disclosure) (Eugen Honey, partner, Bowman Gilfillan Attorneys, 17 February 2009).

141 In eight EU member states: France, Spain, Italy, Belgium, Sweden, Romania, Estonia and Lithuania.

Table 3.2 The eight elements of the franchise-specific pre-contractual regulatory environment in the EU: Constituent elements of the pre-contractual disclosure requirements of franchise-specific laws in the EU

	Corporate Inform-ation	Trade Marks	Character-istics of the Business Format	Details of the Franchise network[1]	Earning Claims	Dispute History	Summary of Contract-ual Terms	Market Analysis
France[2]	✓[3]	✓	✗	✓[4]	✗	✗	✓	✓
Spain	✓	✗	✗	✗	✓	✗	✓[5]	✓[6]
Italy	✓[7]	✓	✓	✓	✓[8]	✓	✗[9]	✗
Belgium	✓	✓[10]	✗	✓	✗	✗	✓	✓[11]
Sweden	✓	✓	✗	✓	✗	✗	✓[12]	✗
Romania	✓	✗	✗	✗	✓	✗	✓	✗
Estonia	✗	✗	✗	✗	✗	✗	✗	✗
Lithuania	✗	✗	✗	✗	✗	✗	✗	✗

Notes:

✓ – required
✗ – not required

1 This includes a list of the networks' outlets, the 'chain' of franchisees, the name and address of each franchisee in the network.
2 Only applies if there is exclusivity or quasi-exclusivity.
3 It requires details of the franchisor company and its directors, banking references, the main stages in the development of the company and the network, the professional experience of the managers and the financial details for the previous two years.
4 The French law also requires details of any potential competitors linked to the franchisor in the area.
5 Spain is the only member state with a franchise-specific law that does not require a copy of the franchise agreement to accompany the disclosure document.
6 The Spanish Royal Decree requires disclosure of a 'general description of the sector of activity of the franchise' (Royal Decree 2485/1998 Article 3) which is interpreted by local practitioners as an obligation to define 'the market conditions of the franchise network' (American Bar Association (ABA Book) 2002, workshop 9, p. 139).
7 The Italian law requires disclosure of all relevant corporate information relating to the franchisor that is not detailed in the franchise agreement including, when requested by the franchisee, the franchisor's balance sheets for the three previous financial years.
8 The Italian law imposes a duty of 'loyalty, fairness and good faith' in relation to earning claims.
9 In Italy a copy of the franchise agreement must accompany the disclosure document.
10 The Belgium law goes further and requires details of all intellectual property. Article 4 para 1 1° of the Law Governing Pre-contractual Information Within the Framework of Commercial Partnership Agreements. See Appendix 10.
11 The Belgian law requires forecasts as to the current state of both the local and national market. This applies to all franchisors seeking to do business in Belgium, even if they are based elsewhere and the agreement is not subject to Belgian law. The disclosure must include information on 'the market in which the activities are carried out', as well as on 'the market share of the sector' 'from both a general and a local point of view'. It also requires disclosure of details of the amortisation of the franchisees' investment. This is a heavy burden to impose on the franchisor.
12 The Swedish law requires details of all tied goods and services.

Table 3.3 Consequences of failure to comply with franchise-specific pre-contractual disclosure requirement in EU

	Consequences of failure to comply	Right of action	Burden of proof
France	Invalidity Financial penalty Damages	Franchisee can file suit for declaration of invalidity and damages within five years	Defective consent must be established
Spain	Invalidity Financial penalty Damages	Franchisee can file suit for declaration of invalidity and damages	Defective consent must be established
Italy	Invalidity Damages	Franchisee can file suit for declaration of voidness and damages	Deliberate non-disclosure and defective consent.
Belgium	Invalidity	Franchisee can file suit for declaration of voidness within two years. Can sue for damages	Strict liability
Sweden	Specific performance	Franchisee can apply to Swedish market court for order of specific performance	Strict liability
Romania	Damages	Franchisee can sue for damages	Defective consent

Notes: Breach of franchise laws outside the EU generally leads to rescission and/or the imposition of fines. In the Canadian provinces of Alberta, Ontario, Prince Edward Island and New Brunswick a failure to give the required disclosure allows the prospective franchisee to rescind the franchise agreement by giving notice to the franchisor the earlier of either 60 days after receiving the disclosure document or no later than two years after the franchise is granted (Alberta Franchises Act Section 13; The Arthur Wishart Act (Franchise Disclosure) 6(1) and (2); The Prince Edward Island Franchises Act Chapter 36 Bill 43 Section 6(1); The New Brunswick Franchises Act s 6(1)). If there is a misrepresentation in the disclosure document as a result of which the franchisee suffers a loss the franchisee has a right of action in damages against the franchisor and/or every person who signed the disclosure document (Alberta Franchises Act Section 13; The Arthur Wishart Act (Franchise Disclosure) 6(1) and (2); The Prince Edward Island Franchises Act Chapter 36 Bill 43 Section 6(1); The New Brunswick Franchises Act s 6(1)). A franchisee is deemed to have relied upon any information detailed in the disclosure document (Alberta Franchises Act Section 13; The Arthur Wishart Act (Franchise Disclosure) 6(1) and (2); The Prince Edward Island Franchises Act Chapter 36 Bill 43 Section 6(1); The New Brunswick Franchises Act s 6(1)).

An analysis of the French[142] disclosure laws and those in Spain,[143] Italy,[144] Belgium,[145] Sweden[146] and Romania[147] shows that franchisors are obliged to make disclosure to potential franchisees about information in eight distinct

142 Law No. 89 – 1008 dated 31 December 1989. L330–3C.

143 Article 62 of Act 7/1996.

144 Law of 6 May 2009, No. 129.

145 Law of 19 December 2005 (modified 27 December 2005) governing pre-contractual information in the framework of agreements of Commercial Partnerships.

146 The Disclosure Act 2006.

147 Government Ordnance 52/1997 as approved and modified by Law 79/1998.

areas, a set number of days before the franchise agreement is entered into.[148] There is no real norm in these six EU member states or in any of the other 21 non-EU jurisdictions that impose a disclosure obligation on the franchisor,[149] but certain common themes do exist.

(b) A comparison of the basic elements

3.41 As can be seen in the above tables, there are eight basic elements that create the franchise-specific pre-contractual regulatory environment in the EU, although their precise details and the consequences of non-compliance vary between each of the member states. The French Loi Doubin, as the first EU franchise-specific law, is perhaps the most influential.[150] The other five member state laws are generally similar, but notably unlike the French law, do not require exclusivity or quasi-exclusivity. All of the disclosure laws have a general sweep-up provision. Under the French law the information disclosed must be 'sincere' and permit the other party to 'contract in full knowledge of the facts'.[151] The combination of these two requirements places a heavy burden on the discloser, because false information can be 'sincere' if the error was made in good faith, but would not permit a contract to be made 'in full knowledge of the facts'. The vague nature of the terms such as 'sincere' introduces an element of uncertainty which can only be reduced by giving as much information as possible.[152] The requirement to present information on 'the general (and local) state of the

148 Spain: A disclosure document must be issued to the potential franchisee 'at least twenty days prior to signature of the franchise agreement or pre-agreement, or payment by the future franchisee to the franchisor of any consideration'.
Italy: The Italian franchise law requires that at least 30 days before the date of execution of the franchise contract, the franchisor must deliver to the franchisee a copy of the contract.
France: 20 days before signature of the agreement.
Belgium: Disclosure must be made at least one month before closing.
Sweden: The Swedish Disclosure Act 2006 requires the franchisor to disclose to potential franchisees in writing, within a reasonable period of time before closing, such information on the nature of the agreement and such other information which, according to the circumstances, may be required. A reasonable period of time is considered to be at least 14 days.
Romania: The Romanian law is the least burdensome of all the EU member state disclosure laws and fails to state a time at which disclosure must be made.

149 The time at which disclosure must be given tends to range between ten and 30 days before signing although this does vary in some jurisdictions. In Brazil the offering circular must be delivered to a prospective franchisee at least ten days prior to the execution of a franchise agreement. Malaysia and Taiwan opt for the same period, whilst Korea requires only five days and other countries require longer. The Canadian states all require 14 days, Vietnam 15 days, China 20 days (South Africa is proposing the same time) and Mexico a rather excessive 30 days. Japan and Indonesia lay down no minimum period of time.

150 In the case of an exclusive or quasi-exclusive agreement it requires disclosure, 21 days before signing of details of the franchisor company and its directors, banker's references, the main stages in the development of the company and the network; the professional experience of the managers and the financial details for the previous two years; details of its trade marks; a summary of the contractual terms of the agreement; details of the network and a market analysis.

151 Article 1(1).

152 Olivier Gast, Chapter on Law and Practice in the European Community in Abell, *European Franchising*, p. 611.

market for the products or services which are the subject of the contract, and the prospects for development of this market' can be particularly problematic. It requires details of the market in which both the franchisee and its competitors are operating rather than simply the state of the franchisor's business. Although Article L.330–3 of the French Commercial Code is a domestic public policy law and therefore generally applies to all exclusive and quasi-exclusive agreements concerning a franchise that will be performed in France, a decision of the Paris Court of Appeals has held that the disclosure obligation under the Loi Doubin does not apply to international franchise agreements that are not governed by French law.[153] As regards enforcement of the law, the French courts of appeal have taken two different tracks as to the manner in which the disclosure law is to be applied.[154] Some took the view that mere non-compliance by the franchisor with the legal requirement was enough to render the agreement null and void[155] whilst other courts held that such non-compliance can only lead to annulment of the contract if it gives rise to defective consent on the part of the franchisee.[156] The Cour de Cassation opted for the second, subjective approach in 1997 and 1998,[157] so Article 330–3 is to be interpreted according to the doctrine of defective consent, which provides that the courts should focus on the validity of consent rather than compliance with technical formalities.[158] The burden of proof lies with the franchisee.[159] A similar approach has been adopted in Spain, Italy and Romania. Non-compliance with either the obligation of utmost good faith or to provide full information may lead to both criminal and civil sanctions in France. Article 2 of the implementing Decree imposes a penalty in Class 5 for failure to provide the required information (currently a fine of between €1500 and €3000 and/or between ten days' and one month's imprisonment). Article 2(2) prescribes the enhanced penalties in Class 5 for a second or subsequent offence (in this case a fine of between €6000 and €12 000).[160] A claim for damages for failure to make pre-contractual disclosure cannot be based on contractual grounds. As a

153 Paris Court of Appeals, 30 November, 2001, JCPE no. 3, 2002, p. 29. Contrast the Swedish disclosure obligation which applies to foreign franchisors entering the Swedish market even if the agreement is not subject to Swedish law.

154 Marot, Y., 1999, 'Prolongements de l'arrêt de la Chambre Commerciale du 10 Fevrier 1998 sur l'information pre-contractuelle en matière de contrat de franchise', Receuil Dalloz, Chron. p431' in Bueno Diaz, O., 2005, 'Franchising in European Contract Law'. Sellier. European Law Publishers p. 67.

155 Based on Article 6 of the Civil Code which provides that parties cannot deviate from a mandatory rule. See, for example, CA Paris 7 April 1993, D. somm, p. 75, obs D. Ferrier.

156 A subjective approach based upon the franchisee's 'actual knowledge'. For example, see CA Colmar 9 March 1990, D. 1990, somm, pp. 232 ff., obs J.-J. Burst.

157 Cass. Com. 2 December 1997, D. 1998, somm., p. 334, obs D Ferrier and Cass. Com. 10 February 1998, D. 1998, somm, p. 334. Cass. Com. 10 Feb 1998, Bull. Civ. IV No. 81 confirmed by Cass. Com, 7 July 2004 No. 02–15950.

158 Article 1109.

159 Cass. Com. 7 July 2004 No. 02–15950.

160 Article R.25 of the Criminal Code.

franchisor may only be liable in tort Article 1382 of the Code Civil applies which sets out that any claims from damages are time-barred after five years from the time that the claimant knew or should have known about the damage.[161] There is little case law on the criminal sanctions for failure to comply with article L. 330–3. One suspects that the main reason is that the statute of limitations limits the period during which action can be taken to only one year. Providing information that is deliberately misleading will amount to fraud under Article 405 of the Criminal Code. Unlike the other EU member states with franchise-focused laws, Spain and Lithuania seek to reduce a mismatch of expectation between franchisor and franchisee (and so reduce the risk to franchisees), by requiring registration of appropriate documentation on public registers. This is fairly common in non-EU jurisdictions such as China,[162] Russia,[163] Indonesia,[164] Malaysia,[165] Moldova[166] and 14 of the States

161 The Spanish courts follow the French lead and focus on a subjective test based on the general doctrine of defective consent (Bueno Diaz, O., 2005, *Franchising in European Contract Law*, Sellier – European Law Publishers. p. 86). Although the Spanish franchise law does not list the civil effects of the failure to make proper pre-contractual disclosure, it is possible that if a court considered the missing (or false) information to be fundamental (i.e. information that is essential for the franchisee to form its consent), the franchise agreement could be declared null and void (SAP Barcelona de 21 de septiembre de 2004 (AC\2004\1952)). If the missing information was not fundamental to the decision whether or not to enter into the franchise agreement, the agreement would not be declared null and void, but it would be still voidable. It therefore largely depends on the type of information that is missing in order to determine the impact on the validity of the contract.

162 Franchisors who sell franchises in China need to file MOFCOM together with, amongst other things, a sample franchise contract and the index of the Franchising Operation Manual. An application has to be made within 15 days after the execution of the franchise agreement (Article 8 of the Administration Regulations and Article 5 of Administration Rules on Commercial Franchise Filing – Decree of Ministry of Commerce 2007 (No 15)).

163 In Russia, a franchise agreement must be registered with the tax authorities which maintain the register of Commercial Concessions in order to be valid against third parties (Russian Civil Code Part II Chapter 54 Article 1028(2)).

164 Uniquely, in Indonesia, the franchise law provides that the franchisee rather than the franchisor must register the franchise agreement and disclosure statement at the Ministry of Trade within 30 days of the effective date of the franchise agreements (Regulation of the Minister of Trade No 12/M-DAG/PER/3/2006 dated 29 March 2006, which revoked The Provisions on and Procedure for the Implementation of Franchised Business Registration (*Decree of the Minister of Industry and Trade No. 259/MPP/Kep/7/1997, dated July 30, 1997*) Chapter III, Article 11.1). Failure to register resulted in the revocation of the franchisee's trade licence (Regulation of the Minister of Trade No 12/M-DAG/PER/3/2006 dated 29 March 2006, which revoked The Provisions on and Procedure for the Implementation of Franchised Business Registration (*Decree of the Minister of Industry and Trade No. 259/MPP/Kep/7/1997, dated July 30, 1997*) Chapter VI Article 22). Franchise licences between a foreign franchisor and a master franchisee are registered.

165 In Malaysia both the franchisor and the franchisee are required to become involved in the registration process. The franchise agreement, the letter of intent (which has replaced the disclosure document originally provided for), the operations manual, the training manual, a copy of the latest audited accounts and financial statements, and other documents must be registered with the Registrar of Franchises (The Franchise Act 1998 Part II Section 6(1)). The franchisee of a foreign franchisor must also register itself (The Franchise Act 1998 Part VIII Section 55). The problem here is that approval can take up to six months so delaying the franchisor's ability to franchise considerably.

166 In Moldova the franchise agreement must be registered with the State Agency for the Protection of Industrial Property (Article 9(4) of the Moldovan Law on Franchising No. 1335 dated 1.1.1997 provides: 'The franchise

in the USA,[167] but it is doubtful whether it is successful in reducing the risks to which franchisees are exposed.

2. The pre-contractual relationship – other laws

The non-franchise-specific pre-contractual regulatory environment in the EU fails both to adequately re-enforce the economic drivers that attract franchisors and franchisees to franchising and to reduce the inherent consequential risk to an appropriate level. In some member states other laws impact upon the pre-contractual regulatory environment in a manner that reduces some of the risks to franchisees that are inherent in their relationship with the franchisor. However, the lack of a homogeneous approach throughout the EU substantially limits the impact of these on cross-border franchising in the EU. These laws do not reduce the risks to which the franchisor is exposed. Neither do they support the economic drivers that encourage the franchisor or the franchisee to become involved in franchising. Five key elements can be identified in the pre-contractual regulatory environment. Some are evident in all EU member states, whilst others exist in only a handful of them. The most universal element is the obligation placed on franchisors not to misrepresent their franchise to potential franchisees. A related, but less common, element which is found in Germany and those member states over which it has historically had influence, is the obligation placed on the franchisor to disclose relevant information to the potential franchisee. The three other elements comprise an extra contractual obligation of confidentiality placed on franchisees and potential franchisees, obligations imposed on the franchisor to enter into an agreement with a potential franchisee if negotiations pass a certain point and a right for franchisees, in certain circumstances, to withdraw from the contract within a specific time. 3.42

(a) The first element – a duty not to misrepresent facts

The concept of misrepresentation can be divided into two different categories. An obligation not to make false representations and a positive obligation to actively disclose certain facts. The common law maxim of caveat emptor, buyer beware, applies in principle in both law and equity to all bargains struck under English and Scottish law.[168] It applies to the purchase of specific things, upon which the buyer can and usually does exercise his own judgment. It applies also 3.43

agreement is registered with the State Agency for the Protection of Industrial Property') but many do not as 'The franchise agreement is considered to be valid from the day it is signed or from the day determined by the parties' (Article 9(3)) Moldovan Law on Franchising). The validity of the franchise agreement does not depend on its registration with the Agency.

167 See 4.11.

168 *Wallis* v. *Russell* [1902] 2 IR 585 at 615.

whenever the buyer voluntarily chooses what he buys and whenever, by usage or otherwise, it is a term of the contract express or implied that the buyer shall not rely on the skill or judgement of the seller. However, if the potential franchisee relies on the judgement, knowledge and information (i.e. the representations) of the franchisor the maxim caveat emptor does not apply.[169] If the franchisor's representations are incorrect or misleading they can give the franchisee grounds for action against it. In some ways misrepresentation can be seen as the common law equivalent to a very limited form of pre-contractual duty of good faith. Indeed, misrepresentation appears in various forms in certain civil jurisdictions as a part of the general pre-contractual duty of care or good faith. Although in general terms there is no positive legal obligation of franchisors under common law to disclose anything about the franchise to a potential franchisee, the commercial reality is that the franchisor makes the franchisee aware of the characteristics of the franchise system[170] and discloses relevant information to potential franchisees so they are aware of what is involved in the running of the franchise. There is a general contractual principle that one must avoid making misrepresentations which induce a party to enter into a contract.[171] In some circumstances silence can amount to a misrepresentation. If the franchisor breaches this principle the contract will be voidable and the franchisee can rescind the contract and, in some circumstances, claim damages. There are three differing types of misrepresentation in English and Scottish law. Fraudulent,[172] negligent[173] and innocent[174] misrepresentations all give rise to slightly different consequences. A misrepresentation is a false statement of past or existing fact given by a franchisor to a franchisee which induces the franchisee into a contract. It must be a statement of fact, past or present, and not merely a statement of opinion, an intention, as these only show that the opinion or intention is held by the person expressing it.[175] A mere statement of opinion which proves to have been unfounded will not be treated as a misrepresentation.[176] However, a statement of opinion or intention that is not honestly held by the franchisor,[177] or could not reasonably be held by it given his knowledge of the facts, may be regarded as a statement of fact and may constitute a misrepresentation.[178] It is also the case that a statement of the intentions of a

---

169 *Jones* v. *Just* (1867–68) L.R. 3 Q.B. 197.

170 *The Encyclopaedia of Forms and Precedents*, Fifth edition, 2003 reissue, V 16(4) Agency and Distribution, 44 [111].

171 Professor Beale, H. (General editor), 2002, *Chitty on Contracts*, 28th edition, Sweet & Maxwell, 6–001.

172 *Derry* v. *Peek* (1889) 14 App Cas 337.

173 *Hedley Byrne & Co Ltd* v. *Heller & Partners Ltd* [1963] 2 All ER 575; Misrepresentation Act 1967 (England).

174 Misrepresentation Act 1967 s.2(2).

175 *Strachan & Henshaw Ltd* v. *Stein Industrie (UK) Ltd (No 2)* (1997) 87 BLR 52.

176 *Hummingbird Motors Ltd* v. *Hobbs* [1986] RTR 276.

177 *Edgington* v. *Fitzmaurice* (1885) 29 Ch D 459.

178 *Chitty on Contracts*, 6–005; *Economides* v. *Commercial Union Assurance Co plc* [1998] QB 587; *Smith* v. *Land and House Property Corp* (1884) 28 ChD 7.

third party is a statement of fact and can constitute a misrepresentation as above.[179] The prohibition on mis-selling franchises in the United Kingdom is based on an implied representation that there are reasonable grounds for holding an opinion, even if that opinion is honestly held.[180] Mere 'advertising puff' does not amount to a representation of fact.[181] The overall principle is that statements are not treated as representations where, having regard to all the circumstances, it is unreasonable for the franchisee to rely on the franchisor's statements rather than his own judgement.[182]

The distinction between fact and opinion has become much less important since *Esso Petroleum Ltd* v. *Mardon*.[183] Esso granted 'solus agreements' to licensees. It offered a forecast of the probable sales of a petrol station, based on an estimated throughput of petrol, to a prospective franchisee. The estimate was produced before Esso was made aware that the local authority would not give permission for the pumps to front onto the main road. The station was built backwards and Esso failed to adjust the estimate. The franchisee did all it could in attempting to reach the projected throughput but never managed to even reach half of the estimate provided by Esso. The difference was attributable to the positioning of the pumps at the station. The forecast was held to be a warranty which had been breached and a negligent misrepresentation by Esso as they 'had special knowledge and skill ... [and] much more experience and expertise at their disposal ... to make a forecast'[184] than the franchisee. Even the loss sustained under a second re-negotiated contract was held to be attributable to the original misrepresentation as it resulted from an attempt of the franchisee to mitigate its losses.[185] In certain circumstances representations may be implied and, if false, lead to an effective misrepresentation. This becomes an issue when, considering all the circumstances, it has been impliedly represented by the conduct of the franchisor that there exists some state of facts different from the truth.[186] There is no legal duty on the franchisor to disclose material facts to the franchisee, however dishonest such non-disclosure may be. However, if a franchisor makes a statement which is literally true but is misleading because of other facts that have been omitted it can give rise to an action for misrepresentation by partial disclosure.[187] The same is true where there has

179 *Smelter Corp of Ireland Ltd* v. *O'Driscoll* [1977] IR 305.

180 *Brown* v. *Raphael* [1958] Ch 636.

181 *Dimmock* v. *Hallett* (1866) 2 Ch App 21.

182 *Harlingdon and Leinster Enterprises Ltd* v. *Christopher Hull Fine Art Ltd* [1991] 1 QB 564.

183 [1976] QB 801.

184 *Per* Lord Denning in ibid.

185 See also *Le Grove* v. *Deatker, Current Law Cases January 21, 1980* [1981] C.L.Y. 31.u, *Stephen Frank Fallon* v. *Shell (UK) Ltd* [2000] All ER (D) 2287 and *Williams* v. *Natural Life Health Foods Ltd* [1997] 1 IBCLC 131.

186 *Spice Girls Ltd* v. *Aprilia World Service BV* [2002] EWCA Civ 15.

187 *Nottingham Patent Brick and Tile Co* v. *Butler* (1886) 16 QBD 778.

been a change of circumstances that makes a previously made statement false; the initial statement is regarded as a continuing representation. In this situation, if the franchisor knows of the change in the facts, there will be a misrepresentation if it fails to disclose it to the potential franchisee.[188] There is conflicting case law as to whether this duty to disclose applies to a change in the intention of the franchisor,[189] but it appears likely that it does. In a situation where a statement was made innocently but falsely and later the franchisor discovers the true facts, failure to alert the franchisee changes the innocent misrepresentation to a fraudulent misrepresentation.[190] A franchisor will not be held liable for a misrepresentation unless it is material in the sense that it induces the franchisee into the contract. Therefore the franchisee must rely on the statement made to him. If it relies upon its own judgement or investigation the franchisor will not be liable.[191] However, the franchisor will not escape liability merely by inviting the franchisee to discover the truth if the invitation is rejected and the statement is still relied upon.[192] It is not necessary for the representation to be the sole reason for the franchisee entering into the contract. If it is actively present in the mind of the franchisee when entering the contract then it is material in inducing him to enter the franchise agreement.[193] In some circumstances the franchisor may be deemed to be under a duty of care to comply with the pre-contractual representations it makes to potential franchisees.[194] In the UK any attempt by the franchisor to escape or limit its liability for misrepresentation must satisfy the requirements of reasonableness as set out in the Unfair Contract Terms Act 1977.[195] In order to satisfy the reasonableness test, the franchisor[196] must prove that the term is a 'fair and reasonable one to be included having regard to the circumstances which were, or ought reasonably to have been, known to or in the contemplation of the parties when the contract was made'.[197] Fraudulent misrepresentation cannot be excluded.[198] The use of entire agreement and no reliance clauses to exclude liability for misrepresentation is not always successful[199] and it is the evidence as a whole, including any such no reliance clause, that will win the day.[200] A no reliance clause will not

---

188 *With* v. *O'Flanagan* [1936] Ch 575.

189 Compare *Traill* v. *Baring* (1864) 4 De GJ&Sm 318 and *Ray* v. *Sempers* [1974] AC 370 with *Wales* v. *Wadham* [1977] 1 WLR 199.

190 *Davies* v. *London Provincial Marine Insurance Co* (1878) L.R. 8 Ch. D. 469.

191 *Attwood* v. *Small* (1839) 6 Cl & Fin 523n.

192 *Redgrave* v. *Hurd* (1881) 20 Ch D 1.

193 *Edgington* v. *Fitzmaurice* (1885) 29 Ch D 459.

194 *MGB Printing & Design Ltd* v. *KallKwik UK Ltd* QBD – 31 March 2010 – [2010] EWHC 624 (QB).

195 S.11 (1).

196 Misrepresentation Act 1967 s.3.

197 Unfair Contract Terms Act s.11 (1).

198 *Thomas Witter Ltd* v. *TBP Industries Ltd* [1992] 2 All ER 573.

199 Ibid.

200 *Cremdean* v. *Nash* (1977) 244 EG 547.

serve its purpose unless the franchisor can show that he entered the contract with the belief that the franchisee did not rely on the representations.[201] The English courts have recognised the efficacy of no reliance clauses in franchise agreements. For example, in the case of *Fleet Mobile Tyres Ltd* v. *Stone & Another*[202] the High Court Judge held that, whilst a no reliance clause does not guarantee complete protection, the franchisee's task of proving that he did, in fact, rely on a pre-contractual statement in the face of a clear statement in the agreement that he did not, is made very much more difficult. However, the recent case of *Quest 4 Finance Limited* v. *John Maxfield and Others*[203] shows that a misrepresentation claim will not always be defeated by a no reliance clause. Although the *Quest* case did not relate to a franchise agreement, the principles will apply to any commercial contract. In *Quest*, the court held that the Claimant could not rely on a no reliance clause to defend itself from a misrepresentation claim when the terms of the contract entered into clearly contradicted information given in the Claimant's brochure and the Defendant showed that he had relied on the statements in the brochure. In *MGB Printing & Design Ltd* v. *KallKwik UK Ltd*[204] it was established that the franchisor owed the franchisee a duty of care because of the proximate nature of the relationship and the foreseeability of damage. This duty of care extended to pre-contractual representations and the clauses excluding contractual liability for misrepresentation did not exclude tortious liability. A misrepresentation by the franchisor renders the franchise agreement voidable *ab initio* by the franchisee. Depending on the type of misrepresentation the franchisee may also claim damages. In fraudulent misrepresentation cases the franchisee may be able to recover all direct loss which can be shown to have resulted from the false statement. This is without regard for the usual requirements of remoteness that the loss be reasonably foreseeable or in reasonable contemplation of the parties.[205]

It is not only the common law jurisdictions of England, Scotland, Ireland and Cyprus that rely upon the concept of misrepresentation to regulate the pre-contractual relationship. As franchise agreements are regarded as 'atypical' agreements, German statutory law does not specifically provide for misrepresentation in franchising and so the general statutory provisions of the German Civil Code and the German Commercial Code apply. Intentional misrepresentation can trigger claims for contractual[206] and other damages,[207] tort claims,[208] **3.44**

201 *Watford Electronics Ltd* v. *Sanderson CFL Ltd* [2001] EWCA Civ 317.

202 [2006] EWHC 1947.

203 [2007] EWHC 2313.

204 QBD – 31 March 2010 – [2010] EWHC 624 (QB).

205 *Doyle* v. *Olby (Ironmongers) Ltd* [1969] 2 QB 158; *Smith New Court Securities Ltd* v. *Citibank NA* [1997] AC 254; *Clef Aquitaine SARL* v. *Laporte Materials (Barrow) Ltd* [2000] 3 All ER 493.

206 Art. 280 sec. 1, 241 sec. 2, 311 sec. 2 BGB.

207 The Unfair Competition Act (UWG).

the right to rescission[209] and criminal charges.[210] Misrepresentation by the franchisor is regarded as a breach of the franchisor's duty to take into account the rights, legal interests and other interests of the franchisee[211] when negotiating a contract, resulting in the franchisor's liability for damages if the misrepresentation resulted in defective consent and resulted in damage to the franchisee. This (contractual/pre-contractual) liability applies regardless of whether the misrepresentation has been negligent or fraudulent. The quantum of the claim is determined by Art. 249 BGB: the franchisor must place the franchisee into the position that would have existed if the misrepresentation had not occurred. In some cases, this includes loss of profit (e.g. if the franchisee gave up employment in order to enter into the franchise contract).[212] Contributory negligence of the franchisee is taken into consideration. Such contributory negligence can be assumed if the franchisee has specific business experience and fails to evaluate the information provided by the franchisor accordingly. Alternatively, the franchisee can choose to rescind the contract which eventually may result in higher payments by the franchisor.[213]

The burden of proof that the information provided has been true and accurate, rests with the franchisor. This reversal of the burden of proof is due to the superior knowledge of the franchisor.[214] A franchisee has a right to rescind the contract if the fraudulent misrepresentation caused the franchisee to enter into the franchise contract. Fraudulent intention can be assumed if the franchisor is aware that the information provided by him may be wrong and fails to inform the franchisor about the uncertainty, if the franchisor knows, or suspects, that the incorrect information is being relied upon by the franchisee when deciding whether or not to enter into the contract.[215] The right of rescission[216] does not depend upon the franchisee suffering damages. Rescission has to be claimed within one year commencing at the time the franchisee discovers the misrepresentation.[217] Rescission renders the franchise agreement void. As a consequence, the franchisee can claim for reversal of the transaction according to the law of unjust enrichment.[218] The rescission has no effect on single sale contracts for goods which the franchisee made during the franchise period.[219] The

208 Art. 823 sec. 2 BGB.
209 Art. 123 sec. 1, Art. 124 BGB.
210 Art. 263 German Criminal Code – fraud.
211 Articles 241 sec. 2, 311 sec. 2 BGB.
212 *Giesler, Nauschütt*, Franchiserecht, 2.ed. 2007, p. 368 (Rn 54a).
213 Ibid.
214 Ibid.
215 Palandt, BGB, 69.ed. 2010, § 123 Rn 11.
216 Ibid.
217 Art. 124 BGB.
218 Art. 812 sec. 1 BGB.
219 Giesler, Nauschütt, *Franchiserecht*, 2.ed. 2007, p. 506 (Rn 251).

franchisor may also be liable for damages.[220] It may also be a criminal offence[221] if the franchisor (i) intended to cause an error, (ii) intended to obtain for himself or a third party an unlawful material benefit, and (iii) caused damage to the franchisee's property/assets. Fraud requires the franchisor to intend to obtain an unlawful material damage and a pecuniary detriment on the side of the franchisee.[222] It is punished by a term of imprisonment of up to five years or a fine. If the misrepresentation is regarded as 'misleading advertising' the franchisor may be liable for damages[223] regardless of whether the misrepresentation is intended or negligent. Untrue/overstated information is regarded as being misleading if it addresses issues such as the essential characteristics of the goods or services; the reason for purchase; the nature, attributes or rights of the entrepreneur; any statement or symbol in relation to direct or indirect sponsorship; the need for a service, part, replacement or repair; compliance with a code of conduct; the rights of consumers.

Misrepresentation can be about facts or future prospects[224] and the courts have found the following examples in respect of franchising:[225] false statement of franchisor that there is a high number of successful franchisees;[226] misinformation about the market success of the franchise system to date;[227] false statement of franchisor that there are already customers existing in the specific trading area;[228] wrong information about presumably needed capital resources;[229] and providing exorbitant turnover statistics and describing them as a conservative estimate.[230] Many of the EU member states take the same general approach to misrepresentation.[231] Misrepresentation can help to reduce

220 Articles 823 sec. 2 BGB.

221 Article 263 sec. 1 of the German Criminal Code.

222 Palandt, BGB, 69.ed. 2010, § 123 Rn 2.

223 Articles 5, 3, 9 of the German Unfair Competition Act.

224 Note that the franchisee is still bearing the risk of future prospects not proving true; C.f. Giesler, Nauschütt, *Franchiserecht*, 2.ed. 2007, p. 358 (Rn 45).

225 C.f. Giesler, Nauschütt, *Franchiserecht*, 2.ed. 2007, p. 338 (Rn 23d).

226 OLG München, judgment from 13.11.1987 – 8 U 2207/87.

227 OLG Hamburg, judgment from 17.04.1996 – 5 U 137/95 (not published).

228 LG München, judgment from 31.07.2001 – 4 O 21318 (not published).

229 LG Hannover, judgment from 12.12.1995 – 14 O 267/94 (not published).

230 OLG München, judgment from 16.09.1993 – 6 U 5495/92; NJW 1994, 667ff.

231 In Malta an essential element of a valid contract is consent, and it is clear that a contract is not valid if the consent of one of the contracting parties is procured through the provision of incorrect information (Article 974 of the Maltese Civil Code). Latvia also relies upon it together with concepts of fraud and deceptive practices which give the franchisee the right to either claim cancellation of the franchise agreement (Article 1461 of the Latvian Civil Law) or sue for damages (Article 1779 of the Latvian Civil Law; the Latvian parliament intend to change their approach and adopt a franchise-specific law that will require franchisors to give their potential franchisees prior disclosure of the nature of the franchise, evidence of the validity of the rights to be granted, details of the franchise networks and details of the terms of the franchise agreement, particularly the financial terms). In Estonia a right of action for misrepresentation is available to franchisees under the Civil Code Act Chapter 7 of the Law of Obligations Act, which provides that a person who entered

the risk that franchisees are induced to enter into a franchise on the back of false or inaccurate representations by the franchisor that it will be able to deliver those economic drivers that the franchisee is looking for from a franchise. In theory it can offer franchisors similar protection.

(b) The second element – a duty to positively disclose relevant facts

3.45 Whereas all EU member states prohibit misrepresentation in the sense that a party may not make false or misleading statements which may entice the other party to enter into a contract, only some civil jurisdictions go further and require a contractual party to make active pre-contractual disclosure. In Germany,[232] once contractual negotiations commence a pre-contractual relationship of trust is immediately established. This imposes on the parties a pre-contractual duty of care in providing pre-contractual disclosure to each other. The statutory foundation of this obligation, according to some commentators and case law, can be found in Article 242 BGB.[233] Both the franchisor and franchisee are under a duty to provide such information to each other as is reasonably necessary to enable the other party to make an informed decision as to whether or not they enter into the franchise agreement with the other party ('*culpa in contrahendo*'). The doctrine of *culpa in contrahendo* means that the franchisor has to provide and prepare site studies, profit and turnover forecasts and other

---

into a transaction based on fraudulent misrepresentation may rescind the contract. If the contract is not yet concluded, then a claim against a fraudulent franchisor can be made under the Law of Obligations Act. This provides that persons who engage in pre-contractual negotiations, or other preparations for entering into a contract, shall take reasonable account of the other's interests and rights (Section 14 subsection 1 of the Law of Obligations Act). The second sentence of the same subsection states that the information exchanged by the persons, in the course of preparation for entering into the contract, shall be accurate. If one of these rules is not followed by the franchisor, then the franchisee has the right to claim for damages (Section 14 (1) of the Law of Obligations Act). In Slovenia, the duty of good faith exists but only applies in the event that the franchisor has made a misrepresentation and provided misleading or inaccurate information to the potential franchisee. In which case, the franchisee can rescind from the contract within one year from learning of the misrepresentation and can also claim damages for any loss suffered (Article 7 of the Slovenian Civil Code). Despite its civil law system there is no express duty of good faith in Denmark and misrepresentation or fraud must be established (Law no 781 of 26.08.1996). Bulgaria also embraces the concept of misrepresentation (The Bulgarian Obligations and Contracts Act 275 of 22.11.1950). In Finnish law (Unfair Business Practices Act (1061/78)) for example, the Unfair Business Practices Act prohibits, 'the use of false and misleading expressions concerning one's own business operations or those of another party if the said expression is likely to affect the demand for or supply of a product or harm the business of another' (Section 2 of the Unfair Business Practices Act (1061/78)). The Court can prohibit an ongoing misrepresentation and impose a conditional fine. Fraudulent misrepresentation gives rise to the right to rescind the entire agreement (Hanna-Maija Elo, 'Finland' in: Getting the deal through – Franchise 2008, p. 36 para. 17). In addition to the Unfair Business Practices Act, a franchisee may also claim damages under the Tort Liability Act as a result of the unlawful behaviour by the franchisor (which includes misrepresentation). In order to prove the claim the franchisee will have to show that it has suffered loss as a result of the actions taken by the franchisor (Hanna-Maija Elo, 'Finland' in: Getting the deal through – Franchise 2008, p. 36 para. 17).

232 Article 311 BGB.

233 For commentary see Farnsworth, E.A., 1994, 'Good Faith in Contract Performance', *Good Faith and Fault in Contract Law*, edited Beatson and Friedman – Clarendon Paperbacks, p. 172. See judgments of 2 January 1920, RGZ 97, 326 and 1 March 1928 RGZ 120, 351.

financial information. This burden is particularly heavy for foreign franchisors who have no knowledge of the German market and have no experience of running a business there. There are several examples of foreign franchisors with no knowledge or experience of the German market giving their German developer or master franchisee such information as they had about the franchise business's performance outside of Germany and subsequently finding that this has resulted in them falling foul of the *culpa in contrahendo* doctrine.[234] Even if the franchisee is an experienced business person, the franchisor is under an obligation to provide information regarding the details of the franchise system.[235] Technically disclosure should also be the other way round (e.g. where the franchisee withholds important information),[236] but in practice of course it is the franchisor's duty that usually becomes the basis of a dispute. The franchisor has to provide all available information regarding the profitability of its franchise system.[237] It is not considered sufficient for the franchisee to have had the opportunity to visit other businesses within the system in order to gain his/her own impression. It has also been regarded as a breach of the disclosure obligations to provide a misleading quote regarding the number of franchises that have failed within the contractual territory. Breach of the duty of disclosure will lead to a cause of action against the franchisor. The franchisee will have the right to withdraw from the contract and claim damages in a sum equal to all expenses incurred in performing the contract (subject to the deduction of profits).[238] However, the franchisee cannot claim for loss of the profit that it

234 For example, the US family restaurant franchise Applebee's.

235 Giesler, Franchiseverträge, Rn. 206.

236 Palandt BGB, § 311 Rn. 20.

237 OLG München NJW 1994, S. 667ff; Braun NJW 1995, S. 504, 505. The plaintiff claimed for refund of the franchise licence fee. The agent of the franchisor had provided untrue information on revenue and profit and assured that the figures were accurate and proven. In the materials provided it was stated that a 'cautious' profit expectation would be between 8000 and 15 000 DM/month. The plaintiff entered into the franchise contract without having conducted its own research or calculations before conclusion of the contract. He rented a salesroom, bought two cars for delivery services and paid a franchise fee of 22 800 DM. Nine months after the conclusion of the franchise contract, the franchisee cancelled the Franchise Agreement and claimed for damages (franchise fees, price of cars). The defendant argued that a certain amount must be deducted from the damages as the plaintiff failed to assess the information on its own. The judges dismissed this notion, arguing that if one assures that certain figures are proven and accurate the other party can rely on such assurance. There are two key lines in the judgment: (i) that a franchisor must provide true and comprehensive information on the profitability of a system, and (ii) the franchisee's claim must not be reduced because of contributory negligence when the franchisee (thoughtlessly/frivolously) trusts in the statements of the franchisor without conducting its own research.

238 BGH NJW 1981, S. 1673ff; Schulze, in: Schulze/Dörner/Ebert, *BGB Kommentar*, 5th edition 2007, § 311 Rn. 20 and Flohr, BB 2006, pp. 389, 392. A German municipality issued an invitation to tender for building a gym by a general contractor. The plaintiff, a general contractor, instructed an architect to prepare the tender. After the architect had finished his work, but before the official opening date of the tender, the municipality (the defendant) withdrew the invitation. The plaintiff claimed for reimbursement of the costs of the architect. The Federal Court of Justice confirmed the judgment of first instance, cancelling the judgment of the court of appeals. Even though the court found that there has been a pre-contractual relationship resulting in fiduciary duties of both parties, the court denied that there had been a loss on the plaintiff's side, as he would have

would have made had the contract continued.[239] Generally speaking a franchisee who has suffered a loss can demand to be restored to the position he would have been in if the breach had not occurred. Normally the franchisee will argue that it would not have entered into the contract if it had been aware of the full facts. He will ask for his money back and for rescission of the contract. The duty of pre-contractual disclosure starts at the point where the franchisor and the potential franchisee meet for the first time and the franchisor presents his franchise system in detail.[240] This can happen, for example, through an advertisement, information material or participation in a fair. It is the franchisor's responsibility to ensure that the information it presents reflects the truth and that it has released all necessary information.[241] However, Section 311(3) of the Civil Code provides that the franchisee's right to claim for damages is not only against the franchisor, but also against any third parties who have established a fiduciary relationship with the franchisee, and hence influenced the franchisee's conduct during the contract negotiations and his/her decision to enter into the contract. In particular, managers of franchise brokers can be liable personally in damages. Theoretically the obligation could apply to franchisees but it is the more experienced party (here the franchisor) that is under an obligation to make available information to the less experienced party (usually the franchisee). In case of a violation of the duty to make pre-contractual disclosure, the franchisee can either claim damages or rescind from the contract provided that the franchisee can prove that entering into the agreement led to a loss. The ordinary limitation period for a claim based on *culpa in contrahendo* is three years.[242] This is a right distinct from the right of rescission which arises in the case of a right to rescind from the contract due to fraudulent misrepresentation. If the right to rescind is to be based on fraudulent misrepresentation alone without proof of damages, then this right has to be exercised within one year following the discovery of the fraudulent misrepresentation.[243]

---

incurred costs for the architect even if the invitation to tender had not been cancelled. Even had the invitation not been cancelled, the plaintiff would not have been sure that his effort would have resulted in the acceptance of his tender.

239 Schulze, in: Schulze/Dörner/Ebert, *BGB Kommentar*, 5th edition 2007, § 311 Rn. 20 and Flohr, BB 2006, pp. 389, 392.

240 Giesler, Franchiseverträge, Rn. 207.

241 OLG München NJW 1994, S. 667ff.

242 Sections 195, 199 of the German Civil Code.

243 OGH 19.01.1989, WBl 1989, 131; Liebscher/Petsche, *Frachchising in Österreich* (2. Auflage 2002), S. 112. Flohr, *Franchise-Vertrag*, S. 10. The defendant claimed, by way of counterclaim, that the plaintiff, although having agreed to non-compete in the area of the franchise business, has had a third party opening up another franchise in the area. The defendant claimed that, because of that, the revenue that has been expected has never been achieved. However, the non-compete agreement, as well as the extent of the fiduciary duty of the franchisor, was irrelevant to the decision as the shop of the third party had been in another district of the city, miles away from the defendant's premises and thus neither covered by the non-compete agreement, nor by a (possible) fiduciary duty. This is an Austrian case. The court, although it had been considering the question whether the franchisor's fiduciary duty would prohibit the franchisor from allowing for another franchise close

Similar duties to make full disclosure are found in other civil law jurisdictions such as Estonia,[244] Greece,[245] Hungary,[246] the Netherlands,[247] Portugal,[248] 3.46

to the franchisee's premise (and showed some sympathy for that position) has eventually not decided upon the question as it was irrelevant for the case at hand. The judgment did not address the fiduciary duty of the franchisee, but the one of the franchisor.

244 In Estonia general pre-contractual disclosure requirements are found in section 14 of the Law of Obligations Act and they apply to franchise contracts. The main rule of disclosure is enacted in subsection 2 of section 14, which provides that persons who engage in pre-contractual negotiations or other preparations for entering into a contract shall inform the other party of all circumstances which are of essential interest to the other party of the contract, taking into account its purpose. However, there is no obligation to inform the other party of circumstances which it could not reasonably be expected to be informed of.

245 There is a strong German influence on Greek law, so, unsurprisingly, parties in Greece must act in accordance with the requirements of good faith and business ethics (Article 281 of the Greek Civil Code and Yanos Gramatidis, Chapter on Greece in Mendelsohn, *The International Encyclopaedia of Franchising Law*, p. 6). During the pre-contractual period, the franchisor is required to provide data on comparable activities in its system and a full set of information on how much the prospective franchisee will have to financially contribute. However, it is up to the franchisee to draw conclusions on the prospects of entering and trading on the market and to evaluate the reputation of the franchisor's business. If prospective franchisees draw the wrong conclusions based on the correct information, the franchisor will not be liable. However, if the franchisor deliberately makes a misrepresentation, it will be liable (Yanos Gramatidis, Chapter on Greece in Mendelsohn, *The International Encyclopaedia of Franchising Law*, p. 20). A party which has been misled, threatened or defrauded by the other contractual party may seek the annulment of the contract and/or compensation under the conditions provided (Articles 140, 147 and 150 of the Greek Civil Code). The conclusion of the agreement must not be a result of mistake, threat or fraud (Articles 140, 147 and 150 of the Greek Civil Code).

246 Hungarian law also imposes strict control over the pre-contractual relationships in accordance with good faith principles (Section 206 of the Hungarian Civil Code). It requires the parties to act reasonably and imposes a duty of disclosure on both franchisor and franchisee (Section 206(4) of the Hungarian Civil Code). If the franchisor fails to disclose information which is relevant to the agreement, the franchisee who enters into a contract can challenge the disclosure within one year after misdisclosure comes to light in writing. If the challenge is successful the agreement can be treated as null and void 'ab inito' and the parties are put back into the position they were in before entering into the contract (Sections 210, 235–237 of the Hungarian Civil Code). Alternately, the agreement can be affirmed and damages opted for (Section 339 of the Hungarian Civil Code).

247 In Dutch law the pre-contractual relationship is also governed by the principle of good faith, or reasonableness and fairness (Article 6:248 subsection 1 of the Dutch Civil Code). A party may annul an agreement if the agreement was concluded on the basis of incorrect understandings (provided that certain conditions are met) (Article 6:228 of the Dutch Civil Code). The parties are obliged to take reasonable steps to ensure that an agreement is not entered into by mistake (Supreme Court of 15 November 1957 (NJ 1958, 67 (Baris/Riezenkamp)). Although the principle of reasonableness and fairness does not mean that the franchisor is always obliged to provide the franchisee with a projection of the franchise's financial performance, in some circumstances such an obligation may arise (LJN: AD7329, C00/118HR (Paalman/Lampenier)). Parties are entitled to assume that the information which has been provided by the other party is correct and so any forecasts provided by the franchisor should be based on thorough market and location research which was carried out with due care (e.g. 18 June 1999, Prg 1999, 5211 (Schouten Fashion B.V./Brown Fashion B.V.) and 14 April 1998, Prg 1998/4976 (Aviti/Kinderparadijs)).

248 In Portugal, the parties must act in good faith during their negotiations and have to provide all and any necessary information prior to the execution of a franchise agreement although there is no law which clearly states what needs to be disclosed (see Article 762 of the Portuguese Civil Code). No false or misleading information about the franchisor's business or those of its franchisees should be submitted to potential franchisees (Santos Cruz/Krupenski, IBA Legal Practice Division International Franchising Committee Newsletter, May 2007, p. 24). As in Germany, the *culpa in contrahendo* doctrine means that non-compliance with the general rules on disclosure will lead to liability ('Outline of franchise issues in Portugal', questionnaire with answers provided by Jose Alves Do Carmo, associate, Barrocas Sarmento Neves).

Lithuania,[249] Slovakia,[250] Austria,[251] and the Czech Republic.[252] A slightly lesser duty is found in Estonia.[253] However, pre-contractual disclosure of material facts is not required in all civil jurisdictions.[254] In the common law jurisdictions of England, Scotland, Ireland and Cyprus there is no duty to make pre-contractual disclosure. This positive obligation to disclose reduces the risks to which franchisees are exposed. It does not reduce the risks to which franchisors are exposed and imposes a substantial burden upon them. It could support the drivers that attract franchisees to franchising but will not support those that attract franchisors to it.

---

249 The Lithuanian Civil Code imposes a duty to disclose certain information based on the general duty of good faith during contract negotiations (Lithuanian Civil Code Article 6.163(1)). It states in very general terms that all parties to the negotiation must disclose to each other the information they possess, which is essential for the conclusion of the contract (Lithuanian Civil Code Article 6.163(4)).

250 Slovakian law arrives at a similar position via a different route. Section 43 of the Slovakian Civil Code obliges the parties to resolve anything which could possibly result in a dispute at a later stage in advance. The parties therefore need to disclose certain facts before entering into a contract. Misrepresentation, whether intentional or unintentional, means that the innocent party has a right to rescind from the contract if it has relied on the false information while making the decision to enter into the agreement (Sections 40a and 49a of the Slovakian Civil Code).

251 Although it is not explicitly provided for under Austrian law (Petsche, A., S. Riegler and W. Theiss, 2004, 'Franchising in Austria', *International Journal of Franchising*, Volume 2, Issue 3), it is historically accepted that franchisors have a similar duty of disclosure under the doctrine of *culpa in contrahendo* (Ibid., Petsche, Riegler and Theiss, p. 3, doctrine derives from §918AGBG). The disclosure duty of the franchisee is limited to properly answering the questions asked by the franchisor. This means that the franchisor is carrying a considerably greater disclosure duty. The franchisor must provide the franchisee with appropriate information in particular regarding market opportunities, sales forecasts and profitability calculations. If the franchisor provides faulty or insufficient information it may be liable under the doctrine of *culpa in contrahendo* (OGH 19.01.1989 WBl 1989, 131; Petsche, Riegler and Theiss, 2004, p. 10, p. 5). However there are limits to the scope of this duty of pre-contractual information. In one decision the highest Austrian civil court decided that a franchisor does not have to provide a prospective franchisee with a detailed market survey before giving an estimate regarding the turnover (OGH 19.01.1989, WBl 1989, 131). Failure to comply with these disclosure obligations entitles the franchisee to damages caused by the disclosure or the lack of it (this entitlement is based on the concept of *culpa in contrahendo* which derives from § 918 AGBG).

252 Whilst there are no express good faith pre-contractual duties of disclosure, under Czech law, if a franchisor causes damage to its franchisees by intentionally withholding relevant information, it will be unethical and render it liable for any resulting damages (Section 424 of the Czech Civil Code). This amounts to an indirect positive duty to disclose. Failure to disclose relevant information to potential franchisees may amount to misrepresentation inducing them to enter into the franchise contract (Section 49 (a) of the Czech Civil Code) and so entitling them to challenge the validity of the franchise agreement.

253 In Estonia (Section 94 subsection 3 of the General Part of the Estonian Civil Code Act – June 1994 and Section 14(2) of the Law of Obligation Act), on the other hand, the prohibition on misrepresentation is closely linked to a duty to take reasonable account of the other's interests and rights. Consequently a franchisor must inform a potential franchisee of all circumstances that are of essential interest to the potential franchisee. Although there is no obligation to inform the other party of any circumstances of which they could not reasonably expect to be informed this is still significantly different to an obligation not to make false representations.

254 For example, 'Poland' in *Franchising – Getting the Deal Through*, 2008 ed. Zeidman, P.

(c) The third element – the right to withdraw

The application of consumer protection law to franchising means that in some member states franchisees are entitled to a 'cooling-off period' after signing a franchise agreement. Many consumer rights such as product liability are regulated at EU level,[255] resulting in a harmonised approach throughout the EU member states. In some EU jurisdictions, such as Germany, franchising has triggered a debate over exactly what a consumer is, resulting in franchisees enjoying protection that was not originally intended for them. Germany treats individual franchisees as consumers if they are entering into substantial financial commitments. Franchisees that start a business for the first time are treated as if they were consumers. Consequently they have, and must be notified of, cooling-off rights in accordance with the consumer protection legislation in Germany.[256] A consumer may withdraw from a contract within two weeks of its execution[257] if it contains a long-term purchasing commitment. Section 507 of the Civil Code extends the cooling-off right to individual franchisees setting up a new business for the first time (but not companies) if they fall below a €50 000 threshold. This means that a start-up franchisee enjoys protection if the value of the long-term purchase commitment does not exceed this amount during the life of the franchise agreement.[258] If this threshold is exceeded then the franchisee will lose its right of withdrawal. The franchisee has to be notified in writing by the franchisor of his rights of withdrawal including its commencement date, its two week duration, the fact that timely dispatch of the withdrawal notice will suffice to comply with the withdrawal period, the required form and content of the withdrawal notice and the name and address of the recipient of the withdrawal notice. If notification of the franchisee's withdrawal right is provided after conclusion of the contract, the withdrawal period is extended to one month.[259] The period does not commence until the day after the franchisee is notified of his/her right of withdrawal. If the instruction is not provided in a clear manner, the withdrawal period is extended to six months. If no notice of the right of withdrawal is given, the right becomes a perpetual one.[260] Some German commentators[261] suggest that the €50 000 threshold is 3.47

255 Council Directive 85/374/EEC on the approximation of the laws, regulations and administrative provisions of member states concerning liability for defective products [1985] OJ L 210 7.8.1985.

256 Until 31.12.2001 cooling-off rights were governed by the Consumer Credit Act (VerbrKrG). As of 01.01.2002 the Act has been incorporated in the Civil Code. However, court decisions dealing with the former Consumer Credit Act are still referred to. The Consumer Credit Act was the national implementation of Council Directive 87/102/EEC.

257 Sections 505 (1), 355 of the Civil Code BGH NJW 2003 S. 1932ff.

258 Palandt BGB, § 507 Rn. 7.

259 Section 355 (2) of the Civil Code.

260 Section 355 (3) of the Civil Code; Timmerbeil NJW 2003, S.569, 570.

261 Section 505, 355 Giesler, Franchisevertraege 2. Auflage 2002, Rn. 131 with further references; Palandt BGB, § 507 Rn. 7; Möller, in: Beck Online Commentary BGB (Bamberger/Roth), § 507 Rn. 8; other opinion Schürnbrand, in: *Münchener Kommentar BGB*, 5th edition 2007, § 507 Rn. 7.

not appropriate in the context of a franchise relationship. It is argued that a small franchisee whose long-term purchase commitment may very well exceed €50 000 is not any less vulnerable than a franchisee where the value of the purchase commitment does not exceed the threshold figure. The basis for this argument is a decision by the German Supreme Court: in connection with the former German Consumer Credit Act[262] a franchisee has the right of withdrawal irrespective of the amount of the purchasing agreement.[263] However, a ruling of the ECJ makes clear that German application of consumer legislation to franchising cannot be imposed on other EU member states.[264] The Italian Consumer Code[265] provides, amongst other things, that a consumer is a 'natural person ... acting for purposes which are outside his/her trade, business or profession'[266] and a professional is a 'natural or legal person ... acting for purposes related to its trade, business or profession ...'[267] In the case of *Francesco Benincasa* v. *Dentalkit Srl*,[268] a German franchisee sought a declaration from a German court against an Italian franchisor that the agreement between them was void, despite the fact that it was subject to the jurisdiction of the Italian courts. The Claimant invoked Article 14 of the Brussels Convention 1968, which states that if a consumer files an action against a contractual counterparty, the court in the Claimant's domicile has jurisdiction. The franchisee claimed that it was a consumer as it was not carrying on the business when the contract was concluded. The ECJ held that whilst reference must be made to the contractual party's position and the type and aim of the contract, 'a plaintiff that concluded a contract with a view to pursuing a trade or profession ... in the future, may not be regarded as a consumer'. The application of consumer protection legislation can substantially reduce the risks that franchisees expose themselves to in entering into a franchise. However, the way in which such legislation is applied to franchising varies from member state to member state, so reducing its impact on cross-border franchising, as illustrated by the *Francesco Benincasa* v. *Dentalkit Srl* case. Not only does it not reduce the risks that franchisors take on when franchising their business, but it increases them in some member states by overprotecting franchisees. However, Germany is not the only member state that applies consumer protection legislation to impose a cooling-off period in franchising. In the UK, franchisors which extend

262 BGH NJW 1995, S. 722, 724 (,Ceiling Doctor').

263 Austria follows the German lead in applying consumer law to individual franchisees (Section 1 subsection 3 of the Austrian Consumer Protection Act, ('Konsumentenschutzgesetz', in short 'KSchG')). A franchisee that is a founder of a new business will enjoy the same protection as a consumer (Liebscher/Petsche, *Franchising in Österreich*, p. 77), including a right of withdrawal (Austrian Consumer Protection Act S.1 553), however, if an existing business is restructured or enlarged the consumer law will not apply (OGH 21.01.1981 SZ 54/10).

264 Case C-269/95 *Francesco Benincasa* v. *Dentalkit Srl* [1997] ECR I-3767.

265 Legislative Decree 206/2005.

266 Article 3.

267 Ibid.

268 Case C-269/95 [1997] ECR I-3767.

credit and/or hire out goods or equipment to non-corporate franchisees must comply with the Consumer Credit Act 2006. This act is complex and wide ranging. It allows the courts a wide discretion to re-write credit agreements that are 'unfair' to non-corporate franchisees. Franchisors must be licensed, the franchise and other agreements must comply with the complex set form prescribed by the law and they must be executed in accordance with very specific requirements which include a 'cooling-off' period for the franchisee. Franchisors must also send out annual statements to their franchisees for all 'fixed sum' credit – this includes hire purchase and conditional sale agreements.

The UK's Fair Trading Act 1996[269] also impacts upon franchising seeks to prevent consumers joining multi-tier trading schemes and imposes a complex procedure on recruitment. It generally prohibits consumers selling on to other consumers further down the pyramid and making a markup on the goods. It aims to prevent the lower tiers being stuck with overpriced stock that they cannot sell on to end users. Any franchise that has more than two levels in the UK must comply with the Act's provisions.[270] Exemptions are granted[271] for those franchisors (and others) who operate single-tier schemes and for pyramids in which all the parties trading in the UK are registered for VAT.[272] Franchisees in non-excluded schemes that do not comply with the detailed requirements of the act are free to leave the franchise at will without restriction. 3.48

(d) The fourth element – confidentiality

A number of EU member states impose a duty of confidentiality on potential franchisees as the 'quid pro quo' for the franchisor having to make disclosure to it.[273] English law imposes no duty of confidentiality and it is an entirely contractual matter. Article 18 of the German Unfair Competition Act imposes a duty of confidentiality upon potential franchisees and prohibits the use of 3.49

269 As amended by the Trading Schemes Act 1996 and the Trading Schemes (Exclusion) Regulations 1997 SI 1997/31.

270 The Trading Schemes (Exclusions) Regulations 1997 SI 1997/31 Regulation 3.

271 The Fair Trading Act 1973 s.188 (6)(b) and the Trading Schemes (Exclusions) Regulations 1997 SI 1997/31 Regulation 3.

272 The aim being to protect small franchisees whose turnover is below the VAT threshold.

273 In Hungary a duty is placed on the franchisee as the quid pro quo for the franchisor's duty of disclosure and is regulated by the Civil Code (Section 81 of the Hungarian Civil Code). In the Czech Republic all information disclosed is protected by the Civil Code (S.271 Czech Commercial Code, Skrdlik, WiRO 2005, p. 369). The Polish Code imposes a similar obligation (Polish Civil Code 72^1 § 1 KC) as does the Lithuanian Civil Code (Lithuanian Civil Code Article 6.164(1)), the Slovenian Code (Slovenian Civil Code Article 1040Z), the Slovakian Commercial Code (Slovak Commercial Code, Section 271) and the Estonian Code (Estonian Law of Obligations Act Section 14(4)). In Belgium both parties are placed under a duty of confidentiality as regards information that they obtain 'with a view to entering into a [franchise] agreement, and may not use the information, either directly or indirectly, other than for the purposes of the commercial partnership agreement to be entered into' (Article 6 of the Law governing pre-contractual information within the framework of commercial partnership agreements).

samples and technical guidelines supplied by the franchisor to compete with it or their disclosure to third parties. This element potentially reduces substantially the risks to which franchisors are exposed by the heterogeneous nature of the approach taken by member states. It does not reduce the risks to which franchisees are exposed. Nor does it support the economic drivers that attract franchisors and franchisees to franchising.

(e) The fifth element – obligation to execute an agreement

3.50 Some jurisdictions penalise the franchisor if, once negotiations with a potential franchisee have developed, the franchisor does not grant it a franchise. German law has developed rules regarding good faith in negotiations, with the Courts consistently holding that a late withdrawal from negotiations without good cause and frustration of reliance investment will entail liability.[274] In France, Courts consider that an agreement has been formed once the parties have reached an agreement on essential points.[275] Based upon the concept of a duty of good faith commentators[276] suggest that French law has used tort law to establish that the parties are subject to a duty to negotiate in good faith[277] but

> once the negotiations have reached a mature stage the parties are subject to a contractual obligation ... to continue to negotiate in good faith. This obligation is sometimes express, but most often implicit in the structure of the preliminary dealings ... the obligation strengthens as negotiations proceeds. Its extent grows: it makes one party furnish information to the other, it prevents his putting up unacceptable proposals with the aim of ... causing a break-off of negotiations, or of merely pretending to negotiate seriously, while in fact he has decided to deal with a competitor, it compels him to work towards the reaching of a definite decision within a reasonable period.[278]

The essential points vary from one contract to another, but in the context of franchising, essential points are generally the provision of the trademark, the transfer of know-how and the financial arrangements. As the franchisor usually provides a potential franchisee with a draft of the franchise agreement as part of its pre-contractual disclosure, without an express statement by the franchisor that the information provided is only for discussion purposes and that an agreement will not be formed until the express acceptance of the franchisor, the

---

274 (1) Keutner, G., 1990, 'Reliance, Promissary Estoppel and Culpa in Contrahendo: A Comparative Analysis', 10 *Tel-Aviv U Stud in Law* 79 and (2) Beatson, J. and D. Friedmann, 1994, 'From Classical to Modern Contract Law', in *Good Faith and Fault and Contract Law*, Clarendon Paperbacks, p. 38.

275 E.g. Cass req., 1 December 1885, Grands arrêts, no. 146.

276 Cohen, N., 1994, 'Pre-Contractual Duties: Two Freedoms and the Contract to Negotiate in Good Faith and Fault in Contract Law', ed. Beatson and Friedmann, Clarendon Paperbacks.

277 Cass. Com, 20 March 1972, JCP 1973.2.17543; Ghestin, J., *Traité de Droit Civil, Les Obligations* (2nd Edition 1988) no 228, p. 252.

278 Jauffiet-Spinosi, C., 1989, 'The Domain of Contract – French Report', in *Contract Law Today: Anglo-French Comparisons*, D. Harris and D. Tallon (eds), pp. 113, 131.

franchise agreement could be deemed to be concluded if the franchisee agrees to the proposed terms. If negotiations are terminated wrongfully, the party terminating the agreement may be held liable.[279] Generally, the more advanced the negotiations are, the more difficult it will be for franchisors to terminate negotiations without incurring liability as the more the negotiations progress, the more the other party's confidence that an agreement will be reached is protected.[280] The French courts take the view that the damage corresponds to the costs incurred during the negotiations and sometimes even the lost chance of entering into an agreement with another party is taken into consideration. Under recent case law, however, a party has been refused a claim of compensation for the loss of the chance to obtain revenue from another agreement that it did not enter into.[281] Once an agreement is concluded, it is the franchisor's duty to perform the agreement. If the franchisor fails to do so, the franchisee can claim damages under Article 1142 of the Civil Code, but cannot require specific performance. Both claims for damages are claims in tort and subject to Articles 1382 and 1383 of the Civil Code. Some of the other EU member states take a similar approach.[282]

3. The ongoing franchisor/franchisee relationship

The regulatory environment in the EU fails both to adequately re-enforce **3.51** the economic drivers that attract the parties to franchising and to reduce the inherent consequential risk to an appropriate level. The legal environment as it impacts upon the ongoing franchisor/franchisee relationship does not adequately support and re-enforce the economic drivers that attract franchisors to franchising. Nor does it adequately reduce the consequential inherent risks to franchisors. It does reduce the risks to which franchisees are exposed and support some of the economic drivers that attract them to franchising in some member states. However, the lack of a homogeneous approach in all member states substantially reduces its impact on cross-border franchising in the EU. The relevant legal regulatory environment

279 Cass. com., 26 November 2003, Bull. civ IV, no. 186.

280 Cass. 1re civ., 14 June 2000, no. 98-17494.

281 Cass. com., 26 November 2003, Bull. civ. IV, no. 186.

282 In the Netherlands if the franchisor unreasonably breaks off negotiations for a franchise agreement, he can, depending on the phase of the negotiations, be held liable in damages to the other party or even be obliged to continue negotiations with the other party (Article 6: 248 Dutch Civil Code). When considering such a case the courts consider: (i) the extent and manner in which the party that broke off negotiations gave rise to such legitimate expectation, (ii) the terminating party's justified interests; and (iii) any unforeseen circumstances that arose during the course of the negotiations (Supreme Court (Hoge Raad), in its decision of 18 June 1982, NJ 1983/723 (Plas-Valburg)). A similar approach is found in Hungary, where such failure may lead to an award of damages (Section 6 of the Hungarian Civil Code).

comprises the duty of good faith, anti-trust, unfair competition and consumer law. Neither the UK, Germany nor France have specific laws that impact upon the franchisor/franchisee relationship. Although franchise laws in non-EU jurisdictions, for example Indonesia,[283] Malaysia,[284] Russia,[285] Ukraine,[286] Georgia[287] and Vietnam,[288] commonly regulate the contents of franchise agreements, only four of the EU member states (Italy, Romania, Lithuania and Estonia) have franchise-focused laws which do so.

---

283 In Indonesia, a franchise agreement must contain the following (Regulation of the Minister of Trade No 12/M-DAG/PER/3/2006 dated 29 March 2006, which revoked The Provisions on and Procedure for the Implementation of Franchised Business Registration (*Decree of the Minister of Industry and Trade No. 259/MPP/Kep/7/1997, dated July 30, 1997*) Chapter II, Article 7.1): the name, address and domicile of the company of each party; the name and position of each party authorised to sign the agreement; the name and type of right over intellectual property, invention or a unique business characteristic, for example a management system, a selling or display method or a distribution method which constitutes a special characteristic which is the object of a franchise; the rights and obligations of each party and the aid and facility given to a franchisee; the marketing area; the period of the agreement and the method of and the requirements for the extension of the agreement; the method for settling a dispute; mutually agreed basic provisions which may result in the termination or expiration of an agreement; compensation in the event of agreement termination; the procedure for the payment of compensation; the use of domestically produced goods or materials produced and supplied by small scale enterprises; nurturing guidance and training for franchisees.

284 Malaysia simply prohibits discrimination between franchisees in respect of the charges offered or made for franchise fees, royalties, goods, services, equipment, rentals or advertising services if such discrimination will cause competitive harm to a franchisee who competes with a franchisee who receives the benefit of the discrimination, unless it can be objectively justified (the Franchise Act 1998 Part III Section 20). It also requires that termination must be for good cause, be by written notice, and offer an opportunity to remedy a breach (The Franchise Act 1998 Part IV Section 30(1)) cited as cause for termination must be given. A franchisor refusing to renew or extend a franchise at the end of its term must compensate the franchisee if it does not waive the post-termination restrictive covenants or give the franchisee six months' prior notice of the termination or non-renewal (The Franchise Act 1998 Part IV Section 32).

285 In Russia the law lays down the rights and obligations of both parties to the agreement by merely stating the essential elements of the franchise relationship (Russian Civil Code Part II Chapter 54 Articles 1030 to 1033). Somewhat unusually it does grant a right of renewal to franchisees properly performing their agreements (Russian Civil Code Part II Chapter 54 Article 1035). There is some case law on this point which suggests that the requirement can be circumvented in some circumstances (Decision of the Federal Arbitrazh Court of East-Siberian District (FAS VSO decision) of 16.10.2003, Case No. NA19–3914/03–13-FO2–3459/03-C2). However, it permits termination of a franchise agreement upon six months' notice by either party (Russian Civil Code Part II Chapter 54 Article 1035). It also surprisingly provides that transfer of a franchise agreement to another franchisee does not constitute cause for termination (Russian Civil Code Part II Chapter 54 Article 1037).

286 In the Ukraine the law (Civil Code, Chapter 76 Articles 1115 to 1129) imposes statutory liability of the franchisor for defective products sold by the franchisee. This is symptomatic of Socialist legal traditions and is also found in (Latvian and Estonian) franchise law.

287 The Georgian Civil Code (Adopted on 26 June 1997, Book Three, Special Part, Title One, Chapter Seven (Articles 607–614)) specifies the obligations of the parties including confidentiality and the liability of the franchisor.

288 In Vietnam early termination is possible in accordance with the conditions set out in Article 16 of the Commercial Law of 2001. Article 16 provides that amongst other things a franchisee has the right to unilaterally terminate the franchise agreement if the franchisor breaches its obligations specified under Article 287 of the Commercial Law.

Despite occasional passing suggestions that an EU relationship law for franchising would be appropriate one has never been seriously considered.[289] The Romanian, Lithuanian, Estonian and Italian[290] laws all specify core terms that must be in a franchise agreement, all of which are found in all of the sample franchise agreements considered above.[291] Only the Lithuanian Code imposes

289 For example, there was a proposal by the Austrian Standards Institute to the European Committee for Standardisation to overcome this inconsistency by drafting a set of European standards for franchising, focusing on terminology and market practices. The European Committee for Standardisation develops voluntary European standards which are national standards in each of its 30 member countries, which comprise all 27 EU member states, Norway, Switzerland and Iceland (www.cen.eu/cenorm/members/national+members/members.asp). The Austrian Standards Institute suggested that the lack of qualitative guidelines for franchising has led to the failure of numerous franchise systems and claims that the legal framework of franchising in Europe is underdeveloped, Frignani, A. and M. Mendelsohn, 2009, 'Project to Standardise Franchising Terminology and Marketing Practices', *International Journal of Franchising Law*, Volume 7, Issue 2, p. 27). However, it produced no evidence to support these claims and seems to have been ignored by the Committee for Standardisation.

This is probably because European standards are designed for technical processes and products rather than business formats. The wide spectrum of commercial structures that come within the term franchising and the differing sectors in which they are applied all militate against there being any meaningful common standards. This is the problem faced by the national franchise associations.

290 The Italian Franchise law provides that in case of disputes, before filing suit or commencing arbitration, the parties must undertake to seek conciliation in accordance with the rules of the local chamber of commerce (Law of 6 May 2004, No. 129 Article 7). Similar provisions are found in some non-EU jurisdictions such as Canada and South Korea. (In Canada the New Brunswick Franchises Act is the first of the provincial statutes to provide for a comprehensive dispute resolution mechanism (S.8(1) of the New Brunswick Franchises Act 2007 (26 June)). The South Korean franchise law also provides for a dispute resolution mechanism and establishes a Franchise Transaction Dispute Mediation Committee (Korean Act on Fairness in Franchise Transactions Chapter IV).

291 Article 4(1) of the Romanian Ordinance specifies the issues that must be dealt with by the franchise agreement (Articles 4(1), (2) and (3) respectively; Herzfeld & Rubin (Romania) S.R.L., Romania's New Franchising Law in 'The Romanian Digest') and states the general principle that the franchise agreement must define, free of any ambiguity, the obligations and liabilities of each of the parties. It does not impose minimal terms. There is no standard form prescribed for franchise agreements. Article 5 of the Ordinance states that a franchise agreement must be in writing and contain clauses in respect to the object of the contract; the rights and obligations of the parties; the financial conditions; the term of the contract; and the modification, prolongation or termination of the contract. Article 6(1) of the Ordinance provides a list of general principles that a franchise agreement must include concerning term, renewal, termination, transfer and the franchisor's pre-emptive rights on a transfer. The Lithuanian Civil Code also requires certain contractual terms to be detailed in the franchise agreement (Lithuanian Civil Code Articles 6.769, 6.770(1), 6.771), all of which are found in the sample franchise agreements, although some of them, such as the provision of ongoing assistance can be contracted out of (Lithuanian Civil Code Article 6.770(2)). The Estonian Law of Obligations (Section 375 Chapter 19) takes a similar approach to the Romanian law and requires franchise agreements to address certain issues, all of which are found in the sample franchise agreements (Section 376–378 of the Law of Obligations Act). It does not impose minimal terms. The Italian law requires that all franchise agreements must specify (Law of 6 May 2004, No. 129 Article 3.3) the exact amount of the franchising fee and of the franchisee's investment; the method of payment of royalties and the determination of a possible minimum turnover to be guaranteed by the franchisee; an exact identification of the exclusive territory granted to the franchisee, if any; a description of the know-how; a description of the services to be provided by the franchisor, such as technical and commercial assistance, planning and training; and the contractual conditions relevant to the renewal, termination and the transferability of the contract.

certain minimum provisions which were not found in any of the sample agreements considered above.[292]

(a) The duty of good faith

3.52 The duty of good faith has a substantial impact upon the economic drivers and consequential inherent risks in the ongoing franchisor/franchisee relationship. It seeks to deliver a degree of equilibrium to the inherent tension within the franchise relationship between the desire of both parties to obtain the best commercial deal for themselves and a need to have a good ongoing commercial relationship based upon a modicum of mutual trust. It exists in many of the EU member states but not all, and even in those jurisdictions that do acknowledge a duty of good faith it is frequently interpreted in different ways.

Good faith 'lacks a fixed meaning, because it is loose and amorphous'[293] and some see it as 'an elusive term best left to lawyers and judges to define over a period of time as circumstances require'.[294]

There are generally considered to be three main 'families' of law in Europe[295] – German, French and English. Each take a different approach to the concept of good faith.[296] These each have a different impact upon the economic drivers and consequential risks associated with franchising.

i. English law

3.53 As Bingham, LJ commented:[297]

---

292 It grants franchisees an automatic right of renewal if they are not in breach. The only exception is if the franchisor undertakes not to enter into a franchise agreement with another franchisee in the same territory within the next three years (Lithuanian Civil Code Article 6.774(1) and (2)). If the franchisor wishes to enter into an agreement with another franchisee in the same territory before the three year term has passed, the franchisor must either offer the existing franchisee renewal of the contract on equivalent terms, or compensate the existing franchisee for its loss connected to the expiration of the contract (Lithuanian Civil Code Article 6.774(2)). It also provides that in the event of death of either franchisor (unlikely as mostly corporations) or franchisee, its rights and obligations under the franchise agreement will be transferred to its heir, provided that the latter is an entrepreneur and continues to undertake an entrepreneurial activity within six months from the date of inheritance, failing which the agreement will be terminated. Its most noteworthy, and inappropriate, provisions relate to the franchisor's liability. A franchisor can be held liable for claims against the franchisee with respect to the quality of goods (works, services) sold by the franchisee under the franchise agreement (Lithuanian Civil Code Article 6.773(1)). The franchisor is also jointly and severally liable for any faults in goods manufactured by the franchisee under the franchise agreement (Lithuanian Civil Code Article 6.773(2)). These provisions undermine the fundamental concept of the franchisee's independence.

293 Juenger, F.K., 1995, 'Listening To Law Professors Talk About Good Faith: Some Afterthoughts', *Tulane Law Review*, Vol. 69, pp. 1253–4.

294 Powers, J., 1999, 'Defining the Indefinable: Good Faith and the United Nations Convention on the Contracts for the International Sale of Goods', *Journal of Law and Commerce*, Vol. 18, p. 333.

295 Op. cit., Whittaker and Zimmerman, p. 48.

296 Ibid.

297 *Interfoto Picture Library Ltd* v. *Stiletto Visual Programmes Ltd* [1988] 1 All ER 384 at 352 (CA).

> in many civil law systems, and perhaps in most legal systems outside of the common law world, the law of obligations recognises and enforces an overriding principle that in making and carrying out contracts parties should act in good faith. This does not simply mean that they should not deceive each other, a principle which any legal system must recognise; its effect is perhaps most aptly conveyed by such metaphorical colloquialisms as 'playing fair', 'coming clean' or 'putting one's cards face down on the table'. It is in essence a principle of fair and open dealing.

Although civil law systems all adopt the principle of good faith based upon the Roman concept of 'bona fides',[298] they interpret it in a variety of ways. Common law theory takes a far more literal approach to contracts using classical interpretative tools such as 'plain meaning'. However, although it has 'little room for a notion as malleable as the implied covenant of good faith',[299] common law abhors certain acts such as misrepresentation that amount to breaches of good faith.

In contrast to the civil law jurisdictions in the EU, English law has always been reluctant to adopt an overriding principle of good faith, although there are elements of it to be found in certain aspects of it, such as the concept of equity and the dictates of EU Directives.

There has been much debate whether good faith is the behaviour of one who acts with a 'pure heart and empty head'[300] or merely the 'prudence and causation of a reasonable man'.[301]

However, the English courts seem to agree that,

> the concept of a duty to carry on negotiations in good faith is inherently repugnant to the adversarial position of the parties when involved in negotiations[302]

and that it is

> as unworkable in practice as it is inherently inconsistent with the position of a negotiating party.[303]

298 Litvinoff, S., 1997, 'Good Faith', *Tulane Law Review*, Vol. 71, p. 1645, 1652–3.

299 Van Alstine, M.P., 1999, 'Of Textualism, Party Autonomy and Good Faith', *William and Mary Law Review*, Vol. 40, No. 4, pp. 1223–312.

300 *Sir John Lawson* v. *Weston* 170 ER 640 (KB 1801) *per* Lord Kenyon.

301 *Gill* v. *Cubitt* (1824) 3 B. & C. 466, 107 ER 806.

302 Lord Ackner in *Walford* v. *Miles* [1992] 1 All ER 453 at 460.

303 Ibid at 461.

Nevertheless, although English law has not committed itself to any such overriding principle[304] it has 'developed piecemeal solutions in response to demonstrated problems of unfairness',[305] which amount to a species of good faith. In other words, the law is suffused with good faith but does not use it as a general legal basis for intervention.[306] The common law rules of mistake, misrepresentation and duress all require the fairness and honesty that are indicative of a general duty of good faith. The principles of equity are also similar to the concept of good faith. Their origins lie in the jurisdiction of the Chancellor who would grant remedies to mitigate the harshness and rigidity of the common law.[307] The rules of promissory estoppel, specific performance, injunctions, consideration, undue influence and more recently the notion of unconscionable bargains[308] all focus on the need for honesty and fairness and so have all led to a whittling away of the common law principles. Therefore, in certain circumstances equity works almost as much as a corrective instrument as the principle of good faith does in civil jurisdictions. It can take a restrictive, adaptive and collateral approach. The courts have also seriously interfered with the express terms of contracts as regards exclusion and exemption clauses,[309] whilst statutes, such as the Partnership Act 1890 and the Unfair Contract Terms Act 1977 also impose good faith principles. The case of *Fleet Mobile Tyres Limited* v. *Stone and Another (trading as Tyre 20)*[310] shows how in franchise disputes, although English law will not imply into a franchise agreement an obligation on a franchisor to act fairly or reasonably towards their franchisees, the courts can look beyond the strict wording of a franchise agreement and utilise less known legal principles of equity in order to protect what the court considers to be the 'innocent' party. The impact of the European Union upon English law must also not be dismissed. It means that the continental notion of good faith now impacts on discrete local legislation. The Uniform Law of International Sales Act 1967, the Commercial Agents (Council Directive) Regulations 1993 and the Unfair Terms in Consumer Contracts Regulations 1999 all contain provisions of the concept of good faith.

---

304 The doctrine of 'Uberrima Fides' in insurance contracts and the concept of good faith in partnership and agency are notable exceptions.

305 *Interfoto Picture Library Ltd* v. *Stiletto Visual Programmes Ltd* [1988] 2 WLR 615 *per* Bingham LJ at 621.

306 Op. cit., Whittaker and Zimmerman.

307 Halsbury's Laws of England, Contract Vol. 9 No. 612.

308 *Hughes* v. *Metropolitan Rly Co* (1877) 2 App Cas 439; *Cross* v. *Cross* (1983) 4 FLR 235; *Stiff* v. *Cassell* (1856) 2 Kay & J. 279; *Maythorn* v. *Palmer* (1864) 11 Jur NS 230; *Nocton* v. *Lord Ashburton* [1914] AC 932; *Credit Lyonnaise Bank Nederland NV* v. *Burch* [1997] 1 All ER 144, CA.

309 Halsbury's Laws of England, Contract Vol. 9 No. 614.

310 (2006) EWCA Civ 1209. The House of Lords refused an application by the franchisor, Fleet Mobile Tyres, to appeal against a controversial decision by the Court of Appeal which allowed a franchisee to terminate its franchise agreement following a forced re-branding by the franchisor. Deducting more than the agreed 6% from the franchisee and changing its brand focus were such fundamental breaches in the opinion of the Court of Appeal that they entitled the franchisee to terminate.

It should perhaps not come as a surprise then that the Law Commission indicated in 1999 that it was considering a commercial code that would force English lawyers and judges to think about general legal principles such as good faith.[311] Whether such a code ever sees the light of day however, remains to be seen.

As regards franchising, perhaps the biggest difference between the civil concept of good faith and the common law de facto implementation of such a duty is that common law does not relieve franchisees from responsibility for their own actions.

The common law use of good faith does not have a significant impact upon the franchisor/franchisee relationship and does not significantly support the economic drivers that attract franchisors and franchisees to franchising or reduce the consequential risks to which they are exposed.

Over time, legislation has reduced common law's inherent sympathies towards 'laissez-faire' in commerce, to such an extent that one should acknowledge the existence of a loose and implied form of good faith in those EU member states that have a common law system. A good example of the equivalent of a duty of good faith being inferred into a franchise agreement under English law is provided by two cases. In *MGB Printing* v. *KallKwik*[312] the court implied an obligation on the franchisor to ensure that it provided services to the franchisee using reasonable skill and care on the basis of 'business efficacy'. In *Stream Healthcare* v. *Pitman*[313] the court ruled that services should be provided to the franchisee by the franchisor when reasonably required or requested. Section 13 of the UK's Sale of Goods Act can also be applied to reach a similar result, as it provides that services must be supplied with reasonable care and skill.

ii. The German approach to good faith

In Germany, the concept of good faith is extremely sophisticated and far **3.54**
reaching. It has 'been used as a convenient legislative peg on which to place a whole raft of developments by German courts to deal with perceived problems either technical or social ... It remains a "general principle" of German contract law ... but its effects have been worked out and elaborately classified into particular categories (known as *Fallgrupen*)'.[314] Each category takes a markedly

311 Law Commission Report No. 259 'The Law Commission Seventh Programme of Law Reform', 16 June 1999 at paras 1.12–1.16.

312 2010 EWHC 624 para 43.

313 [2010] EWHC 216 (Ch).

314 Whittaker, *The Draft Common Frame of Reference – An Assessment*, Commissioned by Ministry of Justice, Appendix II p. 138.

different approach. In order to understand how these various interpretations of the duty of good faith work together one commentator has broken them down into three different approaches,[315] 'collateral', 'restrictive' and 'adaptive'. This categorisation is subjective. More often than not a particular provision contains elements of two or three different approaches. A black and white categorisation is usually not possible. Most jurisdictions follow the 'restrictive approach' to a certain extent, whereas the 'collateral approach' is primarily confined to pre-contractual disclosure and most heavily used in countries which have a long-standing tradition of protecting the weaker party. An 'adaptive approach' is the least common and tends to be used in the circumstances in which the English law concept of 'frustration' of contract would be applied. There is an important distinction between '*Treu und Glauben*' (objective good faith) and '*guter Glaube*' (subjective good faith) which has to do with knowledge. *Treu und Glauben* has become an 'open' norm and although not a legal rule with specific requirements takes shape in the way it is applied.[316]

iii. The collateral approach to good faith under German law

3.55 In Germany, Article 311 BGB takes a 'collateral approach'. It imposes totally new obligations on the parties to the agreement and in doing so can reduce the risks to which both the franchisor and franchisee is exposed. In Germany, the franchisor has certain continuing implied obligations[317] which include advising, instructing and supervising the franchisee. The franchisor also has a fiduciary duty to refrain from interfering in the franchisee's business, especially if the franchisor is active himself in the same market area.[318] Thus encroachment and the adequacy of support are dealt with. The franchisee's main duty of good faith and fair dealing is to pay the royalty and other fees to the franchisor. In return he receives access to the franchisor's know-how, trademark equipment and so forth. Usually the franchisee will be obliged to purchase certain kinds of products from the franchisor. Even without a non-compete clause the business secrets of the franchisor will be protected by the franchisee's fiduciary duties to the franchisor.[319] Accordingly the risks to which the franchisor is exposed are reduced.

iv. The restrictive approach to good faith under German law

3.56 The duty of *Treu und Glauben*[320] takes a 'restrictive approach' to the concept of good faith. It requires that a franchisor is

315 Kroppholler, *Studienkommentar BGB*, 10th edition 2007, § 242 Rn. 1.

316 Hesselink, 2004, 289.

317 See Chapter 1. Introduction; BAG 30.05.1978, BB 1979, 325.

318 Op. cit., Petsche, Riegler and Theiss, 2004, pp. 3, 4.

319 BGH, WBl 1989, 131.

320 Article 242 of the German Civil Code ('BGB').

> bound to perform its obligations according to the requirements of good faith, ordinary usage being taken into consideration.[321]

It seeks to restrict the ability of parties to the agreement to exercise their agreed contractual rights in an unreasonable manner.

This means that the franchisor must exercise its discretion reasonably for it to be considered valid by the German courts. It can be a substantial fetter on the ability of the franchisor to act in the best interests of the franchise network as a whole rather than an individual franchisee. What may seem to be reasonable in the context of a bilateral relationship between the franchisor and a particular franchisee may be totally unreasonable in the context of a multilateral relationship between the franchisor and all of its franchisees. Article 138 BGB provides that a legal transaction which offends good morals (*contra bonas mores*) is void. It seeks to adjust the terms agreed by the parties to the agreement to new and unforeseen circumstances that arise so if the franchisor exploits the predicament, inexperience, lack of judgement or considerable (economic) weakness of the franchisee or gains a financial benefit which is clearly disproportionate to its performance the agreement will be void. Agreements which breach the duty of *Treu und Glauben* in Article 242 of the German Civil Code are therefore void under Article 138. This is clearly far from the English concept of *caveat emptor* and the freedom of the parties to negotiate the contractual terms of their relationship is thus limited.[322] The German courts have ruled that the following did not comply with the principle of good faith and fair dealing: lack of consideration;[323] if the franchisor's obligations are merely discretionary;[324] if the franchise system is based on pyramid selling or multilevel marketing systems;[325] if the franchisee is obliged to buy overpriced goods or an excessive amount of them;[326] or provisions granting the franchisor access to the franchisee's accounts twice a month (on the basis that this unduly restricts the franchisee's entrepreneurial freedom).[327]

v. *The adaptive approach to good faith under German law*

The prime example of the 'adaptive approach' is Section 313 BGB which **3.57**
stipulates that, if circumstances upon which a contract was based change

321 Raymond, Y., 1994, *Sourcebook on German Law*, 1st edition, Routledge Cavendish, pp. 304–305.

322 But see the decision in *Fleet Mobile Tyres Limited v. Stone and Another (Trading as Tyre 20)* (2006) EWCA Civ 1209 which shows that the English courts will not always implement the strict letter of a franchise agreement.

323 LG Paderborn NJW-RR 1987,S, 672f; LG Karlsruhe NJW-RR 1989, S. 822f.

324 BGH NJW-RR 2000, 1159ff.

325 OLG München NJW 1986, S.1880ff.

326 Giesler, Franchiseverträge, Rn. 60.

327 Giesler, ibid, Rn. 62.

substantially after the conclusion of the contract and if the parties would not have concluded the contract or would have done so on different terms if they had foreseen the change, adaptation of the contract can be claimed if a party cannot reasonably be expected to continue to be bound by the contract in its unaltered form. German courts will only make very limited use of the adaptive powers under this provision in situations in which the English courts might apply the concept of 'frustration'. It is used to save a contractual relationship rather than to invoke termination from the beginning. This has the potential to re-enforce the economic drivers that attract both franchisors and franchisees to franchising and reduce the consequential risks. The German concept of good faith has a substantial impact upon the franchisor/franchisee relationship and, as is evident from the above, reduces the risks to which both franchisor and franchisee are exposed and re-enforces the economic drivers that attract franchisees to franchising.

vi. The French approach to good faith ('bonne foi')

3.58 The restrictive, adaptive and collateral approaches to a duty of good faith can be found in differing combinations and degrees in most of the civil jurisdictions in the EU despite the fact that some of them have a very different historical perspective and approach to the concept of good faith. In France, although the general concept of good faith or *bonne foi* is found in Article 1134 of the French Civil Code, until the last quarter of the twentieth century it was substantially limited by the judicial view that 'if a person says something it is fair'.[328] Since the late part of the last century, the doctrine has become controversial amongst French lawyers.[329] Increasingly the legal profession seems to be advocating that it should be more interventionist and less 'liberal' to ensure more 'socially' appropriate outcomes, although some feel that this interferes too much with contractual freedom.[330] Other provisions of French law also contain notions of good faith.[331] The ascendancy of the interventionist school is evidenced by the fact that although the wording of the provision only requires good faith in the performance of the contract,[332] French courts have extended this obligation to

---

328 ('Qui dit Contractuel dit juste') Whittaker, The 'Draft Common Frame of Reference – An Assessment', Appendix II p. 139.

329 See Flour, J. and J. Aubert, 1994, *Les obligations, L'acte juridique*, 6th edition, pp. 289–90 and Demogue, R., 1931, 'Traité des obligations en general'.

330 Whittaker, The 'Draft Common Frame of Reference – An Assessment', Appendix II p. 139 and Mazeaud, 'La politique contractuelle de la Cour de Cassation', in *Libres Propos sur les Sources du Droit – Mélanges en l'honneur de Philippe Jestaz* (Paris: Dalloz-Sirey, 2006), p. 371.

331 Article 1135 of the Civil Code, Articles 111-1 and 113-3 of the Consumer Code and Article 330 of the Civil Code.

332 See www.legifrance.gouv.fr for a translation by Georges Rouhette, Professor of Law, with the assistance of Dr Anne Rouhette-Berton, Assistant Professor of English.

impose a duty of good faith at the earlier stages of pre-contractual negotiations,[333] the formation of the contract[334] and even its termination.[335] The notion of good faith has also been used by the French courts, in 'restrictive' and 'adaptive' and 'collateral' manners, to import morality and justice into contracts commonly by way of interpretation and implied terms. Although no judge can award an injured party more than the law allows under the contract, it is possible to prevent a party from exercising the fullest rights which the law would otherwise permit him to do. The French Courts have taken a 'restrictive approach' and held that a party who has acted in bad faith cannot require the other party to perform the contract as if nothing had happened or claim damages.[336] French courts have the power to terminate the contract when requested by the victim of the unfair behaviour.[337] In addition, a French court can prevent the breaching party from relying on a limitation or exclusion of liability clause when it acts in a deceptive manner.[338] A restrictive approach was taken by the courts when an open price term to be determined by the franchisor was deemed enforceable under French law only so long as it is proportional.[339]

An 'adaptive approach' to the concept of good faith comes into play when there is a change in circumstance which prevents a distributor from being competitive. The French duty of good faith requires the supplier in these circumstances to renegotiate the terms of the contract in order to allow it to be competitive.[340] A more recent case raised an important doctrinal debate around a possible duty of 'solidarity' between the parties (suggesting an adaptive approach to good faith) but the French Supreme Court failed to clearly state its position on the question.[341] One party claimed that good faith imposed an obligation to renegotiate, when a change in circumstances significantly altered the initial balance of the contract. The Supreme Court rejected the claim on the basis that the imbalance already existed when the contract was formed, so failing to clarify whether or not the courts have the power to vary the terms of a contract in such

333 Cass. com. 26 November 2003, Bull. civ. IV, No. 186, (*Manoukian* case).

334 Cass. com. 4 February 2004, no. 00–21.319: Juris-Data no. 2004–022354; D.2005, p. 151 – In this case the franchisor was held liable for failure to provide pre-contractual information necessary to allow the franchisee to enter into the contract with full knowledge of the facts.

335 Cass. com. 11 July 1978, no. 76–13752; Cass. com, 23 Mai 2000, no. 97–10553 – A franchisor may refuse to renew the franchise agreement, but should not let the franchisee believe that the agreement will be renewed whereby inducing him to make investments in the franchise.

336 Cass 1re ch. civ., 16 February 1999 no 96–21997, Bull. Civ. I no. 52 p. 34.

337 Benabent, A., *Les contrats spéciaux civils commerciaux*, Ed, 2008, no 456, p. 202.

338 Cass. com., 3 April 2001 no 98–21233, Bull. civ. IV, no. 70.

339 Cass. ass. plen. 1 December 1995 no. 91–19.653, Bulletin 1995 A. P. N° 8 p. 15.

340 Cass. com. 3 November 1992 CCC. 1993 no. 45 in a fuel supply agreement; Cass com. 24 November 1998, RTD civ. 1999, 98 in a commercial agency contract.

341 Cass. 1re civ., 16 March 2004, n° 01–15.804, D. 2004, p. 1754.

circumstances. There are no cases which suggest that the concept of *bonne foi* can be applied to prevent encroachment by the franchisor.

3.59 The French courts have also considered adopting a collateral approach to the duty of good faith. From the formation of the contract until the end of the contract, a franchisor has the continuing duty to support its franchisees with commercial and technical assistance.[342] A lack of advice and support during the start-up period can lead to the termination of the agreement.[343] The level of support which needs to be provided depends on the needs of each franchisee and therefore needs to be adapted.[344] The French concept of good faith has a substantial impact upon the franchisor/franchisee relationship and, as is evident from the above, reduces the risks to which both franchisor and franchisee are exposed and re-enforces the economic drivers that attract franchisees to franchising.

vii. Comparison of the different concepts of good faith

3.60 The German and French law of good faith supports the economic drivers that encourage franchisees to become involved in franchising and reduces the risks to which both franchisees and franchisors are exposed. However, the lack of a homogeneous approach in other member states greatly reduces the impact on cross-border franchising in the EU. Different jurisdictions have different ideas about what good faith is and the existence of a general doctrine of good faith does not guarantee a particular outcome. The German approach is influential in those jurisdictions in which it has a historical connection such as Greece[345] and

342 Philippe le Tourneau, *Les contracts de franchisage*, 2e édition, Litec 2007, no. 89.

343 CA. de Reims, 8 November 2000, no. 2000–152146, SARL L'âge d'or expansion.

344 CA. de Douai, 2e ch., 6 September 2007, no. RG: 06/177, Phildar-Le Donnant, D., 2007, p. 2303.

345 The Greek Civil Code (Article 288) in a verbatim translation of Article 242 BGB. Also, Article 200 of the Greek Civil Code reflects Article 157 BGB. The terms of the franchise agreement must not unduly restrict the freedom of the franchisee or allow the franchisor to exploit the need or inexperience of the franchisee to obtain for himself or a third person benefits which are clearly disproportionate to the franchisor's obligations (Article 179 of the Greek Civil Code). To do so would be contrary to public policy (Articles 174 and 178 of the Greek Civil Code). The parties must also act towards one another with loyalty, fairness and good faith (Article 281 of the Greek Civil Code). The franchisee may not assign its obligations to a third party (Article 715 of the Greek Civil Code) and must provide the franchisor with information about its business (Article 718 of the Greek Civil Code). The franchisor has a general obligation to assist the franchisee in the exercise of its activities and supply him with documents, brochures and other information in order to enable him to promote the franchise system (F.I.C. of Salonica 1671/71, JCL (1972) 52). In return, the franchisee has to pay the fees and royalties agreed and has a duty of confidentiality which continues after the termination of the agreement (Articles 200 and 288 of the Greek Civil Code as well as Law 146/14 on unfair competition). In the absence of a specific provision to the contrary in the franchise agreement, the franchisee is under an obligation not to compete with his franchisor during the duration of the agreement (Article 919 of the Civil Code F.I.C. of Athens 11486/80 JCL (1981) 50, 131).

Austria[346] and is also gaining influence over certain jurisdictions that were previously more influenced by French law, such as Italy[347] and the Netherlands.[348]

The French Civil Code has historically been the most influential civil code in Europe. Belgium was formerly directly subject to the French Civil Code but, perhaps due to German influence, has relied more on Article 1134 than the French.[349] The Spanish Civil Code Article 1258 provides that contracts give rise not only to obligations to accomplish what has been expressly agreed but also the results that are in accordance with good faith, custom and the law. Whilst Article 7, inter alia, provides that rights must be exercised in conformity with the requirements of good faith. Whittaker and Zimmerman observe that the relationship between member state laws is changing.[350] While Italian reports cite French decisions they also show the influence of the German doctrine of good faith. Belgian law often differs from French law despite its common historical roots. Dutch law has abandoned French law for German influences and Austrian law, whilst mostly following German law, nevertheless differs from it in some aspects of good faith. Although some jurisdictions, such as Poland,[351]

346 Although the Austrian Civil Code does not refer to '*Treu und Glauben*' it does refer to honest business usage which is used to determine the circumstances under which a contract has been concluded (ABGB § 863) and how they should be interpreted (ABGB § 914). The Austrian Supreme Court has used these two rules as a route to asserting that '*Treu und Glauben*' and reliance on honest business usage are ethical principles which are so generally acknowledged that they may be applied without having been included in the Civil Code. There are subtle differences from Article 242 BGB (Whittaker, S. and R. Zimmerman, 2000, *Good Faith in European Contract Law*, CSICL Cambridge University Press, p. 51).

347 Whittaker and Zimmerman, 2000, p. 53.

348 The old Dutch Civil Code reflected Article 1134 of the French Civil Code. However, the new Civil Code (Articles 6:248; 6:258 and 6.2) shows more of a German influence and has been described as 'the culmination of the statutory career of the concept of good faith'.

349 Op. cit., Whittaker, S. and R. Zimmerman, 2000, p. 52.

350 In the Netherlands, all contracts must be construed and performed in good faith (Article 6:248 Dutch Civil Code (the rules of reasonableness and fairness (*redelijkheid en billijkheid*)). However, a contractual provision of a franchise contract will only be set aside on the basis of 'good faith' in limited situations. For example, if the provision concerned is manifestly not in accordance with the character of the franchise contract, or if the franchisee could not be aware of the breadth of the provision concerned. It has been established by case law that in certain circumstances it may be contrary to good faith to invoke an exclusion of liability clause (Judgment of 19 May 1967, (Supreme Court) 'Hoge Raad' (HR), 1967 (Dutch Court Reporter) 'Nederlandse Jurisprudentie' (NJ) No. 261; Judgment of 20 Feb. 1976, HR, 1976 NJ No. 261; Judgment of 18 Dec. 1981, HR, 1982 NJ No. 71; Judgment of 7 May 1982, HR, 1983 NJ No. 509).

351 Polish Civil Code Art 56. Under Polish law, Art. 56 KC imposes a duty of good faith and provides that; 'an action produces not only those effects expressly intended by it, but also those arising from law, principles of community life and accepted customs'. Thus the parties to the franchise agreement are bound by not only the express contractual terms but also those implied by law. These obligations can be collateral, adaptive or restrictive. An example of the franchisor's collateral obligations is the requirement to provide the franchisee appropriate assistance both at the beginning of the relationship, in form of both initial and ongoing training. This obligation arises from the need to enable the franchisee to effectively exercise rights granted it in the franchise agreement (in particular the intellectual and/or industrial property rights). Without the franchisor's appropriate advice and guidance the franchisee would not be able to put the contractual provisions into effect (Bagan-Kurluta, Umowa franchisingu Monografie prawnicze, pp. 77, 79). Revealing or taking advantage of

the Czech Republic,[352] Finland,[353] Malta,[354] Bulgaria[355] and Portugal[356] follow the German lead as regards good faith; others, such as Denmark,[357]

---

the franchisor's trade secrets or obtaining them from an unauthorised person, if it may harm or endanger the entrepreneur's interest, is deemed to be an act of unfair competition (Art 11 § 1 ZNKU). Breach of this duty of confidentiality entitles the franchisor (Art. 18 ZNKU) 'to end the infringement and to prohibit further violation; to eliminate the consequences of the infringement by requiring the infringer to make an appropriate public declaration or declarations; pay damages according to general compensation rules and account for any profits made according to general unjustified enrichment rules'. Breach can lead to imposition of a fine or a custodial sentence of up to two years' imprisonment (Art. 23 ZNKU). Damages are limited to the actual loss directly resulting from the unsuccessful continued negotiations (Article 72¹ § 1 KC). The Polish Act Against Unfair Competition (ZNKU (*Ustawa o zwalczczaniu nieuczciwej knokurencji*)) may also apply.

352 Czech Civil Code Art 6–228(1). In the Czech Republic the doctrine of good faith means that a contractual obligation is enforceable only to the extent that it does not conflict with 'principles of fair dealing'. Given the lack of precedence in franchise matters, judges have wide discretion in defining whether or not a term is fair (Marc, P. and W. Theiss, 2004, 'Franchising in the Czech Republic', *International Journal of Franchising Law*, Volume 2, Issue 6 , pp. 25–34, 27).

353 Section 1 of the Finnish Unfair Business Practices Act (1978). In Finland, the duty of good faith is well protected. Section 36 of the Contracts Act (228/1929) imposes a duty of good faith and states that unfair contract terms may be adjusted or set aside if their application leads to an unfair result. The rest of the contract may also be adjusted or declared terminated under this provision, if it is unfair to enforce the rest of the contract after the adjustment of a contract term (Section 36 of the Contracts Act (228/1929)). The Act on Regulating the Contract Terms between Entrepreneurs (Section 38 of the Act on Regulating Contract Terms between Entrepreneurs (1062/1993)) provides that the use of an unfair contract term in contracts between business parties is prohibited, if one of the parties is in a weaker bargaining position and therefore needs protection (Hanna-Maija Elo, 'Finland' in: Getting the deal through – Franchise 2008, p. 37 para. 22). It is difficult to predict the way in which the courts will amend a contractual term to make it more reasonable (Petri Rinkinen, 'Franchising Legislation in Finland', www.franchising.fi/ukindex). In one case the courts declared it possible for a franchisee to terminate the franchise agreement on the grounds that the franchise business was no longer profitable, even though this was not a contractual ground for termination. It was also held to be unreasonable to charge franchising fees for a period once a franchisee had already ceased trading (Vaasa District Court judgment, dated 20.11.2003 in the case of *Kotipizza Oy* v. *Ekosmart Ky*). The Act on Regulating the Contract Terms between Entrepreneurs also prohibits unfair contract terms if one of the parties is in a weaker bargaining position (Hanna-Maija Elo, 'Finland' in: Getting the deal through – Franchise 2008, p. 37 para. 22). Unfair terms will be adjusted in accordance with the general rules of adjustment under the Contracts Act (Riitta Ahonen, 'Unconscionability and adjustment of unfair contract terms' (Master's book, University of Joensuu, 2004) p. 9) by the Market Court (Section 1(1).3 of the Market Court Act and Section 2(3) of the Act on Certain Proceedings before the Market Court) by way of an injunction and a conditional fine (Hanna-Maija Elo, 'Finland' in: Getting the deal through – Franchise 2008, p. 37 para. 22).

354 Maltese Civil Code Article 993.

355 Bulgarian law recognises a duty of good faith, which only has an impact on the ongoing franchise relationship. The parties to a franchise agreement or any other commercial agreement for that matter owe each other a duty of good faith when exercising their rights under the agreement. In addition, although the parties may freely determine the content of the franchise agreement and the parties' obligations, a contract may not contravene the mandatory provisions of law and the duty of good faith. Article 26(1) of the Bulgarian Obligations and Contracts Act stipulates that a contract which contravenes or circumvents the law as well as a contract which infringes the duty of good faith shall be null and void. This means that Bulgarian law recognises a restrictive approach to good faith as well as possibly an adaptive approach.

356 In Portugal, the ongoing relationship between franchisor and franchisee is governed by general contract law particularly the principle of good faith (Article 762 of the Portuguese Civil Code). This requires honesty of intention, the absence of malice, the absence of a desire to defraud or to seek an unconscionable advantage and a duty to supply to the franchisee all the information and cooperation which is needed for the performance of the agreement and discharge of the obligations by and of the other parties ('Outline of franchise issues in Portugal', questionnaire with answers provided by Jose Alves Do Carmo, associate, Barrocas Sarmento Neves).

Latvia[358] and Slovenia[359] make far less use of the doctrine. Only Romania has a franchise-specific duty of good faith.[360] No other EU member state franchise law contains such a provision. Given the quasi-fiduciary and long-term nature of the relationship between a franchisor and its franchisee, the flexibility of some form of duty of good faith may be appropriate. However, this needs to be tempered by a degree of commercially appropriate certainty. The wide range of ways in which the doctrine currently manifests itself in the EU and the resulting lack of certainty means that it can have a negative impact on franchising between member states.

(b) The regulation of vertical restraints

The EU law's focus on the public interest when regulating the vertical restraints **3.61** found in the franchisor/franchisee relationship means that it undermines the economic drivers that attract franchisors to franchising but it does potentially

357 The general starting point in Danish law is the principle of freedom of contract, but this general rule has been restricted over time, notably by the Danish Contracts Act (Law no 781 of 26.08.1996). The most important provision in relation to franchise agreements is Section 36, which provides that a contract may be found entirely or partly void if it, or specific clauses in it, are found to be 'unfair' to one of the parties. Although this duty of good faith is very rarely applied by the courts to contracts between business partners. It is an assessment based on the facts in each individual case. It may therefore be applied to modify the franchise agreement (Christensen, L.A., 2008, *Franchising in Denmark*, International Franchising, Kluwer Law International, p. 9). For example, although a franchise agreement may prohibit or restrict the right to transfer the franchise, the combination of an unusually long notice period and a prohibition against transferring the franchise may be considered unfair and, hence, be set aside (Sondergaard, *Franchising in Denmark*, p. 10).

358 Latvian Civil Code Art. 14. Section 14 of the Latvian Civil Law regulating leases is not restricted to real estate but also applies to franchise agreements (Article 2113 of the Latvian Civil Law). The franchisor is responsible for the quality of the rights granted to the franchisee (Article 2135 of the Latvian Civil Law). The franchisee is required to use the rights of the lease 'wisely and with care' (Article 2150 of the Latvian Civil Law) and has to exercise them according to the purpose of the intended agreement (Article 2151 of the Latvian Civil Law). This is interpreted widely, and includes preserving the franchise's distinct image. It means that the franchisor has the right to ensure that the franchisee complies with the franchisor's business and marketing concept ('Legal framework of franchising development in Latvia' on the website www. franchising%20.lv/new_site/lt/legislation_latvia. html). There is a general duty to fulfil all responsibilities and rights in good faith (Article 1 of the Latvian Civil Law).

359 Article 5 of the Slovenian Civil Code.

360 Article 3 of the Romanian Ordinance provides that a franchise agreement must include the principle of fairness, stating that it must reflect the interests of the members of the franchise network, as well as protect the franchisor's interests. This idea of fairness is further reflected in Article 7 of the Ordinance, under which the franchisor, in case of breach, has to notify the franchisee in writing of the breach and grant him a reasonable time to remedy the contravention of the franchise agreement. (The Canadian Provinces, China, South Korea and Malaysia impose a duty of good faith on both the franchisor and the franchisee which impacts upon what the franchisor is permitted to do during the relationship. In Canada all franchise agreements impose upon the parties a duty of fair dealing in its performance and enforcement (Alberta Franchise Act Section 7, The Arthur Wishart Act (Franchise Disclosure) 3(1); The Prince Edward Island Franchises Act Chapter 36 Bill 43 s.3; The New Brunswick Franchises Act s.3). In South Korea, both parties to a franchise transaction must exercise good faith in the performance of their duties and the Act enumerates several specific franchisor and franchisee duties (Fair Franchise Transactions Act, Chapter II Article 4). In Malaysia both the franchisor and the franchisee are under a duty of good faith to each other and must 'act in an honest and lawful manner' and 'endeavour to pursue the best franchise business practice of the time and place' (The Franchise Act 1998 Part IV Section 29 (1)).

support some of the economic drivers that attract franchisees to franchising. It does nothing to reduce the consequential inherent risks to franchisors or franchisees. All relevant EU member state anti-trust law is based on the concepts contained in Article 101 of the Treaty on the Functioning of the European Union (TFEU) (formerly Article 81 of the Treaty of Rome). Like all competition law it seeks inter alia to regulate vertical relationships to ensure that they do not contain terms which are against the public interest.

Article 101(1) of the TFEU prohibits:

> ... all agreements between undertakings, decisions by associations of undertakings and concerted practices which may affect trade between Member States and which have as their object or effect the prevention, restriction or distortion of competition within the common market ... [361]

These include attempts to directly or indirectly fix purchase or selling prices, sharing markets or sources of supply and applying dissimilar conditions to equivalent transactions with other trading parties, thus placing them at a competitive disadvantage. A franchise agreement incorporating measures restricting the ability of franchisees to trade freely potentially falls foul of Article 101(1). If an agreement falls foul of Article 101(1), Article 101(2) provides that the agreement will be void and that the parties may be subject to a substantial fine. The English decision in the *Crehan* case[362] makes it clear that if a franchisee suffers loss as a result of his franchise agreement breaching Article 101(1) of the Treaty of Rome, the franchisor may, as well as being liable for a fine, also be liable in damages to the franchisee.

3.62 The ECJ in *Pronuptia de Paris GmbH* v. *Pronuptia De Paris Irmgard Schilligallis* undertook the first detailed analysis of the application of Article 101 to franchise agreements.[363] It found that restrictions intended to protect the franchisor's know-how and to maintain the identity and reputation of the franchise network are not incompatible with Article 101(1),[364] in so far as they are 'indispensable' to achieving such protection. However, restrictions causing the division of markets between the franchisor and franchisee or between franchisees constitute an infringement of Article 101(1) as could attempts at price-fixing. Essentially the court's decision in *Pronuptia* drew a line between those clauses which it deemed to be necessary for the maintenance of the

361 See the EC Treaty Article 81(1).

362 Case C-453/99 *Courage Ltd* v. *Bernard Crehan* [2002] QB 507, [2001] All ER (EC) 886.

363 Case 161/84 *Pronuptia de Paris GmbH* v. *Pronuptia De Paris Irmgard Schillgallis* [1986] ECR 353, [1986] 1 CMLR 414.

364 Ibid., paras 16, 17.

identity and reputation of the franchise network and for the protection of intellectual property (IP) rights and know-how, and those clauses which it deemed to be prima facie anti-competitive such as those aimed at retail price maintenance. The court required Pronuptia to remove a clause requiring the franchisee not to harm the brand image of the franchisor by its pricing level.[365]

There are five decisions which have been instrumental in developing the attitude of both the ECJ and the Commission to certain provisions common to franchise agreements. These are the *Pronuptia* case discussed above, *Yves Rocher*,[366] *Computerland*,[367] *Servicemaster*[368] and *Charles Jourdan*.[369] Each involved a franchise agreement notified to the Commission under Article 101(3). The Commission took positive views of exclusivity, some forms of territorial restraints and post-term restrictions. However, retail price maintenance was not viewed favourably. In both *Pronuptia* and *Yves Rocher* there were clauses inserted into the agreement, at the Commission's request, allowing the franchisees to set their own retail prices. This is consistent with the ECJ's and Commission's general attitude to price-fixing, which will normally lose an agreement the benefit of the exemption under Article 101(3) from the prohibition in Article 101(1). In *Pronuptia* itself, the ECJ held that the fact that the franchisor had suggested prices to the franchisee would not in itself constitute a restriction upon competition, subject to the proviso that there had not been a concerted practice between franchisor and franchisee, or between the franchisees themselves as to the imposition of such prices. The network effect of anti-competitive vertical practices was considered by the courts.[370] However, it 3.63

365 Ibid, para. 12(c).

366 Case C-126/91 *Schutzverband Gegen Unwesen in der Wirtschaft* v. *Yves Rocher GmbH* [1993] ECR I-2361.

367 *Computerland Europe SA Franchise Agreements, Re*, Case IV/32.034, [1989] 4 CMLR 259.

368 *Servicemaster*, OJ [1988] L332/38, [1989] 4 CMLR 581.

369 *Charles Jourdan*, OJ [1989] L35/31, [1989] 4 CMLR 591.

370 *Delimitis* v. *Henniger Brai* (Case 233/89 [1991] ECR1–935). In this case the ECJ elaborated on network effect of anti-competitive vertical practices. A two-stage test was outlined to clarify when the network effect of vertical agreements was in breach of Article 81(1) of the Treaty of Rome (now Article 101(1) TFEU).

1. Having regard to the economic and legal context of the agreement at issue, is it difficult for competitors who may enter the market or seek to increase their market share to gain access to the national market for the distribution of beer in premises for the sale and consumption of drinks? Taking into account: number of outlets tied to the national producer in relation to the number of untied outlets; duration of the commitments entered into; quantities of the product to which those commitments relate; proportion between those quantities and the quantities sold by free distributors (Note: the fact that, in that market, the agreement in issue is one of a number of similar agreements having a cumulative effect on competition constitutes only one factor amongst others in assessing whether access to that market is indeed difficult.)

2. Does the agreement in question make a significant contribution to the sealing-off effect brought about by the totality of those agreements in their economic and legal context? The court will examine whether there are 'real concrete possibilities' for a new competitor to penetrate the bundle of contracts by acquiring a supplier already established on the market together with its network of sales outlets or to circumvent the bundle of contracts by opening new outlets.

If the examination above reveals it is difficult to gain access to the relevant market, then the court will assess the extent to which a particular agreement contributes to the cumulative effect on competition.

is submitted that its ambivalent attitude towards networks is of little relevance to franchising because (as detailed in the first franchise block exemption)[371] franchising is pro-competitive as it allows the entry of new competitors into the market.[372] If a franchise agreement prima facie contravenes Article 101(1), it may be able to take advantage of three exemptions. Firstly, Article 101(3) provides that the prohibition contained in Article 101(1) does not apply to agreements, decisions or concerted practices which contribute to improving production or distribution of goods, or promoting technical or economic progress whilst allowing consumers a fair share of the resulting benefit and not imposing unnecessary restrictions (i.e. restrictions unnecessary to the attainment of the above objectives) or otherwise enabling the parties to eliminate their competition to a substantial degree. Secondly, under the 'de minimis' principle an agreement will only infringe Article 101(1) if it has an 'appreciable' effect on trade.[373] The 1997 Notice on Agreements of Minor Importance (the 'Notice')[374] provides guidance on how parties are to evaluate whether their activities are having an appreciable effect on trade. Paragraph 9 sets out qualitative thresholds in relation to the aggregate market share of those involved. Article 101(1) will not apply to vertical agreements where the aggregate market share of participating undertakings is less than 15% of the relevant market.[375] Even if an agreement contains price fixing or territorial restrictions it will not necessarily lose the benefit of the exemption if the parties' aggregate market share does not exceed the relevant threshold. The Commission will not take action in these instances unless national authorities urge it to do so.[376] Thirdly, there is the Vertical Restraints Block Exemption.[377] Article 2 provides that Article 101(1) does not apply to 'agreements or concerted practices' entered into by undertakings operating at different levels of the production or distribution chain. Key points to note about the application of the Regulation are the exemption is only available to suppliers with a market share of less than 30%; it applies to both exclusive and non-exclusive arrangements; services and goods are included; multi-party agreements are covered; some vertical agreements between competitors at the same level will be exempt and

371 Regulation EU 40 87/88 op. cit., p. 12.

372 Commission Regulation (EEC) No. 4887/88 (OJ 1988 L 359/52).

373 The 'de minimis' principle was first introduced by the ECJ in the case of *Völk* v. *Établissements Vervaecke Sprl*, case 5/69 [1969] ECR 295.

374 Notice on agreements of minor importance which do not fall within the meaning of Article 85(1) of the Treaty establishing the European Community OJ [1997] C 372/13.

375 Commission Notice (EC) on agreements of minor importance which do not appreciably restrict competition under Article 81(1) of the Treaty Establishing the European Community (*de minimis*) OJ (2001/C 368/07).

376 Notice on agreements of minor importance which do not fall within the meaning of Article 85(1) of the Treaty establishing the European Community OJ [1997] C 372/13.

377 Commission Regulation (EC) No 330/2010 on the application of Article 101(1) of the Treaty Establishing the European Community to categories of vertical agreements and concerted practices OJ L 102. 23.4.2010 pp. 1–7.

suppliers may impose maximum price restrictions on buyers (but not minimum price restrictions). Franchising itself is not expressly mentioned in the Regulation, but franchise agreements are covered by the Regulation as they are vertical agreements. However, franchise and other vertical agreements cannot benefit from the exemption if they contain so-called 'hard-core' restrictions, as set out in Article 4 of the Regulation. These include inter alia certain territorial restrictions, price-fixing and restrictions on cross supply. Article 5 of the Regulation sets out 'black-listed' restrictions such as non-compete clauses. However, the inclusion of such clauses will not lose an agreement for the protection of the block exemption altogether; as long as the offending term is deleted or modified the exemption will still be applicable to the remainder of the agreement. Exclusive territories are not permitted, although a location clause is allowed. Franchisees must be free to actively promote their sales to end users wherever they are located. According to the Commission's current guidelines[378] on the application of the block exemption, the area outside which mobile outlets may operate can also be restricted.[379] During the term, non-compete clauses of more than five years are not permitted unless the franchisor is the landlord of the franchisee.[380] This will often not be the case. At the same time the Guidelines on the block exemption provide that a non-compete clause relating to the goods or services supplied under the franchise agreements, whilst not exempted under the block exemption will not be caught by Article 101(1) as long as the franchisor is not dominant in the market and the restraint is necessary 'to maintain the common identity and reputation of the franchised network'.[381] A post-term non-compete clause may be imposed if it relates to goods or services which compete with the goods or services dealt with by the franchisee under the terminated agreement; is limited to the premises from which the franchisee operated during the contract period; is indispensable to protect the franchisor's know-how; and is for a period of one year after termination. This may present a problem for some franchise agreements with terms that have post-termination provisions that relate to a 'territory'. If the franchisor cannot rely on the de minimis or small and medium-sized undertakings exemption then the post-restriction will be unenforceable. The franchisor will need to amend the agreement. Franchisees may not be restricted from selling the brands of particular competing suppliers. Quality specifications may, however, be laid down. The 30% market share test applies to the franchisor's market share. The franchisor's market share includes connected undertakings and relates to the sales value of the contract goods or services, together with competing goods or services. The benefit of the exemption will not be lost

378 Commission Notice – Guidelines on Vertical Restraints Official Journal C 130, 19.05.2010.
379 Ibid.
380 Ibid.
381 Ibid, para 200(2).

if the 30% share rises to 35%. If the market share rises above 35% however the exemption will only continue to apply for one further year. These two dispensations cannot be combined. Article 7 of the Regulation enables national authorities to withdraw the benefit of the block exemption where the effects of the agreements are felt in particular in that Member State and it constitutes a discrete geographic market. Where the geographic market is wider than a single Member State the Commission reserves the exclusive right to withdraw the benefit of the exemption.[382]

3.64 Antitrust laws properly regulate potentially anti-competitive aspects of franchising, although they can at times be overrestrictive and overlook some of the pro-competitive aspects of franchising. EU antitrust law erodes the economic drivers that attract franchisors to franchising as it places franchise chains at a disadvantage compared to corporate chains. Resale Price Maintenance is a hardcore restriction under the Vertical Restraint Block Exemption[383] and was ruled against in both the *Pronuptia* and *Yves Rocher* cases.[384,385] Concerted practices having as their direct or indirect object the establishment of a fixed or minimum resale price or a fixed or minimum price level to be observed by the franchisee are not permitted. They are considered to be 'per se' anti-competitive. Contractual provisions or concerted practices that enable the franchisor to directly establish the franchisee's resale price are also forbidden. Likewise other commercial practices that may have the same effect are prohibited. Examples include the franchisor fixing the franchisee's margin, fixing the maximum level of discount the franchisee can grant from a prescribed level, making the grant of rebates or reimbursement of promotional costs by the franchisor subject to the observance of a given price level, linking the prescribed resale price to the resale prices of competitors, threats, intimidation, warnings, penalties, delay or suspension of deliveries or contract terminations in relation to observance of a given price level. Measures to identify price-cutting franchisees, such as the implementation of a price monitoring system, or the obligation on retailers to report other members of the franchise network who deviate from the standard price level are also prohibited as are measures which may reduce the franchisee's incentive to lower the resale price, such as the supplier printing a recommended resale price on the product or the franchisor obliging the franchisee to apply a most-favoured-customer clause. Thus only the provision of a list of recommended prices or maximum prices by the

382 Commission Regulation (EC) No 330/2010 on the application of Article 101(1) of the Treaty Establishing the European Community to categories of vertical agreements and concerted practices OJ L 102. 23.4.2010.

383 Ibid Article 4(a).

384 [1981] OJ L8/49. [1988] CMCR 592.

385 Technically, it is possible to justify the retail price maintenance on the grounds of efficiency under Article 81(3), but this has proved to be theoretical rather than practical.

franchisor to the franchisee is permitted. In contrast to this, those businesses which have sufficient financial and management resources to expand their network on a corporate, rather than franchised basis are free of all these restrictions. EU competition law gives vertically-integrated corporate chains a monopoly of the ability to deliver a price promise that potentially leads to them being seen as a more consistent and reliable supplier and hence stronger brand than franchised brands that cannot deliver the same price consistency. This in turn disadvantages not only the franchisor but also their franchisees and ultimately consumers. This view is supported by the Chicago School of antitrust analysis, which acknowledges that retail price maintenance has positive, consumer-welfare enhancing aspects. In contrast to the EU's 'per se' approach, the Chicago School advocates an analysis of each individual retail price maintenance provision on its merits, under a 'rule of reason' approach which assumes the practice to be permitted until proven otherwise. The OECD has also recognised that, in the specific context of franchise agreements, retail price maintenance can have desirable effects. In its report on 'Competition Policy and Vertical Restraints: Franchising Agreements'[386] the OECD acknowledged that although

> vertical price restrictions are often suspected of being anticompetitive as well as undesirable for limiting the freedom of franchisees to set prices ..., such price restrictions may generate the same benefits as territorial restraints[387]

which it deems to be

> reducing intra-brand competition and giving franchisees more adequate incentives to provide desired levels of service, at least from a profit-maximising point of view.

It considers that if

> there is enough competition from other brands and retailers, either from competing franchises or from non-franchised rivals, franchisees will have incentives to provide the best possible bundle of prices and services ...

It suggests that

> by limiting intra-brand competition, and, accordingly, by increasing franchisees' expected profits, territorial restrictions (and vertical price restrictions) can give would-be franchisees greater incentives to invest in specific skills and effectively enter a market ... if they reduce intra-brand competition sufficiently.

386 OECD, 'Competition Policy and Vertical Restraints: Franchising Agreements'.

387 Ibid, p. 196.

It concludes that

> the stricter the restriction, the more intra-brand competition is reduced, increasing both the incentives to exert effort and the efficiency gains obtained.[388]

It then continues by dismissing the concern that vertical price restraints may be used by cartels to sustain collusion, explaining that such action is less of a risk in the context of franchising than with more loosely organised distribution arrangements. It states

> In the case of franchisees, price restrictions applied only to franchisees following relatively uniform methods of retailing are unlikely to block the development of new retailing methods and most likely will reduce intra-brand rather than inter-brand competition.[389]

It considers that

> price restrictions may promote efficiency by improving vertical co-ordination between franchisor and franchisees

And

> can be an alternative to territorial restrictions for encouraging franchisees to provide adequate efforts and services – an alternative that does not generate double mark-up problems. In any case, the better the alternatives available to consumers from other brands and retailers, the less likely that franchise control over services will increase profits but reduce consumer surplus.[390]

It concludes that

> As with territorial restrictions, price restraints can serve desirable functions most effectively when prices are well controlled. This supports sometimes not only 'suggested' or 'recommended' prices, accepted by some competition authorities for their usefulness in communicating information to consumers and franchisees, but also true price restrictions. Also, it should be noted that one possible anticompetitive use of price control often cited – sustaining a dealer cartel – is in fact a type of horizontal agreement and in principle could still be controlled as such even if the 'per se' ban on vertical price restrictions were lifted.[391]

---

388 Ibid.
389 Ibid.
390 OECD, ibid, p. 197.
391 Ibid.

Price (and non-price) vertical restraints are unlikely to be anti-competitive or reduce economic efficiency when the franchise system faces substantial upstream and downstream competition. Where there is sufficient inter-brand competition, vertical price restraints within franchise networks should not generally raise competition concerns. Such an approach could be implemented without creating uncertainty or resulting in high costs of analysis or litigation. The instances in which franchises face strong inter-brand competition are identifiable by clear criteria, for example market shares of the franchise in the upstream and downstream markets, the concentration of players in these markets, and evidence of dynamic market competition such as recent entry of the franchise in question, recent entry and growth of other upstream suppliers, retailers or franchisors providing substitutable products, and substantial fluctuations in market shares.[392] The rule of reason approach to price restrictions in franchising has now been embraced by the US courts, which for the previous 100 years held such restrictions to be 'per se' illegal.[393] In December 2006, the US Supreme Court granted review in the case of *Leegin Creative Leather Products, Inc* v. *PSKS, Inc.*[394] In this case a small manufacturer of ladies' accessories such as handbags and shoes required that all its retailers 'pledge' that they would comply with the pricing policy. One of the retailers acceded to the pledge, but then discounted the product line and was subsequently suspended as a Leegin distributor. The brief filed by the Federal Trade Commission (FTC) and the Department of Justice at the Supreme Court argued that

> because the effects of retail price maintenance can be either anti-competitive or pro-competitive depending on the facts in the given case, a per se rule is clearly inappropriate.[395]

The Supreme Court held[396] that the manufacturer's decision to agree with its retailer on the resale price of its products was no longer 'per se' unlawful, and was instead subject to the rule of reason. It is interesting for present purposes to consider the arguments advanced by Leegin. In support of its argument it suggested that minimum resale pricing can result in pro-competitive effects, such as: in giving retailers the incentives to provide necessary service levels; promoting product sales; eliminating free riding by rival retailers; and inducing capital and employment investments which are needed for innovation in the

---

392 OECD, ibid, p. 186.

393 Since the 1911 US Supreme Court decision in *Dr. Miles Medical Co* v. *John D. Park & Sons Co*, 220 U.S. 373 (1911).

394 (No. 06–480) 171 Fed. Appx. 464.

395 Brief of the United States as Amicus Curiae supporting petitioner, paras 3–4.

396 (No. 06–480) 171 Fed. Appx. 464.

development of new products. Leegin argued that because these effects promote inter-brand competition, maintenance of the 'per se' rule is inappropriate. Whilst it may be the case that the US legal environment is not directly analogous to that pertaining in the EU, the OECD and most economists and scholars recognise that retail price maintenance may enhance distribution efficiencies and increase competition. It is therefore reasonable to suggest that, in order to improve the regulation of franchising in the EU, the Commission should change its absolutist rule on retail price maintenance and carefully consider the important role which a uniform pricing policy plays in assisting franchisors (which as stated above, tend to be small or medium sized companies) to compete effectively with large integrated companies. To this end the Commission should follow the OECD's suggestion for a 'simple rule', such as the block exemption, which allows franchisors to use retail price maintenance in certain circumstances. Happily the guidance notes to the new Vertical Restraints Block Exemption[397] suggest that the Commission may have been influenced by the OECD's suggestion. This makes it more likely that efficiency arguments may be run with more success in whatever forum they are being pursued, be it the Commission, national competition authorities, EC or national courts, all of which have the ability to apply Article 81(3) directly. Indeed there have been other signs of a greater willingness on the part of the Commission and EC courts to look at the economic realities of retail price maintenance in a more favourable light, such as in the Court of First Instance's judgment in the *GSK Spain* case[398] on the issue of restrictions designed to limit parallel trade in the pharmaceutical area. The Court of First Instance annulled the Commission's decision fining GSK on the grounds that the Commission had failed adequately to consider the specific legal and economic context of the distribution of the pharmaceuticals. Nevertheless, whatever the Commission's view of retail price maintenance as expressed in the Vertical Restraint Block Exemption Guidelines, it remains an object-type restriction and therefore hard to justify.

(c) The impact of unfair competition and confidentiality law

3.65 The Unfair Competition and Confidentiality laws impact upon the economic drivers and consequential inherent risks in some jurisdictions but there is a lack of homogeneity which dilutes this impact on cross-border franchising in the EU. In addition to a franchisee's good faith duty not to compete with its franchisors, all jurisdictions recognise that as a fundamental part of the bargain between a franchisor and its franchisees the franchisor can, during the term of the relationship and for a period after its termination, require that a franchisee

397 Commission Notice – Guidelines on Vertical Restraints Official Journal C 130, 19.05.2010.

398 Case T-168/1 *GlaxoSmithKline* v. *Commission*, judgment 26 September 2006.

should refrain from competing with the franchisor or misusing the franchisor's confidential information. In some jurisdictions such as England, it is a purely contractual term which can be absolute during the term of the agreement but must be reasonable in terms of time and scope after termination. In others such as Germany,[399] the non-compete and confidentiality obligations during the term are imposed by law as is the post-term right to use confidential information. An obligation of confidentiality is imposed upon the franchisee during the term under Article 18 of the German Unfair Competition Act. This stipulates that the use of samples, technical guidelines (drawings, models and templates) for the purpose of competing with the disclosing party is prohibited. It is also prohibited to disclose such material to third parties without authorisation. In case of violation, the Courts can impose a fine or give the violator a prison sentence of up to two years. All other confidential information is protected by the implied duty to protect the franchisor's interest[400] which is yet another example of the collateral approach to good faith.

A number of other member states take a similar approach.[401]

(d) The impact of prohibited terms

3.66 The prohibition of terms by unfair contract terms provisions does tend to support the financial drivers that encourage franchisees to become involved in franchising and reduce some of the inherent consequential risks they expose themselves to. Although the duty of good faith has the greatest impact upon the fairness of contractual terms in franchise agreements, some consumer laws have a similar impact. The Unfair Contract Terms Directive (1993/13/EEC) means that there is a generally common approach to unfair contract terms in the EU. These provisions can apply to franchise agreements. Although there is no general legal requirement in the UK for a franchise agreement to be either fair or reasonable, the Unfair Contract Terms Act 1977 ('UCTA') provides that a franchisee who has signed a standard form franchise agreement can challenge a term that excludes or limits liability for breach of contract and the clause will only be enforceable if it is fair and reasonable. This will change if the Unfair Contract Terms Bill ('UCTB') becomes law in the UK. It will allow individuals and micro-businesses (businesses employing nine or fewer staff) to challenge any standard term of franchise agreements if the clause in question has not been negotiated between the parties and is not the main subject matter of the

399 Article 18 of the German Unfair Competition Act.

400 Sections 675 (1), 611, 241 (2) BGB.

401 For example Italy: Under the Italian Franchise Law franchisees and their employees are subject to a duty of strict confidentiality about the franchising business, during and after the term of the agreement (Law of 6 May 2004, No. 129 Article 5.2).

contract or the price.[402] In the UK franchisees also enjoy an implied term that any goods purchased from the franchisor are of satisfactory quality.[403] This implied term can be excluded by contractual terms provided that such exclusions are reasonable.[404] However, the Unfair Contract Terms Act 1977 provides that a franchisee who signs a standard form contract can challenge an unreasonable exclusion or limitation of its rights. Likewise, in Ireland, when a franchisee purchases goods from its franchisor there will be an implied term that they will be of satisfactory quality and fit for normal use.[405] Articles 305–310 of the German BGB which deal with unfair contract terms are at least partially applicable in an business to business relationship[406] such as a franchise agreement. Very often the franchisee is considered to be the 'weaker party'[407] and is protected by the unfair contract terms provisions.[408] Over the years, the courts have developed a list of clauses which are null and void because they violate unfair contract terms provisions. These prohibited terms include those that leave the franchisor's contractual performance duties entirely to his discretion;[409] restrict the entrepreneurial freedom of the franchisee unless they are necessary to ensure the franchisor's corporate identity;[410] empower the franchisor to reduce the size of the franchisee's territory or end its exclusivity if the franchisee is not able to reach a certain target and without giving the franchisee the opportunity to make up for missed targets;[411] and provide the franchisor with short notice termination rights. A period of notice of three month is null and void[412] whereas a notice period of one year or a little less is not.[413] This means that many terms that are commonly used in common law franchise agreements are void (and account for some of the 'softer' language in the five German franchise agreements considered in the sample in Chapter 2 above). Effectively the Courts 'negotiate' for the franchisee, where the franchisee itself cannot, as failure to comply results in the provisions being struck out completely rather than applying a blue pencil approach. Sections 339, 340 of the German Civil Code permit the imposition of penalty clauses that take effect if a party is

402 Many franchisee businesses are micro-businesses. The new law will not affect existing franchise agreements or franchise agreements with a total transaction value of more than £500 000 (including the initial franchise fee and all ongoing royalties).

403 Section 14 Sale of Goods Act 1979.

404 Section 6(3) Unfair Contract Terms Act 1977.

405 Sections 12 to 15 of the Sale of Goods Act 1893 as amended by the Sale of Goods and Supply of Services Act 1980.

406 Palandt BGB, Überbl. v. § 305, Rn. 11.

407 §§ 305 to 310 BGB, formerly the German Unfair Contract Terms Act.

408 Sections 307, 308 and 309 of the Civil Code.

409 BGH NJW-RR 2000, 1159ff; Giesler, Franchiseverträge, Rn. 111.

410 Giesler, ibid, Rn. 108.

411 BGH NJW 1984, S. 1182ff.; Giesler/Nauschütt, Franchiserecht, Chapter 9, Rn. 84 and 89.

412 BGH NJW-RR 2003, S. 1635, 1638 ('Apollo-Optik').

413 Giesler, *Franchiseverträge*, Rn. 119.

in breach of the contract.[414] The penalty must not be excessive and if it is agreed upon in a standard form agreement (see the above) it must not be unduly burdensome in terms of Section 307 of the Civil Code.[415] If agreed upon in standard contract terms a contract penalty can only apply to negligent or intentional non-performance.[416] A clause that seeks to impose an excessive penalty is void. Germany is not the only EU jurisdiction that takes this approach.[417] However, not all jurisdictions take this approach to franchisees. The ECJ, in *Francesco Benincasa* v. *Dentalkit Sr.*,[418] confirmed that under Italian law franchisees are self evidently not consumers and that they should not therefore be regulated by consumer laws. If, as inexperienced individuals dealing with sophisticated corporations, they require protection, such protection should be crafted specifically for them. The imposition of consumer laws on franchising is inappropriate and risks damaging the legitimate interests of both franchisors and franchising as a whole.

4. The termination of the franchisor/franchisee relationship

On the termination of the franchisor/franchisee relationship the legal environment in the EU does not support any of the economic drivers that encourage franchisors to become involved in franchising and does not significantly reduce any of the risks that franchisors are exposed to. However, it excessively reduces the risks to which franchisees are exposed to and over-re-enforces the economic drivers that encourage them to become involved in franchising. **3.67**

(a) The contractual right to terminate a franchise agreement

Termination is the ultimate means by which both franchisor and franchisees can enforce their contractual rights against each other and so support the economic drivers and reduce the consequential inherent risk in franchising. However, the right to terminate is regulated in a number of different ways in EU member states. In the event that a party breaches the contractual terms of the franchise agreement, subject to the nature of the breach and the impact of **3.68**

414 Grüneberg, in: Palandt BGB, 69th edition 2010, Vorb. § 339 Rn. 1ff.

415 Ibid, Rn. 12.

416 Palandt BGB, § 309 Rn. 39.

417 In Portugal, the Law of General Contractual Clauses (LGCC) (Decree no. 446/85 of 25 October as amended) also applies to all standard form contracts which have not been negotiated by the parties and cannot be contracted out of (Santos Cruz/Krupenski, IBA Legal Practice Division International Franchising Committee Newsletter, May 2007, p. 24). Even if the parties have chosen a foreign law to govern the agreement, the LGCC will apply where the agreement is more closely connected with Portugal than any other country. This means in practice that whenever the franchisee, its assets and the establishment are located in Portugal, the LGCC will apply with the consequence that a certain set of clauses is prohibited such as: exclusion to the right of compensation; or any provisions which goes against the principle of good faith. Clauses which do not comply with the LGCC are null and void.

418 Case C-269/95 *Francesco Benincasa* v. *Dentalkit Srl* [1997] ECR I-3767.

the concept of good faith, employment law and commercial agency law, all EU member states allow the party not in breach to terminate the agreement and/or sue for damages. In the UK franchisees and franchisors have the right to terminate the franchise agreement if the other party has committed a repudiatory breach or has breached a term of the agreement which is of major importance. Franchise agreements will commonly contain clauses preventing the franchisor competing with the franchisee's business during the term of the franchise agreement. Such a condition of the contract would be regarded as a term of major importance. A repudiatory breach is one that goes to the root of the contract and shows the breaching party's intention not to honour its obligations under it. When it is implied, the test is whether the franchisor has acted in 'such a way as to lead a reasonable person to the conclusion that he does not intend to fulfil his part of the contract'.[419] It must be established that the breaching party has made it clear beyond reasonable doubt that it no longer intends to perform its part of the franchise agreement, otherwise the franchisee may be in breach of the contract itself.[420] Following such a breach the party not in breach has the choice of whether to treat the contract as continuing (affirmation of contract) or to bring the contract to an end '*ab initio*' (as if it had never been in force), but it must exercise this right within a reasonable time of the breach or else it will be held to have affirmed the franchise agreement.[421] However, the party not in breach can take a period of time to make its mind up about what to do.[422] There is no prescribed way to accept the breach[423] but it is usually done by the party not in breach communicating to the other party that it is terminating the contract.[424] A repudiatory breach can occur before the time for performance (an anticipatory breach). If the franchisee affirms the contract, such affirmation is irrevocable and the party cannot go back upon the decision not to terminate the contract.[425] Where there has been a breach of a term which goes to the root of the contract and amounts to repudiation the party not in breach may terminate the contract '*ab initio*'.[426] For the breach of a lesser term, however, the party's right to terminate will depend on the consequences of the breach.[427] If the party not in breach accepts the breach, the contract will be terminated for the future as from the moment the acceptance of the breach is communicated to the breaching party. The contract is treated as having come

---

419 Devlin J in *Universal Cargo Carriers Corporation* v. *Citati* [1957] 2 QB 401, 436.

420 *Mersey Steel and Iron Co* v. *Naylor, Benzen & Co* (1884) 9 App Cas 434.

421 *Cox Toner (International) Ltd* v. *Crook* [1981] IRLR 443.

422 *Per* Rix LJ in *Stocznia Gdanska SA* v. *Latvian Shipping Company (no 2)* [2002] EWCA Civ 889.

423 *Vitol SA* v. *Norelf Ltd* [1996] AC 800; *Stocznia Gdanska SA* v. *Latvian Shipping Company* [2001] 1 Lloyds Rep 537.

424 *Heyman* v. *Darwins Ltd* [1942] AC 356.

425 *Bentson* v. *Taylor Sons & Co* [1893] 2 QB 274.

426 *Poussard* v. *Spiers and Pond* [1876] 1 QBD 410.

427 *Hong Kong Fir Shipping Co Ltd* v. *Kawasaki Kisen Kaisha Ltd* [1962] 1 All ER 474.

into existence (obligations and performance that occurred before the breach are not affected) but that it has come to an end discharging future obligations.[428] Courts interpret contractual termination clauses in light of the commercial purpose that was intended to be served by the clause.[429] For a non-repudiatory breach, the franchisee can only recover loss that is suffered at the date of termination and not future loss.[430] For a repudiatory breach, damages for future loss can be recovered.[431] Where the terms of the franchise agreement provide that the right of termination for a specified breach can be exercised upon notice given to the breaching party, such notice must be sufficiently clear and unambiguous to constitute a valid notice.[432] Breach of the franchise agreement will usually lead to an award of damages. It is possible for franchise agreements to provide for specific sums to be payable on the occurrence of certain breaches (liquidated damages). In principle such clauses are only valid[433] so long as they do not constitute a penalty designed to enforce the offending party to compensate the innocent party for its loss[434] and are a genuine pre-estimate of loss.[435] In Germany there is a distinction between serious and less serious breaches. A party can terminate the franchise agreement without notice depending on the particular circumstances and an objective evaluation of the interests of the franchisor and the franchisee.[436] This is similar to the distinction between material breach of a substantial term and other breaches. Termination without notice is reserved for irremediable material breaches of substantial terms. Non-payment of the franchise fee is deemed remediable and therefore requires notice unless the payment is more than six weeks overdue.[437] The period can be longer or shorter depending on the amount outstanding.[438] Although termination without notice is possible in some circumstances,[439] termination is rarely without some form of notice. The party in breach must be given a clear opportunity to remedy the breach.[440] Termination must take place within a reasonable time of notice.[441] The Federal Supreme Court has ruled that two

428 As *per* Lord Wilberforce in *Johnson* v. *Agnew* [1979] 1 All ER 883 at 889.

429 *Ellis Tylin Ltd* v. *Co-operative Retail Services Ltd* [1999] BLR 205; *Mannai Investment Co Ltd* v. *Eagle Star Life Assurance Co Ltd* [1997] AC 749; *Investors Compensation Scheme Ltd* v. *West Bromwich Building Society* [1999] All ER (D) 23.

430 *Financings Ltd* v. *Baldock* [1963] 2 QB 104.

431 *Yeoman Credit Ltd* v. *Waragowski* [1961] 1 WLR 1124.

432 *Allam & Co Ltd* v. *Europa Poster Services Ltd* [1968] 1 WLR 638.

433 *Cellulose Acetate Silk Ltd* v. *Widnes Foundry* [1933] AC 20.

434 *Dunlop Pneumatic Tyre Co* v. *New Garage and Motor Co Ltd* [1915] AC 79.

435 *Philips (Hong Kong) Ltd* v. *A-G of Hong Kong* (1993) 61 BLR 49; these were first laid down by Lord Dunedin in *Dunlop Pneumatic Tyre Co Ltd* v. *New Garage and Motor Co Ltd* [1915] AC 79.

436 Palandt BGB, 69th edition 2010, § 314 Rn. 7.

437 KG Berlin BB 1998, S. 607ff (‚Burger King').

438 Giesler/Nauschütt, 2nd edition 2007, Franchiseverträge, Rn. 253.

439 Palandt BGB, §314 Rn. 7.

440 § 314(2) BGB; KG Berlin BB 1998, S.607ff ('Burger King').

441 § 314(3) BGB; Palandt BGB, §314 Rn. 10.

months can be reasonable[442] but after eight months the right of termination is deemed to have been waived.[443] This is not dissimilar to the English concept of waiver.

3.69 In France, any material breach by the franchisor may lead to the termination of the contract by the franchisee. Jurisprudence provides useful examples of what amounts to a material breach. Failure to enable the franchisee to use the trademark,[444] the transmission of specific know-how and the permanent provision of assistance of the franchisee are considered as fundamental to a franchise agreement. A material breach of one of these conditions by the franchisor may lead to the termination of the agreement.[445] An abusive unilateral modification of the financial conditions of the contract,[446] breach of the territorial exclusivity granted to the franchisee[447] and abandonment of the concept proposed to the franchisee[448] have also all been held to be material breaches that justify termination of the franchise agreement by the franchisee.[449] All jurisdictions allow termination for breach on reasonable notice.[450]

442 BGH NJW 1994, S. 722ff.

443 BGH NJW 1985, S. 1894, 1895 ('McDonalds').

444 – Not grant any right to use the trademark to the franchisee – Paris Court of appeal, 20 May 1988, 20 ans de jurisprudence de la franchise, n° 26.
– Abandoning the trademark and gives priority to another trademark – Rouen Court of appeal, 9 November 2000, Lettre européenne des réseaux commerciaux, 1er trim 2001.
– Not defending the trademark against infringements or does not renew the registration of the trademark – Versailles Court of appeal, 9 December 1987, Cah. Dr. Entr. 1988, 2, 42.
– Drastically changing its brand strategy – Commercial Court of Paris, 3 October 2000, L'Off. de fr. N° 32, p. 124.
– Failing to support or pass on his know-how to the franchisee – Cass. Com. 24 May 1994 no 92–15846, Contracts. Conc. Consom. 1994 No. 190.
– Not passing on his know-how to the franchisee – Cass. Com. 24 May 1994 no 92–15846, Contracts. Conc. Consom. 1994 No. 190.

445 Paris Court of appeal, 20 May 1988, 20 ans de jurisprudence de la franchise, n° 26.

446 Rouen Court of appeal, 13 October 1994, Jurisdata 050353.

447 Cass. Com., 27 March 1990, Bull. Civ. IV n° 96.

448 Paris Court of appeal, 7 June 1996, Jurisdata 022009.

449 However, the practicalities of termination are far more mechanistic in France and as a matter of principle, termination must be declared by a court. However, there are two exceptions to this principle of judicial termination. Firstly, the *Cour de cassation* has been ruling since 1998 that a party may unilaterally terminate the agreement 'at his own risk' without going to court when the breach is such that it makes it impossible to continue with the agreement (Cass. Civ. 1e, 13 October 1998, Bull I n° 300, p. 207). Secondly, a termination clause may be included in the franchise agreement stating that it can be terminated for breach without going to court.

450 In Belgium the general rules for the termination of an agreement apply to franchising agreements. Fixed-term agreements can terminate due to effluxion of time, whilst agreements of indeterminate length (which include fixed-term agreements that have been renewed several times) can only be terminated by giving reasonable notice. Breach of contractual terms by one of the parties entitles the other to terminate the agreement and claim damages (Belgian Civil Code Article 1184). Only a serious breach of the franchise agreement will entitle the other party to immediately terminate the franchise agreement, without having to give a reasonable term of notice. However, the parties to the agreement can provide for automatic termination when certain conditions or events occur (Cass., 19 April 1979, Pas., 1979, I, 981; Court of Commerce Brussels, 22 November 1985,

Distinctions are made between material breaches of substantial terms and lesser breaches in terms of the consequences of the breaches, particularly the required notice period and the right to remedy the breach.[451]

Other member states make similar distinctions.[452]

(b) The impact of good faith on termination

The duty of good faith can limit a franchisor's ability to terminate in some jurisdictions.[453] In Germany termination for good cause may result in the **3.70**

BRH, 1987, 120 and Court of Commerce of Neufchauteau, 10 December 1985, BRH, 1987, 123). The death or bankruptcy of one of the parties will result in the termination of a franchise agreement as it is a contract *intuita personae*, unless there is a clause granting successors a right to continue the franchise agreement. Greek law also requires that termination must be on reasonable notice, taking into account the particular circumstances. A period of 6 to 12 months will usually be considered reasonable (Yanos Gramatidis, 'Greece' in: Getting the deal through – Franchise 2008, pp. 46–51). In Estonia, the franchisor may terminate the contract by giving reasonable notice unless otherwise prescribed by the franchise agreement (Law of Obligations Act s.195 subsection 3 ('ordinary termination')). Termination without notice is permissible, in particular if the terminating party cannot reasonably be expected to continue performing the contract due to the nature of the breach (Law of Obligations Act s.196 subsection 1 ('extraordinary termination')). The agreement must be terminated within a reasonable time of the notice. In Malta, if the franchise agreement expires, the franchisor may be obliged to renew it under a duty of good faith (Maltese Civil Code Art 993 See Chapter 9 p. 150), if the franchisee has substantially invested in the franchise and has not been able to amortise that investment. In Latvia, the general principle of *pacta sunt servanda* applies to franchise agreements, i.e. the franchise agreement can be terminated by mutual agreement or for the reasons set out in the franchise agreement. However, an agreement may also be terminated unilaterally if 'excessive loss' is suffered by one party (for example the price of the purchase (lease) is less than half of its actual value) and *mala fide* of the other party can be proven (Articles 2170, 2042, 2043 of the Latvian Civil Law). In Austria, as a Franchise Agreement is a continuing obligation it can be terminated 'for an important reason at anytime'. No party can be forced to continue the contractual relationship if it has lost faith in the other party or the other party is in default (Section 918(2) and *per analogiam*. Sections 1117 and 1162 ABGB).

451 For example, under Slovakian law (Section 345(1) of the Slovakian Commercial Code 513/1991 amended on 7 January 2002) although a fundamental breach gives rise to a right to terminate on notice, a non-fundamental breach entitles the party in breach to a reasonable time in which to remedy the breach. (The parties may deviate from these presumptions subject to there not being a substantial imbalance between their rights to terminate.) This distinction also usually impacts upon the rights of the party not in breach and the precise moment from which termination is effective (i.e. from the date of termination or 'ab initio'). Likewise, as in Greece (Yanos Gramatidis, 'Greece' in: Getting the deal through – Franchise 2008, p. 50 para. 24) termination for good cause can also lead to the party in breach being under an obligation to pay damages (Article 673 of the Greek Civil Code and Article 330 of the Greek Civil Code), although wrongful termination will generally result in damages (F.I.C. of Athens 401/77, JCL (1971) 200).

452 Polish law takes a similar approach and distinguishes between termination of an agreement with effect from the date of termination ('*Wypowiedzenie*') (cancellation) and material breach of substantial obligations which might give rise to repudiation of the agreement (ab initio) ('*Jednostronne odstąpienie od umowy*'; Art. 491 KC; Bagan-Kurluta, Umowa franchisingu Monografie prawnicze, p. 125). The parties can expressly stipulate both circumstances in which the rescission is permissible (Bagan-Kurluta, ibid, p. 128), and a period during which they have the right to rescind the contract (in consideration for paying an agreed amount of money) (Art. 395 KC). However, unlike English and Irish law, freedom of contract is limited by the principle of good faith which requires the franchisor to allow the franchisee an opportunity to remedy the failure. Only if the franchisee refuses to perform its obligations, may a franchisor terminate the franchise agreement with immediate effect (Polish Franchise Organisation under www. franchiseportal.pl). The right to terminate the contract for material breach cannot be excluded (see 'Civil Law in Poland', on the website of the Commercial Law Center Foundation of Poland, www.prawo.org.pl). Estonian law recognises not only the right to terminate a contract

franchisor having to pay compensation to the terminated franchisee. If the upfront franchise fee is not just a contribution towards the franchisor's costs in incorporating the franchisee into the system, but also a fee for the know-how and goodwill of the franchise and for other ongoing costs incurred by the franchisor, the upfront franchise fee is partly repayable as far as there has been only partial consideration.[454] According to the principles of good faith,[455] upon termination there is also an obligation on the franchisor to repurchase any stock the franchisee was contractually committed to buy from the franchisor,[456] unless the franchisor has terminated for a material breach of the franchise agreement.[457] The French concept of good faith takes a restrictive approach to the termination of a franchise agreement and determines that a reasonable notice period needs to be given. As a general rule, the longer the franchise agreement has run the longer the notice period will have to be. L. 442–6 I of the Commercial Code prohibits a sudden termination of a well-established business relationship and obliges the terminating party to give sufficient notice to the other party in order to allow it to reorganise its activity and to find alternative solutions. Failing that, the terminating party may be held liable and may have to pay damages to the other party. Wrongful termination generally gives rise to damages. In the UK good faith has no impact upon termination.

---

on reasonable notice (Section 116, section 195 and section 196 of the Estonian Law of Obligations) (unless otherwise prescribed by law or the contract) (Estonian Law of Obligations Act Section 195(3)) as well as the right to terminate for fundamental breach (what amounts to fundamental breach is listed in Section 116(2)(1–5) of the Estonian Law of Obligations) without notice (Estonian Law of Obligations Act Section 196(1)), although a set procedure must be followed (Estonian Law of Obligations Act Section 106). Termination must be within reasonable time and is effective from the date it takes place (Estonian Law of Obligations Act Section 195(2)). The legal remedies available include damages (Estonian Law of Obligations Act Sections 115 and 127 to 140) and rescission (Estonian Law of Obligations Act Section 111). In Denmark, the franchise agreement may be cancelled if a party is in substantial breach of the contract (Sondergaard, *Franchising in Denmark*, p. 10). There is no legislation specifically dealing with termination. If the question is not addressed in the franchise agreement, each of the parties may terminate the agreement on 'ordinary' notice which is typically three months.

453 In Dutch law the right to terminate for breach is subject to the principle of reasonableness and fairness (Article 6:248 Dutch Civil Code). Termination contrary to good faith is null and void, although if the contravention of the duty of good faith is merely inadequate notice, the Court may convert the termination into a valid one by altering the date on which termination would take effect. Termination can also be on grounds not provided for in the agreement (Article 6:258 Dutch Civil Code) as well as breach of contract (Article 6:265 Dutch Civil Code). Case law on dealers/distributorship contracts suggests that if the franchisee has made important investments in the franchise which he has been unable to write off and the franchisor terminates only for technical reasons and is unwilling to negotiate fair termination conditions, the Dutch Courts might protect the franchisee against such termination (compare Judgment of 26 January 1989 Court of Appeal Amsterdam, 118, KG, 1989). Termination of the franchise agreement on inadequate notice gives rise to damages equivalent of the expected net loss of profits of the franchisee over the appropriate notice period.

454 OLG Frankfurt NJW-RR 1995, S. 1395ff; Giesler, Franchiseverträge, Rn. 272.

455 Section 242 of the German Civil Code.

456 Op. cit., Giesler, Rn. 276.

457 Ibid.

(c) The impact of employment law on termination

Many EU jurisdictions struggle with the concept of franchising. They find it hard to reconcile the obligation of a franchisee to follow the franchisor's system and directions with the independence of a stand-alone business. As a consequence they apply aspects of employment law to protect franchisees. Despite the fact that the franchisees invest in their own business they are deemed to be employees. This has an impact on the franchisor's ability to terminate the agreement for breach. This is perhaps due to the fact that some jurisdictions have extremely strict employment laws and some employers are suspected by the courts of using a veil of franchising to camouflage what is nothing more than an employment contract, and so escape the rigorous controls of the law. Certainly a small number of franchises do look rather 'thin' with little or no know-how and offering little or no training and support. However, this is not true of the majority of franchises. This underlying distrust of the description of individuals as franchisees is very evident in Germany, where franchisees cannot be contractually restricted more than is necessary to ensure the proper functioning of the franchise system.[458] If the franchisee is restricted more than this, he/she can be viewed as an 'employee in disguise'[459] and so considered as an employee of the franchisor, placing on the franchisor all of the consequential obligations, particularly the liability to pay social insurance and the obligation to report all staff members to the Inland Revenue, health insurance funds and social security institutions. There is also an obligation to deduct income tax and social insurance contributions of the employee's salary. This can be expensive. A franchisee is seen as an employee in terms of Section 23 of the German Termination Protection Act (KSchG), if the franchisee is financially dependent on the franchisor and in need of protection like an employee. Simply adhering to the corporate identity of the franchise system does not mean that the franchisee will be considered as an employee.[460] As long as the franchisee is in control of its own business and can, for example, determine its sales prices, employ its own staff, sell the products and services for its own account and in its own name and determine its own working hours it will not be considered to be an employee.[461] The more the franchisee's day to day conduct is regulated by the franchisor the more likely it is that the franchisee will be considered as employee. This is especially so if the franchisor is the only supplier/customer of the franchisee and if the franchisee has no employees of its own.[462] A franchisee can be self-employed even though the franchisee is contractually committed to fit out the premises according to the franchisor's instructions, needs the 3.71

458 BGH, Beschluss vom 4.11.1998 – VIII ZB 12–98 (so-called Eismann-Entscheidung).

459 Giesler, *Franchiseverträge*, Rn. 165ff; Flohr, DStR 2003, 1622–1626; Skaupy, NJW 1992, pp. 1785, 1789f.

460 Flohr, BB 2006, pp. 389, 390.

461 Ibid.

462 BGH NJW 1999, S. 218, 220 (‚Eismann').

permission of the franchisor to refurbish the premises, is tied to the franchisor as regards the goods it sells/uses in his/her business, must use the advertising material provided by the franchisor, must employ such numbers of individuals so as to be able to keep the business open during the statutory opening times. However, these guidelines are not conclusive. The Courts always stress that each contract is individual and all circumstances of the individual case must be considered.[463] French law also follows the same approach as Germany. If the franchisor interferes in the franchisee's business beyond what is necessary to ensure the proper functioning of the network the franchisee may be regarded as an employee especially where the degree of supervision is such that the franchisee appears to be subordinated to the franchisor, regardless of what is stipulated in the agreement.[464] Even where the franchisee is not subordinated to the franchisor the provisions of the French Employment Code may also apply[465] if the franchisee's business consists essentially in the sale of goods; there is a supply exclusivity or quasi-exclusivity to the benefit of the franchisor and the franchisee carries on his business in premises made available or approved by the franchisor under its conditions and prices. If the franchise is deemed to be an employee, the franchisor may be prosecuted for illegal employment and required to pay social security contributions for the past three years and late payment penalties; the statutory minimum salary to the franchisee; holidays, overtime and dismissal compensation. A similar approach is found in several other member states such as Austria,[466] Finland,[467] the Netherlands,[468]

463 BGH NJW-RR 2003, S. 277, 280; BAG NJW 1997, 2973ff.

464 Cass. Soc., 17 April 1991 no 88–40121, Dr. Soc. 91, p. 516.

465 Article L. 7321–2 of the Labour Code – Cass. Soc., 4 December 2001 no 99–41265, Société France Acheminement, JCO G 2002, p. 1241.

466 OGH, RdA 1980, 136. In addition, if the Austrian Labour Law Court considers an individual franchisee to be a 'quasi-employee' it will assume and exercise jurisdiction over disputes arising from the Franchise Agreement (Op. cit., Petsche, Riegler and Theiss, 2004, p. 3). If a franchisee loses his ability to make independent business decisions it might be seen as a violation of 'bonos mores' and therefore void the whole Agreement.

467 Finnish employment legislation can also affect the franchisor–franchisee relationship (Hanna-Maija Elo, 'Finland' in Getting the Deal Through – Franchise 2008, p. 37 para.22) where a single private person or entrepreneur enters into a franchise agreement or where the franchisee is a company but owned and run totally by one person. This is because the franchisor is giving orders and instructions to the franchisee and the latter is getting 'paid' by the franchisor through the issuance of its service fees which are only paid back in parts to the franchisor in the form of franchise fees.

468 In the Netherlands franchisees may be treated as employees by both the courts and the tax authorities. Pursuant to Article 7:610 of the Dutch Civil Code, there is a contract of employment and franchisees may be considered to enjoy employee protection rights (such as protection against unfair dismissal, minimum wages and minimum holidays), if the franchisee has to perform the work personally, the franchisor is obliged to pay the franchisee and there is a relationship of supervisory authority between the franchisor and the franchisee. Fortunately the Courts rarely take this view. However, the tax authorities apply similar criteria and are more inclined to assess a case on the factual circumstances than the civil law judges. It is therefore more likely that a franchise agreement will qualify as an employment agreement from a tax perspective than under employment law. The tax authorities put particular emphasis on the franchisee's ability to have the work performed by someone else. In order to get confirmation that a franchise agreement does not qualify as an employment relationship from a tax law perspective, the franchisee can file an application for a Declaration of Income Tax

Greece,[469] Sweden,[470] and the Czech Republic.[471] This approach clearly reduces the franchisor's ability to terminate for breach and so undermines the economic drivers that encourage it to become involved in franchising and does not reduce the consequential inherent risks the franchisor is subject to. The English and Scottish courts have not considered the case, but it is considered unlikely that they would see bona fide franchisees as employees.[472]

(d) The impact of commercial agency law on termination

The EU Commercial Agency Directive[473] provides that a commercial agent is a person acting in the name of and for the account of its principal and so clearly does not therefore apply to franchising. Merely labelling an agent a franchisee will not enable the principal to circumvent the provisions of the Directive as they focus on the form rather than the substance of the relationship. There are **3.72**

Status (*Verklaring Arbeidsrelatie (VAR)*) with the Dutch tax authorities. A VAR will safeguard the franchisee of payment of employee insurance contributions and wage tax contributions.

469 Greece takes a similar approach and under certain circumstances, a franchisee may be identified as an employee on the basis that certain elements arising from a contract for independent services may be regarded as 'work' and thus fall into the scope of Article 648 of the Greek Civil Code (Yanos Gramatidis, 'Greece' in: Getting the deal through – Franchise 2008, pp. 46–51).

470 Given Sweden's strong tradition of protecting the rights of employees, it is not surprising that the application of employment law to franchise agreements was one of the most controversial issues in the 1987 official report (Chapter 3 p. 41). The topic was not within the scope of the Government Report, but reappeared in the discussions in the Cabinet on the proposal that was to be put forward to the Parliament. However, the matter in question on both occasions was not whether or not a franchisee can be an employee but the right for employees of the franchisee to negotiate directly with the franchisor. Such a measure was rejected by the Ministry (Prop. 2005/06:98 pp. 18–19). He concluded that the question of employees' influence arising under such similar conditions should be discussed separately (ibid). Thus, the franchisee's employee cannot negotiate directly with the franchisor (Lagen (1976:580) om medbestammande i arbetslivet. Prop. 2005/06:98 pp. 9–10).

471 In the Czech Republic, the franchisee is considered to be a 'controlled party' and so the franchisor can be liable for its actions (Marc and Theiss, 2004, pp. 25–34) even though the franchisee is not its employee. The franchisor can avoid liability only if it can show that the action or transaction would have been undertaken by an independent party acting with due care (ibid., Marc and Theiss, pp. 25–34).

472 *Ready Mixed Concrete (South East) Ltd* v. *Minister of Pensions and National Insurance* [1968] 2 QB 497 concerns the definition of a contract of service rather than a contract for services. The company had engaged an independent haulage contractor to deliver the concrete to customers but that contract was terminated and RMC decided to introduce a scheme whereby concrete was delivered by owner-drivers working under written contracts. The owner-drivers entered into a hire purchase agreement with Readymix Finance Ltd to purchase a lorry but the mixing equipment on the lorry was the company's property. The driver paid for the hire-purchase of the lorry, and its maintenance. Therefore, because the driver had assumed at least part of the economic risk under the contract, he could not properly be said to have a 'contract of service' and hence was not an employee. The court established that a contract of service exists if these three conditions are fulfilled:
(i) The servant agrees that, in consideration of a wage or other remuneration, he will provide his own work and skill in the performance of some service for his master.
(ii) He agrees, expressly or impliedly, that in the performance of that service he will be subject to the other's control in a sufficient degree to make that other master.
(iii) The other provisions of the contract are consistent with its being a contract of service.

473 Council Directive (EC) 86/653 on the Coordination of the Laws of the Member States Relating to Self-Employed Commercial Agents [2004] OJ L 382.

numerous examples of this.[474] However, some jurisdictions go much further than this and apply commercial agency law to franchises by analogy as a matter of course. In Germany, if the franchise has the characteristics of an agency or distributorship, it will be treated accordingly. However, the courts go much further than this and use the doctrine of analogy to extend the rights of a commercial agent to franchisees. Commercial agents are entitled to compensation upon termination of the agency agreement.[475] The Federal Supreme Court has held that a distributor may also claim this compensation upon termination.[476] Several of the lower courts (including decisions by the Higher Regional Courts) have ruled that this provision can be applied by analogy to certain forms of franchise agreements too.[477] As a result, franchise agreements which integrate the franchisee into the sales organisation of the franchisor are likely to attract compensation claims. Such a claim must meet two basic criteria. Firstly, like a commercial agent, the franchisee must be obliged to leave his established clientele to the franchisor. Secondly, the franchisor must be able to use the franchisee's customer base upon the termination. If the franchisee cannot identify his clientele by name or address (as is usually the case with a walk-in fast food business) a market analysis showing that there are regular customers is necessary to support a claim.[478] The actual scope of compensation differs depending upon the average profit of the franchisee in the past and how far the profits are related to the established clientele that the franchisee leaves to the franchisor.[479] Compensation is limited to the average annual profit of the last five years.[480] A discount is made to the 'general pulling power of the brand'. Compensation has to be claimed within one year of termination.[481] A simple letter is enough to preserve the right. Section 90a of the Commercial Code, that deals with an agent's rights on termination regarding restrictive covenants is also applied by analogy to franchising.[482] There are many examples of

---

474 E.g. under Danish law Act no. 272 of 2 May 1990 on Commercial Agents and Travelling Salesmen ('Handelsagentloven'); Op. cit., Christensen, *Franchising in Denmark*, pp. 18–19 and in Malta Articles 49 to 56 Commercial Code.

475 Section 89b of the Commercial Code (Germany).

476 BGH NJW 1985, S. 3076, 3077; 1983, S. 2877, 2878.

477 LG Frankfurt am Main 10.12.1999, Az: 3/8 0 28/99 (http://www.kuestner-van-manteuffel-wardeck.de/htm/de/html/Uebersicht.pbp?aid=17158idp=52); Giesler, 2002, Rn. 145; Köhler, NJW 1990, pp. 1689–97, 1689; Haager, NJW 2002, pp. 1463–75, 1471.

478 Köhler, ibid, pp. 1689–97, 1693.

479 Giesler, ibid, Rn. 148.

480 Section 89b (2) Commercial Code (Germany).

481 Section 89b (4) Commercial Code (Germany).

482 See below.

commercial agency law being applied to franchising.[483] The German approach is unsurprisingly also found in those member states which are heavily

483 'Aquella' (Federal Court of Justice, judgment of 12 November 1986 – I ZR 209/84 (DB 1987, p. 1039, 1040)). The plaintiff has been a franchisee for mobile mineral water distribution franchise 'Aquella'. The franchise contract contained a post-contractual non-competition clause for the period of two years, without providing for financial compensation. The plaintiff applied for the declaration that (i) the non-competition clause is *contra bonos mores*, and, in the alternative, that the non-competition clause is only valid if the defendant pays compensation in the amount of annual earnings for two years. The Federal Court of Justice dismissed claim (i), but approved the claim for compensation (ii). Even though the court clearly indicated that the provisions governing commercial agents (Art. 84ff. HGB) do not apply for franchise contracts automatically, the court held that the application of Art. 90a sec. 1 clause 3 German Commercial Code (hereinafter: HGB) is applicable by analogy in the case under consideration. Art. 90a sec. 1 clause 3 HGB provides for a waiting allowance if a commercial agent is obliged to omit business activities by a non-competition clause. According to the court, the obligation to pay a waiting allowance would serve to cover the agent's costs of living for the period of time he is contractually bound to the non-competition clause. The court pointed out that, because of the economic dominance of the franchisor, franchisees would often be forced to accept non-competition clauses. According to the court, the situation of the franchisee in this particular case was comparable to the commercial agent's position as presumed in Art. 90a HGB: The defendant specified the way its marks had to be used and the routes the franchisees had to take. Vis-à-vis the customers the franchisee did not disclose his legal independence. For the customers, it did not become clear that each franchisee acted in its own name and on its own behalf. Advertising measures were directed and executed by the franchisor. The court stated that this would give rise to the assumption that the situation under consideration comes as close to the legally protected interests of a commercial agent that the application of Art. 90a sec. 1 clause 3 HGB by analogy must be regarded as necessary. 'Chain Contracts between Franchisor and Franchisee' (Federal Court of Justice, judgment of 17 July 2007 – VIII ZR 59/01 (NJW 2002, p. 1554f)). The appellant, a former franchisee of an US car rental franchising system, has been sued by its German subsidiary for disclosure of information, and for cease-and-desist from using the company's marks after the company decided not to renew the franchise contract after 12 years of contractual relationship. The company gave notice of the non-renewal only two weeks before expiration of the contract. By way of counter-claim the appellant (franchisee) applied for (i) the declaration that the plaintiff and its mother company are obliged to pay all damages which have arisen out of the non-renewal of the franchising contract causally determined by not having granted a termination period of at least one year, and (ii) disclosure of all advertising allowances paid by automotive manufacturers and importers to the plaintiff and/or its mother company. The Federal Court of Justice ordered the respondents to pay damages which have arisen out of the non-renewal of the franchising contract without granting a termination period of six months. The court held that Art. 89 HGB, according to which a period of cancellation of six months is required when the contractual relationship lasted for more than five years, is applicable to the franchise contract at hand. The court stated that commercial agency law can be applied by analogy to franchise agreements if the fundamental idea of a specific commercial agency law provision applies for the franchise agreement at stake because the interests of the franchising parties are identical to those governed by the respective commercial agency law provision. The court argued that Art. 89 HGB serves to grant a protection period within which the commercial agent may seek a new principal, or a new field of business. Such a period would be a necessity for a franchisee, too, if its business operations were tailored to the sales and distribution concept of the franchisor. In the case, the franchisee was obliged to use the standard contract templates of the franchisor, its marks, and to employ a standard design for the business premises as well as for the outfit of its employees. According to the court, these obligations resulted in a comprehensive integration into the franchisor's distribution system which would not allow for readjustment on short notice. Even though the franchising contract has been entered into in 1984 only for a period of three years, and subsequently been renewed for periods of two or three years, these 'chain contracts' would have to be regarded as one contractual relationship if the terms have not been altered, or subject to negotiations, before the renewal has been agreed on. Thus the contract must be regarded as having been entered into 1984, not the date of the most recent renewal (December 1993), which would have resulted in a cancellation period of three years. 'Beer Delivery Contract' (Federal Court of Justice, judgment of 15 December 1993, VIII ZR 157/92). In the decision the Federal Court found that Art. 89a HGB (termination for causes) is applicable by analogy to

influenced by German law, such as Portugal[484] and Austria.[485] However, this approach can also be found in certain other member states that are not so heavily influenced by German law.[486]

3.73 Clearly this approach substantially restricts the franchisor's ability to terminate for breach and so undermines the economic drivers that attract franchisors to

---

franchise contracts. However, since 2001 Art. 314 German Civil Code provides for a general regulation, thus Art. 89a HGB has since become meaningless.

484 In Portugal, the agency law also applies to franchise agreements in respect of termination and compensation, unless any foreign law referred to in the contract is more favourable for the franchisee (Article 38 of Decree No. 178/86 of 3 July as modified by Decree No. 118/93 of 13 April). This means that unless the foreign law offers even more protection, the Portuguese Agency Law will apply irrespective of a valid choice of foreign law. Where the performance of the franchisee is similar to that of an agent and the franchisor maintains the franchisees' customers after the termination of the agreement (Supreme Court of Justice, proc. No. 06a4416, dated 9 January 2007), franchisees are entitled to compensation upon termination due to their loss of goodwill. This view is endorsed by commentators (Antonio Pinto Monteiro, Direito Comercial – Contratos de Distribuicao Comercial, Coimbra, 2002, pp. 163–70 and L. Miguel Pestana Vasconcelos, O Contrato de Franquia (Franchising), Coimbra, 2000 pp. 95–8). Compensation will be calculated on the basis of lost profits, lost investment opportunities and employee obligations, etc. although the franchisee may require that they are calculated upon the basis of the average monthly income it received during the preceding year multiplied by the period of the Agreement still to run. Some commentators suggest that if this provision applies, it will entitle franchisees to compensation upon termination of the Agreement, even if it was terminated for good cause and carried out in accordance with the terms of the Agreement. The theory is that this compensation is on account of the franchisee's loss of goodwill (Article 33 of Decree 178/86 of 3 July as modified by Decree Law 118/93 of 13 April). A franchisee may also be able to successfully claim compensation for wrongful termination. A franchisor will only evade this liability, if the contract terminates by way of effluxion of time in accordance with express notice provisions or if there are none, on reasonable notice (which can be between one month and a year depending upon the duration and 'importance' of the Agreement) and good cause.

485 Austrian commercial agency law likewise applies to franchising by analogy (Section 24 (formerly Section 25) of the Austrian Commercial Agent Act ('Handelsvertretergesetz', in short 'HVertG') OGH 10.4.1991 WBl 1991, 332; OGH 5.5.1987 – *Stefanel* – ÖBl 1987, 152; OGH 21.10.1987 NRSp 1988/3 1; Liebscher/Petsche, *Franchising in Österreich*, p. 79) and on termination of the franchise agreement entitles the franchisee to compensation in respect of the clients that it brought into the franchise system. The franchisee is also entitled to be reimbursed those investments he was obliged to make by the franchise agreement. However this claim will be limited in regard to the degree of amortisation unless it terminated the Agreement itself or if the Agreement was novated or transferred to a third party (Section 454 Austrian Trade Law ('Handelsgesetzbuch', 'HGB')).

486 For example, Spanish agency law (Law 12/1992, of 27 May, regulating Agency Agreements complies with the obligations imposed on EU member states by Directive 86/653/EEC of 18 December 1986 on the coordination of the laws of the Member States related to self-employed commercial agents) can also be applied to franchising by analogy (Sections 9.1 and 10.1 of Law 12/1992, of 27 May, on the Agency Agreement). Franchisees can be awarded compensation for termination of their agreement based on the theory of unfair enrichment (*Vid.* STS, Sala de lo civil, Sección 1ª, 22 de marzo de 1988 (RJ 1988\224)), although there seems to be a distinct lack of certainty. Although recent judgments of the Spanish Supreme Court (STS, Sala de lo civil, Sección 1ª, 26 de octubre de 2005 (RJ\2005\8147), STS, Sala de lo civil, Sección 1ª, 27 de octubre de 2005 (RJ\2005\8043), STS, Sala de lo civil, Sección 1ª, 5 de febrero de 2004 (RJ\2004\639)) have refused to apply Section 28 (which sets out the entitlement to compensation upon termination) of the Agency Law by analogy, other judgments (STS, Sala de lo civil, Sección 1ª, 21 de noviembre de 2005 (RJ\2005\7677), STS, Sala de lo civil, Sección 1ª, 18 de marzo de 2004 (RJ\2004\2147), STS, Sala de lo civil, Sección 1ª, 26 de abril de 2004 (RJ\2004\2714), STS, Sala de lo civil, Sección 1ª, 20 de mayo de 2004 (RJ\2004\2786)) have taken the contrary view. The rationale usually proposed for extending the compensation beyond agents to other distributors and franchisees is that: (i) all these agreements belong to a general category which can be called

franchising and does not reduce the risks to which the franchisor is exposed. In France, the courts have not shown any signs of applying commercial agency law to franchising. However, in some member states, such as the UK,[487] it is clear that the agency regulations do not apply to franchising.

(e) Post-termination restrictive covenants

In Germany, the law of commercial agency is applied by analogy. This means that the right to restrict a franchisee after expiry of the franchise agreement comes at a price with the franchisee being entitled to compensation. The franchisee may agree to post-termination non-compete obligations for a maximum of two years after termination. In return the franchisee can claim compensation[488] under the commercial agency laws which are applied by analogy as detailed above.[489] The obligation to pay compensation can be avoided by the franchisor if it waives the non-compete in writing at least six months before the end of the contract period. If the franchisor gives less than six months' notice of the waiver it is required to pay compensation for each month difference between the mandatory period of six months and the actual notice period given.[490] If the franchise agreement is terminated for material breach, the non-breaching party can waive the non-compete restriction on one month's written notice.[491] Any contract terms excluding these rights of the franchisee are null and void.[492,493] In France, whereas courts are very strict regarding 3.74

'distribution agreements'; (ii) all these distributors (agents, exclusive distributors and franchisees) are distributing not their own products but those of the principal, and (iii) they are all charged with finding new customers for the products. However, these common features are not present in all these agreements in equal measure, so depending on the circumstances of each particular case the right to compensation may or may not be recognised by the court. Although compensation is mandatory for agency agreements in Spain, it is optional for distribution and franchising agreements, due to the principle of party autonomy (Section 1255 of the Spanish Civil Code). Compensation may be excluded. Thus, if the right to compensation by way of analogy is recognised for franchisees, franchisors can expressly exclude compensation in their franchise agreement.

487 Also Latvia and Slovakia: Article 45 of the Latvian Commercial Law. A franchisee is considered an entrepreneur whose franchise is included in the franchisor's distribution network and who is obliged with regard to the franchisor to sell the latter's goods on its own behalf and at its own expense. A similar position exists in Slovakia where the general view seems to be that provisions concerning commercial agents in the Commercial Code do not apply to franchise agreements (Frolkovic, P. and L. Biksadsky, 2005, 'Franchising in Slovakia', *International Journal of Franchising Law*, Volume 3, Issue 2, pp. 3–11) because franchisees generally enter into contracts in their own names and on their own accounts.

488 Section 90a (1); Baumbach/Hopt, HGB, § 90a Rn. 18.

489 BGH NJW 1987, S. 612, 613; Flohr, 3rd edition, Franchisevertrag, p. 193; Giesler, Franchiseverträge, Rn. 149ff; OLG Celle, BB 2007, p. 1862; also see above.

490 Hopt, in: Baumbach/Hopt, *HGB Kommentar*, 33rd edition, 2008, § 90a Rn. 23; Section 90a (2) German Commercial Code.

491 Section 90a (3) Commercial Code.

492 The right to claim for appropriate compensation according to Section 90a does not exclude the right to claim for compensation upon termination under Section 89b of the Commercial Code – Hopt, in: Baumbach/Hopt, *HGB Kommentar*, 33rd edition, 2008, § 90a Rn. 18.

493 In Austria, there are limits to post-term termination clauses deriving from antitrust law. The Austrian courts generally recognise the possibility of the application of agency legislation to franchise agreements by analogy

non-compete covenants binding employees, they take a less stringent view on non-compete undertakings by non-employees, notably franchisees. For such covenants to be enforceable they must be limited in time and/or space and the restriction must be proportionate to the legitimate interests of the franchisor.[494] It is possible that in the future the French courts follow the German example and rule that in order for non-compete covenants to be enforceable against individuals the franchisor must pay them compensation, as is the case with employment agreements.[495] However, this is not currently the case.[496] In 2002, the Supreme Court ruled that a franchisee was an ongoing business,[497] which prevented the franchisee from claiming any compensation. The restrictions on post-termination restrictive covenants detailed in the EU Vertical Agreements Block Exemption[498] obviously have some impact, although it is greater in some

for situations where the franchisee has a similar position to an agent. As post-term non-competition provisions under Austrian agency law are null and void (§ 25 HVertG), it is possible that depending on the structure of the contractual arrangement under the franchise agreement, a post-term non-competition clause may be void for that reason.

494 Cass. Com., 4 January 1994 n° 92–14121, D. 1995, p. 260; Cass. Com., 16 December 1997 n° 96–10859, Contr. Conc. Consom., March 1998, n° 39 ; Cass. Civ. 1e, 11 May 1999 n° 97–14493, Contr. Conc. Consom., October 1999, n° 137.

495 Cass. Soc., 10 July 2002, Dr. Soc., November 2002, n° 11, p. 949.

496 Cass. Com., 1 July 2003, JCPE, n° 22, 27 May 2004, p. 869.

497 Cass. Civ. 3e, 27 March 2002, Bull. III, n° 77, p. 66.

498 EC Regulation No 2790/1999, OJ L 336, 29.12.1999 on the application of Article 81(3) of the Treaty to the categories of vertical agreements and concerted practices OJ L 336, 29.12.1999. For example, the laws of the Czech Republic also provide that although the parties can decide the grounds on which the franchise agreement can be terminated, post-termination restrictions must comply with the limitations set forth in the Vertical Restraints Block Exemption and not exceed one year after the termination of the agreement. Finnish law (Section 38 of the Contracts Act (228/1929)) provides that a contract which unreasonably prevents or restricts competition by imposing an obligation not to engage in a certain activity or not to conclude an employment contract with a person engaging in such activity will not bind the party which has accepted the obligation (Section 38 of the Contracts Act (228/1929)). General EU competition law principles also apply (Petri Rinkinen, 'Franchising Legislation in Finland', www.franchising.fi/ukindex). In Greece, after the expiration or termination of the franchise agreement, a franchisee may no longer take advantage of the franchise system (Section 719 of the Greek Civil Code) and the franchisee's freedom to compete is subject to the law on unfair competition (Article 919 of the Greek Civil Code as well as to Law 146/14 on Unfair Competition). Covenants not to compete are *prima facie* valid unless they are contrary to public policy (Article 178 of the Greek Civil Code). They will be held admissible by the courts as long as the non-compete provisions may be considered reasonable and in accordance with the general principles of law, such as good faith, ethical behaviour and protection from the abuse of rights (Yanos Gramatidis, 'Greece' in: Getting the deal through – Franchise 2008, p. 46). Since there is no definition of what is 'reasonable' in this context, the courts will determine this question on a case-by-case basis. As long as a covenant not to compete is of limited duration and applies only to a specific restricted territory, it should be valid under Greek law (F.I.C. of Athens 11486/80 JCL (1981) 50, 131, F.I.C. of Athens 14284/81, JCL (1982) 144, F.I.C. of Heraklion 158/86, JCL (1987) 38). The franchisor, on the other hand, is under the obligation to purchase some products and goods back from the franchisee. The purchase price in this respect will be the stock value of the product. However, there is no obligation to purchase all remaining goods, especially a large stock of inventory (Dimitros Stefanos Kostaki, 'Termination of a franchise agreement and adherent obligations' in Franchise Success under www.franchise-success.gr). Confidential information is protected in Greece by an implied duty of confidentiality which continues after the termination of the contract and which is based on the principles of good faith, commercial practice and the special nature of the franchise agreement (Articles 200 and 288 of the Greek Civil Code as well as Law 146/14 on Unfair Competition).

jurisdictions than others. In the UK provisions in franchise agreements that limit the franchisee's right to operate a competing business after the termination of the franchise agreement will be void unless they are reasonable.[499] The burden of proving that a restriction is reasonable lies with the franchisor who wishes to enforce the clause. If such a clause is considered unreasonable and it will be unenforceable, it does not mean that the entire contract is void. The parties must continue to perform the other obligations under the contract.[500] There is debate as to whether unreasonable parts of a non-compete clause can be severed. However, some courts have achieved this effect by constructing the clause by reference to circumstances existing at the time the contract was made and not necessarily giving it its literal meaning.[501] The restraint imposed must be reasonable in terms of the length of time and the geographical area which the restraint covers. In *Dyno-Rod plc and Zockoll Group Ltd* v. *Reeve*[502] both a period of twelve months and the extent of the restriction limited to the territory the franchisee was permitted to operate the franchise were considered reasonable.[503] In *Prontaprint plc* v. *Landon Litho Ltd*[504] a covenant not to engage in a similar business within a radius of half a mile for three years was held to be reasonable. Similarly in *KallKwik Printing (UK) Ltd* v. *Bell*[505] a clause preventing involvement in competing businesses for a period of 18 months and within a radius of 700 metres of the centre was upheld. In the UK confidentiality is entirely a contractual matter. The nature of the franchise relationship means that it is only equitable that franchisees are generally obliged to restrict themselves to the franchise and not be involved in competing businesses. It is also appropriate for a former franchisee to be restricted from competing with its former franchisor for a reasonable period of time as otherwise it is inevitable that the franchisors' know-how could be abused and that former franchisees will benefit from a 'springboard' effect.

F. EMPIRICAL RESEARCH INTO THE REGULATORY ENVIRONMENT

Empirical research was undertaken for this book involving a selection of franchisors who are, or plan to, franchise in more than one EU member state. The results of this research are set out in the Appendix at the end of this chapter. The majority of franchisors in the sample would welcome some form of **3.75**

499 *Nordenfelt* v. *Maxim Nordenfelt Guns and Ammunition Co Ltd* [1894] AC 535.

500 *Wallis* v. *Day and another* [1835–42] All ER Rep 426.

501 *Littlewoods Organisation Ltd* v. *Harris* [1978] 1 All ER 1026.

502 [1999] FSR 148.

503 This was also considered reasonable in the Court of Appeal in *Office Overload Ltd* v. *Gunn* [1977] FSR 39.

504 [1987] FSR 315.

505 [1994] FSR 674.

EU-wide franchise-specific statutory regulation of franchising instead of a self-regulatory regime or the application of general member state laws to franchising which many see as creating a barrier to inter-state franchising. They believe that the statutory regulation of franchising in France and Spain seems to have had no adverse impact on franchising there.

3.76 The results set out in the Appendix to this chapter suggest that the majority of franchisors surveyed in France,[506] Spain,[507] Germany[508] and around a third of those surveyed in the UK[509] are in favour of the EU-wide statutory regulation of franchising and felt that it would improve the quality of regulation. Interestingly, of those who responded to the survey in both Germany and the UK a significant minority had no clear opinion of whether or not it was a good idea. The French and Spanish respondents generally felt that statutory regulation of pre-contractual disclosure is more effective than self-regulation in preventing abuse of franchisees[510] whilst a small majority of German respondents[511] and just over a third of UK respondents[512] shared this view. It is noteworthy that none of the French franchisors surveyed and only one of the Spanish franchisors surveyed felt that the statutory regulation of franchising in their jurisdiction had adversely impacted upon their business. This belief in the EU-wide statutory regulation of franchising is not a recent trend. Research carried out back in 1991[513] showed that even then the majority of franchisors surveyed in ten EU member states believed that franchising should be regulated by law.[514] The vast majority of these believed that any franchise-specific regulation should be EU, rather than nationally, based.[515] Despite the national variances, research in those member states in which franchising is most prevalent (the UK, Germany, France and Spain) seems to suggest that the majority of franchisors believe that franchising should be regulated statutorily in the EU and that voluntary regulation does not provide an appropriate level of protection. The results of this survey suggest that leading practitioners also believe that statutory regulation of franchising is more effective than self-regulation and that the EU should regulate franchising throughout the EU in a

506 96%.

507 92%.

508 56%.

509 32%.

510 88% in France and 80% in Spain.

511 52%.

512 40%.

513 Op. cit., Abell, *European Franchising*, p. 46 – 1282 franchisors in ten member states surveyed with a response rate of 25%.

514 88% in Portugal; 57.6% in Spain; 85.7% in the Netherlands; 100% in Denmark; 65% in the UK; 66.7% in France; 69.4% in Germany and 50% in Belgium.

515 60.4% in the UK; 70.5% in France; 84.6% in Spain; 100% in Portugal; 66.6% in Italy; 75% in Germany; 66.6% in Denmark; 88% in the Netherlands; 90% in Belgium.

uniform manner rather than leaving it to individual member states to enact their own franchise law.

G. CONCLUSION

3.77 The regulatory environment in the EU is partly responsible for franchising's underachievement in the single market. Franchising needs to be regulated and the contractual and regulatory environment in the EU (both self-regulatory and legal), within which franchising operates, does not adequately protect and re-enforce the economic drivers that attract franchisors and franchisees to become involved in franchising. Nor does it adequately reduce the consequential inherent risks. In some cases it overprotects the franchisees, so increasing the risks to franchisors and eroding the economic drivers that attract them to franchising in the first place. The contractual environment tends to support and re-enforce the economic drivers that encourage franchisors to become involved in franchising and reduces their consequential risk to a reasonable level. However, it does not always re-enforce the economic drivers that encourage franchisees to become involved in franchising and it fails to reduce the consequential risks for franchisees adequately. Self-regulation of franchising does not work. Although the BFA sees its mandate as seeking 'to deliver self-regulation frameworks and then (delivering) that product to prospective franchisees', it seems to have achieved little. Such intransigence gives little credibility to those advocating self-regulation. If the franchisor's trade body fails to respond to its members' request for a higher level of self-regulation, how can self-regulation be expected to gain the confidence of either the public or the legislature? Historically it has been unwilling to take steps to enforce its code of conduct.[516] These are substantial flaws in the BFA's credentials as an effective self-regulatory body. The inevitable conclusion is that franchising needs to be legally regulated in the EU and that voluntary regulation will never be able to provide franchisees, potential franchisees or indeed franchisors with the level of protection that they require. Much is made, by those who advocate self-regulation, of the difficulties and delays created by legal regulation. Self-regulation of franchising in the EU is not transparent, consistent, accountable or proportionate.[517] Even the most mature national franchise associations are struggling to make the change from representing the interests of franchisors to representing those of franchising. Even if they successfully make that change, they only account for just over a fifth of franchisors in the EU. Given the international nature of franchising, any self-regulatory system must cover all 27

516 Between 1997 and 2007 the BFA expelled fewer than five members.

517 www.berr.gov.uk/whatwedo/bre/index.html, accessed 08.10.2009.

EU member states, and that is extremely unlikely to happen in a consistent manner given the current state of national franchise associations in the EU. There is a lack of suitably experienced, authoritative, fully representative and sufficiently resourced franchise associations. Even the Director General of the BFA admits that self-regulation is 'simply not viable on a pan EU basis';[518] one is led to conclude that the self-regulatory environment in the EU does not adequately support the economic drivers or reduce the consequential risks inherent in the franchisor/franchisee relationship. Despite clear and substantial differences between the civil and common law approaches to drafting commercial contracts franchise agreements exhibit a uniform architecture which comprises provisions detailing the grant made by the franchisor to the franchisee, the term and renewal, targets, the obligations of both parties, confidentiality, non-competition, transfer, product and services ties, goodwill and termination. There is a contractual asymmetry due to the multi-lateral nature of the franchise relationship (each franchisor having several/many franchisees) and the long-term, dynamic and changing nature of the franchisor/franchisee relationship. The contractual environment in the EU supports the economic drivers that encourage franchisors to become involved in franchising. It does not adequately support all of the economic drivers that encourage franchisees to become involved in franchising. It provides for a brand, a format and support but it does not impose a qualitative measure for the format or assistance provided. The contractual environment in the EU reduces the consequential risk inherent for the franchisor to a reasonable level, but it does not do so for the franchisee. The self-regulatory environment does not effectively support or re-enforce the drivers that attract either franchisors or franchisees to franchising. Neither does it reduce the consequential inherent risks for either party. The self-regulatory environment in the EU is marked by a complete lack of homogeneity, the lack of a clear or consistent approach to enforcement, a significant conflict of interest between the interests of franchisors and franchising as a whole and an inability to have any influence whatsoever on nearly 80% of franchise chains in the EU, as they are not members of the national franchise associations. The regulatory environment in the EU seeks by way of franchise-specific laws in six member states to reduce risks to which franchisees are exposed by ensuring that they have sufficient information to allow them to take a view of the adequacy of the business format and the support delivered by the franchisor to its franchisees and the franchisor's historical approach to encroachment. Its success in reducing those risks is dependent on the franchisee carefully considering the information it receives, particularly the feedback from existing franchisees, and is compromised by the inevitable fact of life that the franchisor's historical conduct may not be indicative of its future behaviour. The

518 Brian Smart in an interview with the author on 18 September 2008.

lack of homogeneity of approach between the different EU member states further substantially dilutes its impact on cross-border franchising. The lack of any uniform approach to pre-contractual disclosure further weakens the impact of franchise-specific laws. They do not seek to reduce the risks of informational asymmetry and moral risk to which the franchisor is exposed. Some regulatory regimes seek to redress this imbalance by imposing a duty of pre-contractual disclosure on the potential franchisee[519] but that is not part of the EU pre-contractual regulatory environment. The economic drivers which attract franchisors into franchising and those that attract franchisees to it are neither supported nor eroded in any particular way by the pre-contractual disclosure franchise-specific regulatory environment in the EU. Non-franchise-specific laws impact upon the pre-contractual regulatory environment in the EU in five distinct ways. They impose a duty not to misrepresent facts, an obligation to disclose relevant information to potential franchisees, an extra-contractual obligation to disclose relevant information to potential franchisees, an extra-contractual obligation of confidentiality, an obligation to enter into the franchise agreement once negotiations have passed a certain point and a right to withdraw from the contract within a limited time period. Each member state takes a different approach to each of these issues resulting in the lack of any homogeneous approach. This in turn substantially weakens their impact upon cross-border franchising within the EU and creates a technical barrier to franchising between EU member states. The ongoing franchisor/franchisee relationship in the EU is impacted by a regulatory environment that comprises a duty of good faith, anti-trust, unfair competition and consumer law. The common law and civil law take very different approaches to the concept of good faith. Whereas the German and French approach is loose and amorphous, based upon the Roman law concept of bona fides, the common law takes a far more literal approach to contracts, using a variety of legal tools to ensure fairness on the relationship. However, even with the civil approach to the concept of good faith differences exist between member states. The influence of Article 101 of the TFEU means that all member states take a similar approach to the regulation of vertical restrictions within the franchisor/franchisee relationship whereas Unfair Competition and Confidentiality lie very substantially on a member state by member state basis. Unfair contract term provisions are harmonised by the Unfair Competition Terms Directive. Thus there is a

519 In Vietnam not only does the franchisor have to disclose information to the franchisee, but so does the franchisee to the franchisor. In order to assist a franchisor when deciding to grant commercial rights, Article 9 of the Commercial Law provides that, upon receiving a reasonable request from the franchisor the franchisee is under an obligation to supply the franchisor with information about itself. The earlier Chinese franchise law (the Measures for the Regulation of Commercial Franchises issued by the Ministry of Commerce of the People's Republic of China, 31 December 2004, Chapter III Article 9) also provided for this but it was dropped (without any explanation) from the most recent Chinese statute.

complete lack of harmony between the various regimes seeking to regulate the franchise relationship by statute in the EU. Some issues, deemed worthy of specific regulation in certain jurisdictions outside of the EU are not dealt with at all.[520] Franchisors embarking upon a European 'roll out' of their concept must expect to encounter delays and costs that are a direct result of this heterogeneous approach – an artificial barrier to pan-European expansion. The duty of good faith has a significant impact upon the economic drivers that encourage franchisors and franchisees to become involved in franchising and reduces the consequential inherent risk. The lack of homogeneity through the EU greatly dilutes this impact on cross-border franchising. The regulation of vertical restraints has an undermining impact upon the economic drivers that encourage franchisors to become involved in franchising. The legal regulatory environment in the EU does not support any of the economic drivers that encourage franchisors to become involved in franchising and does not significantly reduce any of the risks that franchisors are exposed to. However, it over-reduces the risks to which franchisees are exposed and over-re-enforces the economic drivers that encourage them to become involved in franchising. All member states recognise the right to terminate for breach, although some (e.g. France) are more formulaic in how it has to be exercised than others. However, the duty of good faith in some member states, such as Germany, overprotects franchisees, entitling them to refunds of upfront fees on termination in some circumstances. An inappropriate use of employment law in some member states can also overprotect some franchisees. Likewise the application by analogy of commercial agency law in Germany erodes the economic drivers that attract

520 The role of third parties in franchising is not regulated by any of the EU member states. However, there are examples of such regulation in other jurisdictions such as Malaysia (Malaysia governs the activities of Franchise Brokers 'doing business as an agent or representative of a franchisor to sell a franchise to any person for a certain consideration but does not include any director, officer or employee of the franchisor or franchisee' (The Franchise Act 1998 Part I Section 4)), Korea (in Korea the law provides for the registration at the Fair Trade Commission of Franchise Consultants (Act on Fairness in Franchise Transactions Chapter III Article 28) and imposes on them a duty to act 'with dignity' and honesty (Act on Fairness in Franchise Transactions Chapter III Article 30) and they can be struck off for inappropriate behaviour (Act on Fairness in Franchise Transactions Chapter III Article 31)) and Kazakhstan (in Kazakhstan Licence brokers (those 'engaged in mediation activities in the course of concluding and performance of the complex business licence contract') are expressly acknowledged by the law which states that they 'may act both on their own behalf and at their own risk, and on behalf and at the risk of the licensor, licensee or other subjects of franchising relations in consideration for a licence broker's fee which can be payable in the form of a fixed single or periodic payment, fixed payments or otherwise, as provided by the contract' (Law on Complex Business Licence (Franchising) (Law No 330: June 24, 2002) Chapter 3 Article 13)). None of the EU member states stipulate a minimum term for franchise agreements. However, two jurisdictions outside of the EU do. In Malaysia the franchise agreement must be for a minimum period of five years (The Franchise Act 1998 Part III Section 25). In Indonesia, there is a minimum period of five years (The Provisions on and Procedure for the Implementation of Franchised Business Registration (*Decree of the Minister of Industry and Trade No. 259/MPP/Kep/7/1997, dated July 30, 1997*) Chapter II, Article 8) and ten years for master franchise agreements (Cornwallis, R., 2006, 'Indonesia – new franchise regulation', *International Journal of Franchising Law*, Volume 4, Issue 3, p. 5).

franchisors to franchising and excessively de-risks it for franchisees. Post-termination restrictive covenants are an essential element in reducing the risks inherent in franchising for franchisors, but German law applies commercial agency by analogy to erode this protection.

APPENDIX: EMPIRICAL RESEARCH INTO THE REGULATORY ENVIRONMENT

1. What are the main barriers to franchisors expanding into other EU member states? Do you consider the following factors to be very significant, significant or insignificant barriers?

	VERY SIGNIFICANT				SIGNIFICANT				INSIGNIFICANT			
Respondents:	UK (25)	Germany (25)	France (25)	Spain (25)	UK (25)	Germany (25)	France (25)	Spain (25)	UK (25)	Germany (25)	France (25)	Spain (25)
Language	1 (4%)	2 (8%)	6 (24%)	16 (64%)	23 (92%)	1 (4%)	9 (36%)	5 (20%)	1 (4%)	22 (88%)	10 (40%)	3 (12%)
The extra burden created by each member state having different franchise regulations	14 (56%)	15 (60%)	22 (88%)	21 (84%)	11 (44%)	9 (36%)	3 (12%)	4 (16%)	0 (0%)	1 (4%)	0 (0%)	0 (0%)
Finding a suitable master franchisee/ developer	24 (96%)	23 (92%)	22 (88%)	23 (92%)	1 (4%)	2 (8%)	3 (12%)	2 (8%)	0 (0%)	0 (0%)	0 (0%)	0 (0%)
Cost	5 (20%)	8 (32%)	3 (12%)	20 (80%)	13 (52%)	14 (56%)	22 (88%)	5 (20%)	7 (28%)	3 (12%)	0 (0%)	0 (0%)
Different market conditions in each member state	4 (16%)	1 (4%)	8 (32%)	17 (68%)	19 (76%)	22 (88%)	16 (64%)	2 (8%)	2 (8%)	2 (8%)	1 (4%)	6 (24%)
Others	0 (0%)	0 (0%)	0 (0%)	0 (0%)	0 (0%)	0 (0%)	0 (0%)	0 (0%)	0 (0%)	0 (0%)	0 (0%)	0 (0%)

2. What are the greatest risks that a franchisor incurs in deciding to franchise its business?

	Very significant risk				Significant risk				Insignificant risk			
	UK	Germany	France	Spain	UK	Germany	France	Spain	UK	Germany	France	Spain
Protection of your know-how from unauthorised use by the franchisee or their agents outside of the franchise system	2 (8%)	9 (36%)	2 (8%)	1 (4%)	15 (60%)	14 (56%)	3 (12%)	7 (28%)	8 (32%)	2 (8%)	20 (80%)	17 (68%)
Competition from franchisees during the term of the Franchise Agreement	20 (80%)	18 (72%)	20 (80%)	1 (4%)	5 (20%)	6 (24%)	4 (16%)	6 (24%)	0 (0%)	1 (4%)	1 (4%)	18 (72%)
Competition from franchisees after the term of the Franchise Agreement	24 (96%)	14 (56%)	22 (88%)	10 (40%)	1 (4%)	8 (32%)	2 (8%)	14 (56%)	0 (0%)	3 (12%)	1 (4%)	1 (4%)
Under -payment of monies due from franchisees	9 (36%)	22 (88%)	24 (96%)	25 (100%)	15 (60%)	3 (12%)	1 (4%)	0 (0%)	1 (4%)	0 (0%)	0 (0%)	0 (0%)
Franchisees not complying with system	3 (12%)	21 (84%)	12 (48%)	18 (72%)	20 (80%)	3 (12%)	3 (12%)	6 (24%)	2 (8%)	1 (4%)	10 (40%)	0 (0%)
Under- performance by franchisees during term of Franchise Agreement which has a significant impact on the brand	1 (4%)	1 (4%)	11 (44%)	4 (16%)	6 (24%)	21 (84%)	13 (52%)	17 (68%)	18 (72%)	3 (12%)	1 (4%)	4 (16%)

	Very significant risk				Significant risk				Insignificant risk			
	UK	Germany	France	Spain	UK	Germany	France	Spain	UK	Germany	France	Spain
Damage to the franchisee's intellectual property	23 (92%)	23 (92%)	22 (88%)	16 (64%)	2 (8%)	2 (8%)	3 (12%)	9 (36%)	0 (0%)	0 (0%)	0 (0%)	0 (0%)

3. Why did you franchise your business? Do you consider the following factors to have been very significant, significant or insignificant?

	Very significant				Significant				Insignificant			
	UK	Germany	France	Spain	UK	Germany	France	Spain	UK	Germany	France	Spain
Access to working capital	18 (72%)	18 (72%)	16 (64%)	13 (52%)	6 (24%)	4 (16%)	1 (4%)	4 (16%)	1 (4%)	3 (12%)	8 (32%)	8 (32%)
Quicker expansion of the business	22 (88%)	24 (96%)	22 (88%)	24 (96%)	3 (12%)	1 (4%)	3 (12%)	1 (4%)	0 (0%)	0 (0%)	1 (4%)	0 (0%)
Access to better-motivated people	18 (72%)	15 (60%)	15 (60%)	8 (32%)	5 (20%)	5 (20%)	3 (12%)	8 (32%)	2 (8%)	5 (20%)	7 (28%)	9 (36%)
You identified franchising as a profitable business model	24 (96%)	22 (88%)	20 (80%)	16 (64%)	1 (4%)	3 (12%)	4 (16%)	5 (20%)	0 (0%)	0 (0%)	1 (4%)	4 (16%)
Easier way of doing business	0 (0%)	0 (0%)	0 (0%)	0 (0%)	0 (0%)	0 (0%)	0 (0%)	0 (0%)	25 (100%)	25 (100%)	25 (100%)	25 (100%)

4. Which of the following obligations are very significant, significant or insignificant in protecting your business from franchisee abuse?

	Very significant				Significant				Insignificant			
	UK	Germany	France	Spain	UK	Germany	France	Spain	UK	Germany	France	Spain
Non-competition by franchisees during the term of the agreement	20 (80%)	18 (72%)	20 (80%)	1 (4%)	5 (20%)	5 (20%)	4 (16%)	8 (32%)	0 (0%)	2 (8%)	1 (4%)	17 (68%)
Non-competition for a reasonable period after termination	24 (96%)	14 (56%)	23 (92%)	10 (40%)	1 (4%)	7 (28%)	1 (4%)	13 (52%)	0 (0%)	4 (16%)	1 (4%)	2 (8%)
No challenge of franchisor's intellectual property by franchisees	24 (96%)	21 (84%)	20 (80%)	25 (100%)	1 (4%)	3 (12%)	5 (20%)	0 (0%)	0 (0%)	1 (4%)	0 (0%)	0 (0%)
Franchisees being obliged to follow the system	3 (12%)	21 (84%)	13 (52%)	19 (76%)	21 (84%)	3 (12%)	2 (8%)	6 (24%)	1 (4%)	1 (4%)	10 (40%)	0 (0%)
	UK	Germany	France	Spain								
Can you name any other very significant obligations in protecting your business from franchisee's abuse?	Payment of monies due to franchisor 12 (48%)	Payment of monies due to franchisor 6 (24%)	Payment of monies due to franchisor 15 (60%)	None								

5. Are you in favour of the Statutory Regulation of Franchising in the EU?

	UK	Germany	France	Spain
Yes	8 (32%)	14 (56%)	24 (96%)	23 (92%)
No	11 (44%)	6 (24%)	0 (0%)	1 (4%)
Don't know	6 (24%)	5 (20%)	1 (4%)	1 (4%)

6. If franchising is regulated by law, should it be done at an EU level rather than a national level?

	UK	Germany	France	Spain
Yes	6 (24%)	22 (88%)	24 (96%)	25 (100%)
No	18 (72%)	2 (8%)	0 (0%)	0 (0%)
Don't know	1 (4%)	1 (4%)	1 (4%)	0 (0%)

7. Has the statutory regulation of franchising in your country had an adverse impact upon your business?

	France	Spain
Yes	0 (0%)	1 (4%)
No	24 (96%)	23 (92%)
Don't know	1 (4%)	2 (8%)

8. Do you believe that specific statutory regulation of pre-contractual disclosure is more effective than self-regulation in preventing abuse of franchisees?

	UK	Germany	France	Spain
Yes	10 (40%)	13 (52%)	22 (88%)	20 (80%)
No	11 (44%)	8 (32%)	1 (4%)	1 (4%)
Don't know	4 (16%)	4 (16%)	2 (8%)	4 (16%)

9. Do you believe that the legal regulation of duties and obligations of franchisors and franchisees during the term of the franchise agreement would significantly reduce disputes between franchisors and franchisees?

	UK	Germany	France	Spain
Yes	1 (4%)	14 (56%)	6 (24%)	8 (32%)
No	24 (96%)	4 (16%)	14 (56%)	9 (36%)
Don't know		7 (28%)	5 (20%)	8 (32%)

10. Do you believe that statutory regulation of franchising is more likely to improve the quality of franchising than self-regulation?

	UK	Germany	France	Spain
Yes	8 (32%)	14 (56%)	23 (92%)	21 (84%)
No	12 (48%)	7 (28%)	1 (4%)	0 (0%)
Don't know	5 (20%)	4 (16%)	1 (4%)	4 (16%)

11. Do you think that statutory regulation of pre-contractual disclosure in franchising will enable disputes between franchisors and franchisees to be resolved in a more effective manner?

	UK	Germany	France	Spain
Yes	22 (88%)	21 (84%)	18 (72%)	18 (72%)
No	1 (4%)	2 (8%)	3 (12%)	6 (24%)
Don't know	2 (8%)	2 (8%)	4 (16%)	1 (4%)

12. Are franchised businesses disadvantaged as compared to non-franchised businesses as regards:
(a) Their ability to set prices in all of their outlets

	UK	Germany	France	Spain
Yes	19 (76%)	18 (72%)	19 (76%)	18 (72%)
No	3 (12%)	4 (16%)	5 (20%)	3 (12%)
Don't know	3 (12%)	3 (12%)	1 (4%)	4 (16%)

(b) Their ability to control the franchisee's use of the internet

	UK	Germany	France	Spain
Yes	14 (56%)	14 (56%)	4 (16%)	16 (64%)
No	8 (32%)	2 (8%)	15 (60%)	8 (32%)
Don't know	3 (12%)	9 (36%)	6 (24%)	1 (4%)

13. In your experience if prospective franchisees are given lengthy documentation to read giving details about the franchise, its performance and the role of franchisees do they read it?

	UK	Germany	France	Spain
Yes	9 (36%)	3 (12%)	6 (24%)	8 (32%)
No	13 (52%)	13 (52%)	10 (40%)	9 (36%)
Don't know	3 (12%)	9 (36%)	9 (36%)	8 (32%)

14. In your experience do the cultural and commercial differences between different national markets give rise to different problems and issues for franchisors?

	UK	Germany	France	Spain
Yes	20 (80%)	22 (88%)	13 (52%)	12 (48%)
No	2 (8%)	2 (8%)	10 (40%)	8 (32%)
Don't know	3 (12%)	1 (4%)	2 (8%)	5 (20%)

4

IDENTIFYING A CATALYST TO RE-ENGINEER THE REGULATORY ENVIRONMENT

A. BREAKING DOWN BARRIERS TO TRADE IN THE EU

4.1 There may be disagreement about whether a self-regulatory regime is more effective in preventing abuses than franchise-specific regulations. There may also be little empirical evidence to prove irrefutably that franchise-specific disclosure and relationship laws have reduced abuse, sharp practice, commercial failure or the number of franchise disputes. Nevertheless, the lack of a homogeneous regulatory environment in the EU is a barrier to cross-border trade and there is no realistic chance of an EU-wide self-regulatory regime being adopted. Eight EU member states regulate franchising in distinctly different ways. There is also a significant difference in the way that non-franchise-specific laws impact upon franchising.[1] This heterogeneity creates legal barriers to interstate trade within the EU. It is suggested that a regulatory environment comprising harmonised legal eco-systems in each member state would facilitate easier cross-border franchising in the EU. This certainly seems to be the view of

1 See Chapter 3 above.

those most actively involved in franchising in the EU on a day to day basis.[2] The EU 'set itself the goal of making its economy the most competitive and dynamic knowledge-based economy in the world'.[3]

In order to achieve this, it is clear to the Commission that it needs to create an economic environment which is 'underpinned by legal certainty and security … to address the obstacles which prevent businesses and consumers from making the most of the internal market'.

It concludes that businesses 'can operate across borders efficiently to stimulate a more competitive supply of goods and services'[4] and that 'this requires a common approach'.[5]

It has stated plainly that if it

> continue(s) to accept a multiplicity of separate solutions for the same issue there is a risk that the uncertainty and complexity of the legal environment will undermine rather than enable legitimate economic activity.[6]

In other words a regulatory environment of harmonised legal eco-systems is needed to support the single market.

The Belgian Parliament came to a similar conclusion in 1986 when it rejected a bill aimed at regulating franchising in Belgium, believing that franchising was becoming more and more a matter of general European interest and implementing a national regulation risked complicating cooperation between member states.[7] Eight[8] of the 27 EU member states already have franchise-specific legislation creating a heterogeneous legal environment for franchising in the EU. The establishment of a true single market within the EU can only be achieved if all physical, fiscal and technical barriers are removed.[9] The regulation of the distribution of goods or services in different ways by member states inevitably creates technical barriers that cannot be reconciled with the objective **4.2**

2 From a survey of franchisors and professional advisors involved in pan-European franchising and interviews with a number of senior managers and in-house lawyers at companies actively involved in pan-European franchising.

3 Mr Robert Madelin, Director General DG Health and Consumer Protection, European Commission, *A Common Frame of Reference for a more coherent European Contract Law*, Joint European Parliament and Commission Conference, 28 April 2004.

4 Mr Robert Madelin, Ibid.

5 Mr Robert Madelin, Ibid.

6 Mr Robert Madelin, Ibid.

7 From the answer to a Parliamentary question Mr Legnean asked on 11 April 1986.

8 France, Spain, Italy, Lithuania, Estonia, Belgium, Romania and Sweden.

9 See Cecchini/Jacquemin/Catinat, *The European Challenge, 1992: The Benefits of a Single Market; and the Single European Act 1986*.

of creating a single market. The European Commission claims that diversity in the laws across member states leads to higher transaction costs for businesses which discourages consumers and businesses from engaging in cross-border trade and makes it especially difficult for small businesses to exploit economies of scale in the single market. The highly fragmented nature of laws within the European Union generates a need for harmonisation.[10] Although the differences between member states' laws reflect the legal cultures of the various countries, they 'threaten legal certainty and lead to high costs of legal actions; cases of dispute become more likely, and mostly harder to resolve too'.[11]

For those involved in legal cases in foreign countries, such differences are often criticised as incomprehensible. These economic players would like to see the law becoming more compatible with the needs of the business world: simple, rapid and predictable.[12]

The lack of certainty from the combination of international, European and national laws of member states is particularly notable for continental lawyers who are used to the formal certainty of codified law. The codifications of civil law were viewed as the 'science' of lawmaking. As Portalis, the principal draftsman of the French Code civil of 1804, observed:

> Laws are not pure acts of power; they are acts of wisdom, of justice and of reason ... The science of the legislator consists of finding for each area those principles which are most beneficial to the common good.[13]

They believe that change is possible and

> the differences between European continental legal systems and common law in style, method, legal culture, legal thinking and legal training are by no means insuperable.[14]

10 'Quelles juridictions économiques en Europe, du règne de la diversité à un ordre européen' edited by Yves Chaput and Aristide Lévi, CREDA, CCIP, Editions Litec. Quote from Robert Badinter, Emeritus Professor at the University of Paris I in the preface to the study.

11 'Legitimacy Conditions for a European Civil Code', Christoph U. Schmid, Florence/Munich. Here is a link: http://ec.europa.eu/consumers/cons_int/safe_shop/fair_bus_pract/cont_law/comments/5.17.pdf.

12 'Towards a pan-European approach to commercial law', Annabelle Pando and Frédérique Perrotin (1 October 2007).

13 J.-E.-M. Portalis, 1988, 'Discours préliminaire sur le projet du Code civil', in J.-E.-M. Portalis, *Ecrits et Discours juridiques et politiques*, at pp. 23 and 30.

14 See note 8. Though this is claimed by Legrand, P., 1997, 'Against a European Civil Code', *Modern Law Review*, Volume 60, 321.

B. THE PRECEDENT OF COMMERCIAL AGENCY

A heterogeneous regulatory environment in the EU once existed in respect of commercial agency.[15] Before 1986 commercial agents were protected by specific laws in a number of EU member states, particularly France, the Netherlands, Belgium and Germany. The Commercial Agents Directive[16] was introduced in order to harmonise these member state laws once it had been accepted by the Council of Ministers that commercial agents needed specific protection of their rights in relation to their principals. The possibility of each member state regulating agency in a different manner (as is currently the case with franchising) was seen as being in direct conflict with the creation of a single market within the European Community. It amounted to the creation of technical barriers to free trade. The Council of Ministers felt that it was necessary to strengthen the position of the commercial agent in relation to his principal. Independent commercial agents were operating throughout the EU across member state borders. They were seen to be in a weak position when dealing with their principals, although it was acknowledged that this was not always the case. There was evidence to suggest that commercial agents were sometimes being abused by their principals.[17] A European-wide solution was therefore felt to be appropriate. It could not be left to individual member states. The Council of Ministers considered that the differing national laws on commercial agency were detrimental to the functioning of the Single Market. Their statement in the preamble to the Directive[18] is extremely relevant to franchising. Indeed it could have been writing about franchising rather than commercial agency. It states that, **4.3**

> the differences in national laws concerning commercial representation substantially affect the conditions of competition and the carrying-on of that activity within the Community and are detrimental both to the protection available to commercial agents vis-à-vis their principals and to the security of commercial transactions.

---

15 There are some basic similarities between franchising and commercial agency. 'As in the case of commercial agency contracts, the franchise agreement generally brings together a strong party, the principal or franchisor, and the weaker party, the commercial agent or franchisee. Both parties are consistently, before, during and after the commercial collaboration, in this unequal position with each other'. The Belgian House Of Representatives, 28 Jan 2004 – *Draft Parliamentary Bill Relating to Franchise Agreements* (lodged by Mme Trees Pieters) [Doc 51 0747/001].

16 Council Directive (EC) 86/653 on the Coordination of the Laws of the Member States Relating to Self-Employed Commercial Agents [2004] OJ L 382.

17 Consumer and Competition Policy Directorate, *Guidance Notes On The Commercial Agents (Council Directive) Regulations 1993*. The Commercial Agents (Council Directive) Regulations 1993 (S.I. 1993/3053 As Amended By S.I. 1993/3173).

18 Council Directive (EC) 86/653 on the Coordination of the Laws of the Member States Relating to Self-Employed Commercial Agents [2004] OJ L 382.

It continues,

> those differences are such as to inhibit substantially the conclusion and operation of commercial representation contracts where principal and commercial agents are established in different Member States; trade in goods between Member States should be carried on under conditions which are similar to those of a single market, and this necessitates approximation of the legal systems of the Member States to the extent required for the proper functioning of the common market; in this regard the rules concerning conflict of laws do not, in the matter of commercial representation, remove the inconsistencies referred to above, nor would they even if they were made uniform.

It therefore concludes that harmonisation of member state law through a Directive is necessary. Exactly the same conclusion can be drawn about franchising. This is reinforced by the conclusion of the Organisation for Economic Co-operation and Development (OECD) that inefficient or unduly restrictive regulation in the distribution sector (which in its study includes franchising) results in increased direct and indirect costs.[19]

C. EMPIRICAL EVIDENCE

4.4 The BFA/NatWest Survey 2007 which found that legislation was seen by the majority of franchisors as the main barrier to international expansion.[20] Interviews with franchise lawyers experienced in cross-border franchising in the EU support this idea that the lack of a single EU franchise law is 'a substantial problem'[21] for at least some franchisors seeking to establish their businesses in

19 Pilat, D., 1997, 'Regulation and Performance in the Distribution Sector', OECD Economics Department Working Paper No. 180.

20 BFA/NatWest Survey 2007, page 20 – 53% cited foreign legislation as the most significant barrier to international expansion, whilst only 16% cited current EU regulations as a significant barrier.

21 Interview with Christopher Nowak, Vice President and General Counsel, Wyndham Worldwide Corporation (10 March 2006). All of those franchise lawyers interviewed shared the same view. Jane Colton, Vice President & Legal Counsel, Vanguard Rental GmbH (1 June 2006) stated that 'the current form of national franchise laws in the EU makes cross border European franchising unnecessarily complicated. It goes against the whole rationale of the European Union increasing the cost and lead time of franchisors entering other EU member states'. Nunns Moodliar, General Counsel, Hertz Europe Limited said 'Even though the EU is a single market, when Hertz do business in any of the 27 member states we have to undertake particular legal advice which leads to us carrying extra costs and losing time. For any franchisor wanting to expand within the EU, harmonisation of franchise disclosure and other law would be a big benefit. It will make entry into other member states quicker, cheaper and far more certain. From the point of view of both franchisors and franchisees clear and harmonised disclosure in all EU member states is essential. It should be a shop window to the business opportunity and reflect the relevant and important aspects of it without unnecessary clutter. I cannot understand why no one in the Commission has got around to the harmonisation of franchise law – both disclosure and relationship laws. It is a very tangible way of making the single market a reality. I am sure that if there was more harmonisation of franchise law, there would be a good deal more franchising, particularly at the smaller operators level. The differences between the law in each of the 27 EU member states are a disincentive to franchising. They particularly disadvantage smaller member states which are made to seem relatively unattractive to franchisors.

several EU member states and makes pan-European franchising far more difficult than it need be. Although the interviews are not in themselves conclusive evidence of the need for a harmonised approach, they certainly support the evidence detailed above and are therefore worthy of consideration. Franchisors in the UK, Germany, France and Spain seem to feel that the extra burden imposed upon them by each EU member state having different franchise laws is a very significant barrier to their expanding into other EU member states.[22] A clear majority of those surveyed were also in favour of a pan-European approach, although the majority of UK franchisors surveyed, reflecting their jurisdiction's traditional antipathy to European legislation, felt that national legislation was more appropriate.[23]

D. THE MECHANISMS AVAILABLE TO HARMONISE EU MEMBER STATE LAW

There are seven options available for harmonising EU law.[24] These are publication of non-binding model contract rules; a binding or non-binding 'tool box' for EU law makers; a contract law recommendation that would call on EU member states to include a European contract law into their national legal systems; an optional European contract law which could be chosen freely by consumers and businesses in their contractual relations; an EU Directive on the harmonisation of national law; full harmonisation using an EU Regulation and the creation of a European Civil Code, replacing all national law. This book does not intend to consider these options in detail. It does however make the observation that a regulation would not enact a franchise law that fits most easily into the legal environment on all 27 member states, as they vary so widely in respect of franchising.[25] All but two of the other options would have no mandatory effect. There are therefore only two options that merit consideration **4.5**

The result is that franchisors' entry into those smaller member states is usually delayed and sometimes abandoned altogether'. Roger Wilde, Managing Director, ChipsAway Limited 'Why do legislators seem hell bent on making life so complicated for us franchisors? It's hard enough complying with one set of laws and disclosure let alone potentially 27'. Rosalynde Harrison, Head of Legal, Monsoon Limited '(the EU) really needs to sort this one out. There are enough legal problems with doing business in other EU member states as it is, without the nightmare of having to deal with different disclosure regimes in many of them'.

22 See Appendix to Chapter 3. 56% UK franchisors surveyed favoured EU legislation
60% German franchisors surveyed favoured EU legislation
88% French franchisors surveyed favoured EU legislation
83% Spanish franchisors surveyed favoured EU legislation.

23 24% UK franchisors surveyed
88% German franchisors surveyed
96% French franchisors surveyed
100% Spanish franchisors surveyed.

24 Commission Green Paper on policy options for progress towards a European Contract Law for Consumers and Businesses, 1 July 2010.

25 See Chapter 3.

as to which are the most appropriate to deliver a European franchise law – a Directive and a European Civil Code.

1. Directives as the way to harmonise member state law

4.6 The EU has harmonised a number of specific sectors, such as Commercial Agency by way of Directives.[26] Directives are legal acts which member states are required to transpose into national law, but are free to implement as they wish provided the end result is achieved. Article 288 TFEU provides that

> a Directive shall be binding, as to the result to be achieved, upon each member state to which it is addressed, but shall leave to the national authorities the choice of form and methods.[27]

Member states are under a duty to incorporate the aim of each Directive into their national law by the given deadline. Failure to implement a Directive, part implementation or incorrect implementation often lead to a complaint by the Commission to the European Court of Justice.[28] However, it has been suggested by the European Parliament that this sectoral approach does not ensure the proper functioning of the internal market. A more politically focused approach to the harmonisation of member state law has therefore been advocated by the European Parliament.[29]

2. A European Civil Code as the way to harmonise member state laws

4.7 Proponents of a codified legal system claim that it brings 'the legal unity desired by business, lawyers and citizens alike'.[30]

26 Article 249 of the Treaty Establishing the European Union.

27 Directives that have not been transposed in time, or at all, will take 'direct effect'. The doctrine of direct effect only applies vertically to directives. This allows individuals to rely upon the rights asserted in the directive against their member state, regardless of whether the directive has been implemented by such state, which reinforces their effectiveness. However, direct effect does not apply horizontally so individuals cannot assert rights against other individuals as confirmed in the case of *Marshall* v. *Southampton and South West Hampshire Area Health Authority* (Case 152/84) [1986] QB 401.

28 Article 258 TFEU.

29 Resolution of 1989, OJ C 158/400 (Resolution A2–157/89); Resolution of 1994, OJ C 205/518 (Resolution A3–0329/94) and Resolution of 2000, OJ C 377/323 (Resolution B5–0228, 0229–230/2000).

Article 1 of the EP Resolution of 1989 reads: 'Requests that a start be made on the necessary preparatory work on drawing up a common European code of private law, the Member States being invited, having deliberated the matter, to state whether they wish to be involved in the planned unification'.

30 See note 5.

If Europe were to adopt a civil code they argue that

> case law and doctrine would be shifted into a new European framework where they could co-operate more effectively – as it were with economies of scale – something that ought not least to benefit the quality of law.[31]

Although European private law principles are 'uncertain in scope, devoid of conceptual foundations, confused in their policy orientation and disruptive in their effects on national legal systems',[32] some academics believe that with a European code 'the most important basic civil-law questions would be regulated uniformly to the advantage of businesses operating Europe-wide'.[33]

As a result, in 2003 the European Commission established a 'Common Frame of Reference' to establish 'common principles and terminology in the area of European contract law'.[34]

In 2005 the Commission engaged two main groups of academic lawyers to produce a draft Common Frame of Reference which comprised the 'Study Group on a European Civil Code' (the 'Study Group') presided over by Professor Christian von Bar, and the 'Research Group on Existing EC Private law' or 'Acquis Group'.[35] The European Commission believes that contract law reform would encourage cross-border trading and has stated that 'only 8% of consumers buy online from another member state', and

> in addition, 61% of cross-border sales are rejected because traders refuse to serve the consumer's country. This is largely due to regulatory barriers and legal uncertainty about the applicable rules.[36]

The European Commission's work on European contract law, which has found a strong echo in the European Parliament, is therefore an important step towards opening new doors for businesses and helping 500 million consumers benefit from our single market.[37] The Commission consulted on seven options for contract law reform in the European Union. The consultation process closed on 31 January 2011. The options for reform include partial harmonisation

---

31 Summers, ZEuP 7 (1999), 201.

32 Schmid, C., 2010, 'A European civil code as a building block for a European social model?', *European Law Review*, Volume 35, Number 1, pp. 102–12.

33 Ibid.

34 Commission, Action Plan, at para.4.1.1.

35 'A Framework of Principle for European Contract Law?' 125 *Law Quarterly Review* 616–47, (2009).

36 See: http://europa.eu/rapid/pressReleasesAction.do?aged=0&format=HTML&guiLanguage=en&language=EN&reference=IP/10/872.

37 See: http://europa.eu/rapid/pressReleasesAction.do?reference=SPEECH/10/441.

through an EU directive and an EU civil code as a unified replacement for national contract law. The Study Group, backed by the EU Commission, endorse the need to regulate franchising on a pan-EU level 'with the benefit of and from the stand point of current legal science.'[38]

Its Amsterdam Group[39] has therefore presented proposals that regulate commercial agency, distribution and franchising on a European level.[40] However, the adoption of a European Civil Code, which was announced in 2003, has raised much discussion about the political nature of such an initiative. Hesselink identifies four areas of political function in the initiative: the underlying ideology (autonomy or solidarity), the cultural conflict (national or European), power (Levels of Governance) and the symbolism of codification (is Europe united or divided?).[41] The technocratic approach of the Commission, appointing a group of academics to prepare a 'Common Frame of Reference', has not abated concerns that there will be winners and losers in the process without the opportunity for all relevant stakeholders to have any real input.[42] In contrast to the manner in which a European Civil Code may ride roughshod over some member states' legal traditions, a Directive offers a more sensitive and flexible approach to the regulation of franchising. Pierre Legrand explains in his paper[43] that the difficulties of a fully harmonised legal system under a civil code stem from sociological findings that the English 'feel definitely uncomfortable with systems of rigid rules' and the English 'pride themselves that many problems can be solved without formal rules'.[44]

In English law 'legal development is not a matter of inducing rules, terms or institutions out of a number of factual situations and applying these rules, terms or institutions to new factual situations. Rather it is a matter of pushing outwards from within the facts themselves. It is a matter of moving from one *res*, say a public highway, to another *res* like private property'.[45] This explains the House of Lords' opposition to a harmonised code of European contract law.[46]

---

38 http://www.sgecc.net, accessed 14 August 2009.

39 http://ecc.uvtl.nl/.

40 On 23 December 2008 the Commission received the final version of the academic draft CFR.

41 Hesselink, M.W., 2004, 'The Politics of a European Civil Code', *European Law Journal*, Volume 10, No 6, pp. 675–97.

42 Ibid.

43 Op. cit., Legrand, P., 1997.

44 Hofstede, G., 1991, *Cultures and Organisations*, London: McGraw-Hill, pp. 145 and 121.

45 Samuel, G., 1995, *The Foundations of Legal Reasoning*, Antwerp: Maklu, p. 195.

46 The House of Lords EU Committee Report on 'European Contract Law; the Draft Common Frame of Reference', 10 June 2009.

In contrast, some commentators believe that the Germans 'have been programmed since their early childhood to feel comfortable in structured environments' and 'look for a structure in their organizations, institutions, and relationships which makes events clearly interpretable and predictable'.[47]

Likewise, the French believe in 'law with sharp edges, based on suspicion, realism and pessimism which contrasts with English law based on custom and trust'.[48]

These different legal mentalities are the result of deep-rooted differences between the three legal traditions embodied in *case*-oriented English law, *rule*-oriented French law and *concept*-oriented German law.[49] The cultural legal differences are evident in the approach these countries take to harmonisation of EU law. England is used to dealing with fragmentation whereas civil law countries are more comfortable with unambiguous codified law and therefore are more likely to be in favour of full harmonisation. For Legrand 'the adoption of a European Civil Code is arrogant, for it suggests that the civil representation of the world is more worthy than its alternative and is, in short, so superior that it deserves to *supersede* the common law's world-view'.[50]

Directives are important as a method of harmonisation because they preserve the legal and cultural differences of member states. Walter van Gerven argues that 'uniformity should not be an objective in itself, because it is *not*, of itself, a higher good than diversity is'.[51]

The United States provides an example of a country without a civil code that is both unified, stable and coherent. In the European Union's Committee Report on the EU Consumer Rights Directive, Professor James P. Nehf, Professor of Law at Indiana University argues

> that full harmonisation is neither necessary nor desirable ... Consumer legislation in the U.S. varies across the states and ... the consensus among consumer representatives (is) that a state-by-state approach (is) preferred unless there (is) a strong need for uniformity in a particular area of commerce.

47 Op. cit., Hofstede, pp. 121 and 116.

48 'Introduction generale', Siegfried (ed.), *Aspects de la sociétéfrancaise*, Paris: LGDJ, 1954, p. 21.

49 Van Gerven, W., 2008, 'The Open Method of Convergence', *Juridica International*, No. 1, pp. 32–41.

50 Merryman, J., 1985, *The Civil Law Tradition*, Stanford: Stanford University Press, 2nd edition, p. 3.

51 Van Gerven, 2008.

This, he argues, allows for

> a healthy degree of experimentation and an evolutionary approach to consumer protection nationwide. State legislatures ha(ve) been able to react more quickly to emerging consumer problems than the U.S. Congress. In most areas of commerce, the differences among state consumer laws creates few obstacles to cross-border transactions.[52]

There are also examples where codes have failed, in particular the failure of McGregor's English Contract Code.[53] This is often cited as evidence that the common law cannot be codified. To date diversity in the laws of member states has survived attempts at full harmonisation. This has made it possible for member states to experiment in their search for efficient and workable rules, in a similar way to the US.[54] This is one of the reasons that the General Secretariat of the European Council's publication of a consolidated version of the conclusions of the Council on the setting up of a CFR emphasised that both the option of using the CFR to harmonise the contract law of member states by creating a European Civil Code and that of a CFR consisting of complete set of standard terms and conditions of contract law have been rejected in favour of an optional 'tool box' for law makers to use if and when they deem appropriate.[55] The problem with this approach is that it is not mandatory and therefore will not deal with the fundamental problem of heterogeneity in the regulatory environment. Progressing to full harmonisation with no freedom as regards implementation would be a step too far. The proposed European civil code assumes the selection and formulation of contract law rules is merely a technical exercise.[56] It fails to put into context the differences between existing national provisions and European code which would need to be bridged by interpretation. Common law systems do not formulate around rules and as Legrand argues that there is 'much law to be found beyond the rules'.

Consideration of human rights and social and economic customs depends more on judges in their realisation than on legislators. Full harmonisation through a European Civil Code would pose a clear challenge to the identity of member states. It would influence the moral and social values of a community and it

52 European Union Committee – Eighteenth Report, 'EU Consumer Rights Directive: getting it right', Chapter 3, para. 55. Here you can browse the report which was ordered by the House of Lords to be printed 7 July 2009. http://www.publications.parliament.uk/pa/ld200809/ldselect/ldeucom/126/12606.htm.

53 McGregor, H., 1993, Contract Code drawn up on behalf of the English Law Commission (Guiffré).

54 Deakin, S., 2000, 'Regulatory Competition Versus Harmonisation in European Company Law' (ESRC Centre for Business Research, University of Cambridge Working Paper No. 163) (March 2000).

55 The Law Societies Joint Brussels Office. October 2010. The Brussels Office Law Reform Update Series: EU Civil Law.

56 Op. cit., Schmid, C., 2010.

would of course affect a country's legal culture.[57] There is also the question of competence with a move towards full harmonisation. As it stands, EU directives leave governance with the member states' legislators, with disputes handled by national courts. A shift away from directives will inevitably lead to a shift in power with national legislators and national judiciary losing power to Europe. It is doubtful that the European judiciary would have the resources to carry the burden of a code for all 27 member states.

3. A directive is the most appropriate approach to regulate franchising in the EU

Having considered the relative merits and difficulties offered by both directives and a European civil code, it is suggested that directives allow for a middle ground by providing partial harmonisation as they require member states to implement certain laws but give member states the freedom to choose how to implement these into their national law. This flexibility **4.8**

> induces individual states to enter into a 'race to the top' when they would have otherwise have an incentive to do nothing or to compete on the basis of the withdrawal of protective standards known as the 'race to the bottom'.[58]

Directives support the European single market without losing the diversity and deep-rooted legal culture of individual states. By giving member states a number of options for implementation, as well as allowing for the possibility that existing, self-regulatory mechanisms can be used to comply with EU-wide standards, harmonisation through directives actually stimulates regulatory innovation instead of suppressing it.[59] This is a strong argument in favour of the use of directives as a method of harmonisation, as it strikes the balance between traditional national governance and self-regulation of member states and full harmonisation across Europe in support of the single market. Directives are therefore the preferred approach to legal harmonisation in Europe. They allow member states to choose how and in which form they implement laws and directives allow member states to preserve the diversity of their legal culture. They provide a more effective method of harmonisation by recognising that it would be difficult to mould common law principles under the umbrella of a civil code. Further, given that the dynamics of franchising are such that it differs in its nuances in each jurisdiction and the commercial differences between each national market, it would seem appropriate for a pan-EU franchise law to be promulgated by way of a Directive which imposes minimum levels of regulation

57 Ibid.

58 Op. cit., Deakin, S., 2000, 'Regulatory Competition Versus Harmonisation in European Company Law'.

59 Ibid., Deakin, S.

that can be fine tuned to meet any particular needs of each member state rather than a uniform Civil Code or Regulation. However, whether a new EU franchise law can be imposed by way of a Directive or a European Civil Code, the same substantive issues as to what the law contains apply.

E. DIFFICULTIES LIKELY TO BE ENCOUNTERED

4.9 The European Franchise Federation and some of its member national associations will vigorously oppose any proposal to regulate franchising. The BFA has been vociferous in its opposition to regulation[60] and openly boasts that over the past ten years it has

> successfully prevented several misguided attempts to regulate franchising which would have seriously damaged franchising throughout the Common Market.[61]

Indeed, when the Chairman of the EFF suggested that the organisation might support EU-wide regulation of franchising at a statutory level, the BFA led a palace coup to have him and the full board of the EFF removed.[62] Any proposal to regulate franchising at an EU level is therefore likely to face aggressive lobbying in Brussels and elsewhere by the EFF and at least some of its national association members. In Italy, Belgium and Sweden the passage of franchise laws through the respective national legislatures was difficult and suggests issues that may cause difficulties during the adoption of a Directive to regulate franchising.[63] All three jurisdictions endured long-drawn-out and politically

---

60 See Chapter 3.

61 Sir Bernard Ingham, Chairman of the BFA at the BFA Annual Convention, 2005.

62 Riding, B., *Franchise World*, Feb/March 2008, p. 29.

63 In contrast the passage of the franchise laws in France, Spain, Romania, Estonia and Lithuania offers little guidance as to what problems these might be. In France the only substantial amendment to the bill proposing the 'Loi Doubin' was the inclusion in it of a requirement for certain further mandatory pre-contractual information. There was also some discussion on the length of this cooling-off period, and the initial 10-day period in the bill was lengthened by 20 days. On 31 December 1989 the law (the Decree was published on 4 April 1991) was enacted with its first article becoming Article L. 330–3 of the French Commercial Code (see Appendix 2). In Spain the passage of the LRCP bill through the Senate was uneventful except for a couple of amendments. The first amendment proposed that bill include a definition of franchising and was made by the bill's original proponent. It was accepted by the Senate without discussion. The second amendment, proposed by the socialist parliamentary group, unsuccessfully tried to include a further provision regarding 'franchise sales'. The lack of any substantial debate of the Catalan proposal (either in Parliament or elsewhere) suggests that Section 62 merely reflects the LRCP's overall public policy, as stated in the LRCP Preamble. This provides that the law is intended to structure, organise and ensure the adequacy of existing legislation regulating the retail distribution and distribution sectors and to reduce the substantial imbalances that existed between large and smaller companies. Two years later, Section 62 LRCP was further developed by Royal Decree 2485/1998, 13 November and again in 2006 by a further Decree without debate (Royal Decree 419/2006, 7 April amending Royal Decree 2485/1998, 13 November regarding Retail Commerce Planning relating to the regulation of franchising and creating the franchisors' register). Both the Lithuanian and Estonian laws passed through the

divisive debates about detailed aspects of the regulation of franchising in their legislatures. It took seven years and eight bills in Italy, 24 years and five bills in Belgium and 19 years and 12 bills in Sweden to produce a franchise law. The issues that arose in Italy were agreeing a definition of franchising; too strong a franchisee bias in proposed bills;[64] an obligation for franchisors to register with the authorities;[65] the proposed mandatory testing period for franchises with criteria set in stone by statute; the lack of certainty about the need to pilot a franchise and the need for franchisees to make earning claims[66] and give details of investment required.[67] In Belgium the problems comprised a failure to take account of the complexities of the wide number of sectors (including production, industry, distribution and services) that franchising covers; the adequacy of self-regulatory regimes existing under the national codes of ethics was seen as

legislature unnoticed as part of a general legislative preparation for their admission into the EU. No parliamentary debate or commentary can be found in either jurisdiction. Franchising was insufficiently developed in either of the Baltic States to warrant any interest from busy legislatures in the absence of high profile abuse or sharp practice by franchisors. The Romanian experience was similar to that of the Baltic States and there appears to have been no parliamentary debate about the bill at all.

64 On 6 March 1997 Bill no. 2093 was proposed by Senator Ascuitti. Inspired by the franchise laws in France and Spain, it proposed both pre-contractual disclosure and the establishment of a franchisors' register at the Chamber of Commerce. However the bill failed to propose a clear definition of franchising, making it difficult to understand the real nature of the contractual relationship to be regulated. Later the same year, members of the Chamber of Deputies proposed an alternative strongly pro-franchisee anti-franchisor regulation. (Bill no. 3869 of 16 June 1997) (e.g. Article 5 provided that 'the determined time of duration of the contract must guarantee a minimum duration so as to allow the franchisee to depreciate its stocks'; Article 6 provided 'the right for the franchisee to return the stocks and all the tangible assets at certain condition' and Article 7 proposed that 'it establishes a specific regulation with regard to the limitations for the competition rights'). The Bill was strongly objected to by franchisors and their trade body resulting in a further two bills being introduced the following year. Senator Caponi of the Communist Party introduced a bill, similar to, but much briefer than Bill no. 2093 (17 June 1998 Bill No. 3361). A fourth bill was introduced by Senator Gambini of the Left Democratic Party (Bill No. 3666 of 24 November 1998). This was based in part upon the expired EU Franchise Block Exemption and contained many glaring errors (for example, its proposal that a post-term non-compete obligation imposed upon the franchisee would be valid for three years conflicted with Article 3.1(c) of the EU Regulation. This provision stated that the franchisee could not carry out, directly or indirectly, any competitive activity which might endanger the franchisor's business for a reasonable period no longer than one year within the territory where the franchisee had exploited the franchising licence). It attracted little support. However, it did make an impact in one respect. It proposed that franchisors should have proven experience of franchising. This proposal gained currency during the parliamentary process and eventually found its way, in a rather transmuted form, into the final law, published on 30 May 2001.

65 The Italian Parliamentary Report published 30 May 2001, Article 2, para. 1.

66 In July 2002, a new draft of the bill was presented to parliament. It reflected some of the proposals of both the Italian Franchising Association and the government. In November 2002, bill no. 842 was formally reviewed by parliament (for example, amending the definition of know-how so that it included the need for secrecy and substantiality and the amendment of the definition of franchising) and on 14 January 2003, the Commission received governmental approval. The text was unanimously approved on 25 March 2003.

67 In Italy Law no.129 was given Presidential consent on 6 May 2004 and entered into force on 25 May 2004. This was followed by decree 204/2005 regarding the regulation of foreign franchises in Italy. Law of 6 May 2004, No. 129, Article 6.1.

offering a high level of protection for franchisees;[68,69] inaccurate research;[70] inappropriate fetters on the franchisor's ability to maintain quality standards;[71] inappropriate rights of termination for franchisees;[72] restrictions on the franchisor's right of termination.[73] In Sweden, the problems comprised a proposal that employees of the franchisee be allowed to negotiate directly with the employer's organisation to which the franchisor was connected.[74] All of these difficulties need to be borne in mind when considering how the EU regulatory environment should be re-engineered.

F. LESSONS TO BE LEARNED FROM OTHER FRANCHISING REGIMES

4.10 Of the 21 non-EU jurisdictions with franchise-specific laws, the USA and Australia offer the most relevant guidance as to how franchising in the EU might be most appropriately regulated. The USA was the first to regulate

68 From the answer to a Parliamentary question Mr Lagneau asked on 11 April 1986 (Andre Lombart and Paul van Hooghten).

69 The effectiveness of self-regulation was also cited as a reason for not having a franchise law by the Swedish legislators. Parliamentary Standing Committee on Civil Legislation 1992/93; LU.

70 The 30 October Bill, which declared that it was based upon the provisions of the even-then defunct EU Franchising Block Exemption (Commission Regulation (EEC) 4087/88 on the application of article 85(3) of the Treaty to categories of franchise agreements) in order 'to avoid the legislation becoming too complex' (The Belgian House of Representatives, Extraordinary Session, 8 October 2003, Doc 51 0265/001 Developments – Article 2) was fundamentally flawed. It was based upon the false premise that although from the strictly legal point of view franchisees are independent entities, 'in fact from a financial and contractual point of view the franchisee is largely the subsidiary of the franchisor' (The Belgian House Of Representatives, 30 Oct 2003 – Summary page 4).

71 One bill restricted the franchisor's ability to maintain the quality of the franchise by restricting the franchisor's ability to refuse franchisees the right to transfer the franchise agreement to a third party by imposing a requirement that refusal to a transfer must be on 'grounds which he can objectively justify' (The Belgian House Of Representatives, 30 Oct 2003, Clause 7) and stated that 'in case of dispute as to these grounds, either party may request the Commission of Franchise Arbitrators to adjudicate whether the grounds raised by the franchiser are objectively justified' (The Belgian House Of Representatives, 30 Oct 2003, Clause 7). It proposed to prohibit (The Belgian House Of Representatives, 28 Jan 2004 – Article 11 [Doc 51 0747/001]) 'the provision of a post-term non-competition clause; a provision prohibiting the transfer of the franchise agreement to relatives in the first degree, or to prevent its transfer to other third parties when the grounds used by the franchisor are not serious and objective; any requirement for unilateral undertakings by the franchisee; the provision in favour of the franchisor of a right of pre-emption, the period for the exercise of which exceeds one month; any provision requiring the franchisee in cases where a right of pre-emption of the business has been agreed, to communicate the identity of the proposed purchaser to the franchisor; to proceed to value the business beforehand; and to include in the contract an option to purchase'.

72 The proposal that the franchisor would have no right to terminate the franchise agreement for failure 'to comply with an obligation to achieve a certain turnover or a pre-determined volume of sales or any other unilateral commitment by the franchisee' (The Belgian House Of Representatives, 30 Oct 2003, Clause 8.1) and that post-term non-compete restrictions would not be enforceable against a former franchisee unless the franchisor had purchased the franchisee's business (The Belgian House Of Representatives, 30 Oct 2003, Clause 8.2).

73 The Belgian House of Representatives, 17 March 2004, Doc 51 0924/001 Second sitting of 51st Parliament, Article 8.

74 Statens offentiliga (SOU) 1987:17 'Franchising'.

franchising over 38 years ago and has the most complete franchise regulatory regime in the world, whilst Australia has hands on experience of trying to make self-regulation of franchising work before adopting its franchising Code of Conduct, which has legal force under the Competition and Consumer Act. They both have state and federal law and have therefore had to deal with the difficulties generated by the relationship between EU and member state law. The two jurisdictions have, however, chosen approaches that differ in a number of important aspects. Australia has dealt with this by, on the whole, having only federal law deal with the regulation of franchising. The USA has taken a different approach and exhibits a complex mix of both federal and state law. Both jurisdictions therefore offer relevant learning as regards both the form and substance of an EU franchise regulatory regime.

1. The USA

As in the EU, franchise regulation in the USA began on a state level. The first statute regulating franchising as we know it today was introduced in California in 1971.[75] However, by the end of the decade, the US had wholeheartedly embraced the need to specifically regulate franchising. Not satisfied with federal regulation many states adopted their own franchise-specific regulations. The state and federal franchise laws can be divided into three basic types: those that regulate the sale of franchises, those that regulate the relationship between the franchisor and the franchisee and those that require the registration documentation on public registers. Some, such as the Californian law, regulate all three. The preamble of the California Franchise Investment Law[76] states that its intent is prohibiting fraud and providing **4.11**

> each prospective franchisee with the information necessary to make an intelligent decision regarding franchises being offered.

It requires sellers to register a franchise prior to making an offer within the state and deliver an offering circular to the prospective franchisee. In due course 17 other states followed suit with an array of laws varying in reach and complexity. The FTC Rules subsequently introduced a federal dimension to the regulation of franchising in the USA, but the rules do not supersede the state laws, they merely add an extra layer of regulation. Disclosure laws were enacted because of a fear that small investors were not receiving sufficient information about their potential investment before committing themselves.[77] Those that regulate

75 The California Franchise Investment Law (1970) (Cal. Corp. Code Sections 31000 to 31516).

76 Ibid.

77 CCH, *Business Franchise Guide*, p. 457.

relationships and termination were adopted because of a concern that small businesses were being eliminated or taken over unfairly by their franchisors. The need for 'good cause' and 'just cause' were therefore introduced.[78] During the 1970s 14 states[79] plus Puerto Rico adopted relationship laws. These laws focus on prohibiting the termination or non-renewal of a franchise without good cause and prior written notice. They also deal with franchise transfers, impose a duty of good faith, prohibit discrimination between franchisees and allow individual franchisees a private right of redress through injunctive relief and damages. This complex matrix of regulation imposes a substantial burden on franchisors and so since the 1970s there have been some attempts to harmonise the differing franchise laws. Some of these efforts were successful. For example the Uniform Franchise Offering Circular ('UFOC') created by the Mid West Securities Commissioners Association, was copied by the North American Securities Commissioners Association and was widely used in those states that did not have a franchise law until 1 July 2008, when the new FTC (Federal Trade Commission) Rule became mandatory and the Uniform Franchise Disclosure Document (the 'UFDD') replaced the UFOC. However, other attempts, such as for example the Uniform Franchise and Business Opportunities Act, have not been successful. Even though this was adopted by the National Conference of Commissioners on Uniform State Law in 1987, the proposal has yet to be enacted by any state.[80] (A similar fate may await any Common Frame of Reference adopted by the EU.)[81] There have also been numerous attempts to enact federal franchise laws which would replace or harmonise state laws. In 1990 the House Small Business Committee commenced a series of hearings about the need for further federal regulation of franchising. In 1992 the Chairman of the Committee, Representative John J. LaFalce, sponsored federal franchise laws dealing not only with disclosure but also relationship and termination issues. In 1993 Representative LaFalce introduced similar disclosure and relationship bills, but these failed to gain Committee approval. Undaunted by this failure though, the Congressman introduced another similar relationship bill in 1995,[82] which also failed. In 2007 the FTC's Trade Regulation Rule 'Disclosure Requirements and Prohibition Concerning Franchising' became effective. This fine tuned the differences between the FTC Franchise Rule and the UFDD. The complexity of the US regulatory regime is well summed up by the fact that although the FTC Franchise Rule, formally entitled 'Disclosure Requirements and Prohibitions

78 Ibid., p. 458.

79 Koch, D.W., 'The End of Franchising As We Know It'; Federal Bar Association Annual Convention, Cleveland, Ohio, 22 September 2000.

80 CCH, *Business Franchise Guide*, p. 456.

81 See above.

82 CCH, *Business Franchise Guide*, p. 457.

Concerning Franchising'[83] (the new FTC Rule) clearly defines franchising, differing definitions have been adopted by 15 states which have formulated their own franchising laws. The USA is a patchwork of overlapping and sometimes conflicting federal and state franchise laws. What constitutes a 'franchise' varies considerably from state to state and both the 'marketing plan' and 'community of interest approach' are found. The marketing plan definition is more common and is used not only by the majority of states but also the FTC.[84] Most state and federal laws have a 'de minimis' exemption threshold for a franchise fee[85] element. If the franchise fees paid by the alleged franchisee do not reach this threshold, no 'franchise' exists.[86] This lack of uniform approach to defining a franchise greatly increases the uncertainty and expense of franchising in the USA and is therefore a state of affairs that should be avoided in the EU.

2. Australia

The regulation of franchising in Australia rests on three basic pillars contained in the Competition and Consumer Act 2010 (CCA) (formerly the Trade Practices Act (TPA) 1974) and the Australian Consumer law which consists of the Trade Practices Amendment (Australian Consumer Law) Acts No 1 and No 2 (ACL); Sections 51AD and 51AE of the CCA prescribe the Franchise Code and make it mandatory, Section 22 ACL (formerly TPA 51AC) prohibits unconscionable conduct, Section 18 ACL (formerly TPA 52) prohibits misleading or deceptive conduct. There is also a common law duty of good faith. The Franchise Code applies to franchise agreements entered into, renewed or extended after October 1998 and ensures that Section 51 of the CCA is directly 4.12

83 Code of Federal Regulations, Title 16, Chapter 1, Subchapter D, Part 436 (16 CFR 436), promulgated 21 December 1978, effective 21 October 1979 (effective date extended from 21 July 1979, 44 Federal Register 31170, 31 May 1979). Cited as 'FTC Rule'.

84 It has the following elements:
(1) grant of a right to operate a business that is identified or associated with the franchisor's trademark or to offer, sell or distribute goods, services or commodities that are identified or associated with the franchisor's trademark;
(2) the franchisor exerts or has authority to exert a significant degree of control over the franchisee's method of operation or provides significant assistance in the franchisee's method of operation;
(3) the payment of fees is a condition of obtaining or commencing the operation of the franchise.
FTC Rule 436.1(h).

85 The FTC rule provides that a sale is excluded from the scope of the regulation if the total payments required by the franchisee before and during the 6-month period after the business opens do not exceed $500. The amount thresholds under the various state laws range from $100 to $500. The time period over which franchise fees are aggregated for purposes of the amount threshold also vary.

86 In a 1998 decision involving the Illinois Franchise Disclosure Act the US Court of Appeals in Chicago determined that a dealer's payment of more than $1600 for parts and service manuals over the course of eight years satisfied the statute's $500 fee threshold. *To-Am Equipment Co., Inc.* v. *Mitsubishi Caterpillar Forklift America, Inc.*, No. 95 C 0836, US 7th Circuit Court of Appeals (6 August 1998).

applicable to franchising by giving clear definition to what amounts to unconscionable conduct.

The mandatory code is designed to

> ... induce behavioural change on the part of big business to smaller business, and to provide to small businesses that are unfairly treated, adequate means of redress[87]

and

> assist franchisees and franchisors make an informed decision prior to entering into a franchise agreement and to provide a framework for dispute resolution.[88]

The Code regulates the franchising sector by ensuring that franchisors disclose relevant information and documents to prospective franchisees, franchisees are aware of their rights under franchise agreements and appropriate and cost-effective dispute resolution mechanisms are available. It is administered by the Australian Competition and Consumer Commission but may be enforced both by the government and by private civil actions.[89] To date, the Franchising Code is the only mandatory industry Code prescribed under the CCA. Since its introduction, there has been considerable ongoing debate in relation to the certain aspects of the Code. This led to a comprehensive review of the operation of the Code by the Franchising Policy Council. Following recommendations by the Policy Council, some amendments to the Code were made[90] on 1 October 2001. Although the Regulations clarified some areas of concern, they did not address all the concerns of the franchise industry. It was further reviewed by the Federal government in 2006 and again in 2008, when the Commonwealth Parliamentary Joint Committee on Corporate and Financial Services held an enquiry into improving franchising conduct. The government's response to the enquiry was published on 5 November 2009 which led to the creation of an expert panel on franchising.[91] The Franchise Code regulates the franchise relationship in a number of ways. It prohibits the general releases of liability in franchise agreements,[92] requires that franchisors disclose

87 Franchising Code of Conduct – Department of Workplace Regulations and Small Business/Australian Competition and Consumer Commission, 1 July 1998.

88 Ibid, p. 1.

89 See below.

90 Trade Practices (Industry Code – Franchising Amendment) Regulations 2001.

91 Minister of Innovation, Science and Research, Media Release: 'Government Appoints Expert Panel on Franchising and Unconscionable Conduct', 27 November 2009 at http://minister.innovation.gov.au/Emerson/pages/governmentappointsexpertpanelonfranchising.

92 Clause 16 of Franchising Code of Conduct.

materially relevant facts not mentioned in the disclosure document,[93] regulates when the franchisor may withhold consent to a franchise transfer,[94] requires notice of termination and an opportunity to remedy a contract breach cited as the reason for termination,[95] and establishes a mandatory alternative dispute resolution procedure.[96]

3. How successful are the US and Australian systems?

The most striking characteristics of US franchise regulation are not its completeness and attention to detail but its complexity, relative lack of uniformity and obsession with form over substance. None of these recommend themselves as hallmarks of effective and appropriate regulation. **4.13**

According to the Franchise Council of Australia[97] the Australian system

> strikes an ideal balance between contractual freedom and flexibility that encourages growth and entrepreneurial behaviour, and regulatory intervention to support the contractual process and ensure informal and fair bargains are made.[98]

It sees Australia as having 'the most comprehensive franchise regulatory system in the world'[99] and declares that 'it is now widely accepted that Australian franchising is world's best practice in the relationship aspect of the franchisor/franchise partnership'.[100]

It believes that this success is a direct result of the Franchising Code of Conduct and 'Part 2' disclosure requirements. Together with the CCA, it considers these to provide 'comprehensive legal protection from all forms of misrepresentation or illegal behaviour'.[101] It relies upon the low level of franchise disputes in Australia to support these bold claims. At around 1% it is substantially lower than the 6% in the USA estimated by the International Franchise Association.[102] It also points to the success of mediation in settling franchise disputes in Australia. 75% of franchise disputes in Australia are settled by mediation, whereas in the USA arbitration and litigation are the norm. Despite this

93 Ibid. Clause 18.
94 Ibid. Clause 20.
95 Ibid. Clause 21.
96 Ibid. Clauses 24–31.
97 Submission to the Federal Government Review, 15 August 2006.
98 Ibid., Executive Summary 1.1.
99 Ibid., Executive Summary 1.2.
100 Ibid., Part B 1.5.
101 Ibid., Executive Summary 1.2.
102 Ibid., Executive Summary 1.1.

apparent success, the changes being currently adopted[103] evidence the perceived need to continuously reappraise the regulatory regime and ensure that it is fit for purpose. Notably, the Federal Government decided against a mandatory obligation of good faith in franchise agreements on the ground that it would 'increase uncertainty in franchising'. The Minister for Innovation, Industry, Science and Research, Dr Craig Emerson, has announced the establishment of an expert panel to advise what other changes, if any, should be made to the Franchising Code.[104] So the US and Australian regulatory regimes suggest how the EU regulatory environment might be most appropriately re-engineered and what might best be avoided.

G. CONCLUSION

4.14 The European Commission is unequivocal in its belief that a regulatory environment comprising harmonised legal eco-systems is necessary to ensure that franchisors and other businesses can operate across borders efficiently. The current heterogeneous regulatory environment creates obstacles that hinder franchisors from taking full advantage of the single market. The same problem confronted commercial agency and was overcome by the adoption of a directive. Empirical research supports the case for harmonisation. The catalyst for such harmonisation could be either a directive or a common civil code. It is suggested that a directive is more appropriate. This is because the considerable difficulties involved in a common civil code mean that proposals for a non-mandatory common frame of reference have overtaken those for a common civil code and the non-binding nature of such a 'tool box' will not achieve the homogenised regulatory environment required. An examination of existing member state franchise laws suggests that there will be much debate about the substantive content of a franchise directive, whilst consideration of US and Australian franchise law offers suggestions as to what a franchise directive might contain.

---

103 Minister for Innovation, Industry, Science and Research, Media Release, 'Government to Strengthen Franchising Code of Conduct and Unconscionable Law', 5 November 2009 at http://minister.innovation.gov.au/Emerson/Pages governmenttostrengthenfranchisingcodeof conduct.

104 Additional Information on Franchising Code and Unconscionable Conduct Reforms, November 2009 at http://minister.innovation.gov.au/Emerson/Documents/Additional%information%20%on%20Franchising%20Code%20%and%20Unconscionable%20Conduct%20ReformsPdf.

5

RE-ENGINEERING THE REGULATORY ENVIRONMENT FOR FRANCHISING IN THE EU

5.1 Franchising makes a positive contribution to the EU's economy and has the potential to make a still greater contribution. An EU Franchise Directive should therefore promote and support the economic drivers that encourage franchisors and franchisees to become involved in franchising. It should also reduce the risks that face both franchisors and franchisees. In order to achieve this, the EU's regulatory environment should clearly define franchising and be re-engineered by accentuating the influence of three commercial imperatives on the legislative eco-systems. These are market confidence in franchising, pre-contractual hygiene and a mandatory taxonomy of rights and obligations which ensures that an appropriate level of protection is afforded to both franchisors and franchisees. This necessitates a clear definition of what franchising is and a re-engineering process that results in environmental dynamics that are targeted, transparent, proportionate, accountable and consistent.[1] In other words, the fundamental objective of an EU Franchise Directive must be to define franchising as a specific, distinct and uniform business structure, to enable both franchisors and franchisees to access the advantages which encourage them to become involved in franchising and to reduce, but not remove, all of the risks involved. An over-regulated environment with no chance of market failure or financial scandals would be undesirable as it would stifle innovation and competition.[2] It would be undesirable as it would discourage companies from franchising out their businesses. This is supported by recent research in the US[3] which shows that over-regulation leads to a reduction in both the number of franchised units and the total number of chain outlets. Regulation must set, promote, monitor and enforce high standards, in order to contribute to the soundness of the system as a whole and to promote consumers' and institutions' confidence in its strength and integrity.[4] It is therefore important that a balance is struck between the need to afford protection to many of those entering into a commercial enterprise or making a financial investment on the one hand and the commercial risk that naturally arises for anyone wishing to enter into a potentially money making enterprise, on the other.[5] It is suggested that it

1 www.berr.gov.uk/whatwedo/bre/index.html. The UK's Department for Business, Enterprise and Regulatory Reform Better Regulation Executive.

2 FSA, *A new regulator for the new millennium*, January 2000.

3 Klick, Kobayashi, Ribstein, 'The Effect of Contract Regulation: The Case of Franchising', George Mason Law & Economics Research Paper No. 07–03, 2nd Annual Conference on Empirical Legal Studies Paper, FSU College of Law, Law and Economics Paper No. 07/001. Based upon the impact of the Iowa Franchise Law of 1992, which is uniformly regarded as unfavourable to franchisors. In addition to preventing termination at will by the franchisor, Iowa requires that franchisors allow franchisees a right to remedy any defect and restricts waiver and choice of law clauses.

4 Financial Services Authority, an outline, 28 October 1997.

5 One of the draft bills placed before the Belgian Chamber of Deputies, whilst advocating the regulation of franchising acknowledged that; 'As in all commercial sectors, there are clearly franchisees who consider that they have suffered loss as a result of the agreements they have entered into. However ... these franchisees are in the minority, as 70% of franchisees are satisfied with their contracts. It is therefore necessary to place this information

should do this by establishing franchise agreements as 'type' or 'nominate' contracts with mandatory and essential terms that seek to preserve the above advantages and reduce the above risks, create a scheme of incentives to encourage business to adopt franchising as part of their market strategy and create an educational infrastructure to support potential franchisees in deciding whether or not to buy a franchise. This approach has only been adopted by two of the EU member states that have adopted franchise laws.[6] In the rush to regulate franchising in EU member states, be it by franchise-specific legislation or the application of the general law, there has been little thought as regards what the overall purpose of the regulation is, or should be. It rarely goes beyond a general feeling that franchisees are unsophisticated 'consumers' who are often investing their life savings into complex businesses that may be run by unscrupulous business people with a great deal more experience and little regard for the franchisee's welfare. The conclusion drawn is that they therefore deserve some kind of extra protection against being unfairly exploited.

As Terry comments, 'the world has embraced the US franchising concept but not the manner of its regulation'.[7]

This lack of clarity and homogeneity has created difficulties and complications with the regulation of franchising in the EU.

A. DEFINING FRANCHISING

It is suggested that a definition of franchising should follow the Shared Marketing Plan approach and that franchising be established as a new 'type agreement' by adopting an 'Exchange of Benefits' approach, that affords franchisors a number of advantages in return for accepting a reasonable level of regulation. Establishing a working definition of franchising is an essential part of a Directive for at least four basic reasons.[8] Firstly, a clear definition helps would-be franchisees assess, with a greater level of confidence, whether a business proposition is all it appears to be i.e. a definition can become a benchmark for potential franchisees. Secondly, a precise definition makes it easier to understand the size and role of franchising in the EU by differentiating 5.2

which is occasionally tainted with sensationalism in context. This does not mean however that those franchisees suffering loss do not merit protection. The matter should be treated in a way which does not adversely affect either the franchisors or the franchisees'. The Belgian House of Representatives, 30 Oct. 2003, Article 16, Doc 51 9361/001.

6 Lithuania and Estonia. But neither has imposed appropriate mandatory terms.

7 Terry, A., 'Franchise Sector Regulation: The Australian Experience. Economics and Management of Franchising Networks', 26 June 2003, www.univie.ac.at/EMNET. Law Asia Journal 97 (9 December 2004).

8 Felstead, 1993.

it from other types of third party relationships. Thirdly, a sharper definition makes it easier to identify those schemes that are either ill-conceived or fraudulent. Fourthly, a clear definition may help to ensure that any regulation is appropriately phrased.

However, although most of those considering the regulation of franchising generally agree that 'it is necessary to have a clear-cut definition of franchising',[9] this is not the unanimous view.[10]

It is not surprising that all the definitions of franchising reflect the interests and concerns of the bodies or individuals providing them. Legislators are naturally trying to define a type of commercial behaviour that they wish to regulate. Trade bodies are trying to determine what types of business they wish to join them. Academics are more interested in the legal and economic dynamics at play than commercial reality. It is therefore only natural that the definitions emanating from such different sources often exhibit material differences to each other. It must be borne in mind that individuals and organisations will produce a definition that best suits their own purpose. So, a trade association, an academic and a legislator will be seeking to achieve different ends by framing a definition of franchising. It is therefore perhaps inevitable that they will produce definitions that differ from each other. Some, following the French and Belgian lead, question the value of any definition,[11] as it

> is less important than a model or 'ideal type' which will enable the area of economic activity with which we are concerned to be identified.[12]

Definitions can create problems of their own. Immediately a definition of franchising is adopted by the legislature in any jurisdiction, lawyers consider whether it is advantageous or disadvantageous for their clients to be deemed a franchise and then commence drafting their contracts and advising their clients to structure their businesses accordingly. In other words legal definitions can become the issue more than the business practices being controlled by them.

---

9 Italian President Caponi, *Corriere della Sera* on 9 December 1997.

10 The French 'Loi Doubin', Law No. 89–1008 dated 31 December 1989 does not seek to define franchising.

11 Adams and Prichard Jones 1997, p. 23.

12 They offer what they see as the three characteristics of franchising. These are '(1) relatively long term relational contracts (usually five years or more); (2) in which an independent undertaking carries out tasks which were, or might have been, carried out by the franchisor undertaking; (3) a relatively high degree of integration of the franchisee undertaking's business systems and activities and those of the franchisor undertaking' (Ibid).

Alluding to this problem one of the bills placed before the Belgian Chamber of Deputies stated[13]

> the problems encountered by a number of businesses do not arise in franchise networks strictly so called, but rather in commercial situations which are similar to franchise agreements (independent management agreements, sales concessions, know-how licences, commission agencies, commercial partnerships etc). One should therefore be aware that the regulations should apply also to these other distribution systems, which are not limited solely to franchise agreements. Otherwise the regulations would not have their desired effect. What would be the use of regulating solely franchise agreements when most contracts outwardly showing franchise characteristics, but which are not in fact franchise agreements, would not be subject to this regulatory regime? Unscrupulous franchisers would quickly be able to steer clear of franchise agreements by adopting formulas less all-embracing or advanced as the franchise, to the detriment of franchisees, in order to escape regulations which would otherwise defeat this objective. If a new law is to be introduced it must cover all types of agreement closely allied to franchise contracts.

This seems to be the view of the French government as, when it enacted the Loi Doubin to regulate franchising, it opted to avoid the need to define it and instead decided to merely describe the main characteristics of a business that has a network of third parties using the same brand.[14] The Belgian government subsequently opted for the same approach.[15]

Maintaining market confidence in franchising means that an appropriate definition of franchising is essential. This inevitably determines the scope and therefore the commercial impact of an EU Franchise Directive. Although there is debate over whether or not it is worthwhile attempting to define franchising and if so how should it be done, it is suggested that in order to effectively regulate it, a 'clear-cut definition' of franchising[16] is imperative. The difficulty is how best to achieve this push for the black and white in a world of grey. A definition must facilitate the more effective regulation of franchising. The regulative approach proposed is one that not only regulates the actions of franchisors but also extends them certain commercial advantages. The definition must therefore have a qualitative threshold to it. A business can only be a 5.3

13 The Belgian House of Representatives, Extraordinary Session, 8 October 2003: Introduction to Draft Parliamentary Bill Concerning pre-contract information in relation to contracts by which one person grants to another the right to carry on commercial activities (lodged by Mme Anne Brazing and MM. Serge Van Overtveldt and Philippe Collard).

14 Article L330–3 of the French Commercial Code (Article 1 of the 'Loi Doubin', Law No. 89–1008 dated 31 December 1989).

15 Law of 19 December 2005 relative to pre-contractual information in the framework of agreements of commercial partnerships.

16 Italian President Caponi, addressing the Italian Parliament on 9 December 1997.

franchise and therefore enjoy its privileges if it clears that threshold. This is dealt with in the definition by the requirement for a 'track record'. A shared marketing plan or prescribed system approach which borrows from both the European Franchise Federation (EFF)'s definition and the Italian franchise law is suggested as follows:

BOX 5.1

A Franchise exists where

(a) one party (the 'Franchisor') who owns or has the right to license other parties to operate a business format offering, supplying or distributing goods or services or both
(b) grants another party (a 'Franchisee')
(c) the right to carry on a business using that business format under a system or in accordance with a marketing plan substantially determined, controlled and/or suggested by the Franchisor or one of its associates or otherwise assisted by the franchisor or one of its associates (a 'Shared Marketing Plan').
(d) The operation of the business must be substantially or materially associated with a brand owned, used or licensed by the Franchisor or an associate of the Franchisor.
(e) The Franchisee will pay monies to the Franchisor or its affiliate, by way of, for example only:
    (i) an initial capital investment and/or
    (ii) a payment for goods or services and/or
    (iii) an ongoing or periodic fee of any discharge from and/or
    (iv) a training fee and/or
    (v) repayment for a lien made by the Franchisor.
(f) A business using the business format has been operated by the Franchisor or its affiliate for a period of 12 months.
(g) For the avoidance of doubt, a franchise does not include motor vehicle dealerships, employee/employer relationship, agencies, landlord and tenants and co-operatives.
(h) An affiliate is an entity in which the Franchisor has a controlling interest.

It is important to consider the main elements of this definition.

1. Shared marketing plan

5.4 Under this definition, a franchise does not have to expressly prescribe a Shared Marketing Plan:

> Control reserved over terms of payment by customers, credit practices, warranties and representations in dealings between franchisees and their customers, suggest a uniform marketing plan

as do

> provisions concerning collateral services, which may or may not be rendered, or prohibiting or limiting the sale of competitive or non-competitive goods.[17]

The key issue is the imposition of a duty to observe

> the licensor's directions or obtaining the licensor's approval with respect to selection of locations, the use of trade names, advertising, signs, sales pitches, and sources of supply, or concerning the appearance of the licensee's business premises and the fixtures and equipment utilized therein, uniforms of employees, hours of operation, housekeeping, and similar decorations.[18]
>
> A marketing plan or system is 'prescribed' where a specific sales program is outlined, suggested, recommended, or otherwise originated by the franchisor.[19]

So, a sales programme may be 'prescribed' by the franchisor where it 'supplies the franchisee with sales aids or props, such as demonstration kits, films, or detailed instructions for personal introduction and presentation of the product, possibly including the text of a sales pitch and especially where such a program is supported by training materials, courses, or seminars'.[20] This view of a prescribed plan is not unique to California.[21] It is preferable to adopt the broader definitions adopted by States such as Illinois, Rhode Island, Washington and Wisconsin which take the view that the marketing plan or system does not have to be prescribed but it can merely be suggested in substantial part by a franchisor.[22] This is because the benefits being offered to franchisees must not be offered too widely. They must be restricted to well-structured businesses that are clearly providing a business format. Whereas many jurisdictions require the

---

17 California Department of Corporations, Release 3-F (Revised) at B(2)(c) (22 June 1994) ('CA Release 3-F'), reprinted at http://www.corp.ca.gov/Commissioner/Releases/3-F.asp.

18 Ibid.

19 Ibid.

20 Ibid.

21 Indiana, Maryland, Michigan, New York, North Dakota, Oregon and Virginia also define a 'franchise' as existing when: 'A franchisee is granted the right to engage in the business of offering, selling or distributing goods or services at retail under a marketing plan or system prescribed in substantial part by a franchisor.' Cal. Corp. Code at § 31005(a)(1); Indy. Code Ann. at § 23–2-2.5–1(a)(3); Mad. Code Ann., Bus. Reg. § 14–201(e)(1)(i); Mich. Comp. Laws § 445.1502(3)(a); N.Y. Gen. Bus. Law, § 681(3)(a) (1996); N.D. Cent. Code § 51–19–02.5.a(1); Or. Rev. Stat. § 650.005(4 a); Va. Code Ann. § 13.1–559A(1).

22 Il Comp. Stat.815 ILCS 705/3(1)(a); R.I. Gen. Laws § 19–28.1–3(7)(i)(A); Wash. Rev. Code § 19.100.010(4)(a)(i); Wis. Stat. Ann. § 553.03(4)(a)1.

payment of a franchise fee,[23] only some require a minimum payment.[24] It is proposed that there would be no minimum level of fees in the European law as it opens the door to the structuring of payments so as to avoid coming within the definition of a franchise.

2. Trademarks

5.5 The role of the trademarks also needs to be considered. There are a variety of approaches. For example, whereas California requires substantial association with the franchisor's trademark,[25] New York does not require the use of a trademark at all. Rather, a business arrangement will constitute a franchise if the franchisor either offers a marketing plan or permits the sale of trademarked goods or services. In Hawaii, Minnesota and South Dakota, it is sufficient for a franchisor to grant the franchisee the right to use the franchisor's trademark.[26] As the brand is a fundamental element of a franchise, its use is specifically included in the proposed definition. The bigger issue is how the brand is used by the franchisee. The US Federal Trade Commission (FTC) Franchise Rule (which also adopts the shared marketing plan approach) uses the phrase 'identified or associated with' the franchisor's mark as do states such as California that require that the franchisee obtain the right to use the franchisor's mark. For example, 'a service-oriented franchise operated out of a home, as opposed to a storefront, might not have a sign with the franchisor's logo, or unique uniforms associated with the franchisor. Although the franchisee's "association" with the franchisor's mark may be limited (such as the right to use the franchisor's mark on business cards, advertising, and in yellow page listings), it is sufficient to trigger the Rule's disclosure obligations: in such circumstances, the use of the franchisor's trademark leads consumers to identify the business with the franchisor'.[27] States such as California, which uses the phrase 'substantial association' with the mark, recognise that the grant of permission to use a franchisor's trademark in the operation of a business would constitute 'substantial association' with the mark.[28] It is interesting to note that in its Staff Report, the FTC however rejected the need for association to be substantial on the basis

23 Cal. Corp. Code at § 31005(a)(3); Haw. Rev. Stat. Ann. § 482E-6; Indy. Code Ann. § 23-2-2.5-2(a)(3); Mad. Code Ann., Bus. Reg. § 14-201(e)(iii); Mich. Comp. Laws § 445.1502(3)(c); Minn. Stat. § 80C.01.4.3; N.Y. Gen. Bus. Law, § 681(3)(b); N.D. Cent. Code § 51-19-02.5.a(3); Wash. Rev. Code § 19.100.010(4)(a)(iii); Wis. Stat. Ann. § 553.03(4)(a)3.

24 146 815 Ill Comp. Stat. at § 705/3(1)(c); R.I. Gen. Laws § 19-28.1-3(7)(i)(B); Va. Code Ann. § 13.1-559(A)(3).

25 California Department of Corporations, Release 3-F (Revised) ibid.

26 Haw. Rev. Stat. Ann. § 482E-6; Minn. Stat. § 80C.01.4.1.

27 Code of Federal Regulations, Rule 16 Part 436.2.

28 See CA Release 3-F at 3 ('[I]f the franchisee is granted the right to use the franchisor's symbol, that part of the franchise definition is satisfied even if the franchisee is not obligated to display the symbol').

that the need to show 'substantial use' imposes a new and unnecessary burden of proof.[29] The proposed definition overcomes this by requiring that the business is substantially or materially associated with the brand.

3. Minimum standard

The EFF[30] requires that franchisors 5.6

> have operated a business concept with success, for a reasonable time and in at least one pilot unit before starting its franchise network.

The Italian franchise regulation has expanded on that requirement and requires the franchisor to have tested the concept for at least one year before it is franchised.[31] It originates from the non-statutory requirement found in the Code of Ethics of the EFF[32] (and in turn the Italian Franchise Association[33]) for franchisors to have at least one-year's experience of their business formula before embarking upon the roll out of their franchise.[34] No minimum period of time is stated for the testing period. All that is required is that the results are disclosed to potential franchisees in a full and unambiguous manner. The only other jurisdictions in the world which have this requirement are China and Vietnam.[35] Like China, Italy ultimately rejected the suggestion that the pilot

29 Federal Trade Commission Disclosure Requirements and Prohibitions Concerning Franchising Staff, Report to the Federal Trade Commission and Proposed Revised Trade Regulation Rule (16 CFR Part 436) – Bureau of Consumer Protection, August 2004, p. 42.

30 www.eff-franchise.com.

31 Law of 6 May 2004, No. 129, Article 3.2.

32 EFF's European Code of Ethics, 19 September 2008.

33 Regulations of the Italian Franchise Association, effective 1 January 1995, Article 2: 'Prior to the establishment of its own franchise system, the franchisor shall have implemented its formula in the market for a minimum period of one year, with at least a pilot unit, if applicable'.

34 The original proposal (in the draft bill approved by the Senate on 25 March 2003) was far more challenging than the provision finally incorporated in the franchise law. It provided for a two-year testing period carried out through at least two pilot units, located in different cities. The 'Test Period' was deemed to be necessary because, '... cases of inexperience and improvisation may generate a serious litigation ... ' (Senator Gambini in the XIII Legislature). However, there was a fear that the test period – at one point proposed to be three years – would severely compromise the commercial success of franchises as it would rob them of many of the advantages that being first to the market brings and so giving non franchised concepts an unfair commercial advantage. In the first draft it was expressly stated that it had to be piloted in the Italian market. This effectively created a barrier to freedom of trade within the EU so contravening a basic tenet of EU law. There was also concern that the provision would discourage foreign franchisors from entering the Italian market. These concerns were acknowledged and the current text of the law provides that the 'testing period' must be based upon the criteria of reasonableness and flexibility. Following the comments of the Commission for Constitutional Affairs (Remarks made on 7 October 2003) that, 'the present formulation of the law might involve an unjustified limitation of economic initiative' the meaning of 'the market' was also amended to mean any market, be it in Italy, Europe or elsewhere in the world.

35 In China franchisors are required to establish and operate two company-owned units for more than one year before granting franchises to third parties (Article 7 of the Regulation on Administration of Commercial Franchises 2007). In the earlier regulation, the pilot had to be in China, but the current law removed this

should be in its domestic market, due to the commercial inappropriateness of such a provision. It effectively creates a barrier to entry into the market. Subjecting new franchisees to the rigorous regulatory regime proposed by this book from day one has the appeal of being straightforward, but could create substantial barriers to new entrants who are franchising their businesses because, inter alia, they lack capital and/or management resource.[36] It is therefore proposed that before franchisors are required to take on the burden of complying with the proposed franchise regulation and can enjoy the consequential benefits they establish a 'track record'. That is, that they must have operated a business using the business format for twelve months or be operating, either by itself or through franchisees, a total of four outlets. Forbidding a business to franchise out its business without complying with the regulation would be too arduous for new entrants. However, in practice, it is suspected that many new entrants will decide that it is more efficient to seek to comply from day one so as to avoid the duplication of effort involved in redrafting their documentation so soon after starting and in order to take advantage of the 'Exchange of Benefits' offered to established franchisors. Another advantage of the initial period is that it enables potential franchisees to have the opportunity to consider the achievements of a year's trading and base its decision whether or not to buy the franchise partly upon that information. Some commentators have suggested that before granting a franchise to a party within an EU member state a franchisor should operate a pilot operation in that member state for a 12-month period. The justification for this proposal is that without experience of a particular member state a franchisor cannot properly franchise in it, although it is not justified in any meaningful way. If this approach were adopted it would in effect freeze foreign franchisors out of smaller member states such as the Baltic States, the Czech Republic, Slovakia and Slovenia. For this reason it must be rejected. The experience of both Italy and China has been that such a parochial approach is unworkable on a national level. The diverse economic and cultural profile of the EU makes it worthless on an EU level. Given the structures generally used for international franchising it would also seem to be inappropriate to require that testing be carried on in the EU. Such a requirement would probably make it very difficult for smaller non-EU franchisors to

---

requirement, mirroring the debate in Italy as to where the pilot operation has to be. In Vietnam, pursuant to Article 2 of the Commercial Law of 2001, which came into force on 1 January 2006, a franchisor must be a lawfully established enterprise either in Vietnam or in a foreign country and a franchise can only be granted to a franchisee who has a Vietnamese business licence (Article 6 of Decree No 35/2006/ND-CP issued by the Government to regulate franchises). In addition, the franchise system must have been in operation for at least a year before a franchise can be granted. In the case of a sub-franchise granted to a Vietnamese master franchisee, the Vietnamese master franchisee must have operated the franchise business for at least a year before it can grant sub-franchises to unit franchisees (Article 5(1) of the Decree No 35/2006/ND-CP).

36 The so-called Agency Theory and Transaction Cost Theory, supported by empirical evidence obtained from the research done for this book.

enter the EU market. In order to comply with such a requirement smaller non-EU franchisors would probably have to use joint venture structures. Whilst these are often used for more substantial businesses and by more sophisticated players, it is doubtful that they would be appropriate for smaller, less sophisticated and less well-resourced franchisors. Further, with appropriate expert advice, franchisors could work the structure to circumvent the main intent of the regulation by still placing the real burden of the EU pilot operation on the joint venture partner. It is therefore recommended that in order to come within the definition of a franchise a business must have been operated for a 12-month period in any market, not necessarily one in the EU. This avoids burdening small start up businesses with too heavy a regulatory burden, so reducing barriers to entry. Such small businesses are unlikely to have a material adverse impact on the market. However, they should not be able to afford themselves of the benefits afforded to franchisors.[37] The definition of a franchise must focus on substance rather than form. Merely because a business relationship is called a 'franchise' does not mean it should be treated as one if the relationship does not satisfy the definition. 'Misdescriptions' of a business relationship as a franchise should not bring them within the definition of a franchise. This definition aims at both describing the essential elements of the business relationship and 'qualifying' each system on the basis of its track record to enjoy certain privileges extended to franchise systems.

B. ACCENTUATING THE INFLUENCE OF COMMERCIAL IMPERATIVES ON THE EU'S LEGAL ECO-SYSTEMS

It is proposed that, in order to enable franchisors and franchisees to access the 5.7
economic drivers that attract them to franchising and reduce the risks involved, the regulatory environment must accentuate the influence of three distinct commercial imperatives on the legislative eco-systems. It must maintain market confidence in franchising as a way of expanding a business; maintain pre-contractual hygiene by increasing understanding of franchising amongst potential franchisees and ensure that they have access to information that allows them to make an informed decision; and impose a mandatory taxonomy of rights and obligations to protect the fundamental interests of both franchisors and franchisees.[38] These commercial imperatives are not unique to franchising. They

37 Such as retail price control in the network and the ability to control a multi-channel sales strategy.

38 These criteria are based on the Financial Services and Markets Act 2000 (FSMA) which suggests four objectives that apply equally to the regulation of other areas of commerce, including franchising. FSMA 2000 Part 1, Sections 2(1), 3, 4, 5 and 6. The fourth objective, prevention of crime, is not appropriate for franchising due to a comparatively low level of criminal activity in the franchise sector and the adequacy of existing criminal

apply to many regulatory systems and are articulated well in the UK's Financial Services and Markets Act 2000.[39] It is suggested that these three 'commercial imperatives' should have a key influence on the way in which the regulatory environment for franchising in the EU is re-engineered.

1. Identifying the commercial imperatives

5.8 The first 'commercial imperative' is the need to maintain market confidence in franchising and so ensure that it is used as an effective route to market by a wide spectrum of businesses across the single market. Unless franchising is regarded by companies as an attractive way of growing their business both domestically and across borders in the EU, it will never be able to help them expand their networks or make its full potential contribution to the growth of the single European market, which will suffer as a consequence. Market confidence is essential. Maintaining market confidence

> involves preserving both actual stability ... and the reasonable expectation that it will remain stable.[40]

It is therefore essential that the re-engineering of the regulatory environment for franchising in the EU accentuates the influence of this factor on the various legal eco-systems. The second 'commercial imperative' is a matter of pre-contractual hygiene. Unless potential franchisees fully understand what they are getting into when they buy a franchise (that it is not a guarantee of success which allows them to abdicate any responsibility for their own performance), there will always be an inappropriately high level of disputes between franchisors and their franchisees. Increasing understanding amongst potential franchisees means 'promoting awareness of both the benefits and risks' associated with the commercial activity being regulated and, 'the provision of appropriate information and advice'.[41] This means that regulation has an educational role in improving general understanding of franchising amongst potential franchisees and ensuring that relevant information is made available to them in good time and in an appropriate form, so rectifying the severe imbalance of information between potential franchisees and franchisors. It is therefore essential that the re-engineering of the regulatory environment creates an educational infrastructure that ensures that potential franchisees have access to appropriate information and accentuates the influence of this factor on

---

sanctions due to the relative lack of sophistication of crime involving franchising as compared to that involving financial services.

39 FSMA 2000, Part (1) Sections 3, 4, 5 and 6.

40 FSA, *A new regulator for the new millennium*, January 2000.

41 FSMA 2000, Section 4.

the EU's legal eco-systems. It is also essential that potential franchisees are given full access to the information that will enable them to take an informed decision as to whether or not they should purchase a particular franchise. The third 'commercial imperative' is that the terms of the franchisor/franchisee relationship, as captured in the franchise agreement, must afford such protection to the parties that the economic drivers which attract them to franchising are supported and re-enforced and the consequential and inherent risks are reduced to an appropriate level. There should be a mandatory taxonomy for franchise agreements. The appropriate level of protection afforded to franchisees and franchisors can be measured by reference to the differing degrees of risk involved for each party; the differing degrees of experience and expertise that the parties may have; and the general principle that individuals should take responsibility for their decisions.[42] As a result, a franchise directive must aim to ensure that both parties receive clear and adequate information about each other and the risks involved. It must also recognise the parties' responsibility for their own decisions, whilst aiming to ensure that they are not exposed to risks that they should not reasonably be expected to assume. An effective franchise directive must therefore maintain market confidence in franchising, ensure pre-contractual hygiene and provide adequate protection to franchisors and franchisees. All this must be done in a manner that does not stifle innovation and competition.

2. The current impact of commercial imperatives

As is evident from the discussion in Chapter 3 above the EU's current **5.9**
regulatory environment does not focus upon accentuating the impact of these three commercial imperatives on its constituent legal eco-systems. None of the legal eco-systems endeavour to promote market confidence or educate potential franchisees, ensuring that they have an appropriate level of information to enable them to take an informed decision about their prospective purchase and provide adequate protection for both franchisors and franchisees on either an EU-wide or national basis. Whilst EU member state franchise laws all seek, on a member state basis, to reduce misconduct by franchisors and maintain market confidence by imposing a degree of stability in their individual national markets, the lack of uniformity of approach and content means that on an EU level they lead to instability. They all fail to protect the franchisor's legitimate interests. The Loi Doubin[43] requires the proprietor of a network in France working under a common brand to make pre-contractual disclosure 21 days

42 FSMA 2000, Section 5(2).

43 Commercial Code Article L.330-3 (Article 1 of the 'Loi Doubin', Law No. 89-1008 dated 31 December 1989).

before contract. However, it does nothing to try and ensure that this information is imparted in a manner that potential franchises will easily understand or to try and ensure that they are educated about the need to take and follow advice about what is revealed by it. Nor does it identify franchising as a specific form of business and differentiate it from other forms of licensing, agency and distribution. It therefore does nothing to promote market confidence in and encourage the use of franchising in preference to other forms of branded networks. As it deals only with disclosure it also fails to deal with the risks involved for both parties or support the commercial drivers that attract franchisors and franchisees to franchising. German law does not categorise franchising as a 'type agreement' and does nothing to promote it as a way of doing business. Likewise, it does nothing to educate potential franchisees. It does seek to address the way in which the balance of the franchisor/franchisee relationship is reflected in the franchise agreement, although this is from the perspective of there being an inherent imbalance of bargaining power between the parties and a need to apply commercial agency, consumer, employment and other laws to redress the balance in favour of the franchisee. It therefore fails to deal with the commercial imperatives. The 'caveat emptor' approach of English law and a relative lack of relevant jurisprudence means that it fails to promote market confidence in franchising, does nothing to promote pre-contractual hygiene and is loath to interfere in the detail of the commercial bargain struck by the parties. None of the other member states have adequately tackled the commercial imperatives with their franchise-focused laws either.[44]

44 The Spanish law (Act 7/1996 and Royal Decree 2485/1998) provides for both disclosure and the registration of franchise documentation but does not promote market confidence in franchising in any meaningful way. The registration requirement is an attempt to help educate potential franchisees but it fails in part due to its lack of effective implementation and in part to the inherent shortcomings of a registration system. The Spanish law fails to acknowledge the risks accepted by franchisors. The Italian law (Law of 6 May 2004, No. 129 Article 1.1) fails to promote market confidence in franchising and fails to recognise the risks accepted by franchisor or seek to educate potential franchisees. The Belgian law (Law of Commercial Partnerships – enacted in 2005 and came into force on 1 February 2006) takes a very heavy handed and paternalistic approach to protecting franchisees but fails to maintain market confidence in franchising. It fails to recognise the risks accepted by franchisors or the principle that franchisees should be responsible for their own actions and no attempt is made to educate potential franchisees. The Swedish law (Franchise Disclosure Law No. 2006:484 – came into force on 1 October 2006) fails to effectively protect the interest of franchisors and franchisees and also fails to recognise the risks accepted by franchisors and promote franchising as a way of doing business. It also fails to educate potential franchisees about it. Although by adopting a franchise law the Romanian, Estonian and Lithuanian legislatures were in a limited way attempting to promote the use of franchising and educate potential franchisees about it, they have failed. The Estonian (Estonian Law of Obligations Act) and Lithuanian (Lithuanian Civil Code Articles 6.766 to 6.779) laws merely acknowledge the existence of franchising with rather turgid and ineffective provisions. They do not even provide for pre-contractual disclosure. The Romanian law (Ordinance no 52/1997 of 28 August 1997 on the law governing franchising, modified by Law 79/1998) fails to provide franchisees with adequate protection. None of these laws seek to protect the franchisor's legitimate interests.

The regulation of franchising in the other seven EU member states that have specific franchise laws also lacks any real harmonisation and so fails to promote confidence in franchising as a way of exploiting (and so expanding) the single market.

3. The impact of the commercial imperatives on proposals to re-engineer the EU's regulatory environment?

Neither of the two main proposals to re-engineer the EU's regulatory environment for franchising (the Amsterdam Team's proposal for a Common Frame of Reference and UNIDROIT's proposal for a model franchise law) focus on the three commercial imperatives. Although the Study Group describes itself as being composed of experts who work 'with the benefit of and from the standpoint of current legal science',[45] unfortunately it offers no meaningful assistance in identifying how the influence of the commercial imperatives on the legal eco-systems can best be accentuated. This part of the paper is full of broad statements and is dogged by uncertainty. It fails to address the first commercial imperative – maintaining market confidence – as it does not adequately capture franchising's fundamental nature. It defines franchising as **5.10**

> the rights granted by a party (the franchisor) authorising and requiring another party (the franchisee) in exchange of direct or indirect financial compensation to engage in the business of selling goods or services on its own behalf under a system designated by the franchisor ...

45 The European Parliament (OJ C 158 (28.6.1989), resolution of 26 May 1989; OJ C 205 (25.7.1994), resolution of 6 May 1994) supports and some member states (*The Speech by the Dutch Minister of Justice at the opening of the symposium: Towards a European Civil Code, 28 February 1997, 9.45 h. at Carlton Beach Hotel, Scheveningen, Den Haag:* http://www.minjust.nl:8080/C_ACTUAL/SPEECHES/SP0006.htm) support the Study Group on a European Civil Code's aim 'to produce a set of codified principles which constitute the most suitable private law rules for Europe-wide application' (http://www.sgecc.net, accessed 14 August 2009) which will take the form of 'a draft codification ... complete with comments and illustrations explaining the provisions and how they apply' although its technocratic approach to harmonisation of member state law is not without dissent. Following a report by the Parliament's Directorate-General for Research in 1999 (Directorate General for Research working paper 'The private law systems in the EU: Discrimination on grounds of nationality and the need for a European civil code. Comparative study of the systems of private law of the EU Member States with regard to discrimination on grounds of nationality and on the scope and need for the creation of a European Civil Code'. Legal Affairs Series JURI – 103 EN 06–2000), in November 2000 the Parliamentary Committee on Legal Affairs and the Internal Market commenced an initiative to create a Common Frame of Reference ('CFR') which is 'a kind of European contract law toolkit ... (which) ... would draw together in one place best solutions based on the common principles underpinning national contract laws ... (and) ... provide tools which can be picked out and used as required to fix a particular problem'. (Robert Madelin, Director General Health and Consumer Protection, European Commission Joint European Parliament and Commission conference 28 April 2004, *A Common Frame of Reference for a more coherent European Contract Law*). Its day to day work is undertaken by a number of Working Teams concentrating on different areas of law. The so-called Amsterdam Team focuses on Commercial Agency, Franchise and Distribution Law (http://ecc.uvt.nl/).

There is no mention of the brand, the franchisor's control of the franchise or the support provided to the franchisees by the franchisor, which sets franchising apart from mere distribution.[46] Its view of franchising is rooted in the civil law view that it is not a 'type agreement' and so should have the law of 'type agreements' such as commercial agency and distribution applied to it by analogy.[47] It therefore fails to produce recommendations that maintain market confidence in franchising and encourage its use. The Study Group's lack of familiarity with the reality of franchising runs throughout the proposals and its failure to distinguish between franchising, agency and distribution undermines all of the Study Group's recommendations. The Study Group Chapter fails to address the second commercial imperative – pre-contractual hygiene (educating potential franchisees and ensuring that they are given appropriate information) – because although it proposes a full set of rules for franchising, it makes no suggestion as to how potential franchisees can be educated into taking appropriate advice before they enter into a franchise agreement and use the information disclosed to them to make an informed decision as to whether they should enter into the franchise. Further, the rules proposed are both excessive and inappropriate.[48] They fail to deliver an appropriate balance between the economic drivers that encourage the parties to become involved in franchising and the consequential inherent risks. The chapter focuses upon the third commercial imperative, seeking to ensure that the franchisors' and franchisees' interests are protected. Although it proposes certain mandatory clauses that are reasonable and underpin some of the economic drivers of the relationship[49] it fails to appreciate where the balance between the interests of the franchisor and franchisee lies and so seeks to overprotect the franchisee thereby eroding some of the economic drivers that attract franchisors to franchising. It suggests that the franchisee should have a number of appropriate obligations imposed upon it. These include paying all monies due to the franchisor under the contract[50] and informing the franchisor of any threat to its intellectual property rights.[51] It also proposes that the franchisee must make reasonable efforts to operate the franchise business according to the business format of the franchisor, follow the franchisor's reasonable instructions in relation to the business format and the maintenance of the reputation of the network and take reasonable care not

46 However, rather inconsistently, the later provisions do refer to the franchisor providing ongoing assistance to the franchisee. Article 3:101, *Commercial Agency, Franchise And Distribution*, Amsterdam Group 8th Draft (21 May 2003).

47 *Commercial Agency, Franchise And Distribution*, Amsterdam Group 8th Draft (21 May 2003).

48 Ibid., Chapter 3.

49 Some of the provisions are reasonable: for example, if the franchisee is obliged or as a matter of practice required to purchase goods or services from the franchisor or a designated supplier, the franchisor must ensure that the goods or services ordered by the franchisee are supplied within a reasonable time, in so far as practicable provided that the order is reasonable (Article 3:204, ibid).

50 Article 3:301, ibid.

51 Article 3:302, ibid.

to harm the franchise network.[52] The franchisee must also allow the franchisor reasonable access to its premises so as to enable the franchisor to check that the franchisee is complying with the franchisor's business method and instructions and audit the franchisee's accounting books.[53] This recognition of at least some of the risks accepted by the franchisor is very positive. However, it fails to identify other important concerns identified earlier in this study such as non-compete provisions and respect of the franchisor's intellectual property. Unfortunately the Study Group also seeks to impose provisions that are far too burdensome on the franchisor and which undermine the economic drivers[54] that attract franchisors to franchising. On the positive side, the Study Group does impose certain obligations on the franchisor which re-enforce the commercial drivers that encourage franchisees to become involved in franchising. For example, it recommends that the franchisor must grant the franchisee a right to use the intellectual property rights to the extent necessary to operate the franchise business and make reasonable efforts to ensure the undisturbed and continuous use of the intellectual property rights,[55] and that throughout the duration of the contract, the franchisor must provide the franchisee with the know-how which is necessary to operate the franchise business.[56] It also states that the franchisor must provide the franchisee with on-going assistance in so far as it is necessary for the operation of the franchise business, without additional charge for the franchisee. However, its lack of specificity potentially causes problems when it states that any further assistance reasonably requested by the franchisee must also be provided at a reasonable cost. The lack of detail as to what 'further assistance' and 'a reasonable cost' mean will have a direct impact upon the commercial viability of the franchise for both the franchisor and the franchisee.[57] It is an open invitation for endless litigation and uncertainty. Some of the obligations it proposes are far too wide and general. As a result they undermine the economic drivers that attract franchisors to franchising. For example, during the term of the contract the franchisor is required to provide the franchisee with information concerning a number of issues including

52 Article 3:303 ibid.

53 Article 3:304 ibid.

54 For example, it must warn the franchisee, within a reasonable time when it foresees or ought to foresee, that the franchisor's or designated supplier's ability to make the supplies will be significantly less than the franchisee had reason to expect (Article 3:206). This obligation may be difficult to comply with in practice and clearly borrows from existing agency laws. The phrase 'ought to foresee' places an arduous duty on the franchisor that is highly subjective and vague. It is unlikely to encourage companies to franchise their business for fear of continual and unjustified litigation with any disenchanted franchisees.

55 Article 3:201 Commercial Agency, Franchise And Distribution Amsterdam Team ibid.

56 Ibid., Article 3:202.

57 Ibid., Article 3:203.

market conditions, commercial results of the franchise network and characteristics of the goods and services.[58] It is not clear what is meant by 'market conditions' or whether the market is local, regional or national. It is totally impractical and indeed unnecessary to expect a franchisor based in one member state (or indeed outside the EU) to know anything about market conditions in another member state. Indeed, its ignorance of those market conditions may well be one of the reasons that it decided to grant a franchise there in the first place. It is also unclear what is meant by 'commercial results'. It could mean sales figures, balance sheets or profit and loss accounts of the franchisor or all the franchisees on the network. Franchisees are unlikely to welcome having details of their individual businesses shared with other franchisees, who in some circumstances are their most immediate competitors but any lesser level of detail would probably not be of any real use or interest to other franchisees. It also proposes that the franchisor is obliged to make reasonable efforts to promote and maintain the reputation of the franchise network and must design and co-ordinate the appropriate advertising campaigns aimed at the promotion of the franchise network without any additional charge.[59] Yet again this provision is inappropriate. It suggests that the franchisees can abdicate responsibility for promoting their business to the franchisor. That is totally at odds with the whole essence of the franchisor/franchisee relationship. Sadly, the Amsterdam Group's proposals are a missed opportunity. Although some of them do accentuate the impact of the third commercial imperative on the legal eco-systems they fail to appreciate where the balance of interests between franchisor and franchisee lies. Most of its proposals are little more than a distillation of existing European member state jurisprudence. There is no originality of thought: just the regurgitation of ad hoc, ready-made solutions to different problems. It therefore fails to address the commercial imperatives in any meaningful way. For example, it fails either to analyse the fundamental characteristics of franchising or to consider empirical evidence and academic comment about it. As a result, it fails to understand even the basic differences between agency and distribution on the one hand and franchising on the other. This leads it to propose an indemnity for goodwill for the franchisee if the franchisor's business volume has been increased by the franchisee, even when the contract was terminated for non-performance by one party. It also leads the Group to propose that the franchisor must repurchase the franchisee's stock at the end of the contract.[60]

58 Ibid., Article 3:205. The other issues prices and terms for the sale of goods or services, any recommended prices and terms for the resale of goods or services, relevant communication between the franchisor and customers in the territory, advertising campaigns are not problematic.

59 Ibid., Article 3:207.

60 Ibid., Article 1:306 and Article 1:307.

The UNIDROIT Model Franchise disclosure law[61] is the other proposal to re-engineer the regulatory environment for franchising. It was issued in September 2002 and was supplemented by the second edition of its *Guide to International Master Franchise Agreements* which was issued in October 2007. UNIDROIT is an independent intergovernmental organisation. Its model law is meant to represent international best practice. It is therefore appropriate to consider whether it addresses the three commercial imperatives identified above and if so, how successful it is in doing so. The fact that the UNIDROIT model law only deals with pre-contractual disclosure clearly means that it cannot deal with two of the three commercial imperatives. At best it can only deal with the second commercial imperative, pre-contractual hygiene, although even here it is lacking, as it proposes nothing to enable prospective franchisees to better understand any information disclosed to them about their potential purchase. UNIDROIT's model law does propose that certain relevant information is disclosed to potential franchisees. However, it fails to offer any new suggestions as to how to ensure that potential franchisees are informed of the nature of the relationship that they are about to enter into. It is no more than a distillation of what it deems to be best practice from existing franchise legislation around the world. Despite the input of practitioners (or perhaps because of it) the model is the sterile product of administrative endeavour. It lacks in the subtlety, originality and 'context' necessary to effectively ensure that potential franchisees not only receive appropriate information, but that it is delivered in a manner and style that the potential franchisee will be able to understand. It offers no proposal as to how the 'Psychology of Failure' identified by the Australian authorities[62] can be overcome or how potential franchisees can be persuaded to take and follow advice given by appropriately qualified and experienced advisors. It offers no fresh insight into the issues to be regulated or how that regulation must be applied. There is nothing in it that cannot be found in existing franchise laws. It gives no analysis of the commercial imperatives at play in the franchising sector and how to maintain market confidence and encourage new entrants. In short it fails to meet the benchmarks that franchise regulations should aspire to. It is disappointing that so much collective endeavour has resulted in no original thought or proposals. Instead it declares that the 5.11

61 The International Institute for the Unification of Private Law (UNIDROIT) dismissed the suggestion of an International Convention on Franchising, preferring an international code of ethics and a model contract – *Guide to International Master Franchise Arrangements* UNIDROIT (second edition) 2007 originally issued in September 2002, pp xxxiv–xxxv. See www.unidroit. org. UNIDROIT was set up in 1926 as an auxiliary organ of the League of Nations and, following the demise of the League, was re-established in 1940 on the basis of a multilateral agreement, the UNIDROIT Statute. Its purpose is to study needs and methods for modernising, harmonising and co-ordinating private and in particular commercial law as between States and groups of States. It endeavours to prepare models and where appropriate harmonise uniform rules of private law.

62 The Franchise Council of Australia's Submission to the Australian Federal Government Review dated August 2006.

fundamental principle that needs to be addressed is whether potential franchisees are more likely to protect themselves against *fraud* if they have access to truthful, important information before they enter into the franchise agreement. That misses a fundamental point. Fraud is a criminal offence and should be regulated accordingly by the criminal law. Disclosure should be about ensuring that franchisees enter into their franchises giving full informed consent to the obligations they take on and that they acknowledge that they are taking on real risks.[63] It is disappointing that it focuses upon fraud rather than the commercial imperatives. By identifying fraud as the priority they have to some extent circumscribed the thrust of the model law and limited its potential use and impact.[64] The model law merely lists matters to be disclosed 14 days[65] before 'completion' and makes the obvious, but valid, point that legislators must consider the financial burden that new legislation can place upon franchisors and franchisees and compare these to the benefits that will be derived from any new disclosure law.[66] It also provides for annual updating of the disclosure document linked to the franchisor's financial year.[67] It does not propose any set form for the disclosure document but requires that it be in a single document,[68] receipt of which is acknowledged by the potential franchisee in writing.[69] It does, however, recognise the need to ensure that franchisees are not overwhelmed by unnecessary disclosure obligations and although the requirement for disclosure cannot be contracted out of,[70] certain obvious exemptions to the need to issue a disclosure document are proposed. These are sales to those already involved in the franchise, franchisee sales, investments over a certain threshold, sales to potential franchisees of a certain minimum net worth, fractional franchises and renewals.[71] The uninspiring nature of the model law is attested to by the fact that it has been in existence for more than nine years so far but has had no impact on the many franchise laws that have been adopted during that period.[72] Neither the Study Group proposal nor the UNIDROIT

63 UNIDROIT, Model Franchise Disclosure Law, Preamble.

64 See below.

65 UNIDROIT, *Model Franchise Disclosure Law*, Article 3(A).

66 Ibid., Preamble.

67 Ibid., Article 3(B).

68 Ibid., Article 4.

69 Ibid., Article 7.

70 Ibid., Article 10.

71 Ibid., Article 5.

72 In Italy the model law was rejected out of hand by the Senate as a basis for their law because 'it did not reflect Italy's legal tradition or deal with the issues of most concern to them' (Emanuele Rossi, La Scala law office – Milan – EFN Annual Conference, London 24 March 2006). In Sweden, the only jurisdiction that one is aware of having considered the Model Law (due in no small part due to the fact that the UNIDROIT officer heading the project was Swedish), it was rejected as being inappropriate. In 2004 the Swedish Ministry of Justice analysed the UNIDROIT Model Law and considered whether or not statutory provisions on franchising should be adopted in Sweden (Departementsserien Ds 2004:55). A survey was conducted among 60 franchise systems of varying size and within different business sectors (in total 550 questionnaires were distributed, of

model law seek to accentuate the impact of the three commercial imperatives on the legal eco-systems that comprise the regulatory environment for franchising in the EU.

C. ACCENTUATING THE IMPACT OF THE FIRST COMMERCIAL IMPERATIVE – MAINTAINING MARKET CONFIDENCE

In order to maintain market confidence in franchising, a directive must promote **5.12** franchising and the economic benefit that it can deliver both to the economy as a whole and to the companies that use it as part of their market strategy in particular. As the introduction to one of the draft bills placed before the Belgian Chamber of Deputies stated,[73] it is

> essential ... not to interrupt ... the development ... of a commercial formula which having been successfully used in the American market has spread to Europe where there are more than 5000 franchisors and almost 200 000 franchisees generating a turnover of 166 billion euros and employing some 1 500 000 personnel.

Franchising can make the single market a reality not only for large corporates with the capital and manpower to set up in other member states, but also for smaller enterprises that have traditionally done business only in their own national markets. It is suggested that a directive must expressly state that it believes that franchising is a legitimate and respectable form of commerce that adds and has the potential to add further to the successful development of the Single Market by empowering SMEs and others to expand their businesses across national boundaries. It must proactively encourage companies to use franchising as part of their market strategy. Conflicting and confusing regulations impede the efficient functioning of the market and discourage entrepreneurship and commerce. Maintaining market confidence in franchising involves preserving stability in franchising and the reasonable expectation that it will remain stable on an EU level.[74] In order to do this, it is suggested that a new dynamic needs to be imposed on the various legal eco-systems: one

which 310 were replied to) as part of the study. It discussed termination, disputes and pre-contractual disclosure and concluded that there was no need to improve the position of franchisees in terms of statutory rules on termination of franchise agreements. The appropriateness of Arbitration clauses was also considered and the suggestion that they be prohibited in franchise agreements was dismissed. These conclusions were based on the notion that franchisees are legal entities with the ability to negotiate terms and as such should take commercial responsibility for their decision. The Study concluded that a Swedish law based on the UNIDROIT Model Law would not be appropriate, because it would not accord with 'the Swedish model' (Departementsserien Ds 2004:55 page 150).

73 The Belgian House of Representatives, 30 October 2003.

74 FSMA, Chapter 1, para. 2.

which can be called an 'Exchange of Benefits' approach. The challenge of regulation is met by the EU's current legal eco-systems, the CFR and the UNIDROIT Model Law in an almost one-dimensional manner. They all focus on penalising non-compliant franchisors by way of civil and/or criminal penalties imposed through either governmental or private legal action. The EU's legal eco-systems do not seek to encourage franchising by offering franchisors appropriate commercial benefits in return for complying with certain appropriate requirements or recognise the risks faced by franchisors. As a result not only do the EU's current legal eco-systems fail to accentuate the impact of the need to increase market confidence, but being a franchisor has become synonymous with accepting extra legal, administrative and financial burden. They have failed to understand the nature of those involved in franchising. Not all franchisors are successful and wealthy multi-national corporations like, for example, McDonalds or Wyndham. The majority are far more modest organisations. Many are SMEs that are using franchising as a way of enabling themselves to compete meaningfully on the European stage.[75] The equation which helps them to decide whether or not to franchise their business is delicately balanced. By granting franchises, franchisors are exposing themselves to potential abuse by franchisees. In order to be encouraged to franchise their business, companies must be able to see tangible benefits beyond the economic drivers already identified.

BOX 5.2

An Exchange of Benefits approach is an effective way of accentuating the impact of the need for increased market confidence in franchising on the legal eco-systems.

A regulatory environment that not only controls the behaviour of franchisors but also protects them from abuse by franchisees will encourage businesses to take advantage of the single market and potentially transform the regulatory environment in the eyes of franchisors from a costly administrative, financial and legal burden to one which, in return for a reasonable investment, offers substantial financial, commercial and legal benefit. By adopting this 'exchange of benefits' approach, regulators will potentially reverse the focus of the debate about what amounts to a franchise. Rather than businesses seeking to find ways of escaping from being classified as a franchise, they may endeavour to come within the definition. Disputes over whether or not a business amounts to a

75 The BFA has 236 full and provisional members of which only around ten are substantial corporates e.g. McDonalds and the Halifax.

franchise would no longer be characterised by businesses trying to prove that they are not a franchise. They would also include cases where businesses were seeking to prove the opposite. In order for businesses to be able to enjoy these benefits they must come within the definition of a franchise, detailed above. It is suggested that the benefits extended to franchisors should be such as re-enforce the economic drivers that attract them to franchising and reduce the consequential inherent risks to an appropriate level. It is therefore proposed that the benefits offered include requiring franchisees to make pre-contractual disclosure to franchisors (at the franchisor's request), focusing the regulation only where it is needed and reducing the disadvantages that franchisors suffer compared to corporate chains.

1. The benefits extended to franchisors

In order to increase market confidence in franchising and encourage companies to become franchisors, disclosure should not be just a one-way process. The degree of risk involved for both franchisors and franchisees must be reflected in the pre-contractual disclosure requirements of an EU Franchise Directive. Not only should franchisors have an obligation to give pre-contractual disclosure, but they should also have the right to require that franchisees provide them with pre-contractual disclosure too. This will help ensure that the risks to franchisors are taken into account and so encourage more companies to franchise their businesses. Effective disclosure by potential franchisees, should the franchisor require it, helps to ensure that inappropriately qualified individuals are less likely to be placed in a position in which they damage themselves, the franchisor and other franchisees. It also protects franchisors from being 'duped' by prospective franchisees with inappropriate criminal, financial, business or personal backgrounds. The franchisor's risk profile is correspondingly reduced. This will not of course prevent franchisors recruiting poor quality franchisees. It will however help to make it less of a surprise to them when a franchisee turns out to be inappropriate and so ensure that they are more clearly responsible for a poor recruitment. If a franchisee mis-states its circumstances, the blame for the problems should be more equitably shared between the franchisee and the franchisor and so reduce the ability of undeserving franchisees to blame their franchisor for all their problems.[76] **5.13**

76 Curiously, only the Vietnamese franchise regulation requires pre-contractual disclosure by potential franchisees, but unfortunately this is an extremely recent law and so offers no guidance as to its effectiveness. The original Chinese franchise regulation also required it, but this was dropped when the second regulation was adopted. No reason was given for its exclusion.

BOX 5.3

Franchisors should be given the right, but not the obligation, to require that, at least 10 working days before entering into any agreement which obliges or potentially obliges a franchisor to grant a potential franchisee a franchise, the potential franchisee must provide the franchisor with the following information about itself and its spouse/partner, if any, or if it is a limited liability company its shareholders and officers:

(1) Full name and address including e-mail address and telephone number.
(2) Details of education and employment.
(3) Details of business experience including directorships and any direct or indirect shareholdings in privately held companies.
(4) Personal bankruptcy history.
(5) Details of the insolvency of any company in which he/she was a director or shareholder.
(6) Details of family situation including details of any divorce, child maintenance and other such court orders and arrangements, and a signed statement from the prospective franchisee's spouse/partner that they fully support the prospective franchisee's application.
(7) Personal medical history and that of their spouse/partner and children.
(8) Criminal record and that of their spouse/partner.
(9) Details of any judgment against them.
(10) Copy of driving licence and passport.
(11) Banker's reference.
(12) Details of personal assets and those of spouse/partner including details of status of current home and any charges on those assets.

BOX 5.4

The consequences of a potential franchisee failing to supply all such information to any franchisor that has requested it, would be to give the franchisor the right to terminate the franchise agreement on the basis of defective consent[77] within twelve (12) months of the failure coming to the franchisor's attention or within two (2) years of the franchisee signing the franchise agreement, whichever is the earliest.

A franchisee that has made any material or substantial wrongful or lack of disclosure will be deprived of any right to claim damages or other remedy from the

77 This reflects the court's approach to non-disclosure by franchisors under both the French and Spanish disclosure laws and German law.

franchisor unless the franchisor is shown to have intentionally and materially breached the terms of the franchise agreement or intentionally and materially made wrongful or incomplete pre-contractual disclosure to the franchisee.

This should avoid any franchisee being inequitably denied justice due to technical non-compliance and prevent the franchisor from using a franchisee's failures to excuse its own deliberately inappropriate behaviour. It is the obligation of any franchisor to ensure that it is aware of and complies with relevant laws that impose obligations upon it. However, one cannot expect potential franchisees to be aware of any such obligations that are placed upon it as a result of it deciding to become a franchisee. Therefore, if a franchisor decides to take advantage of its right to require pre-contractual disclosure by a potential franchisee, the burden of ensuring that the potential franchisee knows of its obligation must lie with the franchisor.

BOX 5.5

The franchisor must provide the potential franchisee with a written statement informing him/her that it wishes to exercise its right to require disclosure in plain language. This must be delivered to the potential franchisee at least 14 days prior to the date on which the potential franchisee must make the disclosure.

It must also be accompanied by a form, in plain language and in a Question and Answer format, setting out exactly what information is required in order to comply with the obligation, so that the franchisee need only complete the form.

It would be difficult, and indeed pointless, to oblige all potential franchisees to make pre-contractual disclosure regardless of the franchisor's desire for it. The franchisor should therefore have the right to require potential franchisees to make full pre-contractual disclosure and be able to rely upon the veracity of such disclosure if it is made. The franchisor may at its own option decide that it does not need written pre-contractual disclosure from a potential franchisee. It may for some other reason fail to obtain such disclosure from a potential franchisee. In either such case the franchisor will lose its right of redress outlined above. As stated above, if a franchisor wishes to take advantage of its right to pre-contractual disclosure by a potential franchisee, it must deliver a notice to the potential franchisee stating that that is the case and clearly explaining the consequences of it not doing so. This notice should also be stated clearly on the cover sheet of the franchise agreement.

BOX 5.6

Both notices of the potential franchisee's pre-contractual disclosure obligations should be in prominent and easily legible form and read as follows:

'THIS IS A VERY IMPORTANT NOTICE.

YOU MUST READ IT CAREFULLY AND DO AS IT SAYS BEFORE YOU ENTER INTO ANY AGREEMENT WITH US.

IT REQUIRES YOU TO GIVE US CERTAIN INFORMATION ABOUT YOU AND YOUR SPOUSE/PARTNER/SHAREHOLDERS/OFFICERS (IF APPLICABLE).

YOU MUST GIVE THIS INFORMATION TO US AT LEAST 14 DAYS BEFORE YOU SIGN ANY AGREEMENT WHICH ENTITLES YOU TO THE FRANCHISE.

YOU CAN GIVE US THIS INFORMATION BY ACCURATELY COMPLETING THE ATTACHED QUESTIONNAIRE. ALTERNATIVELY, IF YOU CHOOSE TO DO SO, YOU CAN GIVE IT IN ANY OTHER WRITTEN FORM.

IF YOU DO NOT GIVE US ALL THIS INFORMATION, OR IF ANY OF THE INFORMATION THAT YOU GIVE US IS FALSE, INCORRECT OR INCOMPLETE, YOU MAY LOSE YOUR RIGHT TO THE FRANCHISE AND SOME OF YOUR OTHER IMPORTANT LEGAL RIGHTS MAY BE SEVERELY RESTRICTED'.

2. Focusing regulation where it is needed

5.14 The pre-contractual disclosure obligation of franchisors proposed below should not apply to all franchise sales. The proposed EU Franchise Directive must encourage the use of franchising by taking into account its commercial realities. The size, commercial experience and sophistication of some franchisees will mean that they do not require the same level of protection as the majority of franchisees. The role a franchise will play in the overall business interests of some franchisees and the size of the investment being made in the franchise (be it very substantial or minimal) will also have an impact upon whether or not additional protection should be made available to franchisees. Substantial businesses that take on a franchise as an 'add-on' to an existing business and other sophisticated individuals making substantial capital investments are dealing with franchisors on a more even footing and have sufficient commercial experience to mean that they do not need the same level of protection as the more usual type of franchisee. They can rely upon the usual contractual remedies available to businesses. Likewise a small investment by a franchisee may not justify imposing the same administrative burden as a more substantial one.

> BOX 5.7
>
> Franchisors should only be required to make pre-contractual disclosure when it is appropriate and not in the case of fractional franchisees, de minimis franchisees, sophisticated franchisees, large investors, large franchisees and insiders.

(a) Excluding fractional and de minimis franchisees

Fractional franchises are those that are taken on by an existing business which is seeking to expand its product line through taking a franchise. 5.15

> BOX 5.8
>
> If (1) the franchisee or its principals have more than two years of experience in the same line of business or is otherwise already familiar with the products and services to be sold through the franchise; and (2) the parties reasonably expect that the franchisee's sales from the new line of business will not exceed 20% of its total sales.[78] It is proposed that any disclosure requirement be excluded.[79]

A de minimis exemption will ensure that the directive focuses upon those franchisees who have made a personally significant monetary investment and who cannot extricate themselves from the relationship if it becomes burdensome without suffering a financial setback.[80] The threshold will exclude transactions where the prospective franchisee is at risk of losing an amount of money too small to justify imposition of the expense and burden of preparing a disclosure document upon sellers. The threshold proposed is €1000.

---

78 In the original SBP, the Commission reasoned, with respect to fractional franchisees, that pre-sale disclosure is unwarranted where the prospective franchisee already is familiar with the products and services to be sold through the franchise and where the prospective franchisee faces a minimal investment risk. Original SBP, 43 FR at 59707.

79 Section 436.1(g) of the US's updated FTC Rule takes this approach.

80 In the US franchise sales under US$500 are exempted from the pre-contractual disclosure requirement. See 16 CFR 436.2(a)(3)(iii).

BOX 5.9

Any franchisee investing €1000 or less in a franchise should not be entitled to a disclosure document.

(b) Excluding sophisticated franchisees

5.16 Franchising often involves heavily-negotiated, multi-million pound deals between franchisors and highly sophisticated individuals and corporate franchisees with highly competent lawyers.[81] In the course of such deals,[82] prospective franchisees often demand and receive material information from the franchisor that equals or exceeds the disclosures required by the Rule. Such business arrangements do not require the same level of protection as those with similar investors. There are three types of sophisticated investors: those that make a large franchise investment, large franchisees and inside investors. In the USA, large franchise investments[83] are defined as franchises where the initial investment is at least US$1 million.[84] The basis for a large investment exemption is not that 'sophisticated' investors do not need pre-sale disclosure, but that they will demand and obtain material information with which to make an investment decision regardless of the application of any law. Where prospective franchisees are likely to demand and obtain pre-sale material information regardless of external prompting or compulsion, then there is no case for legislative intervention. Such an exemption must, of course, be limited. To ensure that the exemption is not too wide, the US FTC Rule[85] sets forth additional safeguards beyond the mere financial threshold.[86] First,[87] funds obtained from the franchisor (or an affiliate) cannot be counted towards the

81 See FTC Staff Report; Gust Rosenfeld, at 7; J&G, at 7; Marriott, at 2–4; Starwood, at 2–3; 7-Eleven, Notice of Proposed Rulemaking (NPR) 10, at 2; NFC, NPR 12, at 17; IFA, NPR 22, at 7; AFC, NPR 30, at 2–3; Marriott, NPR 35, at 6. See also in September 1997, Advanced Notice of Proposed Rulemaking (ANPR), 18 Tr., Kaufmann at 165; Wieczorek at 187–8; Tifford at 194 (noting that the rule imposes unnecessary costs on sophisticated franchisees and adds unwarranted delay in the high-paced negotiation process, where parties often are anxious to cement their deals quickly to beat out the competition).

82 E.g. hotel franchises such as those offered by Wyndham, Marriott, Intercontinental and the like can require investments of US$10 million and more. Large retail franchises such as that offered by Hamleys require a similar level of investment.

83 See the FTC Rule Section 436.8(a)(5)(i) which has such an exemption for franchise sales over US$1 million exclusive of unimproved land and franchisor financing.

84 At least two US states provide some form of exemption for transactions involving large initial investments. Illinois permits a franchisor to apply for an exemption from both registration and disclosure where the investment for a single franchise unit exceeds $1 million. Maryland exempts franchises that require an initial investment of $750 000 or more from registration, but not from disclosure.

85 FTC Rule, Section 436.8(a)(5)(i).

86 These safeguards were included in the proposed version of this provision. Franchise NPR, 64 FR at 57321 and 57345.

87 Section 436.8(a)(5)(i).

$1 million initial investment threshold. Second,[88] the prospective franchisee must sign an acknowledgement that the franchise sale is exempt from the Franchise Rule because the prospective franchisee will be making an initial investment over the threshold. Although franchisors may find a large initial investment exemption[89] appealing, wealth or the ability to make a large franchise investment does not necessarily equate to business sophistication.[90] The franchisee's business background is arguably more relevant.[91] A large investment exemption would not consider the source of the prospective franchisee's funds, which could be raised through a secured loan, pension fund and so on.

> The fact that a franchisee may be ready to invest a highly leveraged franchise investment does not prove that such a person is so sophisticated that a disclosure document would be of no benefit.[92]

However, on balance it appears that a large investment exemption is warranted and that the size of a prospective franchisee's investment is one measure of its sophistication.[93] It is reasonable to conclude that investment level is a straightforward and unambiguous indication of sophistication. Franchisors need a clear objective standard that will indicate when and under what circumstances the sophisticated investor exemption will apply. An exemption based upon the specific business experience of each individual prospective franchisee would be burdensome to administer. Franchisors would not be able to take advantage of the exemption unless they first verified each prospective franchisee's business background. Similarly, without verification, law enforcers would not be able to discern whether any specific franchise relationship was covered by the directive. This approach could create a regulatory nightmare for both franchisors and franchise law enforcers. A large investment exemption offers tangible benefits

88 Section 436.8(a)(5)(i).

89 E.g. PMRW, NPR 4, at 3; Wendy's, NPR 5, at 2; McDonalds, NPR 7, at 2; H&H, NPR 9, at 4; Baer, NPR 11, at 16; NFC, NPR 12, at 20. Marriott, for example, stated that not only are sophisticated franchisees able to protect their own interests, but the self-interest of others involved in the project, such as bankers, is sufficient to protect those interests as well. Marriott, NPR 35, at 6. See, e.g., Baer, NPR 11, at 16; Gurnick, NPR 21, at 3; J&G, NPR 32, at 3.

90 Stadfeld, NPR 23, at 8; Karp, NPR 24, at 6.

91 Karp, at 7; Karp, NPR 24, at 6–7. See also Stadfeld, NPR 23, at 7–8 ('Being wealthy should not be a basis for being screwed').

92 Karp, ibid, at 8.

93 This view was supported by the Automobile Importers of America submission to the FTC, which observed that 'Prospective motor vehicle dealers make extraordinarily large investments. As a practical matter, investments of this size and scope involve relatively knowledgeable investors or the use of independent business advisors, and an extended period of negotiation. The record is consistent with the conclusion that the transactions negotiated by such knowledgeable investors over time and with the aid of business advisors produce the pre-sale information disclosure necessary to ensure that investment decisions are the product of an informed assessment of the potential risks and benefits of the proposed investment.' 45 FR 51763–64 (5 Aug. 1980).

to franchisors such as those operating a hotel business where the typical franchise investment is likely to exceed the large investment exemption's monetary threshold and will provide regulatory relief in those instances. A large franchise investment exemption, however, will provide only limited relief for franchisors that sell franchises both above and below the threshold. In such instances, the franchisor must prepare disclosure documents in order to sell at levels below the threshold. Obviously deciding what the financial threshold should be is vital. In the USA the FTC concluded that a $1 million threshold strikes the right balance between providing relief for sophisticated investors and protecting consumers. Interestingly, during its review of the FTC Rule no consensus emerged on the appropriate investment threshold for the large investment exemption. Several commentators supported a $1.5 million threshold,[94] whilst others urged a higher threshold[95] so as not to place too many transactions outside the Rule's protection. Others, such as McDonald's suggested that the threshold should be lower.[96] The IFA proposed a $1 million threshold, excluding land.[97] It observed that a 1997 update to the Profile of Franchising identified 52 franchise companies offering franchises with an initial investment exceeding $1 million, excluding land. This equates to 4.4% or less of all franchise systems.[98] Thus, at a $1 million threshold for the exemption, more than 95% of all franchise systems would remain within the ambit of the Rule.[99] Some commentators recommended an even lower threshold.[100] The Commission gave particular weight to the statements offered by franchisors such as McDonald's and Marriott that, in their experience, a $1 million

94 E.g., Baer, NPR 11, at 16; Gurnick, NPR 21, at 3; Marriott, NPR 35, at 6.

95 NASAA recommended a $3 million threshold. NASAA, NPR 17, at 12. Seth Stadfeld added that it is not difficult to invest $1.5 million when there is a down payment plus financing of a substantial portion of the investment. 'Indeed, because they are taking on larger obligations, there is all the more reason and urgency why they should get the material, factual and contractual information that is otherwise available under the Rule.' Stadfeld, NPR 23, at 8. See also NFA, NPR 27, at 3.

96 For example, McDonald's suggested that the threshold should be set at $1 million. 'In our considerable experience, individuals purchasing franchises involving a $1 million investment have a clear understanding of the terms and conditions of the business arrangements and have obtained professional financial and/or legal advice before entering into the franchise agreement.' McDonald's, NPR 7, at 2. See also 7-Eleven, NPR 10, at 3; NFC, NPR 12, at 20; BI, NPR 28, at 13. Wendy's suggested that the threshold be lowered, but did not offer any specific amount. Wendy's, NPR 5, at 2.

97 As discussed below, IFA initially stated that 'real estate' should be excluded in calculating the large investment threshold. IFA, NPR 22, at 7. In its Staff Report comment, however, the IFA clarified that by 'real estate' it means raw, unimproved land. See IFA, at 3.

98 IFA, NPR 22, at 7.

99 The Staff Report recommended a $1 million threshold for the exemption, excluding land and franchisor financing, as discussed below. Staff Report, at 240.

100 PMR&W, NPR 4, at 3 (suggesting a $500 000 threshold). See also Cendant, ANPR 140, at 4 (suggesting a $750 000 threshold); H&H, NPR 9, at 4 (advocating a lowered threshold, but not specifying an amount); Duvall & Mandel, ANPR 114, at 21 (suggesting a $250 000 threshold provided there is a showing that the purchaser, alone or with counsel, can understand the merits and risks of the investment). The Commission rejects this approach as unworkable, because it would require franchisors to make subjective judgements about each purchaser's business acumen.

investment is likely to involve sophisticated investors.[101] A review of franchise investment fees in the UK[102] suggests that a large investment threshold of €500 000 be adopted in the EU Franchise Regulation. The average upfront fee in the UK charged is £45 400.[103] Excluding franchisor financing adds a measure of protection to the prospective franchisee because traditional lenders are very likely to require a due diligence investigation of the offering, whereas the franchisor or its affiliate likely would not.[104] Although there is a risk that excluding financing might discourage franchisors from offering financing to prospects, not to do so could tempt a franchisor to increase the cost of the initial investment to qualify for the large investment exemption, while simultaneously offering to finance the deal itself, all without proper pre-sale disclosures. It is therefore appropriate for the exemption to be dependent upon the franchisee having been given notice of the fact that the franchisor is exempt from the disclosure requirement.

BOX 5.10

Franchisees who invest €500 000 or more (excluding funds obtained from the franchisor or its affiliates) in a franchise and have signed an acknowledgement that the sale is exempt from the disclosure requirement because the initial investment is over the threshold, should be exempted from the disclosure requirement.

101 The Commission has a history of considering and granting petitions for exemption to the Franchise Rule under section 18(g) of the FTC Act. In numerous exemption petition proceedings, the Commission has considered the size of investment as an indicium of sophistication. E.g., Paccar, Inc., 68 FR 67442 (2 Dec. 2003); Rolls-Royce Corp., 68 FR 67443 (2 Dec. 2003); Austin Rover Cars of North America, 52 FR 6612 (4 Mar. 1987); Volkswagen of America, Inc., 49 FR 13677 (6 Apr. 1984); Automobile Importers of America, Inc., 45 FR 51783 (5 Aug. 1980). Based upon this experience in analyzing various franchise systems, the Commission believes that a large investment typically entails a sophisticated purchaser: 'As a practical matter, investments of this size and scope typically involve knowledgeable investors, the use of independent business and legal advisors, and an extended period of negotiation that generates the exchange of information necessary to ensure that investment decisions are the product of an informed assessment of the potential risks and benefits.' Mercedes-Benz of North America, Inc., 57 FR 1745 (15 Jan. 1992) (granting petition for exemption).

102 A review of the 44 franchisees advertised in *Franchise World* Feb/March 2009 No. 169 suggests a range of investment levels from £4000 to £260 000.

103 BFA/NatWest Survey, page 36.

104 Section 436.8(5)(i) of the FTC Rule does not count monies that are obtained through franchisor (or affiliate) financing towards the large initial investment exemption's $1 million threshold.

Large entities negotiating franchise deals – such as airports, hospitals, and universities – do not need the protection afforded by the regulation.[105,106]

The US FTC concluded that both $5 million net worth and five years' experience are necessary to ensure that the Rule continues to protect businesses with limited experience, limited assets, and, by inference, limited prior success. As larger companies often have complex corporate group structures, it is appropriate for a franchisor to consider the prior experience and net worth of the franchisee's affiliates and parents when determining whether the franchisee qualifies as a 'large franchisee'.

> BOX 5.11
>
> The EU Franchise Directive adopts a large franchisee exemption with a threshold of €5 million and a requirement for 5 years' experience.

Where a company wishes to sell a franchise to experienced company personnel with substantial direct management experience of the business, it would be overly burdensome to force the company to have to deliver a disclosure document to them as the only beneficiaries of the disclosures are already knowledgeable individuals. The exemption should be company-specific. A manager of one franchised company should not be deemed to be sophisticated for all franchise sales.

> BOX 5.12
>
> A manager or other officer seeking to purchase a franchise of a particular company is an insider if and, as such, the individual in question has worked in the franchisor for two years or more should be exempted.

3. Reducing the disadvantages franchisors suffer compared to corporate chains

5.17 Franchised businesses are disadvantaged when compared to corporate chains by the franchisor's inability to impose uniform retail prices and restrict the

105 Section 436.8(a)(5)(ii) of the FTC Rule exempts sales to entities who have been in any business for at least five years and have a net worth of at least $5 million.

106 Net worth of an entity can readily be determined from the entity's balance sheet or other financial information, typically submitted as part of the application process.

franchisees' use of the internet. Most franchisors would struggle to expand their businesses through conventional corporate means. Indeed, access to working capital and better-motivated people are why many franchisors in the UK, Germany, France and Spain franchise their business.[107] The average cost of launching a franchise in the UK is £170 000[108] so the financial threshold for entry is fairly low. They are very much at a disadvantage when compared to well capitalized and resourced corporate chains. Uniform pricing is a key element in ensuring the brand integrity of any business and so essential to allow franchise chains to compete effectively with corporate chains. The majority of franchisors surveyed believe that they are disadvantaged compared to non-franchised businesses as regards their ability to set prices in all of their outlets.[109] The presence of uniform prices across the network acts as a key attraction for potential new franchisees.[110] Research suggests that franchisors believe that franchised businesses are disadvantaged as compared to non-franchised businesses with regard to their access to a 'multi-channel sales strategy'[111] due to their inability to set prices in all their outlets and to control the franchisee's use of the internet.[112] The development and execution of an appropriate multi-channel sales strategy that involves the appropriate use of the worldwide web is essential to most businesses. Current EU law does not merely fail to encourage companies to use franchising as part of its corporate strategy, in some ways it positively discourages its use. EU antitrust law discriminates against franchising by denying it rights enjoyed by corporate chains in respect of both retail prices and use of the internet. Given that most franchisors are small or medium sized businesses and that franchising greatly increases the chances of individuals with little or no prior experience of business being successful, this amounts to institutionalised discrimination against small businesses. This discrimination is clearly anti-competitive.

---

107 See Appendix to Chapter 3. In the Survey of Franchisors 72% of UK respondents, 72% of German respondents, 64% of French respondents and 52% of Spanish respondents stated that access to capital was a very significant reason why they franchised their business and 24% in the UK, 16% in Germany, 1% in France and 16% in Spain stated that it was a significant reason. 72% of UK respondents, 60% of German respondents, 60% of French respondents and 32% of Spanish respondents stated that access to better motivated people was a significant reason why they franchised their business, whilst 88% in the UK, 96% in Germany, 88% in France and 96% in Spain saw franchising as being able to help them expand their business more quickly.

108 BFA/NatWest Survey 2007, p. 40.

109 Appendix to Chapter 3. 76% in the UK, 72% in Germany, 76% in France and 72% in Spain.

110 OECD, *Competition Policy and Vertical Restraints: Franchising Agreement.*

111 Delloite LLP & Retail (2007), 'First Cross Channel Think Tank Focuses on Future of Retail Industry'.

112 Appendix to Chapter 3. 56% in UK, 56% in Germany, 16% in France and 64% in Spain thought that franchised businesses are disadvantaged as compared to non-franchised business in respect of their ability to control the franchisee's use of the internet. 32% in the UK, 8% in Germany, 60% in France and 32% in Spain disagreed with this whilst 12% in the UK, 36% in Germany, 24% in France and 4% in Spain did not know.

> BOX 5.13
>
> Franchisors should be allowed to set retail prices for its franchisees and dictate the network's multi-channel sales strategy.

(a) Pricing

5.18 As detailed in Chapter 3 above resale price maintenance is a hard-core restriction under the Vertical Restraints Block Exemption and was ruled against in both the *Pronuptia* and *Yves Rocher* cases. It is considered to be 'per se' anti-competitive by the EU authorities. As a result, vertically integrated corporate chains have a monopoly on the ability to deliver a price promise, so disadvantaging both franchisors and the consumer. The OECD[113] however believes that resale price maintenance by franchisors can be pro-competitive. The US Supreme Court takes a similar view.[114]

> BOX 5.14
>
> The vertical restraints block exemption should be amended to expressly state that franchisors may set retail prices for their franchisees where it promotes efficiency by improving vertical co-ordination between franchisor and franchisees, particularly where there is substantial inter-brand competition.

(b) Multi-channel sales strategy

5.19 The growing importance of a multi-channel sales strategy, particularly online sales and other commercial use of the internet, is clear. Here again, whilst large corporates have freedom to adopt whatever strategy they deem appropriate, franchisors are substantially limited in their commercial options by EU competition law – which provides that every franchisee must be free to use the internet to advertise and sell products. The Commission's apparent inability to understand the dynamic and interactive nature of the worldwide web means that it is using an outmoded approach to try to regulate the latest developments in electronic commerce. The EU Commission considers that the use of the internet is a passive form of promoting sales in the same way as advertising in the local press. It considers that the fact that it may have effects outside one's own territory or customer group results merely from its distribution and accessibility. It is considered to be passive selling and any restriction on it is 'per

113 OECD, Competition Policy and Vertical Restraints: Franchising Agreement.

114 *Leegin Creative Leather Products Inc* v. *PSKS Inc*, (No 06–480) 171 Fed. Appx. 464.

se' anti-competitive. Insofar as a website is not specifically targeted at reaching customers primarily inside the territory or customer group exclusively allocated to another distributor, for instance with the use of banners or links in pages of providers specifically available to these exclusively allocated customers, the website is not considered to be a form of active selling. Unsolicited e-mails sent to individual customers or specific customer groups are also considered to be active selling. By seeing the internet as a passive medium comparable to a journal or newspaper the importance of multi-channel sales strategies is totally missed. Over the past five years the retail market has changed substantially. For example, the percentage of UK retail sales made over the internet as a percentage of total retail sales increased from 2.9% in November 2006 to 3.7% in January 2009.[115] The non-geographical nature of the worldwide web, and practices such as wordstuffing, seeding, using materials that drive traffic to websites, the subtle use of meta tabs cookies and other such practices mean that search engines will pick up sites wherever they are. Websites are not an inert medium. The issues caused for franchise networks because of this restriction and its extra-territorial nature are problematic for franchisors. They erode the exclusivity that franchisees often gave and so discourage some potential franchisees from entering into franchise agreements. The franchisor's ability to control the quality of its franchisees' websites is not enough to enable franchised chains to compete on equal terms with corporate chains in a multi-channel environment. A less dogmatic approach by the EU Commission would be appropriate. As the OECD observed,[116] territorial restrictions can have pro-competitive effects by limiting intra-brand competition and increasing franchisees' expected profits, thereby increasing the incentive for franchisees to invest in specific skills and effectively enter a market. Franchisors currently tend to use the internet to exclude and compete with their own franchisees because (amongst other things) they are unable to structure an overall internet strategy for the franchise network.

BOX 5.15

Franchisors should be given a greater level of flexibility and control over internet strategy so that they can add greater value to both the franchisee's business and their own by being more proactive in the use of the internet to increase operational efficiencies and communication.

115 Retail Sales Business Monitor (SDM28), Office of National Statistics.

116 OECD, *Competition Policy and Vertical Restraints: Franchising Agreements*, p. 196.

This collaborative approach to emerging technologies will strengthen the franchisor/franchisee relationship, rather than weaken it, as it currently tends to do.[117] It is therefore recommended that, to borrow the words of the OECD, the Commission should 'allow franchises to use either price or non-price vertical restraints in situations where the franchise faces strong market competition and collusion'.

D. ACCENTUATING THE IMPACT OF THE SECOND COMMERCIAL IMPERATIVE - PRE-CONTRACTUAL HYGIENE

5.20 Ensuring pre-contractual hygiene is essential. It is suggested that this means ensuring that potential franchisees access appropriate information and are equipped to interpret it in an appropriate manner. In order to be able to decide whether or not to buy a particular franchise potential franchisees must have access to certain basic information. However, no matter how well drafted a disclosure law is, the practical issues that arise on a day to day basis can dilute its potential impact. Regardless of how complete any disclosure law is, at the end of the day its effectiveness does depend to a large extent upon prospective franchisees being appropriately educated and looking after their own interests. No disclosure law can, or indeed should, allow franchisees to abdicate responsibility for their own actions.

> BOX 5.16
>
> Potential franchisees must be able to understand what the information disclosed to them by the franchisor means and take appropriate legal and financial advice. The way to ensure this is to make it very clear what information is required, establish a set form of disclosure document which requires the use of plain language and provide for appropriate penalties to be imposed upon those franchisors who do not comply with the pre-contractual disclosure requirement.

However unless potential franchisees understand the need to take professional advice upon their proposed investment and act upon it, disclosure will have only a limited impact.

117 Dixon, H., 2010, 'The Impact of the Internet on Franchising as a Growth Strategy and the Implications for Franchisors Engaging in E-Commerce', Unpublished doctoral book submitted to the School of Business, Retail and Financial Services, Ulster Business School, University of Ulster.

BOX 5.17

Potential franchisees must be educated into taking and following appropriate advice on their proposed purchase.

1. Educating potential franchisees

This provides critical analysis to the third objective of this book. **5.21**

BOX 5.18

It is suggested that an EU Franchise Directive must provide that potential franchisees are educated about franchising and their responsibilities if they wish to become involved in it.

In its submissions to the Federal Government Review[118] the Franchise Council of Australia (FCA) identified the lack of education and the apparent unwillingness of potential franchisees to look after their own best interests as a substantial weakness in the Australian system of disclosure, 'those involved in franchising and perhaps human nature in general'.[119]

It criticises potential franchisees for not reading the documentation or conducting appropriate due diligence before committing to a franchise. It noted that some of the problems involving disgruntled franchisees brought to its attention may have been avoided if the prospective franchisee had a clearer understanding of the significant risks that were involved in becoming a franchisee.[120] Significant risks may include decisions made by third parties relevant to the business (such as landlords, franchisor and franchisee associates), earnings projections, changing competition, franchisor rights to unilaterally amend the franchise agreement, franchisee rights and obligations on termination or expiration of the franchise agreement, economic cycles, legislative change, franchisor solvency, franchisor rights to unilaterally terminate the franchise agreement and a decision by the prospective franchisee not to take advice before entering into a franchise agreement. This tendency of franchisees to refuse to take advice and carry out

118 The Franchise Council of Australia's submission to the Australian Federal Government Review dated 15 August 2006.

119 Ibid.

120 Stephen Giles, Director of the Franchise Council of Australia, interview with author (11 October 2009).

proper due diligence is a real problem because it means that they do not understand the business, the costs involved, the time and effort required, the impact upon their lives and family, their exposure to risk, or the need to follow the franchise system. Franchisors recognise this 'human' failure in potential franchisees.[121] One option would be to legally require potential franchisees to take appropriate advice. However the difficulties in enforcing such a requirement would be substantial. At the end of the day it would probably only increase the cost and bureaucracy without having any real positive impact.[122] A lack of pre-entry education of franchisees is the real problem, as is the 'psychology of failure' which encourages failed franchisees to blame others for their failure and the willingness of the media to take potshots at franchisors. This view that education is a key factor in the success of regulation is shared not only by the FCA but also the BFA and other franchising associations,[123] franchisors and legal practitioners who specialise in franchising – 'The education of people who are contemplating a franchise is fundamental to franchising's ultimate success and that is why the BFA gives it so much priority through our website, exhibitions, publications and various seminars.'[124] The importance of education was explained by one staff member of the US Fair Trade Commission[125] as follows

> How do you tell a guy who bought into a franchise as a 35 year old father of 2 young children that after 20 years of hard work just at the time that he is having to put his children through college, and with another 5 years of his home loan to pay off, he suddenly no longer has a business? How do you tell him at that time that he should have read the disclosure documents more carefully? That is why education is so important.

(a) Delivery of education to potential franchisees

5.22 Education is important, but how should it be delivered? Due to a variety of factors including their knowledge of franchising, existing infrastructures (in some EU member states) and vested interest in making franchising a success, it is suggested that national franchise associations should be empowered by each

---

121 Peter Neighbour, Franchise Director at LighterLife, 20 February 2008 stated in an interview conducted for this book: 'Some franchisees are simply unwilling to take responsibility for their own decisions. They seem to be totally ignorant of the fact that a franchise is not a 100% guarantee of commercial success regardless of what they do. Whatever you tell them seems to go in one ear and out the other. They see professional advice as an unnecessary luxury. They recklessly jump into an investment with boundless, naïve enthusiasm and then blame anything less than 100% success on the franchisor. The problem for franchisors is that it is not always easy to screen these types out of the recruitment process'.

122 Peter Neighbour, Franchise Director at LighterLife, 20 February 2008 stated that 'It is not a bad idea in principle but it would be a bloody nightmare to enforce and the real risk is that it would just put people off franchising altogether.'

123 See the FFF's 'Les formations pro. Catalogue 2009' at http://www.franchise-fff.com/Seminaires-pro-le-calendrier-2006.html.

124 Interview with Brian Smart, Director General of the BFA, 18 September 2008.

125 Interview with Craig Tregellis, senior administrator of the FTC, ABA Franchise Symposium, October 2008.

EU member state government to ensure that potential franchisees are consistently and persistently offered appropriate education about the franchising facts of life and so increase the likelihood of them understanding what they are entering into and the due diligence they should undertake before becoming committed to a franchise. Where there is no national franchise association, the government should mandate its creation and membership of the EFF. The EFF has some 30 years' experience of seeking to educate the public about franchising and create an appropriate self-regulatory environment. Its failure to adequately do so is due more to the enormity of the task and its lack of any legal 'locus standi' than its knowledge or intent. By relieving the EFF and its member associations of the task of attempting to self-regulate franchising in Europe, an EU Franchise Directive would allow the EFF and its members to focus on educating the public and provide it with a legal mandate to do so. This would give it a greater chance of success and allow the EFF and its members to deliver real benefit to franchising, franchisors, franchisees and the public.

> BOX 5.19
>
> Each national franchise association should be recognised as a legally acknowledged source of best practice in franchising and membership of it as an indication (but not a guarantee) that a franchisor has met certain minimum criteria as regards best practice. They should be charged with educating the public as to the benefits and risks of franchising. They should not however be charged with or be allowed to become involved with the regulation of franchising.

It would be appropriate for the national franchise associations to meet certain basic minimum standards before they are entrusted with this task (such as being a not for profit organisation and being a member of the EFF).

(b) A minimal level of education for potential franchisees

> BOX 5.20
>
> Potential franchisees need to be educated in the basic facts of franchising. These facts are:
>
> 1. The need for franchisees to work hard and for long hours. This is a clear and obvious factor of success in any business.
> 2. The need for franchisees to follow the franchise system. The whole reason for buying a franchise rather than starting a business from scratch is that the franchisor has, through its own experience, identified how the business should be run.

3. The risk of failure and what this could mean in terms of both financial and personal terms. Failure is inevitably a risk in running one's own business. It is fundamentally different from employment.
4. The importance of taking expert legal and financial advice from acknowledged experts before being legally committed to a franchise. In order to make an informed decision, advice is essential.

The national franchise associations should be obliged to create an educational pack for potential franchisees spelling out the franchising 'facts of life'. An EU contribution to the funding of the national franchise associations would be appropriate.

BOX 5.21

The national franchise associations should not only make publications and seminars freely available but also prepare an education pack that would include an audio visual presentation (by way of DVD, podcast or other digital media). All potential franchisees should be directed to this pack by franchisors.

In the UK, the internet is the way that the majority of franchisees find out about specific franchises.[126] It is likely that it plays an important role in other EU member states too, so the educational pack should be available from the web. As 41% of all franchisors responding to the BFA/NatWest 2007 survey stated how important the BFA website is to recruitment, it is in an ideal position to ensure that potential franchisees receive these educational packs.[127] Again, it is likely that the website of national franchise associations in other EU member states has or in due course will have a similar impact on franchise recruitment.

BOX 5.22

The EU Franchise Directive should require all potential franchisees to provide written confirmation that they have watched an audio visual presentation and completed a short Question and Answer 'test', filed with the franchisor, to confirm that they have understood its contents.

126 BFA/NatWest Survey 2007, p. 32.
127 Ibid. p. 17.

This will not totally eliminate the problem of franchisees not understanding what they are getting into, of course, but it should reduce it. Some are cynical of what impact such a system will have. Octavia Morley, former CEO of LighterLife, for example believes that,

> ... it will not make a scrap of difference. Potential franchisees are focused totally upon the excitement of having their own business. We (LighterLife) have a rigorous process to try and make sure that no one enters our franchise with any misconceptions as to what being in business for yourself as one of our franchisees means – but we still fail to get that message across to some of our franchisees. The problem is that many potential franchisees are extremely naïve and point blank refuse to take in anything that might dampen their enthusiasm to become a franchisee.[128]

Whether or not such cynicism is justified, it is suggested that an ongoing educational programme targeted at potential franchisees is appropriate, as part of a larger package of reform. It will certainly do no harm and it is suggested is likely to help ensure that potential franchisees take a more responsible approach when purchasing a franchise.

2. Ensuring quality advice for potential franchisees

It is suggested that a key element of education is ensuring that franchisees take **5.23** advice from advisers with an appropriate level of experience. The FCA noted that in Australia the advice given to potential franchisees can vary and franchisees may rely on advice which is not adequate.[129] There is no evidence to suggest that it is any different in the EU.[130] This is another opportunity for the national franchise associations to play an active role in the regulation of franchising. By allowing affiliate membership of national franchise associations (as the BFA already do) for professional advisers such as lawyers and accountants with relevant experience, a reservoir of more suitably experienced professional advisers will be created. Obviously it is important that such affiliate status is open to all advisers with relevant experience and that the definition of relevant experience be clear and unambiguous. Relevant experience should be defined as having undertaken and successfully completed a short self-study programme on the commercial aspects of franchising set by the national

128 Interview with Octavia Morley, CEO, LighterLife (20 February 2008).

129 FCA submission to the Federal Government Review dated 15 August 2006.

130 The author's personal experience as a franchise lawyer acting for franchisors is that many potential franchisees do not take legal advice and of those that do, many use solicitors with little or no experience or knowledge of franchising. Indeed, he has even known for a potential franchisee to take advice from a personal injury lawyer, who offered to give the advice free of charge in return for the potential franchisee agreeing not to file a professional negligence case against him, in respect of a failed claim concerning injuries incurred in a motor vehicle accident.

franchise association. It would not be appropriate for them to seek to test the technical knowledge of the relevant areas of law or financial accounting. Many franchisors feel that prospective franchisees do not read the pre-contractual disclosure documentation given to them.[131] It would be possible to legally require potential franchisees to read the disclosure document but it is doubtful that this would have any meaningful impact.

> BOX 5.23
>
> If a franchisee is required to invest a sum greater than €20 000, legal and financial advice from advisers affiliated to the national franchise associations should be mandatory. There should be a certificate from the potential franchisee's legal and financial advisors stating that the potential franchisee has taken appropriate advice from them and that they have completed the self-study module. Potential franchisees should also certify that they understand that they are taking a substantial risk if they do not follow appropriate advice and accept that they may be responsible for any loss they suffer as a result of not taking such advice.

As detailed above, the problem is that not all national franchise associations are as well developed as the BFA or the FFF and so such a scheme is unlikely to be effective on a practical level in all EU member states in the immediate future. It will therefore be appropriate for national governments to provide support and encouragement to the less developed national franchise associations. Indeed, the establishment of more effective national franchise associations in those EU member states should be a key part of the 'regulatory package'.

(a) Pre-contractual disclosure

> BOX 5.24
>
> Franchisors should be obliged to deliver standard form pre-contractual disclosure to potential franchisees 15 working days before execution of any agreement which commits the potential franchisee to take up the franchise or payment of any fees in connection with the franchise sale. They should deliver details of the identity and experience of the franchisor, the target market and the franchise network, the terms of the franchise agreement and any earning claims. There should be a five working

131 Appendix to Chapter 3 – 52% of franchisors in the UK and Germany, 40% in France and 36% in Spain believe that franchisees do not read extensive documentation on the franchise.

day cooling-off period. Failure to comply should enable both the franchisee and national regulatory authorities to take action against the franchisor.

The challenge for legislators considering pre-contractual disclosure by franchisors is to secure optimal impact for minimal effort. This can be achieved, at least in part, by focusing on the two key factors of pre-contractual disclosure: timing of the disclosure and the quality of the information disclosed. Beyond certain basic facts, it is suggested that the amount of information disclosed can be largely irrelevant. Indeed, above a certain threshold there is an inversely proportional relationship between the amount of information disclosed and its effectiveness. The greater the volume of information given, the less likely it is that franchisees will analyse it. In this sense 'less' is 'more'. This was certainly the conclusion of the government review of the Australian Franchising Code in 2006,[132] which was launched due to an increase of complaints of more than 100% over a period of five years ending June 2006.[133] An obligation of pre-contractual disclosure is not universally considered to be appropriate.[134] It is considered by some that if a person who has invested in the search for information is forced to give it away to the co-contracting party, he will have an incentive to reduce (or curtail entirely) his production of such information in the future.[135] The law should maximise the production of socially useful information by allowing those who discover it to benefit from it.[136] A conceptual distinction is made between information which has been gained 'with investment' and that which has been 'casually obtained'; although in practice this becomes a difficult distinction to make. In terms of franchisors it would suggest that information about the franchised business, which has been obtained without investment should be disclosed but information about the target market[137] should not. Another approach to identifying what should be disclosed and what should not is advanced by Cooter and Ulen.[138] They distinguish between information that can be used to increase wealth and redistributive facts, that is information that creates a bargaining advantage, that can be used to redistribute wealth in favour of the knowledgeable party but that

132 Review of the Disclosure Provisions of the Franchising Code of Conduct – Report to the Hon. Fran. Bailey M.P., Minister of Small Business and Tourism, October 2006 – Secretariat Office of Small Business.

133 The ACCC reported 252 complaints related to disclosing issues during the period.

134 For example: Kronman, A., 1978, 'Mistake, Disclosure Information and the Law of Contracts', *Journal of Legal Studies*, Volume 7. Posner, R., 1986, *Economic Analysis of Law*, 3rd edition, p. 96 et seq. Atiyah, P., 1989, *An Introduction to Contract Law*, 4th edition, p. 265 et seq.

135 Op. Cit. Kronman, T., 1978.

136 Fabre-Magnan, M., 1995, 'Duties of Disclosure and French Contract Law', Contribution to the 'Economic Analysis' in *Good Faith and Fault in Contract Law*, ed. Beatson and Friedmann p. 108 – Clarendon Paperbacks.

137 As required by the French and Belgian franchise-focused laws.

138 Cooter, R. and T. Ulen, 1988, *Law and Economics*, 3rd edition, HarperCollins.

does not lead to the creation of new wealth. The conclusion is that economic efficiency requires that wealth-creating facts should be disclosed but redistributive ones should not. Cooter and Ulen also identify a third type of fact, so called destructive facts, information that if not disclosed will harm someone's property or person. In franchising detail about the targeted market should be disclosed by the franchisor to its potential franchisees; likewise, facts about franchisee failure and disputes. However, information about the franchisor's margins on products and general profitability should not be disclosed to potential franchisees. Both of these arguments are based upon the economic efficiency of disclosure but, in the case of franchising, come to different conclusions. Perhaps the reality is that economic efficiency is better measured by having regard as to what facts, if disclosed to the potential franchisee by the franchisor, are most likely to avoid the disputes that are occasioned by a mismatch of expectations between the parties. Prospective franchisees are often relatively unsophisticated in terms of business. They lack the relevant education to be able to process, analyse and draw appropriate conclusions from large amounts of financial and other information. They are also often loath to spend money on legal and financial advice at a time when they feel that they need to inject all the financial resources they have into their new business. This 'weakness of those involved in franchising and perhaps human nature in general'[139] underlines the reality that, no matter how complete any pre-contractual disclosure law is, no matter how potential franchisees are educated about franchising and pushed to take appropriate advice, at the end of the day its effectiveness does depend upon the information disclosed being relevant and easy to understand. It also depends upon it being disclosed at an appropriate time during the 'recruitment' or sales process.

(b) Can pre-contractual disclosure help provide adequate protection?

5.24 One of the biggest causes of disputes between franchisors and their franchisees is a '*mis-match of expectation*' caused by inadequate communication between them as to what they are looking for from the relationship. Pre-contractual disclosure seeks to prevent this mismatch by ensuring that franchisees have all relevant information about the franchise before they commit themselves to it. If they have been appropriately educated they can then assess the likelihood of their expectation being met by the franchisor. Effective disclosure by the franchisor helps appropriately educated potential franchisees to more fully understand the franchise relationship that they are entering, as well as the legal and financial commitments they are undertaking. This reduces conflict in franchise systems. As the then Chairman of the BFA said,[140]

139 FCA submission – 15 August 2006.

140 Brian Lewis at the BFA Annual Convention, Warwick University, 30 June 2005.

> Complete transparency during the recruitment process can help avoid most of the problems that franchisors encounter with their franchisees.

This view seems to be supported by many of the franchisors surveyed for this book. A majority believe that appropriate regulation of the pre-contractual process would substantially reduce the amount of franchise disputes.[141]

(c) The US experience of pre-contractual disclosure

The US has the most comprehensive and complex[142] pre-contractual disclosure requirements in the world. It is suggested that its experience supports the view that mandatory set form pre-contractual disclosure can increase the protection afforded to potential franchisees to an appropriate level. It also suggests issues that should be taken into account when considering the EU's legal eco-system and its impact on franchising. Pre-contractual disclosure is regulated at both federal and state level in the US. Predictably these laws are not identical, making life somewhat complex for franchisors. The FTC Rule 436 (the 'Amended Rule')[143] aims inter alia to prevent the misrepresentation of material facts and ensure the presentation of material facts as a franchisor offers franchises to prospective franchisees. Franchisors are required to deliver a disclosure document at least 14 days before the franchisee signs a contract with the franchisor or pays any money, whichever occurs earlier. The FTC is responsible for enforcing the Amended Rule.[144] The Amended Rule provides that the franchise agreement and all related agreements (i.e. supply contracts, leases and security agreements) must be delivered to the prospective franchisee in final form, ready for execution, at least seven days prior to the date on which they are to be executed.[145] The timings of the disclosure vary and under some state laws disclosure has to take place earlier than under the Amended Rule, i.e. **5.25**

141 See Appendix to Chapter 3. 76% in the UK, 72% in Germany, 76% in France and 72% in Spain.

142 The complexity of the US disclosure system is witnessed by the fact that the disclosure document is prepared by reference to no less than six different sources. The Amended FTC Franchise Rule: 16 C.F.R. Part 436; The Statement of Basis and Purpose to the Amended FTC Franchise Rule: 72 Fed. Reg. 15445–15544 (30 March 2007) ('Statement of Basis and Purpose'); The FTC's Frequently Asked Questions, known as 'Amended Franchise Rule FAQs'. See http://www.ftc.gov/bcp/franchise/amended-rate-faqss.shtml ('FAQs'); FTC Staff Advisory Opinions: will be published in CCH's *Business Franchise Guide*. (Note: the FTC is currently using the FAQs to respond to inquiries rather than issuing staff advisory opinions); State franchise registration and disclosure law statutes and regulations (as amended or unamended): See CCH's *Business Franchise Guide* 3000 to 3530, and 5050 to 5490; The North American Securities Administrators Association ('NASAA') Statement of Policy, including Instructions for Filing a Uniform Registration Application Using the 'New FTC Franchise Rule' after 1 July 2008. See http://www.nasaa.org/content/Files/2008UFOC.pdf ('NASAA Statement of Policy').

143 Which came into effect in October 1979, as amended in January 2007 and implemented 1 July 2007 with interim provisions until 1 July 2008. Federal Register Vol 72, No. 61, 15444–15563, 30 March 2007.

144 Section 5 of the FTC Act 1914 as amended.

145 FTC Rule at 436.1(g).

at the first personal meeting.[146] This causes unnecessary complexity on a practical level and so the North American Securities Administrators Association is recommending that these states adopt the FTC rules 14 day requirement in order to simplify matters.[147] The offering circular must have a cover page bearing language specified by the Amended Rule[148] and a table of contents.[149] It must contain comments that either positively or negatively respond to each disclosure question required to be answered under the Amended FTC Rule. The offering circular may take one of two forms. The first is prescribed by the Amended Rule. The second format is the Uniform Franchise Disclosure Document (the 'UFDD'[150]) as developed by the North American Securities Administrators Association. The two formats cannot be combined, but following the amendment of the FTC Rule, the differences between the two are now relatively minor. The Amended Rule format is often shorter and more easily prepared than one following the UFDD format. However, it is accepted in only 42 states.[151] The UFDD format is accepted in all 50 states and complies with the requirements of those states with franchise disclosure laws. Both forms of disclosure are similar to each other. The Amended FTC Rule format and the UFDD both include 21 different items of information. In fact the 21 different items (plus the franchise contract and the receipt) are identical. However, the level of disclosure required differs in respect of certain items. This disharmony makes the disclosure process far more complex than it need be. The UFDD complies with the Amended Rule but the laws and regulations of each state must be consulted in order to ensure compliance with its individual registration and disclosure provisions. This caused a great deal of debate and discussion amongst the US franchise bar during 2007 and 2008. It clearly demonstrates the importance of an integrated and straightforward approach to the regulation of franchising in the EU. Disclosure under the Amended Rule is not necessary in certain circumstances.[152]

---

146 Maryland, Michigan, New York, Rhode Island and Washington.

147 Per Fox Rothschild Newsstand, Elizabeth Sigety, August 2009.

148 FTC Rule at 436.3.

149 Ibid at 436.4.

150 Formerly known as the 'Uniform Franchise Offering Circular' or 'UFDD' (UFDD/UFOC) which has been amended to comply with the Amended FTC Rule.

151 The eight states in which the FTC format has not been accepted for use each require a franchisor to register a franchise offering before beginning sales efforts in the state. They are California, Indiana, Maryland, Minnesota, Rhode Island, South Dakota, Virginia and Washington. Eight other states also have registration or specific disclosure requirements. They are Hawaii, Illinois, Michigan, New York, North Dakota, Oregon and Wisconsin. Texas has a Business Opportunity Law which applies to franchise arrangements. However the Act specifically excludes any arrangement which is defined as a 'franchise' under the FTC Rule if the franchisor complies with the disclosure requirements and prohibitions of the FTC Rule in its operations in the State of Texas and the Secretary of the State has been notified before the offer or the sale of a franchise, §41.004(b)(8).

152 FTC Rule at 436.8.

The FTC has the sole authority to bring actions to enforce the law and disclosure rule and there is no express or implied private right of action under the Amended Rule although parties with an interest in the consumer redress aspects of FTC suits have been allowed[153] to intervene in the FTC action for the limited purpose of addressing those issues. Both civil and criminal penalties may be imposed for violation of the Amended Rule or of the franchise disclosure rule. The Commission may mitigate civil damages in view of the financial condition of the defendant. The corporate veil of a franchisor breaching the disclosure rule can be pierced, rendering individual officers and directors of the entity liable.[154] State disclosure/registration laws generally provide civil remedies and criminal penalties for violations. The civil remedies include rescission and the recovery of legal fees and other costs. A number of states, such as Florida, have laws focused on misrepresentation in the sale of franchises.[155] This makes it unlawful when selling or establishing a franchise to 'intentionally misrepresent the prospects or chances for success of a proposed or existing franchise, the known required total investment for a franchise and efforts to sell or establish more franchises than is reasonable to expect the market or market area for the particular franchise to sustain'. In some jurisdictions, fraud or gross misrepresentation[156] may lead to the award of punitive damages. Rescission is another possible remedy although failure to comply with a disclosure/registration law does not, in itself, void the agreement. It provides a party with the opportunity to rescind or seek damages. In some states, such as Wisconsin, rescission is the exclusive remedy for disclosure violations.[157] In contrast, in California[158] actions to remedy violations such as failure to register are in contract only and not for rescission; only wilful violations give rise to rescission rights under the California statute. The need for a specific franchise law has been discussed in great detail for many years in the USA[159] culminating

153 E.g. *FTC* v. *American Legal Distributors, Inc.*, 1989–2, Trade Cases, 68,867.

154 *FTC* v. *Jordan Ashley, Inc.*, 93 2257-Civ-Nesbitt (S.D. Fla.): three greeting card display rack franchisors, and their three principal officers, were liable for various misrepresentations violating the FTC Act. The liability was extendable to the officers upon demonstration that they had control over the wrongful acts and had some knowledge of the misrepresentations.

155 The Florida Business Opportunity Act, Florida Statutes s 559.802.

156 *Cox* v. *Doctor's Associates, Inc.*, 245 I11. App. 3d 186, a terminated fast food franchisee recovered $1 million in punitive damages for overtly fraudulent oral and printed misrepresentations that amounted to an independent tort.

157 *Lulling* v. *Barnaby's Family Inns, Inc.*, 449 F. Supp. 1353 E.D. (Wisc.1980), a franchisee that rejected rescission on advice of counsel was, in effect, subjected to a take-nothing judgment that allowed the franchisor to gain possession plus damages and costs.

158 *Pizza Time Theatre, Inc.* v. *Topeka Inn Management, Inc.*, CCH, *Business Franchise Guide / 1980–1983* ¶ 7790, (N.D. Cal. 1981).

159 Since 1995 the FTC has considered amending its rule entitled 'Disclosure Requirements and Prohibitions Concerning Franchising and Business Opportunity Ventures' (the 'Franchise Rule'). This process began with a regulatory review in 1995 which was followed by the publication of an Advanced Notice of Proposed Rulemaking ('ANPR') in 1997 and a Notice of Proposed Rulemaking ('NPR') in 1999. As part of these and

in the publication in August 2004 of an FTC Report[160] and the adoption of an amended FTC Rule in 2007. Part of this process involved the preparation of an FTC Staff Report. A large number of franchisors and professional advisers (many of them lawyers practising exclusively in the field of franchising) made lengthy submissions about the need for franchise-specific regulations.[161] Many of them made it clear that pre-sale disclosure 'helps franchisees more fully understand the franchise relationship that they are entering as well as the legal and financial commitments they are undertaking thereby reducing conflicts in franchise systems and potential litigation costs'.[162] The vast majority of these not only supported the need for pre-contractual disclosure[163] but also felt it to be

> a cost effective way to provide material information to prospective franchisees so they can assess the costs, benefits and potential financial risks involved in entering into a franchise relationship.[164]

It was seen as enabling prospective franchisees to

> investigate the franchise offering by providing information that is not available, such as the franchisor's litigation history and franchisee failure rates.[165]

Some commentators expressed the view that repeal of the US Franchise Rule would increase a franchisor's costs and compliance burdens by opening the door for individual states to enact franchise disclosure laws that may be inconsistent, making it difficult for franchisors to conduct business on a national basis.[166] A uniform pre-sale disclosure rule enables prospective franchisees to comparison

---

the FTC Staff Report there were numerous public workshops held by the FTC and some 281 submissions were received by the FTC from interested parties.

160 Disclosure Requirements and Prohibitions Concerning Franchising – Staff Report to the Federal Trade Commission and Proposed Revised Trade Regulation Rule (16 CFR Part 436) – Bureau of Consumer Protection, August 2004 ('the FTC Staff Report') – The report, as required by Section 1.13(f) of the Commission's Rules of Practice, contains the staff's analysis of the rule amendment record and its recommendations as to the form of the final revised Franchise Rule. The Report has not yet been reviewed or adopted by the Commission. The Commission's final determination in this matter will be based upon the record taken as a whole, including the Report and comments on the Report received during the 75-day period after the report is placed on the public record.

161 The FTC Staff Report III A p. 6. These included major franchisors such as Cendant, a publicly traded company that owns several franchise systems such as Howard Johnson, Ramada, Century 21, Coldwell Banker, ERA and Avis-Rent-a-Car, Re/Max, Snap-on-Tools, Little Caesars, The Southland Corporation (7–11), Pepsico Restaurants (Pizza Hut, Taco Bell, KFC), Papa John's Pizza, Forte Hotels and Medicap Pharmacies.

162 The FTC Staff Report III, A p. 6 and H&H, ANPR 28, at 2.

163 62 Fed. Reg. at 9,120; the FTC Staff Report III A p. 6.

164 The FTC Staff Report III, A p. 6.

165 The FTC Staff Report III, A p. 6; e.g. Marks ANPR 19 Sept 97 Tr, at 8–9, 29 and Wieczorek, Rule Review Comments (RR), Sept. 95 Tr, at 62–3.

166 E.g., WA Securities, ANPR 117; Shay, RR, Sept. 95 Tr., at 104.

shop for the best franchise offering[167] and so reduces future disputes. In short, the FTC concluded that 'free and informed consumer choice is the best regulator of the market'.[168]

(d) *The Australian experience of pre-contractual disclosure*

Australia has a highly developed franchise disclosure law. It is suggested that its experience supports the view that mandatory pre-contractual disclosure helps to ensure that the protection is extended to an appropriate level. It also suggests issues that should be taken into account when considering the EU's legal eco-system's impact on franchising. The Australian Franchise Code, originally prescribed by Section 51AE of the Trade Practices Act (TPA) (since 1 January 2011 the Competition and Consumer Act 2010 (CCA) section 51AE) which prohibits unconscionable behaviour, focuses on creating an environment where a prospective franchisee can make an informed business decision whether to enter into a franchise agreement. Its provisions include comprehensive disclosure obligations on the part of a franchisor that intends to enter into, extend or renew a franchise agreement covered by the Code.[169] A franchisor must provide to a prospective franchisee at least 14 days prior to signing a franchise agreement a detailed disclosure document. It must also provide a copy of the Code and a copy of the franchise agreement. The disclosure document requires the franchisor to provide approximately 250 items of information listed under 23 categories. The information required to be disclosed includes details of the franchisor, the business experience of those involved, litigation history, existing franchisee contact particulars, and information concerning intellectual property ownership, any territorial or supply restrictions, marketing or other cooperative funds, range of costs and payments relevant to the franchise and the franchisor's financial position. Section 22 of the Australian Consumer Law (ACL) (previously Section 51AC of the TPA), which prohibits unconscionable conduct, gives legal teeth to the Franchising Code of Conduct. Non-compliance with the Code amounts to unconscionable behaviour and leads to prescribed remedies. This is clean and simple and avoids high levels of confusion in Australia. Other relevant provisions of the Code are a seven day cooling-off period for franchisees;[170] requirement that the franchisor obtain from the prospective franchisee signed statements before entering into a franchise agreement confirmation that the franchisee has been given legal, business and accounting advice, or has been told to obtain that advice but has decided not to; and a requirement that the franchisor provide financial statements for any marketing or other cooperative funds to which franchisees have made financial contributions. The 5.26

167 Kaufmann, ANPR 33, at 3.

168 The FTC Staff Report III, A p. 11.

169 Clause 6 of Franchising Code of Conduct.

170 Clause 13 of Franchising Code of Conduct.

recruitment of franchisees is also regulated by section 18 of the ACL (formerly section 52 of the TPA) which prohibits misleading or deceptive conduct and is a comprehensive provision of wide impact. Franchisors are frequently the subject of claims based on misleading or deceptive conduct in the context of franchisee recruitment,[171] particularly as regards projected turnover and profitability. Section 18 applies the equivalent of a more general duty of good faith in pre-contractual negotiations to prevent prospective and actual franchisees from being misled or deceived by the conduct in question. However, it does not go so far as the German concept of *culpa in contrahendo* to impose a duty of care on disclosure. A failure to observe the standard of conduct required by section 52 has its consequences under Part VI of the CCA (enforcement and remedies), including both remedies available at common law (such as injunctions and damages) and other compensatory remedies under section 87 which apply when loss or damage is likely to be suffered by a franchisee (e.g., orders declaring the franchise agreement void or varied, for specific performance of the franchise agreement, accounting for profits made by the franchisor, payment of other compensation, or refunds or returns of property). The CCA takes the view that advertisements must tell the full story and create an accurate impression. Phrases such as 'conditions apply', 'to approved applicants' and 'special offer' have been scrutinised to ensure that conditions or fine print terms were consistent with the thrust of the advertisement. It is important that the fine print is consistent with the impression created by the advertisement. Any individual who suffers loss or damage as a consequence of a breach of section 51AD of the CCA may seek injunctions under section 80 of the CCA; seek remedial orders under section 87 of the CCA; and/or recover damages under section 82 of the CCA. There are no criminal sanctions for a breach of section 51AD of the CCA. The court may grant an injunction to the Australian Competition and Consumer Commission (ACCC) or any other person on such terms as it deems appropriate if a person has engaged in, or proposes to engage in, conduct that contravenes the Code. A person who suffers loss or damage by the conduct of another person that was done in contravention of the Code, may recover the amount of the loss or damage by action against that other person or any person involved in the contravention. The ACCC cannot bring an action for damages under section 82 on its own behalf, as it is not a person who suffers loss and damage by reason of a contravention of the CCA. Actions for damages pursuant to section 82, for breach of section 51AD, must be brought within six

---

171 Franchisors should also be aware of the prohibitions against:

- offering gifts, prizes or other free items with no intention of actually providing them, or with no intention of providing them as described (section 54).
- bait advertising, which is advertising a product or service at a lower than normal price, where the product is unavailable at that price, or available only in limited quantities (section 56); and
- advertising partial prices (section 53C).

years of the date on which the applicant suffered loss or damage. A breach of the CCA could have very serious consequences for a franchise system. Breaches of the anti-competitive conduct provisions attract fines of up to $10 million per offence for corporations and $500 000 per offence for those individuals involved in committing the breach. Breaches of the consumer protection provisions such as unconscionable behaviour may attract fines of up to $1.1 million per offence for corporations, and $220 000 per offence for individuals.[172] The courts can set aside or vary contracts and make other orders affecting the franchise relationship. Negative publicity and corrective advertising have a significant effect on brands, image and reputation. Such penalties are particularly significant in the franchising sector where a strong brand image is essential. Since the introduction of the Code, the ACCC has commenced and successfully concluded litigation in 15 cases.[173] All cases were found to be in breach of the CCA and the Code, and a variety of remedies were ordered by the courts including injunctions, court orders and the implementation of a trade practices compliance programme. Of these 15 cases, 14 involved a failure by the franchisor to fully comply with the disclosure provisions of the Code. Most cases involved situations where the franchisor did not provide disclosure documents to potential franchisees or, if the disclosure documents were provided, they were misleading or inadequate. Some of these cases also involved franchise systems that wrongly represented themselves as distributorships or licence agreements, to avoid the stringent requirements of the Code. The Code seems to have increased compliance costs for franchisors but has generally been well received. It has also provided an opportunity for those franchisors who comply with the Code and give full disclosure, as a mechanism to avoid or reduce likely claims by franchisees. Compliance with the Code reduces the opportunities for the application of section 51AC. The government is proposing further amendments to the Code, including enhancing the ACCC's powers to conduct random audits of franchisors, enabling the ACCC to alert the public of franchisor's misconduct by issuing public warnings and permitting the ACCC to seek redress on behalf of franchisees where large numbers of franchisees have been affected by the franchisor's non-compliance.[174] In addition, the government is proposing to include a list of examples of specific behaviour in the Code that constitute inappropriate behaviour. These may

172 Government's response to the Report into the Franchising Code of Conduct by the Parliamentary Joint Committee on Corporations and Financial Services, the Trade Practices Amendment (Australian Consumer Law) Bill 2009.

173 Review of the Disclosure Provisions of the Franchising Code of Conduct. Report to the Hon Fran Bailey M.P.

174 Minister for Innovation, Industry, Science and Research, Media Release, 'Government to Strengthen Franchising Code of Conduct and Unconscionable Law', 5 November 2009. http://minister.innovation.gov.au/Emerson/Pagesgovernmenttostrengthenfranchisingcodeofconduct.

include: unforeseen capital expenditure; unilateral contract variation; attribution of legal costs; confidentiality agreements; franchisor-initiated changes to franchise agreements when a franchisee is trying to sell the business.[175] In Australia, pre-contractual disclosure is credited with reducing the number of disputes between franchisors and franchisees. This is in no small part due to the fact that failure to comply with the disclosure process in both these jurisdictions is subject to significant legal sanctions which the authorities are ready, able and willing to apply. The Australian experience suggests that 'prevention' in the form of legally prescribed disclosure can reduce the need for or at least lessen the drastic measures required for a 'cure' in the form of the imposition of penalties.

(e) The French experience of pre-contractual disclosure

5.27 The provisions of the Loi Doubin are detailed above. Its failure to define franchising, the requirement of exclusivity or quasi-exclusivity in order for it to apply and its failure to require disclosure of the details of all ongoing fees that must be paid seem to have reduced the potential impact of the law, and so are not approaches that should be incorporated into an EU Franchise Directive.

(f) What should be disclosed to potential franchisees?

> BOX 5.25
>
> Disclosure must help potential franchisees assess the potential benefits of taking a franchise and reduce, but not remove entirely, the consequential inherent risks involved.

5.28 Current requirements in EU member states, the USA and Australia are helpful in determining exactly what should be incorporated in the franchisor's pre-contractual disclosure document to ensure that it helps to provide adequate protection for franchisees.

Common themes emerge when considering the six European disclosure regulations and the US and Australian franchise regulations. However, the European laws are generally less formulaic and are somewhat narrower in their scope. Some of these differences, such as that concerning the involvement of public figures in the franchise in the USA, are due to cultural and commercial

175 Minister for Innovation, Industry, Science and Research, Media Release, 'Government Appoints Expert Panel on Franchising and Unconscionable Conduct', 27 November 2009. http://minister.innovation.gov.au/Emerson/Pagesgovernmentappointsexpertpanelonfranchising.

differences and so can be ignored. Others, such as exclusivity, reflect the differences in both the saturation/maturity of the markets and the propensity for litigation in each jurisdiction.

BOX 5.26

Disclosure should comprise information about the identity and experience of the franchisor; the franchise network; the terms of the franchise agreement and any earning claims made.

These are all straightforward matters of fact which potential franchisees clearly require and which the franchisor can easily provide and are reflected to some extent in the proposals of both the Amsterdam Team[176] and the UNIDROIT model law.[177] However, it is the quality and relevance of the information and the way in which it is communicated rather than the mere type and quantity of the information that is important. 'More is sometimes less' and as one experienced in-house US franchise lawyer has commented,

> The American UFDD goes far too far, obscuring important and relevant information with masses of less important detail.[178]

BOX 5.27

Details of the identity and experience of the franchise and its directors should include the franchisor's litigation history over the previous 36 months and the bankruptcy history of the franchisor and its directors and substantial shareholders (holding over 25% of the issued shares).

Details of the franchise network should include details of the franchise network in the target market (or, if there is none, an analogous market), including the contact details of existing franchisees and any franchisees that have failed in the previous 12 months.

176 Article 3:102 Commercial Agency, Franchise and Distribution, Amsterdam Team 8th Draft (21 May 2003).
177 UNIDROIT, Model Franchise Disclosure Law.
178 Interview with Christopher Nowak, Vice President and General Counsel, Wyndham Worldwide Corporation (10 March 2006).

There are significant differences between the different EU member states. The proposed obligation should be restricted to knowledge that the franchisor actually has and will not include information that it ought to have.

BOX 5.28

A summary of the terms of the franchise agreement should be detailed in the disclosure document. These are:

- the Initial and Ongoing Fees,
- Intellectual Property,
- Franchise Territory,
- Supply of Goods and Services,
- Marketing and other co-operative funds,
- any financing arrangements provided by the franchisor,
- the Franchisor's Obligations,
- the Franchisee's Obligations and Restrictions,
- Related Agreements,
- Renewal,
- Termination,
- Post-termination restrictions,
- Dispute Resolution,
- Earning claims.

Prospective franchisees want to know their likely level of earnings in the franchise and so this should be covered by the disclosure document. However, a prescriptive approach to what should be disclosed to potential franchisees about their likely earnings (as is found in the US), is not recommended.

BOX 5.29

The Italian approach to earning claims of 'loyalty, fairness and good faith'[179] should be adopted.

This is because artful draftsmen can get around detailed provisions so giving misleading information that complies with the law whilst this general approach makes it more difficult to evade and more adaptable to local conditions.

179 Law of 6 May 2004, No. 129, Article 6.1.

(g) Inappropriate disclosure

BOX 5.30

It is not appropriate to disclose the characteristics of the franchisor's relevant know-how to potential franchisees.

Although the Amsterdam Team recommend this, to do so would compromise the franchisor's trade secrets and so discourage companies from becoming franchisors.[180]

BOX 5.31

The franchisor should not be under an obligation to deliver to the potential franchisee details about the market conditions.

This is contrary to the Study Group's recommendation (and the provision of the French and Belgian disclosure laws). However, to require the franchisors to do so removes from the franchisee responsibility for its own commercial decisions and so encourages the unsuitable individuals and nurtures the blame culture condemned by the Australian government.

(h) Renewal

There is a reasonable case for suggesting that on the renewal of a franchise agreement the incumbent franchisee has sufficient information about the franchised business to make any disclosure document a meaningless and unnecessary administrative burden for the franchisor. This is particularly so for mature systems that are no longer actively recruiting new franchisees. However, the counter argument is, on balance, more persuasive. The renewal of a franchise is an important commercial event which requires the franchisee and the franchisor to carefully consider their options. In order to do this both need accurate and up to date information. The franchise network will have developed during the term of the expiring franchise agreement and the new franchise agreement may differ from the original agreement in important ways. The franchisee's circumstances may have also changed and the franchisor should be given formal notice of these. **5.29**

180 Article 3:102 Commercial Agency, Franchising and Distribution, Amsterdam Team 8th Draft (21 May 2003)

BOX 5.32

The EU Franchise Directive should provide that on each renewal of a franchise agreement the franchisor and the franchisee must comply with the pre-contractual disclosure obligations as if they did not have an existing franchisor/franchisee relationship.

(i) The timing of disclosure

5.30 Timing of disclosure is important. The franchisee must have sufficient time to properly consider it but too long a period risks it becoming out of date and unduly slowing down the commercial process.

BOX 5.33

Delivery of the disclosure document to the prospective franchisee should be 15 working days before the execution of any agreement which commits the prospective franchisee to take up the franchise or payment of any fees in connection with the franchise sale.

This follows the Swedish example[181] and is similar to the approach taken by both the US's FTC Rules[182] and the Australian Franchise Code.

(j) Who should it be delivered to?

BOX 5.34

The disclosure document must be delivered to a 'prospective franchisee'. A prospective franchisee is any person (including any agent, representative or employee) who approaches or is approached by a franchise seller to discuss the possible establishment of a franchise relationship.

This follows the US lead.[183] Representatives of a prospective corporate franchisee must be permitted to accept delivery of the disclosure document on the prospective franchisee's behalf. The requirement that the parties must 'discuss

181 The Swedish law requires a reasonable period of no less than 14 days.

182 See 16 CFR 436.1(g), 436.2(a) and 436.2(c).

183 Section 436.1(r) of the FTC Rule. The term 'franchise seller' is used in lieu of 'franchisor, or franchise broker, or any representative, agent, or employee thereof'. See section 436.1(i).

the possible establishment of a franchise relationship' makes it clear that for an individual to become a 'prospective franchisee' he or she must communicate with the franchisor about a franchise offering. Merely perusing a franchisor's website alone, for example, will not turn an ordinary internet surfer into a prospective franchisee.

(k) *What constitutes delivery of the disclosure document?*

It is important to avoid confusion over whether or not the disclosure document has been delivered. **5.31**

> BOX 5.35
>
> The Directive should lay down a clear and unambiguous definition of what amounts to delivery to the prospective franchisee.

Evidence that the duty of disclosure has been complied with is important in order to prevent any future dispute as to compliance. This issue is dealt with in both the US[184] and Australian[185] legislation. With the increasing use of e-mail and other forms of electronic communication, the Directive must also deal with the issue of electronic disclosure. There are three key issues that need to be considered as regards this.[186] The first issue to be addressed is whether the electronic disclosure document has to be exactly the same as the hard copy document. Enhancements such as audio, video, pop-ups and external links to websites could erode the integrity of the disclosure document so are best avoided although limited electronic enhancements, such as scroll bars, search features and internal links to facilitate franchisee navigation of the document are appropriate. Secondly, there are a multitude of options available to the franchisor: e.g., e-mail, a password-protected Internet site or CD-ROM although e-mail is likely to be the favoured option due to cost efficiency and ease of use. To ensure that a franchise prospect realises that alternative disclosure formats are available, the franchisor should add information to the cover page of the disclosure document indicating that such alternative formats are

184 In the USA Item 23 of the UFDD requires that the last page of the offering circular must be a detachable document acknowledging receipt of the offering circular by the prospective franchisee. The prospective franchisee signs the receipt and returns it to the franchisor. The franchisor is also required to furnish the franchise agreement containing all material terms at least five business days before signing.

185 According to the Australian Franchise Code of Conduct, the last page of the disclosure document must contain 'a statement to the effect that the prospective franchisee may keep the disclosure document', and 'a form on which the prospective franchisee can acknowledge receipt of the disclosure document' (The Code, Annexure 1, item 23).

186 Plave, *LJN's Franchising Business & Law Alert*, April 2007, Vol. 13, No. 7, pp. 1, 2, 4.

available. Thirdly, the greater ease of using electronic disclosure potentially increases the administrative burden of recording who was served with the disclosure document and when. The US requirement for the delivery of disclosure documents to be acknowledged by the recipient[187] has led to detailed provisions as to how this must be effected if disclosure is made electronically.[188]

> BOX 5.36
>
> Receipt of the disclosed document can be acknowledged by any affirmative action by the recipient to authenticate his/her identify and confirm receipt. This could include, for example, a handwritten signature, an electronic signature, passwords or a security code. The fast changing nature of electronic commerce means that this general statement is more appropriate than detailed and specific provisions are likely to become out of date in a short period of time.

(l) What documents should be given to the potential franchisees?

> BOX 5.37
>
> The disclosure document should be accompanied by a copy of the franchise agreement in the form in which it is to be executed.

The franchisor should also provide the prospective franchisee with all other documents required by the franchise agreement to be signed, in the form each is intended to be executed. Whilst this may seem all very obvious and straightforward, in practice complications can arise. The prospective franchisees should receive the franchise agreement in the form in which it is intended to be executed at the same time as they receive the disclosure document. However in practice all documents may not be available in their final form at that time.[189] Research in Australia[190] suggests that despite the requirements of the Code,[191] the final form of such documents sometimes are not provided until after the

187 Statement of Basis and Purpose, Section II.B.2,b, 72 Fed. Reg at 15469.

188 Section 436.1(4) Statement of Purpose, Section III, A21, 72 Fed Reg at 15467 FTC FAQs, Question 15.

189 A similar provision is found in the Australian Franchising Code of Conduct, Part 2, Division 2.1, section 6C and Annexure 1, section 18.

190 Review of the Disclosure Provisions of the Franchising Code of Conduct – Report to the Hon. Fran. Bailey M.P., Minister of Small Business and Tourism, October 2006 – Secretariat Office of Small Business.

191 It requires the franchisor to provide a summary of any requirements under the franchise agreement for the franchisee to enter into other agreements as a result of signing the franchise agreement. These include leases and sub-leases for premises, chattel leases or hire purchase agreements, guarantees, mortgage security deposits, confidentiality agreements and agreements not to carry out business in the area for a time after the franchise

franchise agreement is signed and their existence is only alluded to briefly during preliminary meetings or brushed off as not being of any significance. The Loi Doubin requires that a potential franchisee must be provided with all information which is indispensable for the franchisee to contract with full knowledge of the facts.[192] It is suggested that if there is any material difference between the summary of any such document and the one presented to the franchisee for execution, it should entitle the franchisee to withdraw from the franchise without penalty and cost. Clearly a franchisor may have difficulty providing all documents required to be signed by the franchisor to the prospective franchisee 15 working days before the franchise agreement is expected to be signed. If the documents are available, they should be provided at least 15 working days before the franchise agreement is expected to be signed. A latest draft of documents not available in final form at that time must be provided. When the final draft is ready, a red-lined copy illustrating any changes should be provided. This must be at least five working days before executing the Franchise Agreement and other relevant documents. If necessary, the execution of documents must be delayed to ensure that there are five working days between delivery of the final document and execution.

(m) The accuracy of the information being disclosed

It is important that the standard of the franchisor's liability for drafting the disclosure document is established. If the information disclosed is inaccurate the disclosure process is pointless. The simplest solution would be to place the franchisor under a strict liability to ensure the accuracy of the information it supplies. However, **5.32**

> as anyone who has drafted a (US) Offering Circular can testify, there is no certainty as to the nature of the information that has to be included in the various disclosure sections of the Offering Circular and reasonable persons often differ in good faith as to what has to be disclosed.[193]

The Directive should follow the French and Spanish approach to accuracy of disclosure and focus upon the subjective test of defective consent rather than a technical failure to comply with the technical requirement of disclosure.

agreement is terminated. Federal Trade Commission Rule on Disclosure Requirements and Prohibitions Concerning Franchising and Business Opportunity Ventures (FTC Rule) §436.

192 Commercial Court of Creteil, 9 May 2000, L'Off De la. fr No. 30 p. 94.

193 FTC Staff Report, Baer, NPR 11, at 10.

> BOX 5.38
>
> Even if disclosed information is inaccurate it will be immaterial if the inaccuracy has not led to defective consent being given by the franchisee and that it is a violation for a franchisor to fail to use best endeavours to ensure the accuracy of the disclosed information.
>
> Liability for inaccurate disclosure that leads to defective consent should attach not only to the franchisor, but also to any individual working for or with the franchisor who can be shown to have been responsible for the disclosure of the inaccurate information, who knew (or should have known) the legal or commercial significance of those facts, and was in a position to influence the outcome of the matter.

A secretary could 'know' that incorrect financial performance data was routinely provided to buyers, but neither know the significance of doing so nor be in a position to stop the practice. Failure to comply should lead to the imposition of a fine by the authorities and liability in damages if despite consent being valid the franchisee is disadvantaged in some tangible way. In the interests of clarity and practicality it is also appropriate to impose an obligation upon the franchisor to update the disclosure document on a regular basis.

> BOX 5.39
>
> The Australian approach be adopted by the EU Franchise Directive and that the Disclosure Document be updated within six months of the end of each financial year.

A shorter period might create too much compliance urgency for franchisors without adequate resources to comply.

(n) Language

5.33 The different languages of the 27 member states can create complications with pre-contractual disclosure.

> BOX 5.40
>
> The disclosure document should be in the plain language(s) of the member state in which the franchisee will be operating its business or, in member states in which there is more than one official language, the official language which the franchisee designates as its preference.

For example, a franchisee in Belgium could require the disclosure document to be in Flemish, French or German.

> BOX 5.41
>
> Plain language should be defined as the organization of information and language usage understandable by a person unfamiliar with the franchise business. It incorporates short sentences; definite, concrete, everyday language; active voice; and tabular presentation of information, where possible.

It avoids legal jargon, highly technical business terms, and multiple negatives.[194]

(o) Risk statement

Potential franchisees need to be reminded in clear and unambiguous terms that buying a franchise can be a risky business. There is no guaranteed return on their income and they may lose everything they invest. The proposals regarding educating potential franchisees made above should be re-enforced by a Risk Statement on the disclosure document. If prospective franchisees are made aware of these significant risks then they should be better informed in making their decision about entering a franchise agreement and will be better equipped to manage the risks. **5.34**

The US approach is to ensure that franchisors 'present all material facts accurately, clearly, concisely, and legibly'.[195]

---

194 This definition is based upon the definition of 'plain English' used in Part 436 of the final amended FTC Rule, Section 436.1(o).

195 See UFOC Guidelines, General Instruction 150. The phrase 'plain English' is defined separately in section 436.1(o), consistent with the UFOC Guidelines.

There are no such requirements in the EU member states. It would be appropriate to place on the front of the disclosure document a clear and unequivocal risk statement.

> BOX 5.42
>
> A Risk Statement which identifies known significant risks that could have a material impact on the franchisee should be placed on the front of the disclosure document. It should read as follows:
>
> 'Investing in a franchise can be a risky business. There is no guarantee that your franchise will be a success. You could lose your investment. In order to succeed you will have to work long and hard. It is not a road to instant success and riches. You must think about it carefully before you enter into the franchise agreement. Some of the information you need in order to make an informed decision is contained in this disclosure document. Take your time, read all documents carefully, talk to other franchisees and assess your own financial resources and capabilities to deal with requirements of the franchised business. You should also make your own enquiries, get independent legal, accounting and business advice, prepare a business plan and projections for profit and cash flow and consider an educational course, particularly if you have not operated a business before'.
>
> The front of each franchise agreement should be endorsed with the following statement:
>
> 'This franchise will not provide a guaranteed income to you. In entering into this franchise you are accepting the risk that you may lose your investment. If you get into financial trouble whilst operating your franchised business your franchisor has no obligation to rescue you. It is therefore essential that before entering this franchise you take legal and financial advice from professionals with a proven track record of advising prospective franchisees on their intended investment and that you follow their advice. You must also carefully read the disclosure document. It contains important information that you must read before entering into the franchise agreement. Remember, if your franchised business fails depending upon your circumstances you could end up losing your home and becoming bankrupt.'

(p) Cooling-off period

5.35 A number of jurisdictions with franchise-focused laws impose a 'cooling-off' period on the parties after the execution of the franchise agreement, ranging from five to 30 days.[196] In Germany BGB 507 imposes a cooling-off period in

196 Mexico – Decree No 35/2006/ND-CP, article 142 of Mexico's Industrial Property Law. Malaysia – The Franchise Act 1998, Part III Section 18(2)(h) and 18(4). Taiwan – Article 5 of the Standards Governing Disclosure of Information by Franchisors by the Fair Trade Commission.

certain circumstances as does Austria and the UK. This extra time for a franchisee to reflect upon their decision is a small investment in helping to ensure that franchisees are really committed to making the franchised business a success. It is an investment in favour of franchisor and franchisee alike.

BOX 5.43

A period of five working days following the day on which the franchise agreement is executed by both parties the franchisee has the right to withdraw by written notice, without penalty.

(q) Foreign franchisors

Should an EU disclosure law impact only on franchisors based in the EU or should it also have jurisdiction over those based outside of the EU but granting franchises into member states? The answer to the question about the effect of the franchisor's location may seem an obvious one. However, until a recent change of law, Australia exempted foreign franchisors from the need to provide disclosure to an Australian franchisee so long as the franchisor was resident outside of Australia and only granted one franchise or master franchise to be operated in Australia.[197] The main reason for this exemption seems to have been to ensure that there was nothing that discouraged foreign franchisors entering into the geographically remote and demographically small Australian market. However, it seems that this concern was misplaced and the AFC's recommendation[198] that this exemption be dropped has recently been accepted by the Australian government. If one views individual member states as separate markets then some of the smaller markets such as the Baltic States, Slovenia and Slovakia may merit such treatment. They are demographically small and are noticeably more remote than the western and central member states. Perhaps a US franchisor would appreciate an exemption that removed its obligation to make disclosure to, say, a Latvian franchisee. However, given the size and wealth of the EU as a whole, the justification for such an exemption for foreign franchises entering an EU member state could not be that it is necessary in order to encourage new franchises to enter the EU. One could argue that foreign concepts entering an EU member state for the first time are entirely untested in the target EU market, and therefore do not have that much information about the target market to disclose. There is, of course, some merit in that argument, but it is not sufficiently persuasive. There is a good deal of 5.36

197 Section 5 of the Australian Franchise Code of Conduct.

198 Submission of the Review of the Disclosure Provisions of the Franchise Code of Conduct – 15 August 2006.

important non-market specific information that needs to be disclosed to potential franchisees, in addition to which, as one franchise executive stated,

> whilst for some businesses the details of the business outside of the target member state might well be irrelevant and possibly confusing, for many including our business such disclosure is extremely useful and important to potential franchisees.[199]

All franchisors should give some form of disclosure, although a franchisor with no experience of the market in a particular member state should not be under any obligation to furnish potential franchise information about that member state.

> To expect a franchisor to have a real detailed knowledge of foreign jurisdictions in which it has no operational experience is nonsensical and dangerous. Often it is the franchisor's very lack of such knowledge that leads it to franchise in a foreign jurisdiction in the first place.[200]

Such requirements can create barriers to successful cross-border franchising and show a real lack of understanding of what master franchisees and developers are expected to bring to the party. However, such a franchisor must make some type of disclosure about the business and about how it has fared in at least one market. A Master Franchisee who tries to establish a franchise system in an EU member state from scratch would be compromised by a lack of knowledge of how the system has performed in other markets. A potential franchisee needs the protection afforded to it by formal disclosure and the location of the franchisor is irrelevant. Although a system's performance in foreign markets and other member states may be totally different to its potential performance in a particular member state, so long as such information is furnished to the potential franchisee with an appropriate health warning clearly stating that it is for a different market and that the system may perform very differently in the franchisee's market, it can be useful.

BOX 5.44

(1) A franchisor granting a franchise to a party in a member state in which it is not based (the target member state) should disclose details of its franchise in the target member state.
(2) If a franchisor does not have outlets in the target market it should disclose details of its business in another member state.

199 Interview with Christopher Nowak, Vice President and General Counsel, Wyndham Worldwide Corporation (10 March 2006).
200 Interview with Jane Colton, Vice President & Legal Counsel, Vanguard Rental GmbH (1 June 2006).

(3) If the franchisor does not have any outlets in the whole of the EU, it should disclose details of its franchise in the country in which it is based or another country which it can reasonably justify as being appropriate ('the analogous market').

The disclosure requirement will not apply to franchisors based in the EU granting franchises to potential franchisees who are based outside of the EU. When a franchisor is disclosing details of outlets in a market other than the target member state, it must clearly state that this is the case and that performance in a different market is not necessarily a reliable guide to performance in the target market due to economic, cultural and commercial differences and that the potential franchisee should therefore treat them with caution.

(r) Regular review of the law

BOX 5.45

The EU Directive be reviewed every five (5) years to ensure that the contents of the Disclosure Document continue to be relevant to the market.

It is important that the required contents of the disclosure document and indeed other aspects of it are not fossilised, but are regularly updated to reflect the concerns of the market and so ensure that it continues to meet the benchmarks of good regulation. 5.37

Such reviews have recently been conducted on an ad hoc basis in both Australia and the USA. The disclosure provisions of the Australian Franchising Code were reviewed on behalf of government in 2006[201] due to a marked increase of complaints (more than 100% increase) over the five-year period to June 2006.[202] The US Federal and State franchise laws are being continually reassessed and amended.[203] It is therefore suggested that

201 Review of the Disclosure Provisions of the Franchising Code of Conduct – Report to the Hon. Fran Bailey M.P., Minister of Small Business and Tourism – October 2006 – Secretariat Office of Small Business. The Review, completed on 31 October, was conducted by a committee chaired by Mr Graeme Matthews, National Managing Partner, KPMG Middle Market Advisory, supported by a secretariat from the Office of Small Business and a team from the law firm Corrs Chambers Westgarth.

202 The ACCC reported 252 complaints related to disclosure issues in the five year period – Review of the Disclosure Provisions of the Franchising Code of Conduct – Report to the Hon Fran Bailey M.P. etc.

203 For example: (1) in the last 20 years, Congressman LaFalce has twice proposed stricter federal regulation, (2) the FTC has twice reviewed its FTC Rules as part of the process that ultimately led to the recent changes,

the format of the statutory disclosure document should be reviewed every ten years or so to ensure that as franchising develops along with the sophistication of potential franchisees it also changes to ensure that the disclosures are relevant and useful.

(s) The consequences of inadequate disclosure

5.38 A disclosure law is meaningless unless the consequences of non-compliance are such as to deter franchisors from failing to give full disclosure and afford sufficient remedy to the wronged party. The wronged franchisee always has a right of redress against a franchisor who has made wrongful or inadequate disclosure. However, in some jurisdictions the government agencies have an independent right of action.[204] Failure to make adequate disclosure under disclosure laws[205] is generally sanctioned by nullity/rescission of the franchise agreement;[206] prohibition of further franchising by the

(3) states such as Iowa have adopted new franchise laws, (4) the Supreme Court has relaxed the law on price control in the *Leegin* case, (5) innumerable states have amended their existing franchise laws.

204 In Spain for example, both private parties and the Ministry of Economy and Finance may bring legal action for violation of the disclosure requirements before the administrative courts. In addition, a franchisee can file a request to the government to commence action against a franchisor. The government does not have to do this, but if failure to bring action results in damages to the franchisee, the franchisee may have a claim against the government. In the USA, the FTC itself can bring a civil action for rescission of contract (FTC Act s.19 (15 U.S.C. s57b)). The ACCC also has power to act against offending franchisors. It can bring actions in relation to a violation of the Franchising Code of Conduct or of Section 52 of the TPA. It can order the contract fully or partly void and can refuse to enforce all or any provisions of the franchise agreement.

205 USA: Federal Trade Commission Act; Australia: Trade Practices (Industry Codes-Franchising) Regulations known as the Franchising Code of Conduct enacted as Section 51AE of the Federal Trade Practices Act 1974 (the TPA); Spain: Article 62 of Act 7/1996 and Royal Decree 2485/1998; France: The 'Loi Doubin', Law No. 89–1008 dated 31 December 1989 on Pre-contractual Disclosure; Italy: Law of 6 May 2004, No. 129 Article 1.1; Belgium: Law relative to pre-contractual information in the framework of commercial partnership agreements adopted 19 December 2005, modified 27 December 2005; effective 1 February 2006, Art. 5; Sweden: Disclosure Act 2006; Romania: Government Ordinance No. 52/1997 as amended by Law No. 79/1998.

206 Nullity/rescission of the franchise agreement is a formalistic approach to non-compliance aimed at ensuring that franchisors comply with the disclosure law, sometimes regardless of proportionality. All jurisdictions except Sweden recognise the right for individual franchisees to rescind agreements but not all give the regulatory authorities the same rights. Misrepresentation under English and Irish law can render the agreement void 'ab initio'. Although the Loi Doubin is silent as to the consequences of inadequate or wrongful disclosure, failure to comply can give rise to a retroactive cancellation (Cass. Com., 10 February 1998, Bull. Civ.IV No. 71 recently confirmed by Cass. Com., 7 July 2004, No.02–15950). However, in recent years French courts have only voided or cancelled a franchise agreement if the franchisor's failure to disclose has meant that the franchisee's consent was vitiated (Cass. Com., 10 February 1998, Bull., Civ IV No. 71, recently confirmed by Cass. Com., 7 July 2004, No. 02–15950). Article 1304 of the French Civil Code imposes a time bar of five years from the time that the franchisee begins any action for rescission of contract. Inadequate or incorrect disclosure may give rise to the nullity of the franchise agreement in Spain. Some Spanish courts have declared several franchise agreements to be null and void due to a lack of compliance with disclosure requirements, whereas other courts have deemed the failure to comply with disclosure obligations a mere administrative default. If the misrepresentation has been minor, the Spanish courts will award the franchisee an extraordinary right to terminate the agreement rather than to declare it null and void from the beginning. Failure to disclose may lead the Italian courts to rescind the agreement or declare it null and void. Article 5 of the Belgian franchise law provides that failure to provide the disclosure document enables the franchisee to seek a declaration that the franchise agreement is null and void within two years following the execution of the contract.

franchisor;[207] cease and desist orders and injunctive relief;[208] financial penalties;[209] damages;[210] and criminal sanctions.[211] These sanctions are imposed either by individual franchisees exercising their rights in the courts or by the regulatory authorities who either have a right to take court action against the franchisor or impose an administrative penalty. The Amsterdam Group's recommendation for a model Civil Code was that if failure to make 'full and proper disclosure' leads to a 'fundamental mistake'[212] the franchisee is entitled to

207 In some jurisdictions if a franchisor is a serial offender and is regularly breaching the disclosure obligations the authorities have the right, in the public interest, to disqualify it from granting further franchises. In the UK the Companies Investigation Branch of the Insolvency Service can petition the High Court to place franchisors who misrepresent their businesses to potential franchisees into liquidation. (In November 2008 the Queensbury and Richmond vending franchises were placed into liquidation as a result of the CIB's investigation showing that their recruitment literature centred around untested claims about what franchisees could earn; *Franchise World*, Dec/Jan 2009, p. 6.)

208 In a number of jurisdictions, the courts can make orders for specific performance in addition to fines and awarding damages. However, in Sweden this is the only order that the Market Court can make (Lag (2006:484) om franchisegivares informationsskyldighet). As the right to rescission or damages may not always be immediate enough to provide a franchisee with adequate remedy both the wronged franchisee and the regulatory authority are often able to apply for injunctive relief. For example, in both the USA and Australia, cease and desist orders can be issued by the regulatory authorities and obtained from the courts on application by the franchisee.

209 Financial penalties rather than damages can also be imposed by the regulatory authorities in the USA, Australia and certain EU member states. In the USA, monetary penalties of up to US$10 000 a day for each violation can be imposed (S.5 of the FTC Act (U.S.C. §45)); whilst in New South Wales payment of money is a possible remedy under section 106 of the Industrial Relations Act 1996 (New South Wales). Article 2 of the Loi Doubin provides for specific fines for failure to comply with disclosure obligations (€1500 for a single violation and €3000 for repeat violation) even where intent is lacking, whilst the Spanish government can impose fines of up to €3000 for the first offences, up to €15 000 for repeated violations and if turnover of the franchisor is over €600 000 fines of up to €600 000.

210 Failure to comply with the disclosure obligation usually also gives the franchisee the right to damages. For example, in the UK and Ireland the franchisee can affirm the contract and opt for damages instead of rescission. In the USA, franchisees can bring common law action for damages (even penal damages) against franchisors, but may not be able to obtain rescission or legal fees. The Australian courts will grant damages. Remedies for contravention of the Code or the unconscionable conduct provisions in section 51AC of the TPA may be brought by the ACCC or by a person who suffers loss or damage as a result of conduct. Even if there has been no breach of the code, the conduct of a franchisor may contravene section 52 of the TPA which prohibits a corporation from engaging in conduct that is misleading or deceptive or is likely to mislead or deceive. Franchisees have evoked this to recover losses from failed franchised businesses on the grounds of misrepresentations during the sales process (*Silver Fox Company PTY Limited* v. *Lenards PTY Limited* [2005] FCAFC 131 (19 July 2005); *Cut Price Deli Pty Ltd* v. *Jacques* (1994) 49 FCR 397; 126 ALR 413; (1994) ATPR 46–128). The general limitation period is six years from the date on which the cause of the action accrued. Damages can be claimed under Article 1382 of the French Civil Code (law of tort); but the French courts will only award them in cases of fraud or gross negligence. There are no punitive damages. Actions for damages under tort liability are time-barred after five years from the time that the damage occurred. There is no contractual claim. In Italy, damages can be awarded if there is a direct relation between any loss suffered and the franchisor's failure to disclose. In Romania, civil damages can be claimed for both actual loss and anticipated loss. The time bar for such claims is three years.

211 Some jurisdictions also impose criminal sanctions on franchisors for inaccurate disclosure in some circumstances. In France, criminal penalties can be imposed if fraud, false advertising or abuse of power are involved. Article 515 of the Italian Criminal Code provides for a criminal penalty up to two years of imprisonment or up to €2065.83 in case of fraud. In Romania, intentional misrepresentation can result in criminal charges.

212 Article 4:103 Commercial Agency, Franchise And Distribution, Amsterdam Team 8th Draft (21 May 2003).

damages[213] unless the franchisor had reason to believe that the information was adequate and it was given in reasonable time. It is uncertain what 'full and proper' disclosure, a 'fundamental mistake', 'adequate information' and 'reasonable time' are. Such details are of fundamental importance and their absence renders the proposal both meaningless and dangerous. Such an approach is unlikely to encourage either new franchisors or franchisees. Failure to comply with the disclosure obligation which leads to defective consent being given should enable both the franchisee and the appropriate regulatory authority (e.g. the Department for Business, Enterprise and Regulatory Reform in the UK) to rescind the franchise and related agreements or, in the case of the franchisee, to affirm the agreement and sue for damages instead, subject to certain chronological limitations. The franchisee's right to withdraw from a contractual relationship into which it has been wrongfully enticed is clearly of fundamental importance, although there comes a point at which it must be deemed to have affirmed the relationship. The right to walk away from the franchise due to inadequate disclosure cannot continue in perpetuity.

BOX 5.46

The right to walk away or claim damages due to inadequate disclosure should be restricted so that it must be exercised by the franchisee (or the government agency authorised) within 12 months of the franchisee becoming aware of the failure or 24 months of the date of the franchise agreement, whichever is the later.[214] If the agreement continues after this time the franchisee will be deemed to have affirmed the franchise agreement and so lose both its right to terminate the agreement and the right to sue for damages (as would the government agency). If the franchisee has not taken action by that time the failure to comply with the disclosure obligation could not be sufficiently damaging as to justify the franchisor having access to such remedies. This should encourage a reasonable level of confidence and stability in franchising.

The cut off is necessary to ensure that the franchisor can enjoy a degree of certainty and avoid having to work with the franchisee under the burden of uncertainty for a prolonged period of time.

213 Article 4:117 (2) and (3), ibid.

214 Article 5 of the Belgian law provides similar limitations – as does Section 339 Ptk of the Hungarian Civil Code.

> BOX 5.47
>
> Member state regulatory authorities should have the right to require a franchisor to desist from making wrongful or inadequate disclosure if there is found to be an established pattern of such behaviour. Failure to comply with the prohibition should lead to the imposition of substantial fines on the franchisor and the disqualification of its directors as directors of a company for up to five years.

Penalties for non-disclosure should also be imposed on franchisees. Franchisors should also have the right (but not obligation) to require potential franchisees to give them pre-contractual disclosure.

> BOX 5.48
>
> Failure by a franchisee to comply with a franchisor's request for disclosure by the franchisee will result in the franchisor having the right to terminate the franchise agreement within 12 months of the failure coming to the franchisor's attention or within two years of the franchisee signing the franchise agreement, whichever is the earlier. The franchisee will also be deprived of any right to claim damages or other remedy unless the franchisor has intentionally and materially either breached the franchise agreement or made wrongful or incomplete disclosure to the franchisee.

3. Prohibition on misleading or deceptive behaviour

It is suggested that in addition to set form pre-contractual disclosure, there 5.39
should also be a pre-contractual duty on the franchisor not to do anything which is misleading and deceptive. However, franchisees and potential franchisees are not consumers and should not be allowed to enjoy any consumer rights vis-à-vis their relationship with franchisors. In Germany the pre-contractual duty to make full disclosure (*culpa in contrahendo*) seeks to ensure that potential franchisees are able to make a decision to enter the franchise based on all relevant facts.[215] In the UK it has been suggested that there is a pre-contractual duty of care owed by the franchisor to the franchisee which means that pre-contractual representations are actionable in tort as well as contract.[216] In Australia there is a similar approach taken under the TPA. A

215 BGB 242. Palandt, BGB, p. [103].

216 *MGB Printing & Design Limited* v. *KallKwik UK Ltd* (QBD) – 31 March 2010 – [2010] EWHC 624 (QB).

pre-contractual duty to disclose similar to that found in the Australian TPA would comprise two parts. Firstly, it would impose an obligation to comply with the pre-contractual disclosure required by the EU Franchise Directive. Secondly, it would prohibit all conduct constituting pre-contractual disclosure that could objectively be considered to be misleading and deceptive. The Directive will need to give details of what amounts to misleading and deceptive behaviour. The term 'misleading' is mentioned in many EU directives and is defined in two.[217] These lead one to understand the term to mean 'anything which contains false information and is therefore untruthful or which in any way (including its presentation), deceives or is likely to deceive a person, even if the information is in part factually correct'. The term 'deceptive' is mentioned but is not defined in a number of Directives.[218] Misleading and deceptive behaviour would include a franchisor's statement (whether made publicly or in private negotiations by the franchisor),[219] which although literally true, misleads or deceives or is likely to mislead or deceive. Even reasonable and honest conduct by a franchisor could be misleading or deceptive conduct in certain circumstances.[220] Although a franchisor must be permitted to bargain 'hard',[221] silence by a franchisor may, in all of the circumstances constituted by its acts, omissions and representations, constitute conduct likely to mislead or deceive a franchisee.[222] Representations and opinions by a franchisor, as to future matters, could be misleading unless the franchisor can prove that it had reasonable grounds for making the representation. Such a 'duty to disclose', obliging all

217 Directive 2006/114/EC of the European Parliament and of the Council of 12 December 2006 concerning misleading and comparative advertising states '"misleading advertising" means any advertising which in any way, including its presentation, deceives or is likely to deceive the persons to whom it is addressed or whom it reaches and which, by reason of its deceptive nature, is likely to affect their economic behaviour or which, for those reasons, injures or is likely to injure a competitor'. Directive 2005/29/EC of the European Parliament and of the Council of 11 May 2005 concerning unfair business-to-consumer commercial practices in the internal market and amending Council Directive 84/450/EEC, Directives 97/7/EC, 98/27/EC and 2002/65/EC of the European Parliament and of the Council and Regulation (EC) No 2006/2004 of the European Parliament and of the Council ('Unfair Commercial Practices Directive') states 'a commercial practice shall be regarded as misleading if it contains false information and is therefore untruthful or in any way, including overall presentation, deceives or is likely to deceive the average consumer, even if the information is factually correct, in relation to one or more of the following elements, and in either case causes or is likely to cause him to take a transactional decision that he would not have taken otherwise'.

218 Directive 2006/114/EC of the European Parliament and of the Council of 12 December 2006 concerning misleading and comparative advertising. 2000/520/EC: Commission Decision of 26 July 2000 pursuant to Directive 95/46/EC of the European Parliament and of the Council on the adequacy of the protection provided by the safe harbour privacy principles and related frequently asked questions issued by the US Department of Commerce. 80/271/EEC: Council Decision of 10 December 1979 concerning the conclusion of the Multilateral Agreements resulting from the 1973 to 1979 trade negotiations. Regulation (EC) No 1980/2000 of the European Parliament and of the Council of 17 July 2000 on a revised Community eco-label award scheme.

219 *Bevanere Pty Ltd* v. *Lubidineuse* (1985) 7 FCR 325.

220 *Hornsby Building Information Centre Pty Ltd* v. *Sydney Building Information Centre Ltd* (1978) 140 CLR 216.

221 *Poseidon Ltd* v. *Adelaide Petroleum NL* (1991) 105 ALR 25.

222 *Demagogue Pty Ltd* v. *Ramensky* (1992) 39 FCR 31 and *Fraser* v. *NRMA Holdings Ltd* (1995) 55 FCR 452.

parties to act in an objectively reasonable manner when making the relevant pre-contractual disclosure, would be practical and would work to further ensure that each party receives all the information it needs during the pre-contractual phase to make a decision whether or not to join the franchise/grant a franchise. It would amount to what some commentators call 'good faith purchase'.[223] However, it would preserve the required degree of certainty by falling short of the amorphous duty of a good faith that regulates the ability of the parties to treat with third parties during their negotiations and allows the courts to imply collateral terms as they deem fit. Failure to comply with the pre-contractual disclosure requirements would only amount to misleading and deceptive behaviour if the franchisor would have made a different decision had it been complied with, so following the French and Spanish approach to disclosure of relying upon the need for defective consent rather than a failure to comply with a technical requirement. It is also similar to the English law concept of misrepresentation. Negotiating parties will always have adversarial interests. Each party is interested in making a profit and to get 'the best deal possible'. However, there can be little objection to them having to behave in an objectively reasonable manner when making their pre-contractual disclosures to each other. They would not be under any other pre-contractual duty of good faith that restricts their ability to deal with other parties, as is the case in Germany. Breach of the pre-contractual disclosure requirement would give rise to the remedies detailed above. This will homogenise the pre-contractual disclosure obligations of franchisors in the EU in an appropriate manner delivering a high degree of certainty but avoiding some of the difficulties found under German law. A pre-contractual duty that both focuses upon the disclosure made by the parties and prohibits misleading and deceptive conduct, as articulated above, will serve to maintain market confidence in franchising.

BOX 5.49

Any pre-contractual duty of care or consumer right currently imposed by member state law be disapplied to franchising and replaced with the following provisions in the Franchise Directive:

(1) The proposed parties to a franchise agreement and related documentation must comply with the duty of the pre-contractual disclosure expressly provided for in this Directive. Failure to do so will be deemed to be unconscionable behaviour.
(2) In addition to this all parties must refrain from any misleading or deceptive conduct when making any pre-contractual disclosure. This will include, but

223 Farnsworth, 'Good Faith Performance and Reasonableness under the Uniform Commercial Code', *University of Chicago Law Review*, 1968, Vol. 30, p. 666.

is not limited to, making statements which, although literally true, mislead or deceive or are likely to mislead or deceive.

(3) If the misleading or deceptive behaviour leads to defective consent by the franchisee the courts will be able to make orders preventing such misleading or deceptive behaviour and preventing the franchisor from enjoying the benefits acquired by such behaviour being set aside or varying the franchise agreement or related documents and awarding damages. When considering what remedy to apply the court shall give priority to the best interests of the franchise network as a whole. The parties involved and the regulatory authorities may apply for such remedies.

4. Registration of franchise documentation

5.40 Another way of trying to ensure that potential franchisees have access to relevant information when deciding whether or not to invest in a franchise and enable them to compare what they are being offered with other franchises is to require all franchisors to place key information on a public register. In order for the information to be placed on the register it must be approved by the administrators who administer the register. The idea is that this not only enables potential franchisees to 'comparison shop' but ensures that all franchisors meet certain minimum levels as regards their offerings. It is suggested that such an approach is inappropriate as it is unwieldy and cost-ineffective. The aim of those jurisdictions that require the registration of documentation at a public registry is to ensure that it is reviewed and approved before the franchisor begins offering franchises in that jurisdiction. The general rationale is that 'prevention is better than cure'. The registration authority provides a minimum quality assurance by only registering documents that comply with the law. However this creates substantial challenges for both franchisors and the administrators who run the registry.

BOX 5.50

Registration is not an appropriate way to accentuate the impact of the second commercial imperative on the EU's legal eco-system, and should therefore not be required by the Directive.

In the USA, 15 states[224] require advance registration. Thirteen of these states require that the Disclosure Document and contractual documents be submitted for review and approval before franchises can be offered in those states.[225] The documents have to be modified in slightly different way for each state. This obviously creates a great deal of administrative compliance work for franchisors, and results in not insubstantial costs being incurred. It also results in delay. Franchises cannot lawfully be granted in registration states until the franchisor has complied with the registration requirements. Failure to do so can result in administrative proceedings, public or private civil actions, or even criminal prosecution.[226] Waiting periods of up to 30 days are something imposed in order to give the regulators the opportunity to review the documents filed.[227] The cost and delay is not confined to when the franchise is launched as many states require franchisors to renew a registration or file a report, annually.[228] The consequence of non-compliance can be severe. Officials in some states have the authority, without a prior hearing, to order a halt to franchise sales if there has been a failure to register successfully. Failure to comply with such an order can amount to a criminal offence.[229] In other states, any violation of the registration laws is a criminal offence, regardless of whether there is a stop order in effect.[230] Each state offers exemptions to franchisors but there is no homogeneous approach.[231] The various registration regimes are all implemented by well-financed and heavily resourced state administrative regimes. Registration is a pre-emptive attempt to ensure that franchisors comply with their various legal requirements as regards disclosure and other franchise-specific requirements laid down by the relevant state law. This means that the state administrative

224 These states include California, Hawaii, Illinois, Indiana, Maryland, Michigan, Minnesota, New York, North Dakota, Rhode Island, South Dakota, Texas, Virginia, Washington and Wisconsin. Oregon has specific disclosure requirements but does not require registration. Michigan does not require prior submission and approval of the franchise offering documents.

225 Michigan and Texas do not require this.

226 CCH, *Business Franchise Guide,* p. 641.

227 Ibid.

228 Ibid.

229 Ibid.

230 Ibid.

231 Franchise offerings can be exempt from the registration requirements of state laws based on characteristics of the franchisor, the franchisee or the offering. These exemptions can be conferred by statute, by regulation, or by a state regulator and must be considered in light of a state's registration requirements. One state might declare an offering to be exempt from registration while another simply does not include it within those transactions that must be registered. For example, Illinois excludes from the definition of a franchise a transaction requiring the payment of a fee of less than $500, while Michigan defines the arrangement as a franchise but exempts it from registration. Registration exemptions based on the net worth of the franchisor or the franchisor's holding company are perhaps the most important and exist in nine states (California, Illinois, Indiana, Maryland, New York, North Dakota, Rhode Island, South Dakota and Washington). The experience of the franchisor and the sophistication of the prospective franchisee might also qualify an offering for an exemption.

agencies review the franchisor's application to register the franchise, the proposed disclosure statement, financial statements, the franchise's advertising materials, information about the persons who will engage in the sale of the franchise, the franchise agreement and all other agreements that the franchisee must sign to acquire the franchise. The purpose of the state review of the application is to determine whether the franchisor has complied with all legal requirements; whether all documents contain all of the required information in an understandable form; whether advertising materials contain any prohibited claims or representations; whether the franchise is fraudulent, deceptive, unfair or inequitable and whether the franchisor has sufficient financial resources to fulfil its obligations. The most common problems encountered by the registration authorities are incomplete financial statements, deficient disclosure documents, inconsistent advertisements, illegal activities, outdated information in disclosure, other State-specific issues and flaws in the financial assurance documentation, revenue disclosure, rebate/supplier payments, expense estimates, and assistance with the advertising fund, site selection and training. Most of the agencies also have the power to suspend or revoke any registration. Australia does not have a registration system, but there is some support for such a system by those who believe that if a franchisee enters into a franchise agreement due to misleading material, 'the only recourse it has is to law and, by the time a franchisee is in a position where it needs recourse to law, it usually has no money [to fund a legal action]'.[232] The Franchise Council of Australia recently recommended that the ACCC be empowered to administer a mandatory franchisor registration system requiring annual filing of the most current disclosure material and other prescribed information.[233] However, the Government declined to follow their suggestion on the grounds of cost and practicality. This underscores the problems inherent in any attempt to establish a registration system for franchising, namely the compliance burden placed on franchisors (which would be significant); the difficulties the authorities would have in ensuring the quality or substance of the documents lodged; the potential liability of the authorities if they were seen to endorse and provide credibility to registered franchisors and lodged disclosure documents; and the fact that it would increase the regulatory burden on business. The only mandatory registration regime in the EU is found in Spain.[234] Once an agreement is executed, the

232 The Hon. D.P. Beddall, President of the Franchisee Association of Australia, speaking to the Economic and Finance Committee of the Parliament of South Australia – Hansard Report, 2 April 2008.

233 Submission of the Franchise Council of Australia dated 15 August 2006, Part E8–11.

234 (Royal Decree 2485/1998 Articles 5 to 10). Franchisors must register with the Autonomous Government in the territory where they are headquartered. Franchisors intending to do business in more than one Autonomous Region must be included in the Federal Register under the Directorate General for Domestic Trade of the Ministry of Economy and Finance (Royal Decree 2485/1998 Article 5). The Federal Register includes franchisors registered by the Autonomous Governments (Royal Decree 2485/1998 Article 6). Applications for inclusion in the Federal Register must be made by the Autonomous Governments where the franchisor is

franchisor must register it.[235] However, it has not been successful, despite recent attempts to re-invigorate it.[236] The new law introduces the concept of an 'Established Franchisor'.[237] This is an attempt to distinguish between established franchisors with a track record of demonstrable success and newcomers. Franchisors who have a minimum of four establishments, two of which must be exploited directly by the franchisor, and who have been operating the franchise network for a period of at least two years qualify for the status of 'Established Franchisor'. Failure to comply with the registration obligation can result in the imposition of a fine of between 3000 up to 15 000 Euros subject to a maximum amount not exceeding the total invoicing of the franchisor. The history of the registration of franchise agreements in the EU has not been distinguished by notable success. In Spain franchisors are required to register the franchise agreement and certain relevant information with the relevant authorities[238] and file an annual update.[239] Failure to comply can result in the imposition of a fine. The purpose is to help maintain a certain level of quality amongst franchisors. This has not been achieved. The registration of franchise agreements in Spain

---

headquartered. In Lithuania there is an obligation to register, but it can be contracted out of the franchise agreement, must be in writing, and must be registered in the Register of Legal Entities of the Republic of Lithuania to be enforceable against third parties (Lithuanian Civil Code Article 6.767(1)). If the franchisor is not Lithuanian, the franchise agreement must be registered by the franchisee. This obligation could in theory be contracted out of by the parties, but it would render the agreement legally unenforceable. The practical impact of this is that the franchise agreement must always be registered. The information required to obtain registration with the Franchisor's Registry includes (Echarri, A., 2006, 'New Regulations on the Spanish Franchisor's Registry', *International Journal of Franchising Law*, Volume 4, Issue 3, p. 3: the franchisor's details such as company name, registered office, details of registration with the Spanish Commercial Registry, taxpayer or business identification number; details of the intellectual property rights included in the franchise and a certificate verifying ownership; a description of the franchised business, including the number of franchises in the network and the number of units, indicating whether they are directly operated by the franchisor or franchised, the time period for which the franchisor has been in the franchising business and the name of the franchisees which have left the franchise network within the last two years; if the franchisor is a master franchisee, the name, registered address, legal status, and duration of an agreement for franchisees that have the power to grant subfranchises as well as the master franchise agreement itself (Royal Decree 2485/1998 Article 7). In the event that the franchisor is registered through a representative, proof of its authority must be supplied. Foreign franchisors must submit the original and translated copies of the relevant documents (Royal Decree 419/2006 Article 7(1)(f)). In addition, there are some details which can voluntarily be filed with the Registry for information purposes only, such as (Royal Decree 419/2006 Article 11), a quality standards certificate evidencing compliance with quality standards; adherence to an alternative dispute resolution system; adherence to any franchising codes of conduct; adherence to consumer arbitration systems or other ADR procedure in regard to consumer complaints; other information of general interest.

235 Royal Decree 2485/1998.

236 The first eight years of the Spanish law were confused, with the authorities and franchisors alike being uncertain as to where the documents should be registered. As a result, there was a very low level of compliance with, and no enforcement of, the law. To try and remedy this, Royal Decree No 419/2006 was enacted on 27 April 2006. It has not changed the registration system as such but seeks to improve it. The new law obliges registered franchisors to file a report at the beginning of each calendar year even if the data registered remain unchanged (the new sections 3 and 4 of Article 8).

237 Article 12.

238 Article 62(2) of Act 7/1996.

239 Royal Decree No 419/2006 (new sections 3 and 4 of Article 8).

has not been a success. There appears to be no qualitative or other analysis of the documentation and it has become nothing more than a 'tick the box' administrative task. Registration has become the hallmark of respectability, but without any qualitative consideration of the documentation registered, this has obvious and dangerous implications. The introduction of the concept of an 'Established Franchisor'[240] is a weak attempt to try to remedy this fault by distinguishing between newly established franchisors and those with a track record (regardless of how good that record is). So far it shows little sign of making any impact. One therefore concludes that a registration requirement places a substantial administrative burden (and possibly a substantial cost) on the regulator. It imposes an equally great administrative burden on the franchisor, which has to constantly update the registration to keep it current and so avoid being penalised. This burden would be increased further by the large number of languages used in the EU. Any registry would have to be on a member state basis due to the linguistic differences between member states. It would create financial and technical barriers to the establishment of a true single market within the EU. The cost effectiveness of a registration system is an issue that cannot be ignored. To set up the necessary regulatory framework, train the regulators, keep them updated on all relevant changes, and expect them to regularly audit the registered documents is a substantial and expensive undertaking. Given the size and scale of franchising in the EU, it seems to be an unwieldy and disproportionate response to the issues involved. The contrast between the Californian registration requirements and Spain's feeble attempt at it could not be greater. Neither could the budget of the two systems. The Californian registration system serves to show that a registration law requires the creation of a substantial administrative infrastructure which in turn demands a substantial financial investment. It proved to be impossible to obtain any estimate of the Spanish budget for its registration system other than 'probably not a great deal'.[241] In California the registration of franchising is dealt with by the Department of Corporations, which publishes its annual expenditure. In 2008–09 the Department's total expenditure was US$40 161 000. This deals with many more areas than just franchising. The cost directly attributable to franchising alone in 2008–09 was US$1 456 000.[242] However, this excludes all of the indirect costs involved, such as accommodation, infrastructure, technology support and so on. The Department estimates that it processes up to 600 franchise registrations and renewals each year. There is a charge of US$675 for an application for registration and US$450 for a renewal. If there were 600 applications for registration in one year that would

240 Ibid. (New Article 12).

241 Joana Banda, Jimenez de Parga law offices, Barcelona: 'Franchising in Spain' at EfN Annual Convention 2006.

242 Interview with Tim Lebas, Corporation Deputy Commissioner in charge of franchise registration, Californian Department of Corporations (telephone interview, March 2009).

amount to US$405 000 in fees for applications. If all of these were renewals it would be US$270 000. The professional costs of compliance with the Californian registration requirement are estimated[243] at around US$1500 for the initial filing and US$400 for renewals. These costs are for a state with a population of approximately 36 500 000,[244] the working language of which is English. The EU has a population of approximately 500 000 000 and 23 official languages.[245] The likely cost of a pan-EU registration system is therefore substantial and unlikely to be proportionate to any benefit it might provide. At Californian-type rates, the professional legal costs of filing a franchise in 27 EU member states could be around US$40 500 or €28 196 with US$10 800 or €7518 annual renewal fees.[246] The administrative filing cost in 27 EU member states at Californian levels would be US$18 225 or €12 688 with annual renewal costs of US$12 150 or €8459.[247] Such professional and administrative filing costs would be a real barrier to franchising between EU member states. Although appropriately resourced and well-implemented registration may maintain market confidence in franchising, it is unlikely to encourage companies to use franchising as part of their corporate growth strategy as it will inevitably result in increased costs and bureaucracy.

E. ACCENTUATING THE IMPACT OF THE THIRD COMMERCIAL IMPERATIVE – A MANDATORY TAXONOMY

Accentuating the impact of the need for adequate protection on the EU's legal eco-systems is most effectively achieved by imposing mandatory terms upon the franchise agreement and a prohibition of unconscionable behaviour. The risks that both the franchisor and franchisee are exposed to are detailed in Chapter 2 above. Franchise agreements seek to address these risks but the sample examined above suggests that they do not always deliver sufficient protection. The EU's legal eco-systems need to compensate for this failure. In doing so they need to balance the risks that both parties face with the general principle that both parties are independent and are responsible for their own decisions. Franchisees cannot abdicate their responsibility for their own decisions. A franchise is not a guarantee of success. Good regulation provides adequate not total protection. It is suggested that in order to achieve an 5.41

243 An estimate supplied by leading franchise lawyer, Ken Costello, partner in the LA office at the Bryan Cave law firm.

244 US Census Bureau 2007 estimate blocks http://quickfacts.census.gov/qfd/states/06000.html.

245 http://ec.europa.eu/education/languages/languages-of-europe/index_en.html.

246 At 6 January 2010 exchange rate.

247 At 6 January 2010 exchange rate.

appropriate balance in the franchisor/franchisee relationship it is necessary to re-engineer the EU's legal eco-systems so that the regulatory environment ensures that all franchise agreements contain certain minimum terms which re-enforce the economic drivers that encourage both franchisors and franchisees to become involved in franchising and reduce the inherent consequential risks to both parties to an appropriate level. As evidenced by the sample franchise agreements, a fairly standard architecture has evolved for franchise agreements. They define the rights granted, the term and renewal, the obligations of the parties, confidentiality, non-compete clauses, impose targets, regulate termination, stipulate the ownership of goodwill and set out the franchisee's right to sell its business. However, this architecture fails to fully re-enforce the economic drivers that encourage franchisees to become involved in franchising. It also fails to reduce the inherent consequential risks to which the franchisees are exposed. The legal eco-systems of EU member states do not improve matters. They create a regulatory environment for franchise agreements which reduces their ability to re-enforce the economic drivers which encourage franchisors to become involved in franchising and fails to reduce the inherent consequential risks to which franchisors are exposed. It is therefore suggested that franchise agreements should incorporate mandatory clauses that impose certain obligations upon franchisors and franchisees and grant them certain rights so that the franchisor/franchisee relationship is one which will continue to attract franchisors and franchisees and reduce the consequential inherent risks to an appropriate level. However, that alone will not be sufficient. The franchisor/franchisee relationship is a dynamic one. It changes over time, which means that the contractual terms of the relationship may become dated, irrelevant or even oppressive. A more flexible tool which takes account of the changing nature of the franchise relationship is also needed to ensure that the re-engineering of the legal eco-system is successful. A prohibition of unconscionable behaviour is therefore proposed.

1. The US experience

5.42 At federal level in the USA there are no franchise-specific relationship laws. Twenty states – plus the District of Columbia, Puerto Rico and the Virgin Islands – have enacted laws of general application that govern franchise relationships and terminations. They aim to prevent franchisees being abused by franchisors by preventing discrimination, franchisor competition, market encroachment and dilution, or change of competitive circumstances. They also regulate terminations, cancellations and non-renewals. Some relationship/termination laws also govern alterations in franchise relationships. For example, in Indiana,[248] it is unlawful for a franchise agreement to provide for or allow substantial modification of the franchise agreement by the franchisor without written consent of the franchisee. Many relationship/termination laws require franchisors to be 'fair', 'just', and act with 'good cause', or in 'good faith' when terminating a franchise or not renewing. However, despite vigorous lobbying by franchisees and their advisors there is no regulation of the ongoing franchise relationship at a federal level.[249] Although the FTC Staff Report[250] concluded that

> there is little doubt that some franchisees are dissatisfied with their franchise purchase,[251]

it felt unable to identify how much that dissatisfaction was due to the franchisor and how much was due to 'other factors, such as downturns in the economy or shifting consumer preferences'.

It therefore concluded that 'substantive franchise rulemaking is unwarranted'.[252]

248 Section 1 of the Indiana Deceptive Franchise Practices Law.

249 US franchisees and their advisers commenting on the proposed changes for the FTC Rule suggested that 'the greatest problem in franchising today' is 'post-sale abusive franchise relationships'. They urged that the Rule be amended so as to 'prohibit post-contract covenants not to compete (e.g. Brown, ANPR 4, at 3; AFA, APNR 62, at 3; Slimak, ANPR 130; Leap, ANPR at 1–2; Vidulich, ANPR, 22 Aug 97 Tr, at 21), encroachment of franchisees' market territory (Brown, ANPR 4, at 2; Donafin, ANPR 14; AFA, ANPR 62, at 1; Buckley, ANPR 97; Zarco & Pardo, ANPR 134, at 2), and restrictions on the sources of products or services (e.g. Brown, ANPR 4, at 2; Weaver, ANPR 17; Colenda, ANPR 71; Haines, ANPR 100, at 3; Chiodo, ANPR, 21 Nov 97 TR, at 293–4), among other practices' (The FTC Staff Report III A, p. 7). They also recommended that the Commission prohibit the inclusion into franchise agreements of mandatory arbitration, jurisdiction and choice of law provisions that either impede a franchisee from bringing suit or favour the franchisor (the FTC Staff Report III A, p. 7) Brown, ANPR 4, at 3; Bell, ANPR 30; D. Iuliano, ANPR 56; AFA, ANPR 62, at 3; Johnson ANPR 67.

250 The FTC Staff Report III A, p. 7.

251 Ibid., p. 8.

252 The FTC Staff Report A III, p. 10. This position is supported by a staff review of post-sale franchise relationship issues, as reflected in the Commission's complaint database – the Consumer Information System ('CIS'). During the period 1993 through June 1999, franchisees raised post-sale relationship issues involving 110 companies. The FTC Staff Report concludes that this means that about 95% of the approximately 2500 franchise systems operating in North America at that time did not generate even a single relationship complaint to the Commission. Moreover, the vast majority of companies that were the subject of a complaint generated only one complaint, see Bond's *Franchise Guide* (11th edn. 1998) at 9, 25 (estimating there are 2500 American and Canadian franchisors). Currently, Bond's maintains a database of 2500 North American franchisors, and its *Franchise Guide* (13th edn. 2001) provides information on approximately 2150 of those systems, that in its view, are actively engaged in franchising.

2. The Australian experience

5.43 The Australian approach to regulating the ongoing relationship contrasts to that found in the USA and relies more upon prohibition of unconscionable behaviour and misleading and deceptive conduct. The Australian common law duty of good faith is apparently in a state of some confusion with different states taking different views. There is doubt as to whether a duty of good faith is a broad duty implied into all commercial contracts as held by the *Burger King* v. *Hungry Jack* decision in the New South Wales Court of Appeal,[253] or is implied only where the facts and circumstances of a particular case warrant it, so supporting contractual certainty, as held in *Esso Australia Resources Pty* v. *Southern Pacific Petroleum NL* in the Victorian Supreme Court.[254] In contrast to the common law position however there is absolute clarity under the ACL Section 22 (formerly TPA section 51AC), which prohibits unconscionable conduct and ACL section 18 (formerly TPA section 52) which prohibits misleading and deceptive conduct. Section 22 of the ACL prevents a range of abusive conduct including charging excessive prices for goods supplied to franchisees; secret rebates and commissions from suppliers; encroachment on the franchisee's geographical trading area and failing to provide adequate service and support to franchisees.[255] Unconscionability of conduct has to be judged by reference to seven factors[256,257] which include the relative bargaining position of the parties, the reasonableness of the conditions protecting the franchisors, the franchisee's ability to understand the documents, undue influence, alternative suppliers, discrimination and the amount of negotiation that took place. The most instructive case concerning unconscionable behaviour under Section 22 of the ACL is *ACCC* v. *Simply No Knead*.[258] In this case the company had a number of franchisees to which it supplied training and

253 (2001) NSWCA 187.

254 [2005] VSCA 228. This case rejects the concept of a blanket duty of good faith in favour of contractual certainty. However, the relevance of the common law duty of good faith, no matter how confused it is, has been reinforced by the government's current proposals to insert a new provision in the Franchise Code stating that nothing in the Code limits any common law requirements of good faith in relation to the franchise agreement. Additional Information on Franchising Code and Unconscionable Conduct Reforms, November 2009 at http://minister.innovation.gov.au/Emerson/Documents/Additional%information%20%on%20Franchising %20Code%20%and%20Unconscionable%20Conduct%20Reforms.pdf.

255 Giles, Redfern & Terry, *Franchising Law and Practice*, Lexis Nexis, para 11.0200. Others include fraud and misrepresentation in inducing the contract; unjust terms in the contract; bad faith in the operation of the contract; discrimination in terms of trading between company owned outlets and franchised outlets; failure to address lack of viability of franchise outlets; making substantial increases to renewal fees; unwillingness to discuss and negotiate problems using advertising levies for other purposes; intimidation and victimisation of franchisees; and unfair terminations.

256 ACL section 22 (formerly TPA Section 51AC).

257 The provision excludes from its ambit listed public companies and the acquisition of goods and services of no more than Aus $3 million.

258 *ACCC* v. *Simply No Knead (Franchising) Pty Ltd & Cameron Bates* (2000) ATPR 104 FCR 253.

materials for baking bread and related products in the home. Sandberg J found that the franchisor's behaviour had disclosed 'an overwhelming case of unreasonable, unfair, bullying and thuggish behaviour' against five franchisees. The franchisor's conduct included refusing to deliver products to franchisees; refusing to negotiate with franchisees and discuss matters of concern to them; deleting franchisees' telephone numbers from the Telephone Directory Assistance Service without their knowledge or consent; producing and distributing advertising and promotional material for its products in the territories of the franchisees and refusing to provide current disclosure documents in response to written requests. None of the cases so far suggest, as feared by some,[259] that the courts have taken an over-lenient approach to finding unconscionable behaviour based solely upon a disparity of bargaining power in franchising. Reflecting the common law's distrust of a general concept of good faith[260] there were concerns that equitable notions of unconscionability would pose a real threat to the doctrine of freedom of contract[261] and bring uncertainty to commercial transactions by either enabling[262] or even requiring the courts to make value judgments and expand the notion far beyond the equitable notion as set out in section 51AA.[263] However, so far this does not seem to have happened. Section 22 of the ACL (along with section 51AD of the ACL and the Franchising Code of Conduct) amounts to a legislative attempt to re-engineer the regulatory environment for franchising by accentuating the impact of the economic drivers that encourage franchisees to become involved in franchising.[264]

3. Protecting the franchisor's interests

The franchisor's interests are best protected by re-enforcing the economic drivers that attract them to franchising and reducing the inherent consequential risk that they expose themselves to. As detailed in Chapter 3 above franchise agreements generally endeavour to re-enforce these economic drivers and reduce the inherent consequential risk to a reasonable level. However, some of 5.44

---

259 Finlay, A., 1999, 'Unconscionable Conduct and the Business Plaintiff: Has Australia Gone Too Far?', *Anglo American Law Review*, Volume 28, p. 470.

260 Ibid.

261 Baxt, R. and J. Mahemoff, 1998, 'Unconscionable Conduct Under the Trade Practices Act – An Unfair Response by the Government: a Preliminary View', *Australian Business Law Review*, Volume 26, p. 5; Op. cit., Finlay, 1999; Duncan, B. and S. Christensen, 1999, 'Unconscionability in Leasing Transactions', *Australian Business Law Review*, Volume 27, p. 280.

262 Ibid., Duncan and Christensen, 1999; Cornwall, J., 2000, 'Breach of Contract and Misleading Conduct: A Storm in a Teacup?', *Melbourne University Law Review*, Volume 24, p. 10.

263 Op. cit., Finlay, 1999, p. 470; Cecere, C., 2003, 'Australia section 51AC of the Trade Practices Act: Impact on franchising sector', *International Journal of Franchising Law*, Volume 1, 8–24; Op. cit., Baxt, R. and J. Mahemoff, 1998, p. 5.

264 Corones believes it to be an attempt to limit the ability of franchisors to exploit the vulnerability of franchisees. Corones, *Australian Business Law Review*, 2000, Vol. 28, No. 6, pp. 462–9.

the legal eco-systems that comprise the EU's regulatory environment tend to limit the franchise agreements' ability to reduce the risks. Commercial agency law, employment law and consumer law in some member states inhibit the ability of the franchisor to prevent 'free riding' by terminating erstwhile franchisees. The duty of good faith can also reduce the franchisor's ability to prevent free riding and other misdemeanours, not only by limiting its right to terminate the agreement, but also by removing its ability to make decisions at its sole discretion, without regard for the franchisee's interests. This is particularly pronounced in Germany. Unfair contract term laws can also restrict the franchisor's discretion in respect of how it deals with its franchisees. Antitrust law tends to undermine some of the financial drivers by denying the franchisor the right to determine uniform pricing and multichannel strategies. It is suggested that the Franchise Directive should impose mandatory clauses which re-enforce the economic drivers and reduce the inherent consequential risks to franchisors. In other words franchise agreements should become nominate or type agreements in civil jurisdictions. Although German law does not recognise franchise agreements as nominate agreements, it protects the franchisor's rights to receive fees from the franchisee, recognises the franchisee's obligations to purchase tied goods from the franchisor and protects the franchisor's know-how from abuse by the franchisee.[265] These should be included in the Directive, but by themselves are not sufficient to protect the franchisor's interests. Amongst other things, the Directive should afford appropriate protection to the franchisor's brand. In the original Franchise Block Exemption[266] franchisors could not stop franchisees challenging their intellectual property rights, but could terminate any franchisee who did, thereby accommodating the decisions in both *Windsurfing*[267] and *Moosehead*[268] but delivering a good degree of brand

---

265 BGH, WBI 1989, 131.

266 EU Reg 4087/88 Op. Cit., p. 12.

267 Case 193/83 *Windsurfing International* v. *Commission* [1986] ECR 611 [1986] 3 CMLR 489. Windsurfing International Inc. ('Windsurfing') made certain patent and trademark licensing agreements in relation to its windsurfing sailboards. The scope of the patent granted to Windsurfing in Germany was a matter of dispute. The Commission of the European Communities in its Decision of 11 July 1983 found that clauses in certain patent licensing agreements infringed the Treaty of Rome 1957 Art. 85(1) and fined Windsurfing 50 000 ECUs. The licensing agreement contained a no-challenge clause with regard to the licensor's trade marks and patents (preventing licensees from challenging their validity) which the Commission held to be contrary to Art. 85(1) of the Treaty of Rome.

268 Moosehead–Whitbread Commission Decision of 23 March 1990 OJ L100/32. The licensee was required to acknowledge both the licensor's titles to the Moosehead mark and the validity of its trade mark registrations. This was amplified by an undertaking 'to observe all conditions which may be prescribed by the terms of the registration of the trademarks and also not do any act which would, or may, invalidate such registration or title, nor apply to vary or cancel any registration of the trademarks'. The Commission distinguished between no-challenge obligations pertaining to the ownership of the mark, and those relating to the validity of the mark. The former were not contrary to Article 81, on the basis that whether or not the licensor or licensee has the ownership of the trade mark, the use of it by any other party was prevented in any event and competition would thus not be effected. On the other hand, a no-challenge clause relating to the validity of the mark might be contrary to Article 81, because it might contribute to the maintenance of a trade mark that would be an

protection for franchisors. It is suggested that the Directive should go still further and take a more hands on approach to this serious issue by forbidding franchisees from challenging the validity and ownership of the franchisor's brand.

BOX 5.51

The Directive should ensure that regulatory environment takes into account the economic drivers that encourage franchisors to become involved in franchising and the inherent commercial risks they assume. Franchisees must therefore be placed under a general duty of confidentiality as regards the franchisor's trade secrets, including its know-how, providing that they are not placed in the public domain by or with the consent of the franchisor. This means that franchisees must be under an obligation not to act in an unconscionable manner and, in particular, must:

(1) Not in any way challenge the validity or ownership of the franchisor's intellectual property rights and to keep the franchisor's know-how confidential and only use it in operating the franchise;
(2) Fully and faithfully implement the franchisor's system, including but not restricted to undertaking all training required by the franchisor;
(3) Not compete with the franchisor or its franchisees during the term of the franchisee's franchise agreement;
(4) Not compete with the franchisor or its franchisees for a reasonable time within a reasonable geographical area following the termination of the franchisee's franchise agreement;
(5) Allow the franchisor to purchase the franchisee's business on termination for a reasonable valuation, which will include all premises and fixtures used in the business and stock but exclude all goodwill. The franchisor will not however have an obligation to purchase the franchisee's business;
(6) Allow the franchisor to terminate the franchise agreement for breach without having to pay the franchisee any compensation;
(7) Allow the franchisor to sell, transfer or license its business to a third party subject to that third party purchaser agreeing to honour the franchisor's obligations to the franchisee, without recourse against the franchisor in the event that the assignee/transferee/purchaser fails to honour such obligations;
(8) Purchase tied goods and services from the franchisor or its nominated suppliers.

---

unjustified barrier to entry into a given market. However, only where the use of a well-known trade mark would be an important advantage to a company entering or competing in any given market, and the absence of which constituted an important barrier to entry would a clause restricting the possibility of challenging the validity of the mark come within Article 81(1). In Moosehead, the mark was 'comparatively new to the lager market in the Territory' and the Commission on this basis found that there was no infringement of Article 81(1).

A franchisee's failure to respect these rights of the franchisor should give the franchisor the right to terminate the franchise agreement and sue for damages or loss of future profits.

4. Protecting the franchisee's interests

5.45 As identified in Chapter 2, the key economic drivers that attract franchisees to franchising are an increased chance of success due to access to a proven format, a recognised brand, ongoing support, economies of scale and so on. The inherent consequential risks to which they are exposed are misrepresentation, encroachment, poor quality business formats and inadequate support. The Franchise Directive should impose mandatory clauses which re-enforce these economic drivers and reduce the inherent consequential risks. In civil jurisdictions, franchise agreements should be recognised as 'nominate' or 'type' agreements. Although German law does not recognise franchise agreements as 'nominate' or 'type' agreements, it identifies the franchisees' interests as including receiving advice and supervision from the franchisor,[269] the franchisor refraining from interfering in the franchisee's business[270] and not being forced to pay inflated prices for products supplied by the franchisor.[271] It also prohibits what it deems to be inappropriate rights for the franchisor such as the right to determine what its contractual duties are and reducing or enrolling the franchisee's exclusivity as a result of underperformance without a right to remedy and termination on short notice.[272]

BOX 5.52

The Directive should provide that the franchisor should not act in an unconscionable manner and in particular should:

(1) be the owner of, or have the legal rights to use, the network's trade name, trade mark and other distinguishing identification;[273]
(2) provide the franchisee with a reasonable level of initial training and continuing commercial and/or technical training during the entire life of the agreement;[274]

269 Gesler, *Franchiseverträge* 1. Introduction; BAG 30.05.1978, BB 1979, 325.
270 Petsche, Riegler and Theiss, 2004, pp. 3, 4.
271 Giesler, *Franchiseverträge*, Rn 60.
272 BGB 305–310.
273 As provided for by the European Franchise Federation in their Code of Ethics – www.eff-franchise.com.
274 Ibid. – www.eff-franchise.com.

(3) render reasonable ongoing technical and consulting assistance to the franchisee;[275]
(4) refrain from encroachment on the territory of an exclusive franchisee;[276]
(5) allow the franchisee to sell its franchise on to a third party approved by the franchisor as an appropriate franchisee (subject to the franchisor's pre-emptive right of purchase on the same terms);
(6) not supply goods or services to the franchisee at inflated prices or which are unfit for purpose.

For the avoidance of doubt it should be expressly stated that, as regards their relationship with the franchisor, franchisees and potential franchisees are not consumers and are not entitled to enjoy any of the rights afforded to consumers as regards their relationship with the franchisor.

Termination on short notice or without an opportunity to remedy (unless it was a fundamental breach) would be deemed to be unconscionable. This will ensure that the franchisee obtains what it entered into the franchise agreement to gain.

5. The prohibition of unconscionable conduct

By identifying mandatory provisions for a franchise agreement, and so establishing it as a specific 'type agreement' it is possible to re-enforce many of the economic drivers that attract franchisors and franchisees to franchising and reduce many of the inherent consequential risks they both expose themselves to. However, the dynamic and ever-changing nature of the franchisor/franchisee relationship means that these mandatory provisions by themselves will not reduce those risks to an appropriate level. It is suggested that in order to reduce the risks to both franchisor and franchisee to an appropriate level a more dynamic and flexible approach is also needed: one that can deal with the tensile stresses resulting from the franchise relationship's long term and changing nature. However this in itself brings about other challenges. **5.46**

BOX 5.53

The EU Franchise Directive should expressly disapply to franchising any general duty of good faith found in EU member state law and replace it with a specific prohibition of unconscionable conduct by parties to a franchise, breach of which will enable the courts to act in a restrictive and adaptive manner.

275 As per Lithuanian Civil Code Article 6.770(2).
276 As held by the case of *Scheck* v. *Burger King Corp* 756 F Supp. 548 (S.D. Fla. 1991).

> In order to give effect to this, the EU Franchise Directive should provide that all parties to a franchise agreement and related documentation must refrain from exercising their rights and obligations under the agreement, and must not otherwise conduct themselves, in an unconscionable manner during the term of the franchise agreement.

The franchise relationship's ongoing nature differentiates it from 'one-off' transactions such as the sale of goods, which are 'discrete transactions ... of short duration, involving limited personal interactions and with precise party measurements of easily measured objects of exchange'.[277] Franchise relationships are fundamentally different. They are relational and are characterised by

> long duration, personal involvement by the parties and the exchange, at least in party, of things difficult to monetize or otherwise measure.[278]

As a result

> obligations are not frozen in an initial bargain. They evolve over time and circumstances change. The object of contracting is to establish and define a co-operative relationship, not merely to allocate risk.[279]

This means that

> parties are obliged to behave in a way that promotes the relationship, and ... is consistent with the needs and expectations of both parties.[280]

However, franchise agreements do not evolve or change over the years as the franchise system develops. They are static documents fixed for a term of years. They require mutual performance over a number of years and therefore do not always define the parties' full obligations. Because of their longevity and the multilateral nature of franchising they inevitably vest the franchisor with an amount of discretion as to how the rights and obligations of both parties will be performed. How the franchisor exercises its discretion will inevitably impact upon the franchisees' operation of its business.

> In making discretionary decisions, franchisors can extract value from the franchisees in many ways, such as granting additional franchises in close proximity, raising the price of goods sold to franchisees, increasing rent on the franchisees' locations, increasing

277 Op. cit., Gudel 1998, p. 763.
278 Ibid.
279 Op. cit., Leichtling 1994, p. 671.
280 Ibid. Leichtling quoting Parritt at 717.

> inventory and growth requirements, as well as increasing advertising funds. Conflicts invariably arise when the franchisee perceives the franchisor's exercise of discretion to be unfair.[281]

The implied covenant of good faith is

> the doctrinal tool necessary to bring the resolution of franchise contract disputes into line with the realities of the franchise relationship.[282]

It helps to restrain the franchisor from over-stepping the mark. Its flexibility is what enables it to do this. However it is that very flexibility which also creates the uncertainty that can undermine the economic drivers that attract franchisors to franchising. It is the way in which such a flexible approach has manifested itself in a number of jurisdictions, including Germany, France and (to a limited extent) the USA. It has a substantial impact upon the regulation of franchising in Germany and a number of other EU member states. However, few jurisdictions include it in their franchise-specific regulations, it takes a different form in each jurisdiction. In the USA for example, the doctrine of good faith has very limited impact upon franchising at Federal level. The statutory concept only relates to the supply of goods[283] whilst the common law concept, despite once being the centre of great debate in the celebrated case of *Scheck* v. *Burger King Corp*,[284] seems to be of little real relevance nowadays. The Australian government have failed to accept the Australian Franchise Federation's suggestion that a franchise-specific duty of good faith be adopted. Uncertainty, the flip side of its flexibility, presents a real difficulty in franchising. This is succinctly described by the Australian government in its response to the Commonwealth Joint Committee on Corporation and Financial Services 2008 Inquiry into improving franchising conduct.[285] It is considered that[286] as

---

281 Whitner/Brito/Spandorf, paper at ABA Franchising Forum, Oct. 2007.

282 Hadfield, G., 1990, 'Problematic Relations: Franchising and the Law of Incomplete Contracts', *Stanford Law Review*, Volume 42, pp. 927–92.

283 The Uniform Commercial Code concept of good faith applies only to transactions in goods: Article 2 (§2–102).

284 In this case the court ruled that 'lack of franchisee exclusivity did not allow Burger King to open other neighbouring franchises regardless of their effect on the existing franchisee destroying the right of the franchisee to enjoy the fruits of the contract'. 756 F. Supp. 548 (S.D. Fla 1991).

285 Minister for Innovation, Industry, Science and Research, Media Release, 'Government to Strengthen Franchising Code of Conduct and Unconscionable Law' 5 November 2009 at http://minister.innovation.gov.au/Emerson/Pages Governmenttostrengthenfranchisingcodeofconduct.

286 *Finding a Balance: Towards Fair Trading in Australia* (The Fair Trading Report), May 1997. Review of the Disclosure Provisions of the Franchising Code of Conduct – Report for the Hon. Fran Bailey M.P., Minister of Small Businesses and Tourism – October 2006. AFF's Submission dated 15 August 2006 http://minister innovation.gov.au/Emerson/Documents/Additional%information%20%on%20Franchising%20Code%20% and%20Unconscionable%20Conduct%20ReformsPdf.

> the inclusion of a general obligation of good faith in the Franchising Code would increase uncertainty in franchising. Neither franchisors nor franchisees would be certain of the occurrence of a breach: court proceedings would be required to establish whether or not these had been a breach.[287]

The uncertainty arising from a general duty of good faith was felt to have adverse commercial consequences for franchisees.

> Franchisors would seek compensation for the extra risk they faced through larger franchise fees and more onerous terms and conditions in other parts of the agreement. And banks and other financiers would be more reluctant to provide credit to franchisees and franchisors in these more rising commercial circumstances.[288]

It concludes that a general, undefined, good-faith obligation would only make matters worse for franchisors and franchisees alike. This uncertainty is increased still further given the wide range of ways in which member states interpret that duty of good faith. Similar circumstances involving franchising can therefore lead to very different outcomes in different member states. This does not maintain market confidence in cross-border franchising in the EU or encourage its use as a tool to increase inter-state trade. However, as evidenced by the sample agreements considered above, franchise agreements do not impose heavy obligations on the franchisor to support the franchisee and there is no standard of performance specified. Indeed, the ever-changing nature of the franchise relationship and the demands of the market in which the franchise network operates makes it extremely difficult, if not impossible, to stipulate in detail the support that the franchisor must deliver to the franchisee. This enables unethical franchisors to act unconscionably and abuse their contractual rights. The challenge is balancing the flexibility that good faith delivers with the lack of certainty it presents.[289] Adopting a finely tuned, franchise-specific prohibition of unconscionable conduct would help find this balance. If the EU Franchise Directive could prevent unconscionable behaviour in franchising in a more specific manner, it would reduce the uncertainty. An EU-wide, franchise-specific prohibition of unconscionable conduct could reduce uncertainty and help ensure that member state courts take a more uniform approach to contractual interpretation, so reducing barriers to cross-border franchising. However, that will only be achieved if what amounts to unconscionable behaviour in franchising is clearly spelt out in the Directive. Without this guidance the judicial tradition of each member state is likely to lead to different results in similar circumstances. As the German concept of good faith is the

---

287 Ibid.

288 Ibid.

289 Article 7 of Romanian Ordinance 52/1997 as amended by Law No 79/1998.

most developed and influential one in the EU, its three-pronged approach[290] would certainly be a popular way of preventing unconscionable behaviour in some member states[291] as potentially being the least disruptive option. However, it is difficult to see how such a broad and general ability of the courts to impose new obligations upon parties to the franchise agreement and even change the legal relationship as a result of a change in circumstances will do much to limit uncertainty and so maintain market confidence in franchising. Franchisors would have to accept that the courts could effectively rewrite the franchise agreement at will. There would be no guarantee that the risks to the franchisor's business would be properly recognised and respected. There would be a very real probability that the German tendency to view franchisees as consumers would take hold and reduce the franchisee's obligation to be responsible for its own actions. The differing approach of the German and French courts to good faith also suggests that there would be no uniform, EU-wide approach to how good faith would be applied to franchising. That would severely reduce the positive impact of the Franchise Directive on removing artificial borrowing to the use of franchising as a way of increasing trade between member states. A more focused, better defined prohibition of unconscionable conduct is required: one such as that laid out in the Australian Consumer Law 2011.[292]

BOX 5.54

The Directive restricts the parties from unreasonably exercising their rights in a way that would damage market confidence and discourage new entrants of the right calibre whilst recognising and respecting the risks adopted by both the franchisees and the franchisor.

This will help to strike the appropriate balance between flexibility and uncertainty.[293] The amorphous nature of good faith (which is what many believe makes the implied covenant work, allowing it to be applied effectively on a case by case basis)[294] must be tempered by a reasonable degree of certainty. The EU Franchise Directive must balance the flexibility and uncertainty presented by a

290 Collateral, adaptive and restrictive.

291 Austria, Greece and Portugal.

292 It prohibits unconscionable, misleading and deceptive conduct.

293 The so-called restrictive approach.

294 Iglesias, J., 2004, 'Applying the Implied Covenant of Good Faith and Fair Dealing to Franchises', *Houston Law Review*, Volume 40, p. 1423.

franchise-specific prohibition of unconscionable conduct.[295] Rather than refer to good faith, like the CCA and CLA it should prohibit unconscionable conduct. A detailed description of unconscionable conduct is required to reduce any uncertainty. The prohibition of unconscionable behaviour[296] will impact upon unjust contractual terms, bad faith in the operation of the contract, excessive pricing, hidden rebates and commissions, discrimination between franchisees, encroachment and so on. Prohibiting unconscionable conduct offers a way in which the certainty demanded by the commercial imperatives can be balanced with the flexibility that the franchising relationship requires: a way that is based more on the real commercial needs of the relationship rather than the views of individual judges with little or no understanding of the dynamics of the franchise relationship. Franchisees will be able to take advantage of the prohibition of unconscionable conduct regardless of 'whether they be astute or gullible, intelligent or not so intelligent, well-educated or poorly educated franchisees',[297] although franchisees who are 'extraordinarily stupid' or gullible, or whose reactions are 'extreme or fanciful' are unlikely to be used as the standard against which a franchisor's conduct will be judged.[298] By striking the right balance between flexibility and certainty, an obligation that prohibits unconscionable behaviour by either party to a franchise will maintain market confidence in franchising, re-enforce the economic drivers that attract franchisees to franchising and provide adequate protection for franchisors and franchisees without stifling innovation and competition. As evidenced by the Australian *Hungry Jack* case,[299] even the most reputable franchisors can act in unconscionable ways to further their own best interests. If it is to re-enforce the economic drivers that encourage franchisors to become involved in franchising, an EU Franchise Directive should not grant courts the power to modify agreements which are one-sided and favour the franchisor simply because the franchisee is considered the weaker party and the courts take pity upon it. Franchisees are entrepreneurs even though they might not have a great deal of experience. Unconscionability must be the key. The prohibition of unconscionable conduct is what should enable the courts to restrict the parties' ability to

295 Whilst the Australian Competition and Consumer Act 2011 has not replaced the common law doctrine of good faith, it has substantially reduced its role. The common law doctrine of good faith is 'still evolving and … [lacks] a single definition or standard set of behaviours'. (http://ministerinnovation.gov.au/Emerson/Documents/Additional%information%20%on%20Franchising%20Code%20%and%20Unconscionable%20Conduct%20Reforms.pdf.)

296 Australian Consumer Law Section 51AC.

297 *Campomar Sociedad Limitada* v. *Nike International Ltd* [2005] ETMR 1.

298 Ibid. See also *Telstra Corp Ltd* v. *Cable & Wireless Optus Ltd* [2002] FCAFC 296 and *Taco Co of Australia Inc* v. *Taco Bel 1 Pty Ltd* [1982] FCA 136.

299 [1999] NSW SC1029.

exercise their contractual rights. However, although unconscionability is mentioned in a number of EU directives it is not defined in any of them. It is necessary to define it so as to increase certainty.

> BOX 5.55
>
> For conduct to be regarded as unconscionable, serious misconduct or something clearly unfair or unreasonable must be demonstrated. Unconscionable should mean actions showing no regard for conscience or that are irreconcilable with what is right or reasonable.[300]

Examples of unconscionable behaviour should be detailed so as to keep uncertainty to a bare minimum.

> BOX 5.56
>
> A prohibition of unconscionable conduct should require a party 'not to act capriciously'.[301] It should also require it not to act in a way that allows either party to the franchise agreement to obtain an unreasonably material commercial advantage or suffer a material commercial disadvantage that neither party would have contemplated had they been aware of the change in circumstances that lead to the behaviour in question. It should take account of the varying levels of experience of the parties in seeking to deliver an appropriate level of protection.

Having defined 'unconscionable conduct', in order to reduce uncertainty as far as possible, it is then necessary first to outline the grounds upon which unconscionability will be judged and secondly to provide examples of what will amount to unconscionable behaviour.

> BOX 5.57
>
> The grounds on which unconscionability will be judged should be as follows:
>
> (a) The relative strengths of the bargaining positions of the franchisor and the franchisee.
> (b) Whether, as a result of conduct engaged in by the franchisor, the franchisee

300 *ACCC* v. *Simply No Knead (Franchising) Pty Ltd & Cameron Bates* (2000) ATPR n.68, 40,585.
301 Finkelstein, J. (1999) ATPR 41–703 n.61, 43,014.

was required to comply with conditions that were not reasonably necessary for the protection of the legitimate interests of the franchisor.

(c) Whether the franchisee was able to understand any documents relating to the franchise and the supply or possible supply of the goods or services.

(d) Whether any undue influence or pressure was exerted on, or any unfair tactics were used against the franchisee by the franchisor in relation to the franchise or the supply of the goods or services.

(e) The amount for which, and the circumstances under which, the franchisee could have acquired identical or equivalent goods or services from a person other than the franchisor.

(f) The extent of which the franchisor's conduct towards the franchisee is consistent with the franchisor's conduct towards its other franchisees.

(g) The requirements of 'best practice' as detailed in the European Code of Ethics.

(h) The extent to which the franchisor unreasonably failed to disclose to the franchisee:

  (1) any intended conduct of the franchisor that might affect the interests of the franchisee; and

  (2) any risks to the franchisee arising from the franchisor's intended conduct (being risks that the franchisor should have foreseen would not be apparent to the franchisee).

(i) The extent to which the franchisor was willing to negotiate the terms and conditions of the franchise agreement with the franchisee.

(j) The extent to which the franchisor and franchisee act to protect the legitimate interests of other franchisees and the franchise network as a whole.

BOX 5.58

Examples of unconscionable conduct should include, but not be limited to, the following:

(a) unreasonably encroaching upon an exclusive territory;[302]

302 In *Dymocks Holdings Pty Ltd & Ors* v. *Top Ryde Book Sellers Pty Ltd & Ors* (2000) 217 ALR 615; [2000] NSWSC 390; BC200002404 the court passed direct comment on the issue of encroachment. The case related in part to a dispute between a franchisor and some of its franchisees as a result of the franchisor establishing a website for the purpose of selling books directly to consumers. The dispute was essentially contractual, although it does illustrate how much the Internet market can change in a short period. Dymocks were in essence seeking a court ruling to help them unwind a commercial arrangement they had established in good faith and for valid commercial reasons a couple of years earlier. They had set up their Internet site such that it was to be owned and run by the advertising fund and administered by a joint committee of franchisor and franchisee representatives. Less than two years later it became obvious that the site needed funding on a major scale beyond the capacity of the marketing fund. Dymocks successfully obtained the declaration they sought, to the effect that the franchisor was the legal and beneficial owner of the website, the domain name and the content. However the respondents were awarded damages for breach of contract on the basis of the memoranda sent by Dymocks to the franchisees.

(b) failing to provide the franchisee with a reasonably sufficient level of training and support;
(c) unreasonably withholding, delaying or conditioning consent or approval, forcing franchisees to purchase goods or services at what, on a like for like basis and having regard to the obligations of the franchisor and its affiliates and the full financial and other terms of the agreement, amount to an unreasonably excessive price;
(d) unreasonably refusing to discuss matters of dispute with the other party;
(e) unreasonably terminating a franchise over a dispute of an insubstantial amount of money;
(f) using the confidential information of the franchisor in a manner that is against the best interests of the franchisor or the franchise network;
(g) unreasonably competing with the franchisor or other franchisees in the network in a manner not expressly allowed by the franchise agreement, during the term of the franchise agreement and for a reasonable period after its termination or expiry;
(h) making an unreasonable profit on goods or services supplied to franchisees which they cannot or are not permitted to purchase from independent third parties;
(i) terminating a franchise over a dispute of an insubstantial sum of money;
(j) threatening to terminate franchise agreements rather than negotiate and consider important issues;
(k) unreasonably forcing franchisees to buy supplies from the franchisor at a greater cost than they could buy elsewhere;
(l) preventing franchisees and their staff from wearing appropriate uniforms;
(m) refusing to allocate jobs to franchisees in order to force them into accepting settlements in respect of totally unrelated disputes;
(n) penalising, suspending or threatening to penalise or suspend franchisees because they were associating with other franchisees; requiring franchisees to attend seminars unrelated to the core business of the franchise;
(o) unreasonably refusing franchisees access to its records to ensure all payments due to the franchisees by the franchisor had in fact been made;[303]
(p) unreasonably discriminating against individual franchisees.

The risks to both franchisors and franchisees need to be addressed through an objective analysis of what is reasonable bearing in mind the best interests of the franchise network. As appreciated by the Romanian franchise law the best interests of an individual franchisee or the franchisor may be at odds with those of the majority of franchisees involved in the franchise. In such circumstances it should be the interests of the franchise network as a whole that take priority.[304]

---

303 Many of these are listed in the unreported Australian case of *ACCC* v. *Cheap as Chips Franchising Pty Ltd & P Hudousek* – Gadens Lawyers, Franchising Update, September 1999.

304 Article 3 of the Romanian franchise ordinance expressly states that the duty of good faith requires that the agreement reflects the interests of the members of the franchise network. This seems to suggest that any

If the interests of the network as a whole are not adversely affected by the circumstances then an objective analysis of what is reasonable as regards the parties involved in the dispute should be made. This approach will help avoid the difficulties sometimes presented by Article 242 of the German Civil Code. The duty of *Treu und Glauben* can mean that the interests of a single franchisee can take precedent over those of the entire network. A prohibition of unconscionable behaviour during the term of a franchise agreement that gives priority to the interests of the franchise network as a whole over those of an individual franchisee should maintain market confidence.[305] The prohibition on unconscionable conduct does not focus on 'fuzzy' subjective concepts of honesty, loyalty and good morals but rather upon objectively unconscionable conduct which results in an unanticipated and unreasonable gain or loss for one of the parties. The prioritisation of the interests of the whole network over those of an individual will certainly encourage new entrants as it greatly increases the security of the investment made by both the franchisees and the franchisor. The proposed prohibition of unconscionable conduct therefore strikes an appropriate equilibrium between flexibility and certainty. It presents franchisees with an adequate, but not over-burdensome level of protection against franchisors behaving badly towards them by acting inappropriately within the terms of the franchise agreement. Unconscionable conduct will result in the courts being able to make orders to restrict the party acting unconscionably from enjoying its contractual rights or other benefits resulting from that unconscionable conduct, set aside or vary the franchise agreement and other related agreements, to require the unconscionable conduct to cease and to award damages to the party suffering from the effects of the unconscionable conduct. When considering what remedy to apply the court should give priority to the best interests of the franchise network as a whole, before considering what is reasonably appropriate for the parties in dispute. The parties involved and the regulatory authorities may apply for such remedies.

F. CONCLUSION

5.47 Franchising should be defined in accordance with the Marketing Plan approach that originated in the US and is found in various forms in six of the eight EU member states with franchise-specific regulations. It focuses upon independence, economic interest, the brand, the business format, control and ongoing support. It also includes a qualitative threshold to ensure that the advantages of

---

exercise of the duty of good faith would require that it takes into account the interests of all of the franchisees, not merely the one who is in dispute with the franchisor.

305 This was proposed by the failed Belgian Parliamentary bill of 17 March 2004. Doc 51 0924/001.

being a franchise are only available to businesses that have a track record and that start-up franchises are not overwhelmed with regulatory requirements. A franchise that has not operated the business format for at least 12 months or which is operating less than four outlets will not have to comply with the regulation and cannot enjoy the 'Exchange of Benefits'. In order to ensure that the EU regulatory environment is fit for purpose as regards franchising and so enables franchisors and franchisees to access the economic drivers that attract them to franchising whilst reducing the risks involved to a reasonable level, its legal eco-systems must accentuate the influence of three commercial imperatives. These are maintaining market confidence, ensuring pre-contractual hygiene and imposing a mandatory taxonomy of rights and obligations onto the franchisor/franchisee relationship through the franchise agreement. None of the EU's legal eco-systems currently do this. Likewise, neither do either of the proposals to re-engineer the EU's regulatory environment for franchising made by the Amsterdam Team or UNIDROIT. It is proposed that the EU Franchise Directive actively promotes franchising and accentuates the impact of the need to increase market confidence on the EU legal eco-systems. It should do this by enabling franchisors to require pre-contractual disclosure by franchisees, focusing regulation only where it is required (by excluding fractional franchisees, *de minimis* franchisees, sophisticated investors, large investors, large franchisees and insiders) and allowing franchisees to compete on a level playing field with corporate chains. It should establish this partly by allowing franchisors to set the prices of their franchisees and restrict franchisee sales over the internet.[306] These two provisions will accentuate the impact of the need for increased market confidence in franchising on the EU's legal eco-system. It is suggested that in order to help ensure pre-contractual hygiene potential franchisees must be given access to appropriate information and equipped to interpret it in an appropriate manner. This means that potential franchisees must be educated out of the 'psychology of failure' that encourages failed franchisees to blame others for their own failures. They must understand what they are committing themselves to when they buy a franchise and the need to take and follow appropriate expert professional advice. It is proposed that advisors are required to take short, online, franchise education courses if they are to advise potential

306 Failing a wholesale change in the EU's approach to competition law, Finland has found a way forward on this issue that may suggest a viable compromise. The EU authorities may be willing to accept this more readily than a more fundamental reappraisal of their 'per se' approach. The Finnish Competition Authority issued an exemption on price cooperation by businesses while implementing a campaign of offers intended for consumers (Exemption No. 187/67/2003, dated 14.03.2003). This exemption was valid until 28 February 2008. There is currently no intention to issue a new exemption (Petri Rinkinen, 'Franchising Legislation in Finland', www.franchising.fi/ukindex.html). The effect of the exemption is that price campaigns within a chain are made possible as long as the campaign does not take place for a period of more than two months. In addition, the vendor must maintain the right to sell the product or service at an even lower price at any time (Rinkinen, ibid).

franchisees and that potential franchisees investing more than US$20 000 must produce a certificate from their advisers to prove that they have taken such advice. National franchise associations can play an important part in educating potential franchisees about the facts of life of franchising – they have to work hard, follow the format, risk failure and take and follow expert advice from appropriately experienced professionals. Pre-contractual disclosure should be given in a set form 15 working days before execution or payment, covering details of the identity and experience of the franchisor, the franchise network, the terms of the franchise agreement and any earning claims. It should be in plain language and contain an appropriate risk statement. A copy of the franchise agreement in the form in which it is to be executed should accompany the disclosure document. There should also be a five day cooling-off period after execution. Failure to comply with the disclosure requirements should lead to the right for the franchisee and government authorities to terminate or claim damages within 12 months of the franchisee becoming aware of it or 24 months of the date of execution, whichever is the later, if it resulted in defective consent having been given. Electronic disclosure should be permitted. There should be personal liability for any individual responsible for the disclosure document being inaccurate. Those disclosure obligations should apply to foreign franchisors with no presence in the relevant member state who should be under an obligation to disclose relevant information about analogous markets. There should be a regular review of the law every five years. Failure to comply with the disclosure requirements, if it leads to defective consent, should enable both the franchisee and the appropriate regulatory authority to rescind the franchise and related agreements or claim damages. The claim must be made within 12 months of the franchisee becoming aware of the failure or 24 months of it taking place, whichever is the latest. The regulatory authorities should be able to impose penalties including disqualification. Misleading and deceptive behaviour should be prohibited. Such behaviour comprises failing to comply with the pre-contractual disclosure obligations and making any statement which, although literally true, misleads or deceives is or likely to mislead or deceive. It is suggested that registration of documentation on a public register is not appropriate due not only to the practical difficulties it would give rise to in the 27 EU member states, but also due to the cost-effectiveness of it and the low likelihood of it making any tangible contribution to accentuating the impact of the second commercial imperative on the EU's legal eco-systems. In order to re-enforce the economic drivers that attract both franchisors and franchisees to franchising and reduce the inherent consequential risk to an appropriate level it is suggested that franchise agreements have mandatory clauses imposed on them. Franchisees must not challenge the franchisor's intellectual property, nor compete with the franchisor during the term and for a reasonable period thereafter allow the franchisor the right to purchase the franchisee's business on termination. They must implement the business format, allow termination for cause without compensation, allow the franchisor a pre-emptive right of purchase, impose a duty of confidentiality and purchase tied goods and services from the franchisor or its nominated suppliers. In return the franchisor has mandatory obligations. It must be the owner of or have the right to license the intellectual property rights on which the franchise is based, provide a reasonable level of training, refrain from encroachment, allow the franchisee the right to sell its business (subject to the franchisor's pre-emptive right) and not supply goods or services to the franchisee at over-inflated prices or which are unfit for purpose. In order to take account of the franchise agreement's long term and changing nature unconscionable behaviour must be prohibited. Unconscionable conduct is conduct showing no regard for conscience or that is irreconcilable with what is objectively right or reasonable taking into account the best interests of the franchise network before those of individual franchisees and the franchisor. In order to increase certainty details of the grounds upon which unconscionability will be judged and examples of what amounts to unconscionable conduct should be given in the directive. These proposals could be implemented by the EU Commission adopting the Proposed Draft Franchise Directive detailed in Appendix 1.

6

CONCLUSION

A. THE THREE CONCLUSIONS OF THIS BOOK

6.1 Franchising has failed to fulfil its potential in the EU. This is in part due to the regulatory environment. This failure can be remedied by re-engineering the legal eco-systems that comprise the regulatory environment in the EU. This book draws three distinct conclusions. The first conclusion is that although franchising is a specific, distinct and uniform type of commercial activity with a positive influence in the EU which stimulates economic activity by improving distribution, giving business increased access to other activity by offering economic advantages to all those involved and improving distribution and giving businesses increased access to other EU member state markets, it is not fulfilling its potential to contribute to the realisation of the single market. The second conclusion is that the regulatory environment in the EU is, at least in part, responsible for this underachievement of franchising in the single market. The third conclusion is that the regulatory environment in the EU should be re-engineered to enable franchising to better fulfil its potential in the EU.

B. THE FIRST CONCLUSION

6.2 As explained in Chapter 2, business format franchising is the latest incarnation of a long established business structure. Its importance is acknowledged by a wide range of institutions and it has emerged as an important vehicle for entrepreneurship that has appeal to large corporations and small businesses alike. The 9971 or so franchise networks operating in the EU and the 405 000 or so outlets make a substantial contribution to the GDP of a number of member states, with a roughly estimated total turnover of €215 billion (US$300 billion). It has great potential to stimulate economic activity within the EU by improving the distribution of goods and/or services within and between member states. However, it is over-concentrated in a small number of EU member states and a comparison with the size of franchising in the USA and Australia suggests that its potential to contribute to the single market and the growth of trade between member states is far from being fulfilled at present. An estimated 83.5% of its turnover being concentrated in only 25% of the member states. The economic drivers that lead franchisors and franchisees to become involved in franchising and the consequential inherent risk differ. As detailed in Chapter 2, improved access to both appropriately qualified managerial resource and capital (the Agency, Transaction Cost and Resource Scarcity theories) and other economic drivers such as bulk purchasing, economies of scale and enhanced product development explain why businesses use franchising as part of their commercial strategy. A number of economic incentives resulting in an increased chance of success (such as access to a proven format, a nationally recognised brand, ongoing support, economies of scale and so on) supported by various situational, personality and economic correlatives explain the attraction of franchising to franchisees. There are a number of different risks inherent in franchising for franchisors and franchisees. As explained in Chapter 2, franchisors are exposed to risks arising from information asymmetry and moral hazard (such as underpayment, in-term competition, abuse of the franchisor's brand and non-compliance with the business format), whilst franchisees are exposed to the risk of misrepresentation, encroachment, poor quality business formats and inadequate support. Franchising is a symbiotic relationship between two legally independent businesses that is used in a wide range of sectors and on a broad spectrum of scale and value which can be differentiated from commercial agency and distribution. Chapter 2 establishes that the architecture of franchising comprises six basic features: independence of the parties involved, economic interest, a business format, a brand, control of the franchisee by the franchisor and the provision of assistance to the franchisee by the franchisor. It is distinct from agency and distribution, the main difference being the business format and the ongoing support. These features are not impacted by either economic or sectoral contextualisation. The legal architecture is uniform regardless of the legal system in which the franchise operates. Despite the differing nature of the sectors in which franchising is used these differences do not impact upon the architecture of franchising. Likewise although the value of investment required from franchisees inevitably defines the type of franchisee attracted to each franchise system, the resulting differences in economic bargaining power do not change the fundamental architectural features of franchising. This architecture is subjected to tensile stresses as a result of the long term and ever-changing nature of the franchise relationship. In order to withstand these stresses the franchise agreements give the franchisor a degree of flexibility that can result in abuse of the franchisee.

C. THE SECOND CONCLUSION

6.3 It has been established that the regulatory environment in the EU is partly responsible for franchising's underachievement in the single market. It has established that franchising needs to be regulated and that the contractual and regulatory environment in the EU (both self-regulatory and legal) within which franchising operates does not adequately protect and re-enforce the economic drivers that attract franchisors and franchisees to become involved in franchising. Nor does it adequately reduce the consequential inherent risks. In some cases it overprotects the franchisees, so increasing the risks to franchisors and eroding the economic drivers that attract them to franchising in the first place. As detailed in Chapter 3, the contractual environment tends to support and re-enforce the economic drivers that encourage franchisors to become involved in franchising and reduces their consequential risk to a reasonable level. However, it does not always re-enforce the economic drivers that encourage franchisees to become involved in franchising and it fails to reduce the consequential risks for franchisees adequately. Self-regulation of franchising does not work. Although the BFA sees its mandate as seeking 'to deliver self-regulation frameworks and then (delivering) that product to prospective franchisees', it seems to have achieved little. Such intransigence gives little credibility to those advocating self-regulation. If the franchisor's trade body fails to respond to its members' request for a higher level of self-regulation, how can self-regulation be expected to gain the confidence of either the public or the legislature? Historically it has been unwilling to take steps to enforce its code of conduct.[1] These are substantial flaws in the BFA's credentials as an effective self-regulatory body. The inevitable conclusion made in Chapter 3 is that franchising needs to be legally regulated in the EU and that self-regulation lacking transparency, consistency, accountability and proportionality will never be able to provide franchisees, potential franchisees or indeed franchisors with the level of protection that they require.[2] Even the most mature national franchise associations are struggling to make the change from representing the interests of franchisors to representing those of franchising. Even if they successfully make that change, they only account for just over a fifth of franchisors in the EU. Given the international nature of franchising, any self-regulatory system must cover all 27 EU member states, and that is extremely unlikely to happen in a consistent manner given the current state of national franchise associations in the EU. There is a lack of suitably experienced, authoritative, fully representative and sufficiently resourced franchise

---

1 Between 1997 and 2007 the BFA expelled fewer than 5 members.

2 www.berr.gov.uk/whatwedo/bre/index.html, accessed 08.10.2009.

associations. As even the Director General of the BFA admits that self-regulation is 'simply not viable on a pan-EU basis',[3] one is led to conclude that the self-regulatory environment in the EU does not adequately support the economic drivers or reduce the consequential risks inherent in the franchisor/franchisee relationship. Chapter 3 establishes that, despite clear and substantial differences between the civil and common law approaches to drafting commercial contracts, franchise agreements exhibit a uniform architecture which comprises provisions detailing the grant made by the franchisor to the franchisee, the term and renewal, targets, the obligations of both parties, confidentiality, non-competition, transfer, product and services ties, goodwill and termination. There is a contractual asymmetry due to the multi-lateral nature of the franchise relationship (each franchisor having several/many franchisees) and the long term, dynamic and changing nature of the franchisor/franchisee relationship. The contractual environment in the EU supports the economic drivers that encourage franchisors to become involved in franchising. It does not adequately support all of the economic drivers that encourage franchisees to become involved in franchising. It provides for a brand, a format and support but it does not impose a qualitative measure for the format or assistance provided. The contractual environment in the EU reduces the consequential risk inherent for the franchisor to a reasonable level, but it does not do so for the franchisee. The self-regulatory environment does not effectively support or re-enforce the drivers that attract either franchisors or franchisees to franchising. Neither does it reduce the consequential inherent risks for either party. Chapter 3 establishes that the self-regulatory environment in the EU is marked by a complete lack of homogeneity, the lack of a clear or consistent approach to enforcement, a significant conflict of interest between the interests of franchisors and franchising as a whole and an inability to have any influence whatsoever on nearly 80% of franchise chains in the EU, as they are not members of the national franchise associations. The regulatory environment in the EU seeks by way of franchise-specific laws in six member states to reduce the risks to which franchisees are exposed by ensuring that they have sufficient information to allow them to take a view of the adequacy of the business format and the support delivered by the franchisor to its franchisees and the franchisor's historical approach to encroachment. Its success in reducing those risks is dependent on the franchisee carefully considering the information it receives, particularly the feedback from existing franchisees and is compromised by the inevitable fact of life that the franchisor's historical conduct may not be indicative of its future behaviour. The lack of homogeneity of approach between the different EU member states further substantially dilutes its impact on cross-border franchising. The lack of any uniform approach to pre-contractual

3 Brian Smart in an interview with the author on 18 September 2008.

disclosure further weakens the impact of franchise-specific laws. They do not seek to reduce the risks of informational asymmetry and moral risk to which the franchisor is exposed. Some regulatory regimes seek to redress this imbalance by imposing a duty of pre-contractual disclosure on the potential franchisee[4] but that is not part of the EU pre-contractual regulatory environment. Chapter 3 establishes that the economic drivers which attract franchisors into franchising and those that attract franchisees to it are neither supported nor eroded in any particular way by the pre-contractual disclosure franchise-specific regulatory environment in the EU. Non-franchise-specific laws impact upon the pre-contractual regulatory environment in the EU in five distinct ways. They impose a duty not to misrepresent facts, an obligation to disclose relevant information to potential franchisees, an extra contractual obligation to disclose relevant information to potential franchisees, an extra contractual obligation of confidentiality, an obligation to enter into the franchise agreement once negotiations have passed a certain point and a right to withdraw from the contract within a limited time period. Each member state takes a different approach to each of these issues resulting in the lack of any homogeneous approach. This in turn substantially weakens their impact upon cross-border franchising within the EU and creates a technical barrier to franchising between EU member states. The ongoing franchisor/franchisee relationship in the EU is impacted by a regulatory environment that comprises a duty of good faith, anti-trust, unfair competition and consumer law. Chapter 3 establishes that the common law and civil law take a very different approach to the concept of good faith. Whereas the German and French approach is loose and amorphous based upon the Roman law concept of bona fides, the common law takes a far more literal approach to contracts, using a variety of legal tools to ensure fairness in the relationship. However, even with the civil approach to the concept of good faith differences exist between member states. The influence of Article 101 of the TFEU means that all member states take a similar approach to the regulation of vertical restrictions within the franchisor/franchisee relationship whereas Unfair Competition and Confidentiality laws vary substantially on a member state by member state basis. Unfair contract term provisions are harmonised by the Unfair Competition Terms Directive. Thus there is a complete lack of

4 In Vietnam not only does the franchisor have to disclose information to the franchisee, but so does the franchisee to the franchisor. In order to assist a franchisor when deciding to grant commercial rights, Article 9 of the Commercial Law provides that, upon receiving a reasonable request from the franchisor, the franchisee is under an obligation to supply the franchisor with information about itself. The earlier Chinese franchise law (the Measures for the Regulation of Commercial Franchises issued by the Ministry of Commerce of the People's Republic of China, 31 December 2004, Chapter III Article 9) also provided for this but it was dropped (without any explanation) from the most recent Chinese statute.

harmony between the various regimes seeking to regulate the franchise relationship by statute in the EU. Some issues, deemed worthy of specific regulation in certain jurisdictions outside of the EU are not dealt with at all.[5] Franchisors embarking upon a European 'roll out' of their concept must expect to encounter delays and costs that are a direct result of this heterogeneous approach – an artificial barrier to pan-European expansion. The duty of good faith has a significant impact upon the economic drivers that encourage franchisors and franchisees to become involved in franchising and reduces the consequential inherent risk. The lack of homogeneity through the EU greatly dilutes this impact on cross-border franchising. The regulation of vertical restraints has an undermining impact upon the economic drivers that encourage franchisors to become involved in franchising. Chapter 3 establishes that the legal regulatory environment in the EU does not support any of the economic drivers that encourage franchisors to become involved in franchising and does not significantly reduce any of the risks that franchisors are exposed to. However, it over reduces the risks to which franchisees are exposed and over re-enforces the economic drivers that encourage them to become involved in franchising. All member states recognise the right to terminate for breach, although some (e.g. France) are more formulaic in how it has to be exercised than others. However, the duty of good faith in some member states, such as Germany, overprotects franchisees, entitling them to refunds of upfront fees on termination in some circumstances. An inappropriate use of employment law in some member states can also overprotect some franchisees. Likewise the application by analogy of commercial agency law in Germany erodes the economic drivers that attract franchisors to franchising and excessively de-risks

5 The role of third parties in franchising is not regulated by any of the EU member states. However, there are examples of such regulation in other jurisdictions such as Malaysia (Malaysia governs the activities of Franchise Brokers 'doing business as an agent or representative of a franchisor to sell a franchise to any person for a certain consideration but does not include any director, officer or employee of the franchisor or franchisee' (The Franchise Act 1998 Part I Section 4)), Korea (in Korea the law provides for the registration at the Fair Trade Commission of Franchise Consultants (Act on Fairness in Franchise Transactions, Chapter III Article 28) and imposes on them a duty to act 'with dignity' and honesty (Act on Fairness in Franchise Transactions Chapter III Article 30) and they can be struck off for inappropriate behaviour (Act on Fairness in Franchise Transactions Chapter III Article 31)) and Kazakhstan (in Kazakhstan licence brokers (those 'engaged in mediation activities in the course of concluding and performance of the complex business license contract') are expressly acknowledged by the law which states that they 'may act both on their own behalf and at their own risk, and on behalf and at the risk of the licensor, licensee or other subjects of franchising relations in consideration for a license broker's fee which can be payable in the form of a fixed single or periodic payment, fixed payments or otherwise, as provided by the contract' (Law on Complex Business Licence (Franchising) (Law No 330: 24 June 2002) Chapter 3 Article 13)). None of the EU member states stipulate a minimum term for franchise agreements. However, two jurisdictions outside of the EU do. In Malaysia the franchise agreement must be for a minimum period of five years (The Franchise Act 1998, Part III Section 25). In Indonesia, there is a minimum period of five years (The Provisions on and Procedure for the Implementation of Franchised Business Registration (*Decree of the Minister of Industry and Trade No. 259/MPP/Kep/7/1997, dated July 30, 1997*) Chapter II, Article 8) and ten years for master franchise agreements (Cornwallis, *International Journal of Franchising Law*, 2006, Vol. 4, Issue 3, p. 5)).

it for franchisees. Post-termination restrictive covenants are an essential element in reducing the risks inherent in franchising for franchisors, but German law applies commercial agency by analogy to erode this protection. This book therefore achieves its second objective and establishes in Chapter 3 that the regulatory environment in the EU is in part responsible for the underachievement of franchising in the EU.

D. THE THIRD CONCLUSION

6.4 As detailed in Chapter 4 the European Commission is unequivocal in its belief that a regulatory environment comprising harmonised legal eco-systems is necessary to ensure that franchisors and other businesses can operate across borders efficiently. The current heterogeneous regulatory environment creates obstacles that hinder franchisors from taking full advantage of the single market. The same problem confronted commercial agency and was overcome by the adoption of a directive. Empirical research referred to in Chapter 4 supports the case for harmonisation. The catalyst for such harmonisation should be either a directive or a common civil code. It is suggested in Chapter 4 that a directive is more appropriate. This is because the considerable difficulties involved in a common civil code mean that proposals for a non-mandatory common frame of reference have taken over those for a common civil code and the non-binding nature of such a 'tool box' will not achieve the homogenised regulatory environment required. The regulatory environment in the EU should be re-engineered to enable franchising to better fulfil its potential in the EU. This can be achieved as explained in Chapter 5 and is summarised below. The Draft Proposed Franchise Directive in Appendix 1 suggests how the EU Commission could implement these recommendations. It is suggested in Chapter 5 that franchising should be defined in accordance with the Marketing Plan approach and focus upon:

- independence,
- economic interest,
- the brand,
- the business format,
- control, and
- ongoing support.

A franchise that has not operated the business format for at least 12 months or which is operating less than four outlets will not have to comply with the regulation and cannot enjoy the 'Exchange of Benefits'. As discussed in Chapter 5, in order to ensure that the EU regulatory environment is fit for purpose as regards franchising and so enables franchisors and franchisees to access the economic drivers that attract them to franchising whilst reducing the risks involved to a reasonable level, its legal eco-systems must accentuate the influence of three Commercial Imperatives. These are

- maintaining market confidence,
- ensuring pre-contractual hygiene, and
- imposing mandatory terms onto the franchisor/franchisee relationship through the franchise agreement.

As discussed in Chapter 5, it is proposed that the EU Franchise Directive actively promotes franchising and accentuates the impact of the need to increase market confidence on the EU legal eco-systems by

- enabling franchisors to require pre-contractual disclosure by franchisees,
- focusing regulation only where it is required (by excluding fractional franchisees, de minimis franchisees, sophisticated investors, large investors, large franchisees and insiders),
- allowing franchisees to compete on a level playing field with corporate chains.

It should establish this by

- allowing franchisors to set the prices their franchisees may charge, and
- restricting franchisee sales over the internet.

These two provisions will accentuate the impact of the need for increased market confidence in franchising on the EU's legal eco-system.

As discussed in Chapter 5, it is suggested that in order to help ensure pre-contractual hygiene potential franchisees must be given access to appropriate information and equipped to interpret it in an appropriate manner. It is therefore proposed that

- advisors are required to take short on-line franchise education courses if they are to advise potential franchisees;
- potential franchisees investing more than US$20 000 must produce a certificate from their advisors to prove that they have taken such advice;
- national franchise associations play an important part in educating potential franchisees that they have to
  - work hard,
  - follow the format,
  - risk failure, and

- o take and follow expert advice from appropriately experienced professionals.

Pre-contractual disclosure should

- be given in a set form 15 working days before execution or payment
- cover details of the identity and experience of the franchisor, the franchise network, the terms of the franchise agreement and any earning claims
- be in plain language
- contain an appropriate risk statement
- be accompanied by a copy of the franchise agreement in the form in which it is to be executed
- include a five day cooling-off period after execution
- if not complied with, lead to the right for the franchisee and government authorities to terminate or claim damages within 12 months of the franchisee becoming aware of the non-compliance or 24 months of the date of execution, whichever is the later, if it resulted in defective consent having been given
- enable the appropriate regulatory authority to rescind the franchise and related agreements or claim damages
- allow the regulatory authorities to impose penalties including disqualification
- be allowed electronically
- give rise to personal liability for any individual responsible for the disclosure document being inaccurate
- apply to foreign franchisors with no presence in the relevant member state who should be under an obligation to disclose relevant information about analogous markets.

There should be a regular review of the disclosure law every five years. Misleading and deceptive behaviour (failing to comply with the pre-contractual disclosure obligations and making any statement which although literally true, misleads or deceives or is likely to mislead or deceive) should be prohibited. As detailed in Chapter 5, registration of documentation on a public register is not appropriate due not only to the practical difficulties it would give rise to in the 27 EU member states, but also due to the cost-effectiveness of it and lack of impact. In order to reinforce the economic drivers that attract both franchisors and franchisees to franchising and reduce the inherent consequential risk to an appropriate level it is suggested that franchise agreements have mandatory clauses imposed on them. As detailed in Chapter 5, franchisees must

- not challenge the franchisor's intellectual property,
- implement the business format,

- not compete with the franchisor during the term and for a reasonable period thereafter,
- allow the franchisor the right to purchase the franchisee's business on termination,
- allow termination for cause without compensation,
- allow the franchisor a pre-emptive right of purchase,
- impose a duty of confidentiality, and
- purchase tied goods and services from the franchisor or its nominated suppliers.

The franchisor must

- be the owner of or have the right to license the intellectual property rights on which the franchise is based,
- provide a reasonable level of training,
- refrain from encroachment,
- allow the franchisee the right to sell its business (subject to the franchisor's pre-emptive right), and
- not supply goods or services to the franchisee at overinflated prices or which are unfit for purpose.

In order to take account of the franchise agreement's long term and changing nature unconscionable behaviour must be prohibited. This book therefore achieves its third objective and suggests how the regulatory environment in the EU can be re-engineered to enable franchising to better fulfil its potential in the EU. It does this by proposing to re-engineer the regulatory environment so that it imposes a harmonised approach across the EU which accentuates the impact of the three Commercial Imperatives. The proposed draft Franchise Directive, detailed in Appendix 1, offers a way in which the EU Commission can implement this.

E. CONCLUSION

In conclusion, this book concludes that franchising has failed to fulfil its **6.5** potential in the EU and that this is in part due to the regulatory environment. It recommends seismic changes in the EU's regulatory environment to remedy this failure. This creative destruction of key parts of those parts of the legal eco-systems that impact upon franchising results in a vigorous re-engineering of the regulatory environment in the EU. This re-engineering involves accentuating the impact of three Commercial Imperatives: market confidence, pre-contractual hygiene and a mandatory taxonomy of rights and obligations. This book is focused on the EU, but its recommendations as to how franchising should be regulated may be equally applicable to other jurisdictions and so help their legislatures and judiciaries to enable franchising to fulfil its full potential in their economies.

> 'A perfection of means and a confusion of aims, seems to be our main problem'
>
> *Albert Einstein, 1879–1955*

APPENDIX 1

PROPOSED DRAFT FRANCHISE DIRECTIVE

Council Directive

The Council of the European Communities

Having regard to the Treaty on the Functioning of the European Union.

Whereas, the approximation of the laws of the member states impacting upon franchising is necessary because the existing divergence may distort competition and affect the movement of goods and services within the common market and regulate franchising differently on each member state.

Whereas, business format franchising is a specific, distinct and uniform type of Commercial activity with significant beneficial economic impact in the EU. It stimulates economic authority by offering economic advantages to all those involved, improving distribution and growing business increased access to other member states. However, compared to its scale in other markets business format franchising is not realising its full potential in the single market and there is a disproportionate concentration of it in the larger national economies in the EU.

Whereas, there is a lack of homogeneity between the laws of member states as regards how they regulate business format franchising and these differences create a barrier to business format franchising between member states. Existing member state laws that regulate business format franchising fail to reduce the inherent risks to which those involved in business format franchising are exposed to an appropriate level. These laws also fail to re-enforce the economic drivers that encourage both corporations and individuals to become involved in business format franchising as a way of carrying on business between member states.

Whereas, the harmonisation of member state laws that regulate business format franchising will encourage the use of business format franchising as a way of doing business between member states and remove barriers to it.

Whereas, harmonised laws regulating business format franchising should promote market confidence in it, ensure pre-contractual hygiene during the franchise sale process and impose mandatory rights and obligations on both franchisors and franchisees.

The Commission has adopted this Directive:

Article 1

This Directive applies only to Business Format Franchising

A Business Format Franchise exists where:

1.1 (a) one party (the 'Franchisor') who owns or has the right to license other parties to operate a business format offering, supplying or distributing goods or services or both
(b) grants another party (a 'Franchisee')
(c) the right to carry on a business using that business format under a system or in accordance with a marketing plan substantially determined, controlled and/or suggested by the Franchisor or one of its associates or otherwise assisted by the Franchisor or one of its associates (a 'Shared Marketing Plan').
(d) The operation of the business is substantially or materially associated with a brand owned, used or licensed by the Franchisor or an associate of the Franchisor.
(e) The Franchisee pays monies to the Franchisor or its affiliate, by way of, for example only:
(i) an initial capital investment and/or
(ii) a payment for goods or services and/or
(iii) an ongoing or periodic fee of any discharge from and/or
(iv) a training fee and/or
(v) repayment for a lien made by the Franchisor.
(f) A business using the business format has been operated by the Franchisor or its affiliate for a period of 12 months.

1.2 For the avoidance of doubt, a franchise does not include motor vehicle dealerships, employee/employer relationship, agencies, landlord and tenants and co-operatives.

1.3 An affiliate is an entity in which the Franchisor has a controlling interest.

Article 2

2.1 Franchisors have the right, but not the obligation, to require that (at least 10 working days before entering into any agreement which obliges or potentially obliges a Franchisor to grant a potential franchisee a franchise) the potential franchisee provides the franchisor with the following information about the franchisee and its spouse/partner, if any, or if it is a limited liability company, its shareholders and officers:

(1) Full name and address including e-mail address and telephone number.
(2) Details of education and employment.
(3) Details of business experience including directorships and any direct or indirect shareholdings in privately held companies.
(4) Personal bankruptcy history.
(5) Details of the insolvency of any company in which he/she was a director or shareholder.
(6) Details of family situation including details of any divorce, child maintenance and other such court orders and arrangements, a signed statement from the prospective franchisee's spouse/partner that they fully support the prospective franchisee's application.
(7) Personal medical history and that of their spouse/partner and children.
(8) Criminal record and that of their spouse/partner.
(9) Details of any judgment against it.
(10) Copy of driving licence and passport.
(11) Banker's reference.
(12) Details of personal assets and those of spouse/partner including details of status of current home and any charges on those assets.

2.2 The consequences of a potential franchisee failing to supply all such information to any franchisor that has requested it, is to give the franchisor the right to terminate the franchise agreement on the basis of defective consent within twelve (12) months of the failure coming to the franchisor's attention or within two (2) years of the franchisee signing the franchise agreement, whichever is the earliest.

2.3 A franchisee that has made any material or substantial wrongful or lack of disclosure will be deprived of any right to claim damages or other remedy from the franchisor unless the franchisor is shown to have intentionally and materially breached the terms of the franchise agreement or intentionally and materially made wrongful or incomplete pre-contractual disclosure to the franchisee.

Article 3

3.1 The franchisor must provide the potential franchisee with a written statement informing him/her that it wishes to exercise its right to require disclosure in plain language. This must be delivered to the potential franchisee at least 14 days prior to the date on which the potential franchisee must make the disclosure.

3.2 The statement must also be accompanied by a form, in plain language and in a Question and Answer format, setting out exactly what information is required in order to comply with the obligation, so that the franchisee need only complete the form.

3.3 Notices of the potential franchisee's pre-contractual disclosure obligations should be in prominent and easily legible form and read as follows:

'THIS IS A VERY IMPORTANT NOTICE.

YOU MUST READ IT CAREFULLY AND DO AS IT SAYS BEFORE YOU ENTER INTO ANY AGREEMENT WITH US.

IT REQUIRES YOU TO GIVE US CERTAIN INFORMATION ABOUT YOU AND YOUR SPOUSE/PARTNER/SHAREHOLDERS/OFFICERS (IF APPLICABLE).

YOU MUST GIVE THIS INFORMATION TO US AT LEAST 14 DAYS BEFORE YOU SIGN ANY AGREEMENT WHICH ENTITLES YOU TO THE FRANCHISE.

YOU CAN GIVE US THIS INFORMATION BY ACCURATELY COMPLETING THE ATTACHED QUESTIONNAIRE. ALTERNATIVELY, IF YOU CHOOSE TO DO SO, YOU CAN GIVE IT IN ANY OTHER WRITTEN FORM.

IF YOU DO NOT GIVE US ALL THIS INFORMATION, OR IF ANY OF THE INFORMATION THAT YOU GIVE US IS FALSE, INCORRECT OR INCOMPLETE, YOU MAY LOSE YOUR RIGHT TO THE FRANCHISE AND SOME OF YOUR OTHER IMPORTANT LEGAL RIGHTS MAY BE SEVERELY RESTRICTED'.

3.4 Failure by a franchisee to comply with a franchisor's request for disclosure by the franchisee will result in the franchisor having the right to terminate the franchise agreement within 12 months of the failure coming to the franchisor's attention or within two years of the franchisee signing the franchise agreement, whichever is the earlier. The franchisee will also be deprived of any right to claim damages or other remedy unless the franchisor has intentionally and materially either breached the franchise agreement or made wrongful or incomplete disclosure to the franchisee.

Article 4

4.1 Franchisors are only required to make pre-contractual disclosure when it is appropriate and not in the case of fractional franchisees, de minimis franchisees, sophisticated franchisees, large investors, large franchisees and insiders.

4.2 A franchisee is a fractional franchisee if (1) the franchisee or its principals have more than two years of experience in the same line of business or is otherwise already familiar with the products and services to be sold through the franchise; and (2) the parties reasonably expect that the franchisee's sales from the new line of business will not exceed 20% of its total sales.

4.3 A franchisee is a de minimis franchisee if it pays €1000 or less for the franchise.

4.4 A franchisee is a sophisticated franchisee if it invests €500 000 or more (excluding funds obtained from the franchisor or its affiliates) in a franchise and has signed an acknowledgement that the sale is exempt from the disclosure requirement because the initial investment is over the threshold.

4.5 A franchisee is a large franchisee if it pays an upfront fee of €5 million or more and has at least 5 years' experience of the type of business being franchised.

4.6 A franchisee is an insider franchisee if a franchisor sells a franchise to one of its current or former (someone who has worked in the franchisor for two years or more) managers or other officers.

Article 5

5.1 It is the franchisor's obligation to ensure that if a franchisee is required to invest a sum greater than €20 000, the franchisee takes legal and financial advice from advisers affiliated to the national franchise associations. This obligation is satisfied by the franchisor being presented with a certificate from the potential franchisee's legal and financial advisors stating that the potential franchisee has taken appropriate advice from them and that they have completed the self study module. Potential franchisees must also certify that they understand that they are taking a substantial risk if they do not follow appropriate advice and accept that they may be responsible for any loss they suffer as a result of not taking such advice.

5.2 Franchisors are obliged to deliver standard form pre-contractual disclosure to potential franchisees 15 working days before execution of any agreement which commits the potential franchisee to take up the franchise or payment of any fees in connection with the franchise sale.

Franchisors must deliver details of the identity and experience of the franchisor, the target market and the franchise network, the terms of the franchise agreement and any earning claims. There must be a five working day cooling-off period. Failure to comply will enable both the franchisee and national regulatory authorities take action against the franchisor.

5.3 Potential franchisees must be informed by the franchisor in the disclosure document that:

5.3.1 Franchisees must work hard and for long hours. This is a clear and obvious factor of success in any business.

5.3.2 The franchisees must follow the franchise system. The whole reason for buying a franchise rather than starting a business from scratch is that the franchisor has, through its own experience, identified how the business should be run.

5.3.3 There is a risk of failure and what this could mean in both financial and personal terms. Failure is inevitably a risk in running one's own business. It is fundamentally different from employment.

5.3.4 It is important to take expert legal and financial advice from acknowledged experts before being legally committed to a franchise. In order to make an informed decision, advice is essential.

5.4 Details of the identity and experience of the franchise and its directors must include the franchisor's litigation history over the previous 36 months and the bankruptcy history of the franchisor and its directors and substantial shareholders (holding over 25% of the issued shares).

5.5 Details of the franchise network must include details of the franchise network in the target market (or, if there are none, an analogous market), including the contact details of existing franchisees and any franchisees that have failed in the previous 12 months.

5.6 A summary of the terms of the franchise agreement must be detailed in the disclosure document. These are:

- the Initial and Ongoing Fees,
- Intellectual Property,
- Franchise Territory,
- Supply of Goods and Services,
- Marketing and other co-operative funds,
- any financing arrangements provided by the franchisor,
- the Franchisor's Obligations,
- the Franchisee's Obligations and Restrictions,
- Related Agreements,
- Renewal,
- Termination,
- Post-termination restrictions,

- Dispute Resolution,
- Earning claims.

5.7 All earning claims made by the franchisor must be accurate, fair and made in good faith.

5.8 On each renewal of a franchise agreement the franchisor and the franchisee must comply with the pre-contractual disclosure obligations as if they did not have an existing franchisor/franchisee relationship.

5.9 Delivery of the disclosure document to the prospective franchisee should be 15 working days before the execution of any agreement which commits the prospective franchisee to take up the franchise or payment of any fees in connection with the franchise sale.

5.10 The disclosure document must be delivered to a prospective franchisee, that is any person (including any agent, representative, or employee) who approaches or is approached by a franchise seller to discuss the possible establishment of a franchise relationship.

5.11 Receipt of the disclosed document can be acknowledged by any affirmative action by the recipient to authenticate his/her identity and confirm receipt. This can include, for example, a handwritten signature, an electronic signature, passwords or a security code.

5.12 The disclosure document should be accompanied by a copy of the franchise agreement in the form in which it is to be executed.

5.13 The Disclosure Document must be updated by the franchisor within 6 months of the end of each financial year.

5.14 The language of the disclosure document should be the plain language(s) of the member state in which the franchisee will be operating its business or, in member states in which there is more than one official language, the official language which the franchisee designates as its preference.

5.15 Plain language is the organisation of information and language usage understandable by a person unfamiliar with the franchise business. It incorporates short sentences; definite, concrete, everyday language; active voice; and tabular presentation of information, where possible. It avoids legal jargon, highly technical business terms, and multiple negatives.

5.16 A Risk Statement which identifies known significant risks that could have a material impact on the franchisee must be placed on the front of the disclosure document. It must read as follows:

> Investing in a franchise can be a risky business. There is no guarantee that your franchise will be a success. You could lose your investment. In order to succeed you will have to work long and hard. It is not a road to instant success and riches. You must think about it carefully before you enter into the franchise agreement. Some of the information you need in order to make an informed decision is contained in this disclosure document. Take your time, read all documents carefully, talk to other franchisees and assess your own financial resources and capabilities to deal with requirements of the franchised business. You should also make your own enquiries, get

independent legal, accounting and business advice, prepare a business plan and projections for profit and cash flow and consider educational course, particularly if you have not operated a business before.

5.17

5.17.1 A franchisor granting a franchise to a party in a member state in which it is not based (the target member state) should disclose details of its franchise in the target member state.

5.17.2 If a franchisor does not have outlets in the target market it should disclose details of its business in another member state.

5.17.3 If the franchisor does not have any outlets in the whole of the EU, it should disclose details of its franchise in the country in which it is based or another country which it can reasonably justify as being appropriate ('the Analogous Market').

Article 6

6.1 Inadequate or inaccurate disclosure by the franchisor will entitle the franchisee who received such disclosure and/or the relevant government agency the right to terminate the resulting franchise agreement *ab initio* or claim damages. This right to terminate or claim damages due to inadequate disclosure must be exercised by the franchisee (or the member state regulatory authority) within 12 months of the franchisee becoming aware of the failure or 24 months of the date of the franchise agreement, whichever is the later. If the agreement continues after this time the franchisee will be deemed to have affirmed the franchise agreement and so lose both its right to terminate the agreement and the right to sue for damages (as does the member state regulatory authority).

6.2 If disclosed information is inaccurate it will be immaterial if the inaccuracy has not led to defective consent being given by the franchisee and that it is a violation for a franchisor to fail to use best endeavours to ensure the accuracy of the disclosed information. Liability for inaccurate disclosure that leads to defective consent attaches not only to the franchisor, but also to any individual working for or with the franchisor who can be shown to have been responsible for the disclosure of the inaccurate information, who knew (or should have known) the legal or commercial significance of those facts, and was in a position to influence the outcome of the matter.

6.3 Member state regulatory authorities have the right to require a franchisor to desist from making wrongful or inadequate disclosure if there is found to be an established pattern of such behaviour. Failure to comply with the prohibition will lead to the imposition of substantial fines on the franchisor and the disqualification of its directors as directors of a company for up to five years.

6.4 During a period of five working days following the day on which the franchise agreement is executed by both parties the franchisee has the right to withdraw by written notice, without penalty and receive a full refund of all monies paid by it to the franchisor.

Article 7

All pre-contractual duties of care and consumer rights applied by member states on franchising be disapplied and replaced with the following provisions:

(1) The proposed parties to a franchise agreement and related documentation must comply with the duty of the pre-contractual disclosure expressly provided for in this Directive. Failure to do so will be deemed to be unconscionable behaviour.

(2) In addition to this all parties must refrain from any misleading or deceptive conduct when making any pre-contractual disclosure. This will include, but is not limited to, making statements which, although literally true misleads or deceives or is likely to mislead or deceive.

(3) If the misleading or deceptive behaviour leads to defective consent by the franchisee the courts have the power to make orders preventing such misleading or deceptive behaviour and preventing the franchisor from enjoying the benefits acquired by such behaviour being set aside or varying the franchise agreement or related documents and awarding damages. When considering what remedy to apply the court shall give consideration to the best interests of the franchise network as a whole and not just the best interests of the franchisee concerned. The parties involved and the regulatory authorities may apply for such remedies.

Article 8

Registration of Franchise Agreements, disclosure documents and related documents should not be required.

Article 9

9.1 Franchisors are allowed to set retail prices for their franchisees and dictate the network's multi-channel sales strategy.

9.2 Franchisors can control the franchisee's use of the internet so that they can add greater value to both the franchisee's business and their own by being proactive in the use of the internet to increase operational efficiencies and communication.

Article 10

10.1 Franchise Agreements must provide that the franchisee is under an obligation not to act in an unconscionable manner and, in particular, must:

(1) Not in any way challenge the validity or ownership of the franchisor's intellectual property rights and to keep the franchisor's know-how confidential and only use it in operating the franchise;
(2) Comply with a general duty of confidentiality as regards the franchisor's trade secrets, including its know-how, providing that they are not placed in the public domain by or with the consent of the franchisor;
(3) Fully and faithfully implement the franchisor's system, including but not restricted to undertaking all training required by the franchisor;
(4) Not compete with the franchisor or its franchisees during the term of the franchisee's franchise agreement;
(5) Not compete with the franchisor or its franchisees for a reasonable time within a reasonable geographical area following the termination of the franchisee's franchise agreement;
(6) Allow the franchisor to purchase the franchisee's business on termination for a reasonable valuation, which will include all premises and fixtures used in the business and stock but exclude all goodwill. The franchisor will not however have an obligation to purchase the franchisee's business;
(7) Allow the franchisor to terminate the franchise agreement for breach without having to pay the franchisee any compensation;
(8) Allow the franchisor to sell, transfer or licence its business to a third party subject to that third party purchaser agreeing to honour the franchisor's obligations to the franchisee, without recourse against the franchisor in the event that the assignee/transferee/purchaser fails to honour such obligations;
(9) Purchase tied goods and services from the franchisor or its nominated suppliers.

A franchisee's failure to respect these rights of the franchisor gives the franchisor the right to terminate the franchise agreement and sue for damages or loss of future profits.

10.2 Failure to comply with the provisions of this Article will render the Franchise Agreement null and void *ab initio*.

Article 11

11.1 Franchise Agreements must provide that the franchisor must not act in an unconscionable manner and in particular must:

(1) be the owner of, or have the legal rights to use, the network's trade name, trade mark and other distinguishing identification;[1]
(2) provide the franchisee with a reasonable level of initial training and continuing commercial and/or technical training during the entire life of the agreement;[2]
(3) render reasonable ongoing technical and consulting assistance to the franchisee;[3]
(4) refrain from encroachment on the territory of an exclusive franchisee;[4]
(5) allow the franchisee to sell its franchise on to a third party approved by the franchisor as an appropriate franchisee (subject to the franchisor's pre-emptive right of purchase on the same terms);
(6) not supply goods or services to the franchisee at inflated prices or which are unfit for purpose.

For the avoidance of doubt as regards its relationship with the franchisor, franchisees and potential franchisees are not consumers and are not entitled to enjoy any of the rights afforded to consumers as regards its relationship with the franchisor.

11.2 The front of each franchise agreement must be endorsed with the following statement:

> 'This franchise will not provide a guaranteed income to you. In entering into this franchise you are accepting the risk that you may lose your investment. If you get into financial trouble whilst operating your franchised business your franchisor has no obligation to rescue you. It is therefore essential that before entering this franchise you take legal and financial advice from professionals with a proven track record of advising prospective franchisees on their intended investment and that you follow their advice. You must also carefully read the disclosure document. It contains important information that you must read before entering into the franchise agreement. Remember, if your franchised business fails depending upon your circumstances you could end up losing your home and becoming bankrupt.'

---

1 As provided for by the European Franchise Federation in their Code of Ethics – www.eff-franchise.com.
2 Ibid. – www.eff-franchise.com.
3 As per Lithuanian Civil Code Article 6.770(2).
4 As held by the case of *Scheck v. Burger King Corp* 756 F Supp. 548 (S.D. Fla. 1991).

11.3 Failure to comply with the provisions of this Article will render the Franchise Agreement null and void *ab initio*.

Article 12

12.1 Any general duty of good faith found in EU member state law is disapplied to franchising and replaced with a specific prohibition of unconscionable conduct by parties to a franchise, breach of which will enable the courts to act in a restrictive and adaptive manner.

12.2 All parties to a franchise agreement and related documentation must therefore refrain from exercising their rights and obligations under the agreement, and must not otherwise conduct themselves, in an unconscionable manner during the term of the franchise agreement.

12.3 To be regarded as unconscionable, serious misconduct or something clearly unfair or unreasonable must be demonstrated. Unconscionable means actions showing no regard for conscience or that are irreconcilable with what is right or reasonable. No party should act capriciously or act in a way that allows either party to the franchise agreement to obtain an unreasonable material commercial advantage or suffer a material commercial disadvantage that neither party would have contemplated had they been aware of the change in circumstances that led to the behaviour in question. This must take account of the varying levels of experience of the parties in seeking to deliver an appropriate level of protection.

12.4 The grounds on which unconscionability will be judged are as follows:

(a) The relative strengths of the bargaining positions of the franchisor and the franchisee.

(b) Whether, as a result of conduct engaged in by the franchisor, the franchisee was required to comply with conditions that were not reasonably necessary for the protection of the legitimate interests of the franchisor.

(c) Whether the franchisee was able to understand any documents relating to the franchise and the supply or possible supply of the goods or services.

(d) Whether any undue influence or pressure was exerted on, or any unfair tactics were used against the franchisee by the franchisor in relation to the franchise or the supply of the goods or services.

(e) The amount for which, and the circumstances under which, the franchisee could have acquired identical or equivalent goods or services from a person other than the franchisor.

(f) The extent of which the franchisor's conduct towards the franchisee is consistent with the franchisor's conduct towards its other franchisees.

(g) The requirements of 'best practice' as detailed in the European Code of Ethics.
(h) The extent to which the franchisor unreasonably failed to disclose to the franchisee:
  (1) any intended conduct of the franchisor that might affect the interests of the franchisee; and
  (2) any risks to the franchisee arising from the franchisor's intended conduct (being risks that the franchisor should have foreseen would not be apparent to the franchisee).
(i) The extent to which the franchisor was willing to negotiate the terms and conditions of the franchise agreement with the franchisee.
(j) The extent to which the franchisor and franchisee act to protect the legitimate interests of other franchisees and the franchise network as a whole.

12.5 Examples of unconscionable conduct include, but are not limited to, the following:

(a) unreasonably encroaching upon an exclusive territory;
(b) failing to provide the franchisee with a reasonably sufficient level of training and support;
(c) unreasonably withholding, delaying or conditioning consent or approval, forcing franchisees to purchase goods or services at what, on a like for like basis and having regard to the obligations of the franchisor and its affiliates and the full financial and other terms of the agreement, amount to an unreasonably excessive price;
(d) unreasonably refusing to discuss matters of dispute with the other party;
(e) unreasonably terminating a franchise over a dispute of an insubstantial amount of money;
(f) using the confidential information of the franchisor in a manner that is against the best interests of the franchisor or the franchise network;
(g) unreasonably competing with the franchisor or other franchisees in the network in a manner not expressly allowed by the franchise agreement, during the term of the franchise agreement and for a reasonable period after its termination or expiry;
(h) making an unreasonable profit on goods or services supplied to franchisees which they cannot or are not permitted to purchase from independent third parties;
(i) threatening to terminate franchise agreements rather than negotiate and consider important issues;

(j) unreasonably forcing franchisees to buy supplies from the franchisor at a greater cost than they could buy elsewhere;
(k) preventing franchisees and their staff from wearing appropriate uniforms;
(l) refusing to allocate jobs to franchisees in order to force them into accepting settlements in respect of totally unrelated disputes;
(m) penalising, suspending or threatening to penalise or suspend franchisees because they were associating with other franchisees; requiring franchisees to attend seminars unrelated to the core business of the franchise;
(n) unreasonably refusing franchisees access to its records to ensure all payments due to the franchisees by the franchisor had in fact been made;
(o) unreasonably discriminating against individual franchisees.

Article 13

Each member state must have a national franchise association which is recognised as a legally acknowledged source of best practice in franchising and membership of it as an indication (but not a guarantee) that a franchisor has met certain minimum criteria as regards best practice. They must educate the public as to the benefits and risks of franchising but not the regulation of franchising. The franchise associations must be not-for-profit organisations and be funded by membership subscriptions and member state subsidies.

Article 14

This EU Directive will be reviewed every five (5) years to ensure that the contents of the Disclosure Document continue to be relevant to the market.

Article 15

Member states shall bring into force, not later than two years from the date of notification of this Directive, the laws, regulations and administrative provisions necessary to comply with this Directive. They shall forthwith inform the Commission thereof.

Article 16

Member states shall communicate to the Commission the texts of the main provisions of national law which they subsequently adopt in the field governed by this Directive.

Article 17

Every five years the Commission shall present a report to the Council on the application of this Directive and, if necessary, shall submit appropriate proposals to it.

Article 18

This Directive is addressed to the member states.

Article 19 [grandfathering clause]

Done at Brussels, [ ] 2013

For the Council

The President

[ ]

APPENDIX 2

ANALYSIS OF FRANCHISE AGREEMENTS

The samples represent both civil and common law, a variety of sectors and a range of investment profiles.

A. Jurisdiction

The agreements are of franchisors doing business in the three largest franchise markets in the EU (the UK, Germany and France) and two other jurisdictions in which franchising is common (the USA and Australia). The sample therefore includes agreements drafted under both civil and common law.

B. Sectors

The sample includes franchises in the retail, service, food and hotel sectors. Some are mobile, some are location based.

C. Investment Scale

The sample includes small-scale 'man in a van' job franchises and large-scale hotel and restaurant franchises. It is generally the start up investment rather than the upfront franchise fee that requires most funding. The higher the start up investment the higher the upfront fees tend to be. The upfront fees and the upfront investment costs vary from country to country depending on a wide range of external variables, such as, for example, the cost of real estate. Therefore the exact level of the upfront franchise fee and start up investment are not exactly the same on a like for like basis. This sample details the type of start up investment required, not the exact figure. It categorises them as low, medium, substantial and high. In the UK, low is nothing to £10 000, medium is over £20 000 to £100 000, substantial is over £100 000 to £500 000 and high is over £500 000. In the other countries in the sample it is the same number in the local currency (e.g. £20 000 becomes €20 000 and US$20 000), not the sterling figure converted into the local currency. This is sufficient to give an appropriate understanding of the scale of investment and therefore the type of franchisee involved in each franchise.

Categorisation of Sample by Sectors

	Australia	UK	Germany	France	USA
Hotel	✓	✓	✓	✓	✓
Retail	✗	✓	✓	✗	✓
Other Services	✓	✓	✗	✓	✓
Food/ Restaurant	✓	✓	✓	✓	✓

Categorisation of Sample by Investment Required

	Australia	UK	Germany	France	USA
Low	✓	✓	✓	✓	✓
Medium	✓	✓	✓	✓	✓
Substantial	✓	✓	✓	✓	✓
High	✓	✓	✓	✓	✓

Categorisation of Sample by Mobile/Location Based Criteria

	Australia	UK	Germany	France	USA
Totally Mobile	0	1	1	3	2
Location Based	3	4	4	1	2
Both	2	0	0	1	1

APPENDIX 3

STATUTES OF THE 21 COUNTRIES OUTSIDE OF THE EU THAT HAVE FRANCHISE-SPECIFIC LAWS

Albania

Civil Code of the Republic of Albania Approved by Law no. 7850, dated 29.7.1994

Australia

Trade Practices Act 1974

Competition and Consumer Act 2010

Australian Consumer Law Act No 1 and No 2 (Cth) 2010

Barbados

The Barbados Franchises (Registration and Control) Act

Belarus

Decree of the Cabinet of Ministers of 21 March 2009 N 346 on the registration of license contracts, contracts of a concession and pledge contracts of the rights to objects of the industrial property and contracts of the complex enterprise license (franchise)

Brazil

Law No 8.955 of 15 December 1994 providing for the contract of franchise business, and other measures

Canada

The Alberta Franchise Act 1995, The Arthur Wishart Act (Franchise Disclosure) 2000 (Ontario), The Prince Edward Island Franchise Act 2007, The New Brunswick Franchises Act 2009

China

Regulation on Administration of Commercial Franchise 2007

Georgia

Civil Code Book Three, Title One; Chapter Seven Articles 607–614

Indonesia

The Provisions on and Procedure for the Implementation of Franchised Business Registration – Decree of the Minister of Industry and Trade No. 259/MPP/Kep/7/1997, dated 30 July 1997

Japan

FTC Franchise Guidelines April 2002

Kazakhstan

Law on Complex Business Licence (Franchising) Law No 330 24 June 2002

Korea

The Fair Franchise Transaction Act 2002

Malaysia

The Franchise Act 1998

Moldova

Law on Franchising No. 1335 of 1 January 1997

Mexico

Decree No 35/2006/ND-CP

Russia

Civil Code Pt II Chapter 54

Taiwan

The FTC's Guidelines on Standards Governing Disclosure of Information by Franchisors; 1999

Ukraine

Civil Code Chapter 76 Articles 1115 to 1129

USA

Federal Trade Commission Act 1914.
Federal Trade Commission Franchise Rule.
California Franchise Investment Law (1970) (California Corporate Code Sections 31000 to 31516).
Florida Business Opportunity Act.
Illinois Company Statute.
Indiana Deceptive Franchise Practices Law.
Iowa Franchise Law (1992) and Code 2001 Supplement.
Michigan Company Law.
New Jersey Franchise Practices Act.
New York General Business Law.
Texas Business Opportunity Law.
Wisconsin Fair Dealership Law.

Venezuela

The Pro-Competition Agency Guidelines for the Evaluation of Franchise Agreements, 7 January 2000

Vietnam

Article 2 of the Commercial Law of 2001

APPENDIX 4

EUROPEAN FRANCHISE ASSOCIATIONS AND MEMBERSHIP

The aggregate membership is approximately 1577:

Austrian Franchise Association

45 members

Belgian Franchise Association

30 members

British Franchise Association

350 members

Czech Franchise Association

20 members

Danish Franchise Association

46 members

Finnish Franchise Association

105 members

French Franchise Federation

125 members

German Franchise Association

200 members

Greek Franchise Association

48 members

Hungarian Franchise Association

46 members

Italian Franchise Association

204 members

Netherlands Franchise Association

193 members

Portuguese Franchise Association

24 members

Slovenian Franchise Association

107 members

Swedish Franchise Association

51 members

Ireland Franchise Association

57 members

N.B. Some brands are members of more than one national franchise association.

The number of brands represented by national franchise associations is therefore less than 1577.

The estimated number of brands in the EU is 9971.

BIBLIOGRAPHY

Books

Abell, M. (1991), *European Franchising: Law and Practice in the European Community*, London: Waterlow Publishers

Adams, J. and K.V. Prichard Jones (1997), *Franchising: Practice and Precedents in Business Format Franchising*, 4th Edition, LexisNexis UK Publishing

Amsterdam Group, *Commercial Agency, Franchise and Distribution*, 8th Draft (21 May 2003)

Atiyah, P.S. (1989), *An Introduction to the Law of Contract*, 4th edition, Clarendon Press

Beale, H. (general editor) (2002), *Chitty on Contracts*, 28th edition, London: Sweet and Maxwell

Besanko, D., D. Dranove and M. Shanely (1996), *Economics of Strategy*, 1st edition, New York: John Wiley & Sons

Blair, R. and F. Lafontaine (2005), *The Economics of Franchising*, Cambridge: Cambridge University Press

The Rt Hon Sir Leon Brittan, QC, Vice President of the European Commission (1991) in M. Abell, *European Franchising: Law and Practice in the European Community*, London: Waterlow Publishers

Breyer, S. (1982), *Regulation and its reform*, Cambridge, MA: Harvard University Press

Brousseau, E. and J.-M. Glachant (2002), *The Economics of Contracts: Theory and Application*, 1st edition, Cambridge: Cambridge University Press

Butterworths Encyclopaedia of Forms and Precedents, Vol 16(4) (2003), Franchising Agency and Distribution, Fifth Ed., Millet

Central Clearing House (1980), *Business Franchise Guide*, Chicago

Christensen, L.A. (2008), *Franchising in Denmark*, International Franchising, Kluwer Law International

Collart Dutilleul, F. and Ph. Delebecque (2002), *Civil and Commercial Contracts*, 6th edition, Dalloz, Paris

Cooter, R. and T. Ulen (1988), *Law and Economics*, 1st edition, Lancaster: HarperCollins

Demogue, R. (1931), *Law treaty regarding general obligations*

Diaz, O.B. (2007), *Franchising in European Contract Law, A comparison between the main obligations of the contracting parties in the Principles of European Law on Commercial Agency, Franchise and Distribution Contracts*, European Legal Studies, Volume 8, Sellier European Law Publishers

Diaz, O.B. (2005), *Franchising in European Contract Law*, Sellier European Law Publishers

Dixon, H. (2010), *The Impact of the Internet on Franchising as a Growth Strategy and the Implications for Franchisors Engaging in E-Commerce*, Unpublished doctoral book submitted to the School of Business, Retail and Financial Services, Ulster Business School, University of Ulster

Dnes, A. (1992), *Franchising: A case study approach*, Aldershot: Ashgate Publishing Ltd

Dourma, S. and H. Schreuder (2002), *Economic Approach to Organisation*, 3rd edition, Edinburgh: Pearson Education

Farnsworth, A.E. (1994), *Good Faith in Contract Performance*, Oxford: Oxford University Press

Farnsworth, A.E. (1997), *Good Faith and Fault in Contract Law* (Beatson and Friedmann, eds), Oxford: Clarendon Paperbacks

Felstead, A. (1993), *The Corporate Paradox: Power and Control in Business Franchise*, 1st edition, London: Routledge

Ferrier, D. (2002), *Economic Law*, 3rd edition, Litec

Flohr, Eckhard (2006), *Franchise-Vertrag*, 3rd edition, Munich

Flour, J. and J. Aubert (1994), *The obligations, The legal Act* (6th edn)

Gast, O. (1991), Chapter on Law and Practice in the European Community in M. Abell, *European Franchising: Law and Practice in the European Community*, London: Waterlow Publishers

Giesler, P.J. and J. Nauschütt (2007), *Franchiserecht*, 2nd edition, Cologne

Giesler, P.J. (2002), *Franchiseverträge*, 2nd edition, Cologne

Hall, P. and R. Dixon (1988), *Franchising*, London: Pitman

Hesselink, M., J. Rutgers, O. Bueno Diaz, M. Scotton and M. Veldmann (edited by Study Group on a European Civil Code 2006), *Commercial Agency, Franchise and Distribution Contracts (PEL CAFDC)*, Oxford University Press

Hofstede, G. (1991), *Cultures and Organisations*, London: McGraw-Hill

Hopt, K.J., H. Merkt, M. Roth and A. Baumbach (2007), *HGB Kommentar*, 33th edition, Munich

Hough, J. (1986), *Power and Authority and their Consequences in Franchise Organisations – A Study of the Relationship between Franchisor and Franchisees*, unpublished PhD book, London: University of Westminster

Housden, J. (1986), *Franchising and other Business Relationships in Hotel and Catering Services*, London: Heinemann

Huet, J. (2002), *Treaty of Civil Law, The Main Specific Contracts*, 2nd edition, LGDJ, Paris

ICC Model International Franchising Contract (2000), *ICC International Contract Series*, Paris: ICC Publishing

Jauernig, O. (2009), *Bürgerliches Gesetzbuch Kommentar*, 13th edition, Munich

Korah, V. (1990), *An Introductory Guide to EEC Competition Law and Practice*, 4th edition, Oxford: ESC Publishing

Kosteka, A. (1986–1988), *Franchising in the Economy*, Washington: US Government Printing Office

Kropholler, J. (2007), *Bürgerliches Gesetzbuch Studienkommentar*, 10th edition, Munich

Lagen (1976), *Om medbestammande i arbetslivet*

Leloup, J.-M. (2004), *Franchising, law and practice*, 4th edition, Paris: Delmas

Liebscher, C. and A. Petsche (2002), *Franchising in Oesterreich*, 2nd edition, Vienna

Love, J.F. (2008), *McDonalds: Behind the Arches*, reprint, Paw Print Publishers

Martinek, M., F.-J. Semler, S. Habermeier and E. Flohr (2010), *Handbuch des Vertriebsrecht*, 3rd edition, Munich

Matusky, G. (1990), *The Competitive Edge: How Franchisees Are Teaching the Corporate Elephants to Dance Success*, September, 58–66

Mendelsohn, M. (1999), *The Guide to Franchising*, 6th Edition, London: Cassell

Mendelsohn, M. (2004), *The International Encyclopaedia of Franchising Law*, Richmond Law and Tax Ltd, UK

Mendelsohn, M. and S. Rose (2002), *Guide to the EC Block Exemption for Vertical Agreements*, Kluwer Law International

Merryman, J. (1985), *The Civil Law Tradition: An introduction to the legal system of West Europe and Latin America*, 2nd edition, Stanford University Press

Miguel Pestana Vasconcelos, L. (2000), *O Contrato de Franquia (Franchising)*, Coimbra

Oxford English Dictionary (1933)

Pinto Monteiro, A. (2002), *Direito Comercial – Contratos de Distribuicao Comercial*, Coimbra

Plitt, J.R. (2000), *Martha Matilda Harper and the American Dream: How one Woman Changed the Face of Modern Business*, New York: Syracuse University Press

Prichard Jones, K.V. (1990), *Franchising: Practice and precedents in business format franchising*, 3rd Revised Edition, Butterworths

Raymond, Y. (1994), *Sourcebook on German Law*, 1st edition, London: Routledge Cavendish

Richie, B. (1992), *An Uncommon Brewer – The Story of Whitbread*, London: James & James Ltd

Ritter, L., F. Rawlinson and D. Braun (2000), *European Competition Law: a Practitioners Guide*, Second Edition, Kluwer Law International

Säcker, F.-J. and R. Rixecker (eds) (2007), *Münchener Kommentar zum Bürgerlichen Gesetzbuch*, 5th edition, Munich

Samuel, G. (1995), *The Foundations of Legal Reasoning*, Antwerp: Maklu

Schulze, R. (2007), in R. Schulze, H. Dörner and I. Ebert, *BGB Kommentar*, 5th edition, Nomos Auflage

Schulze, R., H. Dörner, Ina Ebert et al. (2006), *Bürgerliches Gesetzbuch*, Handkommentar, 5th edition, Baden-Baden

Seid, M. and D. Thomas (2006), *Franchising for Dummies*, 2nd edition, Wiley Publishing

Skaupy, W. (1995), *Franchising – Handbuch für Betriebs- und Rechtspraxis*, 2nd edition, Munich

Stanworth, J. and B. Smith (1991), *Barclays Guide to Franchising for Small Businesses*, Blackwell Publishers

Stanworth, J. (1977), 'A study of Franchising in Britain', London, University of Westminster

Thompson, D.N. (1971), *Contractual Marketing Systems*, Heath Lexington Books

von Bar, C., O. Lando and S. Swann (2002), *Communication on European Contract Law and the Study Group on a European Civil Code*, Kluwer Law International

Whittaker, S. and R. Zimmerman (2000), *Good Faith in European Contract Law*, Cambridge: Cambridge University Press

Williamson, O. and S.E. Masten (1999), *The Economics of Transaction Costs*, Cheltenham: Edward Elgar Publishing Ltd

Zeidman, P. (contributing editor) (2008), *Getting the Deal Through: Franchise*, London: Law Business Research

Zweigert, K. and H. Kötz (1998), *An Introduction to Comparative Law*, 3rd edition, Clarendon Press

Articles

Abell, M. and D. Bond (2003), 'The Encyclopaedia of Forms and Precedents', Volume 16, Issue 4, Agency and Distribution, 5th edition, Butterworths

Baer, J., K. Metslaff and L. Weinberg (2004), 'International Treaties, Conventions and Agreements Affecting Franchising', *International Journal of Franchising Law*, Volume 2, Issue 2, 3–42

Baer, J., E. Flohr, L. Polsky and M. Hero (2005), 'Disclosure in International Franchising', *IJFL*, Volume 3, Issue 6, 3–31

Bamberger, H.-G. and H. Roth (eds.) (2011), *Beck'scher Online-Kommentar zum BGB*, ed. 20, Munich

Barrow, C. (1989), 'Franchising', in P. Burns and J. Dewhurst, eds, *Small Business and Entrepreneurship*, London: Macmillan

Bassenge, P., G. Brudermüller, U. Diederichsen et al. (2010), 'Palandt, Bürgerliches Gesetzbuch', 69. Auflage, Munich

Baxt, R. and J. Mahemoff (1998), 'Unconscionable Conduct Under the Trade Practices Act – An Unfair Response by the Government: a Preliminary View', *Australian Business Law Review*, Volume 26

Benabent, A. (2008), *The specific civil and commercial contracts*, Ed, no. 456

Bradash, J.L. (1997), 'Using the Plural Form in the Management of Restaurant Chains', *Administrative Science Quarterly*, Volume 42, No. 2, 276–303

Braun, F. (1995), 'Aufklärungspflichten des Franchisegebers bei den Vertragsverhandlungen', *NJW*, 504

Brickley, J. and F. Dark (1987), 'The Choice of Organizational Form: The Case of Franchising', *Journal of Financial Economics*, Volume 18, 401–20

Brickley, A., F. Dark and M. Weisbach (1991), 'An Agency Perspective on Franchising', *Financial Management*, Volume 20, Issue 1

Bruton, G.D., J.K. Keels and E.L. Scifres (2002), 'Corporate Restructuring and Performance: An Agency Theory Perspective on the Complete Buyout Cycle', *Journal of Business Research*, Volume 55, Issue 9, 709–24

Cane, P. (1987), 'Self Regulation and Judicial Review', *Civil Justice*, Volume 6, 328–33

Carney, M. and E. Gedajlovic (1991), 'Vertical Integration in Franchise Systems: Agency Theory and Resources Explanations', *Strategic Management Journal*, Volume 12, 607–29

Caves, R.E. and W.F. Murphy (1976), 'Franchising: Firms, Markets and Intangible Assets', *Southern Economic Journal*, Volume 42, 572–86

Cecere, C. (2003), 'Australia section 51AC of the Trade Practices Act: impact on franchising sector', *International Journal of Franchising Law*, Volume 1, 8–24

Cohen, N. (1994), 'Pre-Contractual Duties: Two Freedoms and the Contract to Negotiate', in *Good Faith and Fault in Contract Law* (Beatson and Friedmann, eds), Clarendon Paperbacks

Combs, J.G. and D.J. Kitchen (1999), 'Explaining Interfirm Cooperation and Performance: Toward a Reconciliation of Predictions from the Resource-Based View and Organizational Economics', *Strategic Management Journal*, Volume 20, 867–88

Cornwall, J. (2000), 'Breach of Contract and Misleading Conduct: A Storm in a Teacup?', *Melbourne University Law Review*, Volume 24

Cornwallis, R. (2006), 'Indonesia – new franchise regulation', *International Journal of Franchising Law*, Volume 4, Issue 3

Corones, S. (2000), 'Implied Good Faith and Unconscionability in Franchises: Moving Towards Relational Contract Theory', *Australian Business Law Review*, Volume 28, 462

Dant, R.P. and P.J. Kaufmann (2003), 'Structural and Strategic Dynamics in Franchising', *Journal of Retailing*, Volume 79, Issue 2

Duckett, B. (2008), *Franchise World*, Feb./Mar., 19

Duncan, B. and S. Christensen (1999), 'Unconscionability in Leasing Transactions', *Australian Business Law Review*, Volume 27

Echarri, A. (2006), 'New Regulations on the Spanish Franchisor's Registry', *International Journal of Franchising Law*, Volume 4, Issue 3

Eisenhardt, K. (1989), 'Agency Theory: An Assessment and Review', *Academy of Management Review*, Volume 14, Issue 1, 57–74

Elo, Hanna-Maija (2008), 'Getting the deal through – Franchise', Finnish section, Law Business Research Ltd

Emerson, R. (2010), 'Franchise Territories – A Community Standard', *Wake Forest Law Review*, Volume 45, No. 3, 1

Emmerich, V. (1995), 'Franchising', *JuS*, 761

Fabre-Magnan, M. (1995), 'Duties of Disclosure and French Contract Law' in *Good Faith and Fault in Contract Law* (Beatson and Friedmann, eds), Oxford: Clarendon Paperbacks

Farnsworth, E. (1968), 'Good Faith Performance and Reasonableness under the Uniform Commercial Code', *University of Chicago Law Review*, Volume 30

Finlay, A. (1999), 'Unconscionable Conduct and the Business Plaintiff: Has Australia Gone Too Far?', *Anglo American Law Review*, Volume 28

Flohr, E. (2006), *Aktuelle Tendenzen im Franchise-Recht*, BB, 389

Flohr, E. (2003), *Franchise-Nehmer: Arbeitnehmer oder selbstständiger Absatzmittler? Bestandsaufnahme, Kriterien der Selbstständigkeit und Vertragsgestaltung*, DStR, 1622

Frignani, A. and M. Mendelsohn (2009), 'Project to Standardise Franchising Terminology and Marketing Practices', *International Journal of Franchising Law*, Volume 7, Issue 2

Frolkovic, P. and L. Biksadsky (2005), 'Franchising in Slovakia', *International Journal of Franchising Law*, Volume 3, Issue 2, 3–11

Gudel, P. (1998), 'Relational Contract Theory and the Concept of Exchange', *Buffalo Law Review*, Volume 46, 763

Haager, B.C. (2002), 'Die Entwicklung des Franchiserechts in den Jahren 1999, 2000 und 2001', *NJW*, 1463

Hadfield, G. (1990), 'Problematic Relations: Franchising and the Law of Incomplete Contracts', *Stanford Law Review*, Volume. 42, 927–92, excerpted in Richard Craswell and Alan Schwartz (1994), *Foundations of Contract Law*

Hesselink, M.W. (2004), 'The Politics of a European Civil Code', *European Law Journal*, Volume 10, No. 6, 675–97

Hill, C. and C. King (2004), 'How Do German Contracts do as much with Fewer Words?', *Chicago–Kent Law Review*, Volume 79, 889

Hollander, P. (2001), 'Possible Legislative Developments: Is Belgium Doomed to Become a Hell for Franchisors?', *International Journal of Franchising and Distribution Law*, Volume 3, Issue 1, 47–51

Huber, J. (1992), 'Franchising puts small business in the fast lane', *Entrepreneur*, 117–23

Iglesias, J. (2004), 'Applying the Implied Covenant of Good Faith and Fair Dealing to Franchises', *Houston Law Review*, Volume 40, 1423

Iuliana, S. and M. Mihaela (2009), 'The High Impact of Franchising on Economic Affairs in Some of the EU Members', *Annals of Faculty of Economics*, Volume 1, Issue 1, 251–6 (published by the University of Oradea, Faculty of Economics)

Jauffiet-Spinosi, C. (1989), 'The Domain of Contract – French Report', in D. Harris and D. Tallon, *Contract Law Today: Anglo-French Comparisons*, Oxford University Press

Jensen, M.C. and W.H. Meckling (1976), 'Theory of the Firm, Managerial Behaviour, Agency Costs, and Ownership Structure', *Journal of Financial Economics*, 305–60

Juenger, F.K. (1995), 'Listening To Law Professors Talk About Good Faith: Some Afterthoughts', *Tulane Law Review*, Volume 69, 1253–7

Kaufmann, P. and J. Stanworth (1995), 'The Decision to Purchase a Franchise: A Study of Prospective Franchisees', *Journal of Small Business Management*, 22033

Keutner, G. (1990), 'Reliance, Promissary Estoppel and Culpa in Contrahendo: A Comparative Analysis', 10 *Tel-Aviv U Stud in Law* 79

Klein, B. (1980), 'Transaction Cost Determinants of Unfair Contractual Arrangements', *American Economic Review*, 356–62

Klein, B. (1995), 'The Economics of Franchise Contract', *Journal of Corporate Finance*, Volume 2, Issue 1–2, 9–37

Klock, C. (2004), 'Franchising a Good Strategy for a company operating throughout Europe? – Case Study Benetton', University of Abertay Dundee

Knight, R. (1986), 'Franchising From the Franchisor and Franchisee Points of View', *Journal of Small Business Management*, 8–15

Korah, V. (2002), 'The New Vertical Restraints Block Exemption', *Intereconomics*, Volume 37, Number 1, 4–11

Kronman, A. (1978), 'Mistake, Disclosure Information and the Law of Contracts', *Journal of Legal Studies*, Volume 7

Lafontaine, F. (1992), 'Agency Theory and Franchising: Some Empirical Results', *Rand Journal of Economics*, Volume 23, Issue 2, 263–83

Legrand, P. (1997), 'Against a European Civil Code', *Modern Law Review*, Volume 60, Issue 1

Leichtling, A. (1994), 'Why Burger King Cannot Have Its Own Way with Its Franchisees', *University of Miami Law Review*, Volume 48, 671

Le Tourneau, P. (2003), 'The franchising contract', Litec, Paris in O. Bueno Diaz (2007), *Franchising in European Contract Law*, p. 43 Sellier, European Law Publishing

Le Tourneau, P. (1994), 'Franchising', *Economica*, Paris

Litvinoff, S. (1997), 'Good Faith', *Tulane Law Review*, Volume 71, 1652–3

Malaurie, P., L. Aynés and P.-Y. Gautier (2005), 'Civil Law', *Specific Contracts Law*, Paris

Marc, P. and W. Theiss (2004), 'Franchising in the Czech Republic', *International Journal of Franchising Law*, Volume 2, Issue 6, 25–34

Marot, Y. (1999), 'Prolongements de l'arrêt de la Chambre Commerciale du 10 Fevrier 1998 sur l'information pre-contractuelle en matière de contrat de franchise, Receuil Dalloz, Chron. p431' in O. Bueno Diaz (2005), *Franchising in European Contract Law*, Sellier European Law Publishers p. 67

McGregor, H. (2004), 'Contract Code drawn up on behalf of the English Law Commission' (Guiffré, 1993)

Mendelsohn, M. and S. Crossick (1986), 'Franchising in Europe: Consequences of Pronuptia', 14 *International Journal of Business Law*, Volume 12, Issue 7, 220–2

Michael, S. (1996), 'To franchise or not to franchise: An analysis of decision rights and organisational form shares', *Journal of Business Venturing*, Volume 11, 57–71

Minkler, L.P. (1990), 'An Empirical Analysis of a Firm's Decision to Franchise', *Economic Letters*, 34, 77–82

Munchener Kommentar, BGB 4. Auflage 2003, 311 Rn 234

Norton, S. (1988), 'An Empirical Look at Franchising as an Organizational Form', *International Journal of Business*, Volume 61, Issue 2, 197–218

Ogus, A. (1995), 'Rethinking Self Regulation', *Oxford Journal of Legal Studies*

Oxenfeldt, A.R. and A.O. Kelly (1968), 'Will Successful Systems Ultimately Become Wholly-Owned Chains?', *Journal of Retailing*, Volume 44, Issue 49, 69–83

Peterson, A. and R. Dant (1990), 'Perceived Advantages of the Franchise Option From the Franchise Perspective: Empirical Insights from a Service Franchise', *Journal of Small Business Management*, Volume 28, Issue 3, 46–61

Petsche, A., S. Riegler and W. Theiss (2004), 'Franchising in Austria', *International Journal of Franchising*, Volume 2, Issue 3

Portalis, J.-E.-M. (1988), 'Preliminary debates regarding the Civil code project' in J.-E.-M. Portalis, *Law and political written work and debates*

Posner, R. (1986), 'Economic Analysis of Law', *Stanford Law Review*, Volume 39, No. 3

Powers, J. (1999), 'Defining the Indefinable: Good Faith and the United Nations Convention for the International Sale of Goods', *Journal of Law & Commerce*, Volume 18

Purvin, R. (1994), 'The Franchise Fraud', *The American Association of Franchisees and Dealers*, 129

Riding, R. (2003), *Franchise World*, Dec./Jan., 12

Riding, R. (2007) *Franchise World*, Feb./Mar., 16–18

Riding, R. (2009), *Franchise World*, Dec./Jan., 6

Rubin, P. (1978), 'The Theory of the Firm and the Structure of the Franchise Contract', *Journal of Law and Economics*, 21, 223–33

Schmid, C. (2010), 'A European Civil Code as a Building Block for a European Social Model?', *European Law Review*, Volume 35, No. 1, 102–12

Schmitz, D.A. and A.V. Hamme (1988), 'Franchising in Europe: The First Practical EEC Guidelines', 22 *International Journal of Business Law*, 717

Schulz, A. and S. Kozuka (2008), 'The Importance of Cultural Differences When Expanding a Franchise Internationally', *International Journal of Franchising Law*, Volume 6, Issue 2, 5–10

Shane, S.A. (1996), 'Hybrid Organizational Arrangements and Their Implications for Firm Growth and Survival: A Study of New Franchisors', *Academy of Management Journal*, Volume 39, No. 1, 216–34

Smart, B. (2007), *Franchise World*, Feb./Mar., 7

Steward, E. (2001), 'The Four Horsemen of the Apocalypse – The Financial Services Authority and its Statutory Objectives', *Business Law Review*, Volume 22, Number 11, 258–61

Terry, A. (2004), 'Franchise Sector Regulation: The Australian Experience', *LawAsia Journal*, 97 (9 December)

Thompson, R.S. (1994), 'The Franchise Life Cycle and the Penrose Effect', *Journal of Economic Behaviour and Organisation*, 207–18, North Holland

Tikoo, S. (1996), 'Assessing the Franchise Option', *Business Horizons*, May-June, 78–82

Timmerbeil, S. (2003), 'Der neue § 355 II BGB – ein Schnellschuss des Gesetzgebers?', *NJW*, 569

Van Alstine, M.P. (1999), 'Of Textualism Party Autonomy and Good Faith', *William and Mary Law Review*, Volume 40, 1223–312

Van Gerven, W. (2008), 'The Open Method of Convergence', 14 *Juridica International*, Tartu, Estonia, 32–41

Withane, S. (1991), 'Franchising and Franchise Behaviour: An Examination of Opinions, Personal Characteristics and Motives of Canadian Franchisee Entrepreneurs', *Journal of Small Business Management*, Volume 29, Issue 1, 22–9

Whittaker, S.J. (2009), 'A Framework of Principle for European Contract Law?', 125 *Law Quarterly Review*, 616–47

Wormald, C. and A. Scott (2004), 'Stranger in a Strange Land: Contrasting Franchising Alternatives in International Franchising', *International Journal of Franchising Law*, Volume 2, Issue 6, 3–21

Zaid, F. (2004), 'International Franchise Agreements – Research, Risk and Reward', *International Journal of Franchising Law*, Volume 2, Issue 5, 3–20

International references

Clément, J.-P. (1994), *La franchise: Vingt ans de jurisprudence*
Echebarria Saenz, J.A. (1995), *El contrato de franquica, Definicion y conflictos en las relaciones internas*
Hernando Giménez, A. (2000), 'El contrato de franquicia de empresa', Civitas, Madrid
Huet, J. (2002), 'Nous faut-il un "euro" droit civil? (propos sur la communication de la Commission concernant le "droit européen des contrats", et, plus généralement, sur l'uniformisation du droit civil au niveau européen)', Receuil Dalloz, point de vue
Jednostronne odstąpienie od umowy; Art. 491 KC; Bagan-Kurluta, *Umowa franchisingu Monografie prawnicze*, p. 125
Jeol, Michel (1996), *Conclusions to the decisions of the Assemblée Plénière de la Cour de Cessation of 1 December 1995*, D. jur., p. 13ff.
Leloup, J.-M. (2004), *Franchising: Law and Practice*, p. 11
Mazeaud (2006), 'La politique contractuelle de la Cour de Cassation' in *Libres Propos sur les Sources du Droit – Mélanges en l'honneur de Philippe Jestaz,* Paris: Dalloz-Sirey
Palandt (2010), *Bürgerliches Gesetzbuch*, 69th edn

Reports, seminars, research papers and conferences

Aliouche, S. and M. Schlentrich (2005) 'Does franchising create value? An analysis of the financial performance of US public restaurant firms', 19th Annual Conference of the International Society of Franchising
Barkoff, R. and W. Garner (1994), 'Encroachment: The Thorn in Every Successful Franchisor's Side', Annual Forum on Franchising, American Bar Association
British Franchise Association, BFA/NatWest 2007 Franchise Survey, p. 40
Deakin, S. (2000), 'Regulatory Competition Versus Harmonisation in European Company Law' (ESRC Centre for Business Research, University of Cambridge Working Paper No. 163)
Deutsche Bank, Report on Franchising, January 2008
Does franchising create value? An analysis of the financial performance of US public restaurant firms Aliouche, and Schlentrich, Working Paper No. 2005–02 presented at the 19th Annual Conference of the International Society of Franchising, London, England, 20–22 May 2005
French Franchise Federation Report (2010)
Frignani, A. (1996), 'Some Basic Differences Between the Common Law and Civil Law Approach', IBA-IFA 13th Annual Seminar on International Franchising

'General Introduction' (1954), Siegfried (ed), *Aspects of the French Society*, Paris: LGDJ

Klick, J., B.H. Kobayashi and L.E. Ribstein (2007), George Mason Law & Economics Research Paper No. 07–03

Koch, D.W. (2000); 'The End of Franchising As We Know It', Federal Bar Association Annual Convention, Cleveland, Ohio, 22 September

Law Commission Report No. 259, June 16 1999, 'The Law Commission Seventh Programme of Law Reform' at paras 1.12–1.16

OECD (1994), 'Competition Policy and Vertical Restraints: Franchising Agreements', Report, OECD

Olson, Weinberg and Spencer (2010), 'The Annotated Franchise Agreement', Amercian Bar Association 33rd Annual Forum on Franchising

Pilat, D. (1997), 'Regulation and Performance in the Distribution Sector', OECD Economics Department Working Paper No. 180

Plave, L. (2007), *LJN's Franchising Business & Law Alert*, Volume 13, No. 7

Report on the Fourth Meeting of the Study Group on Franchising held on 9–10 December 1999, Study LXVIII –Doc 20, p. 2

Review of the Disclosure Provisions of the Franchising Code of Conduct, Report to the Hon Fran Bailey M.P.

SOAS (1998), London University, IPL Seminar

Terry, A. (26–28 June 2003), 'Franchise Sector Regulation: The Australian Experience', The EMNet-Conference on Economics and Management of Franchising Networks, Vienna, Austria

The French Franchising Association (2003), *All About Franchising: Texts, Numbers, Networks*

Whittaker, S. (2008), 'The Draft Common Frame of Reference – An Assessment', commissioned by Ministry of Justice

Wormald, C. (2010), 'The Basics of Franchising', Field Fisher Waterhouse Annual Seminar on Franchising

Websites

www.berr.gov.uk/whatwedo/bre/index.html

www.bfa.org

www.british-franchise.org/casestudies.asp

www.copecl.org

http://www.corp.ca.gov/Commissioner/Releases/3-F.asp

www.dfv-franchise.com

http://ecc.uvtl.nl/

http://ec.europa.eu/education/languages/languages-of-europe/index_en.html

www.efcommittee.eu (this site no longer exists, so further suggesting the transient nature of the organisation)

http://www.eff-franchise.com/, accessed 14 August 2009
http://www.eff-franchise.com/IMG/article_PDF/article_13.pdf, accessed 7 September 2009
http://www.eff-franchise.com/spip.php?rubrique6, accessed 27 October 2009
http://emnet.univie.ac.at/fileadmin/user_upload/conf_EMNet/2003/papers/Terrypaper.doc, accessed 19 August 2009
http://europa.eu/rapid/pressReleasesAction.do?aged=0&format=HTML&guiLanguage=en&language=EN&reference=IP/10/872
http://europa.eu/rapid/pressReleasesAction.do?reference=SPEECH/10/441
http://www.franchiseverband.com/fileadmin/user_upload/MAIN-dateien/Studien/Franchising_in_Germany_coming_of_age.pdf
http://www.franchise.org.au/lib/pdf/aboutfranchising/WhatIsFranchisingBrochure.pdf accessed 21 August 2009
www.franchising.fi/ukindex.html
http://www.franchise-fff.com/Seminaires-pro-le-calendrier-2006.html
http://www.ftc.gov/bcp/franchise/amended-rate-faqss.shtml ('FAQs')
http://www.kuestner-von-monteuffel-wardack.de/html/Uebersicht.php?aid=17158idp=52 accessed 6 January 2011
http://minister.innovation.gov.au/Emerson/Documents/Additional%information%20%on%20Franchising%20Code%20%and%20Unconscionable%20Conduct%20ReformsPdf
http://minister.innovation.gov.au/Emerson/Pagesgovernmentappointsexpertpanelonfranchising
http://minister.innovation.gov.au/Emerson/Pagesgovernmenttostrengthenfranchisingcodeofconduct
http://www.minjust.nl:8080/C_ACTUAL/SPEECHES/SP0006.htm
http://www.nasaa.org/content/Files/2008UFOC.pdf
www.printweek.com/news/1040784/kall-kwikfranchisees-continue-legal-against-against-ODC
http://www.publications.parliament.uk/pa/ld200809/ldselect/ldeucom/126/12606.htm
http://quickfacts.census.gov/qfd/states/06000.html
http://www.sgecc.net accessed 14 August 2009
http://steconomice.uoradea.ro/anale/volume/2009/v1-international-relations-and-european-integration/39.pdf
http://www.thebfa.org/fpnews/natwestbfasurvey10.asp
http://www.theukfranchisedirectory.net
http://lb7.reedexpo.fr/Data/kmreed_franchise/block/F_23316ac8f1472bf8d16e0ce274b508624c124d19ed45d.pdf
www.univie.ac.at/EMNET

INDEX